D0311935

Hello America!

While millions of people on both sides of the Atlantic listened, the voice of King George V welcomed delegates to the Five Power Naval Conference

CÉSAR SAERCHINGER

Hello America!

Radio Adventures in Europe

ILLUSTRATED

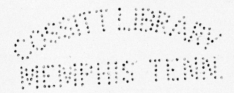
Boston

HOUGHTON MIFFLIN COMPANY

The Riverside Press Cambridge

1938

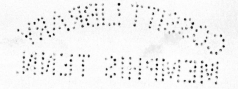

TO

MARION

'The time will come, and that presently, when, by making use of the magnetic waves that permeate the ether which surrounds our world, we shall communicate with the Antipodes.'

— JOSEPH GLANVILL, *The Vanity of Dogmatizing*, 1661

FOREWORD AND ACKNOWLEDGMENT

W HAT do you do all day?' is a question which sympathetic visitors to my office in London used to ask. 'What sort of work is it? How can you spend all your time in Europe, working for American radio? Do you broadcast yourself; if so, why don't we hear it over here?'

This book tries to answer these questions, to tell how the foreign radio representative — a breed of which I happened to be the first — whiles away the heavy hours. For seven years it was said by some of my friends that I wouldn't speak to anyone less than three thousand miles away. I want to assure them that this was not due to uppishness but to genuine preoccupation.

In telling my story I do not pretend to completeness. Others have done as much, and more, for transatlantic radio, for narrowing the spiritual distance between the two great continents of the west. For nearly two years I had the field almost to myself: those were the 'creative' years. Then, in the heat of competition, many things emerged out of the flow of world events, of news, of interests often ephemeral but none the less exciting or amusing, as the case may be.

It is the privilege and the merit of broadcasting to have drawn within its orbit the leading and significant personalities of contemporary life. These personalities have given content to an otherwise soulless machine; it is through personalities — and personages — that I have tried to interpret the somewhat confused activities of these turbulent years. The purely informative chapters on the methods and the structure of international broadcasting have been relegated to the last section of the book, together with those general conclusions and speculations which not even the most matter-of-fact person could forego, if he had for a considerable time been on the inside of the most astounding mechanism ever devised by the human brain. Those who don't care for plain, factual information, or for the wider implications which reside in all functions, manifestations and appearances, may stop short of Part IV, which I consider the most important part of the book.

Acknowledgments, then, are due first of all to my inquiring friends. Beyond that I am grateful to the heads of the Columbia Broadcasting System for affording me the leisure to write this book; to the British Broadcasting Corporation for allowing me to use its library and some of its documentary information, as well as for the untiring courtesy of its staff; to my friendly rivals, Fred Bate and Max Jordan, of the National Broadcasting Company, for essential information concerning their own European activities; to the officials of the broadcasting administrations of the principal European countries, and in particular to Mr. Arthur E. Burrows, secretary-general of the International Broadcasting Union, for their cordial co-operation in the various endeavors which form the substance of my tale.

I want to take this opportunity to thank Frederic William Wile for inveigling me into broadcasting, and Henry Adams Bellows for clinching the deal. Finally I am beholden to my successor, Edward R. Murrow, for access to his records, and no words of gratitude can ever repay the unremitting helpfulness and generous loyalty of that paragon of secretaries, Miss Kathryn Campbell. In the planning of this volume I had the benefit of valuable counsel from Ernestine Evans, while Raymond Gram Swing and Morris Gilbert read the manuscript with discernment tempered by friendly forbearance.

CÉSAR SAERCHINGER

NEW YORK, *January*, 1938

CONTENTS

ILLUSTRATIONS

PART ONE

People

I. AMERICA HEARS KING GEORGE

WHEN the *George Washington* sailed from New York in January, 1930, carrying the American Delegation to the Five Power Naval Conference in London, she also had on board the largest and most variegated complement of newspaper correspondents that had crossed the ocean since the ill-starred Peace Conference at Versailles eleven years before. Among them were two specimens of a type of reporter that had been unrepresented either at Versailles or any of the dozen or more conferences from Spa to Locarno which ushered in the new era of 'open diplomacy.'

This journalistic species — new in the international field — was the radio commentator. He was not represented at any of the previous parleys for the simple reason that he had not yet been invented, although broadcasting — the greatest discovery in mass communication since the invention of printing — had been born in 1920, the very year which saw the conclusion of Versailles and the birth of the League of Nations. It had taken ten years for the new baby to grow up.

During that bitter and turbulent decade, in which a new Europe was laboring to be born, inventors and engineers had been quietly working to perfect the new discovery. While long-suffering, disillusioned humanity was pathetically clamoring for the peace that would not come, the medium through which 'nation might speak peace unto nation' was being made effective by these twentieth-century pioneers. This coincidence may one day appeal to the historian of our time; for the moment we are interested in those two men aboard the *George Washington* who, unwittingly perhaps, were starting a new epoch in the dissemination of thought.[1]

The two men were William Hard, representing the National Broadcasting Company, and Frederic William Wile, who was sent by the Columbia Broadcasting System, then in existence less than two years. Hard was known through America as a brilliant and fearless commentator on political affairs, with a trenchant, witty style; Wile was a veteran journalist of world-wide experience — an American whose pre-war exploits had led Lord Northcliffe to 'discover' him for the *Daily Mail*. Both were worthy members of that hardest-boiled of all newspapermen's fraternities, the Washington correspondents. Short-bodied, long-headed 'Bill' Hard, with shrewd, kindly eyes; rotund and white-haired 'Fred' Wile, a hard-hitting go-getter of benign countenance, were among the most distinctive human animals in that political Noah's Ark — two personalities peculiarly fitted by destiny for a pioneering job.

Their business was to report every few days, by radio, on the progress of the Conference, speaking by way of a nation-wide 'hook-up' direct to the radio audience of the United States and Canada. This was, essentially, no different from the daily cable reporting by newspaper correspondents, except for the medium employed. In effect, they were to telephone their observations from what amounted to little more than a telephone booth within a mile of St. James's Palace, where the Conference met, to a radio control-room in New York, whence their voices were instantaneously retransmitted to the sixty or more broadcasting stations constituting a radio 'chain' and simultaneously broadcast from these stations.

They were thus talking directly to millions of listeners,

[1] For the sake of historical accuracy be it recorded that wireless telephony across the Atlantic was first accomplished in 1915, and the first European radio program was transmitted to America early in 1924; but these and other spectacular developments in wireless communication were admittedly experimental. The first *scheduled* international and short-wave transmission was a part of a symphony concert in Queen's Hall, London, on February 1, 1929, and Senator Marconi's first transatlantic talk for broadcasting was short-waved from Chelmsford, England, on December 12, 1929, six weeks before the opening of the London Naval Conference.

with but a fraction of a second's delay. They had the advantage over their journalistic rivals in the all-important factor of time, and also in the superior power of the spoken over the written word. They could convey, by inflection and emphasis, what no amount of punctuation could suggest; they could capture and hold the interest of their audience by the appeal of their voices instead of relying upon words in cold print.

Indeed, the qualities of their voices were transmitted with startling fidelity. The 'telephone booth' which they used was a small studio in the building of the British Broadcasting Corporation, and they talked, not into an ordinary telephone, but into that amazing instrument, the microphone, which reproduced and magnified their voices so as to carry, besides the meaning of their words, a projection of their personalities.

But their assignment went further. Besides reporting the Conference and projecting their own personalities, they were to introduce the chief actors of the drama itself — the delegates and the leading figures in and about the Conference room — and to transmit an impression of the atmosphere of this important international event. Here is something no writer for a newspaper or a magazine could do.

The fact that radio could do it illustrated at a flash the superior power of the new medium in journalism. It could report at first hand; it could set the scene by means of the spoken word, and it could then present the actors in the scene. Ramsay MacDonald, the British Prime Minister and president of the Conference, Henry L. Stimson, United States Secretary of State and chief American delegate, and others directly concerned could — if they would — give an account of their purposes and acts. The microphone could pick up, from the Conference table direct, the speeches, the rumble of voices, even the whispers and the rustle of papers. And so, for the first time in the history of 'open diplomacy,' at least the formalities were transmitted direct to the public.

THE FIRST WORLD BROADCAST

On the twenty-first of January, 1930, an announcer of the British Broadcasting Corporation ('B.B.C.') said, 'We now take you to the House of Lords,' and there, in the hushed Royal Gallery, the voice of King George V welcomed the delegates of the five great Naval Powers, while millions of people on both sides of the Atlantic listened and heard, for the first time in history, the royal but quite human voice of the man whose personality symbolized the unity of the greatest empire in the world.

It was noon in London, seven o'clock in the morning in New York, four o'clock — long before dawn — on the Pacific coast; yet everywhere men and women rose from their beds to listen, to witness this miracle of science. During the middle of the speech a curious thing happened in New York. By an odd misadventure a mechanic in the Columbia control-room tripped and tore the wire through which the King's voice was being transmitted to the broadcasting stations. With quick presence of mind the control operator picked up the severed strands and held them in his two hands until the break was repaired. In the intervening minutes the body of Harold Vivian formed part of the circuit through which the voice of George V reached millions of listeners.

The King's speech was followed by those of the British Prime Minister, the chief delegates of the United States, France, Italy, Japan, India, and the British Dominions; on the same day Hard and Wile gave their first eye-witness accounts, and from then on, almost daily, radio listeners throughout the United States were able to follow the tortuous path of this Conference, whose half-success, half-failure foreshadowed so much of Europe's and the world's unhappy history of the subsequent years.

Little need here be said of the Conference itself. Many of the world's great and near-great flitted across its flood-lit stage or lingered in the obscure corners behind the wings, dickering, scheming, strutting, threatening, cajoling. Tardieu and Briand, that ill-matched couple representing a still intransigent 'victorious' France; handsome, black-bearded Dino Grandi, with his troupe of admirals and propagandists, for the first time truculently defying Italy's ex-ally, France, and demanding 'parity' with the Big Latin Brother; Makatsuki and Matsudaira, bland, smiling Japanese, cunningly playing one European politician against another, and finally accepting a sham inferiority that would not survive another Conference.

Shadows of Abyssinia and Manchukuo, of violent acts to come and violations being plotted, could have been seen hurrying like storm-clouds across the horizon of that lowering political sky by anyone with a grain of historical prescience. But here was Ramsay MacDonald, self-appointed high-priest of political righteousness; vain, gullible, persistent, and sentimentally attached to Anglo-American friendship, bent on face-saving all round and insisting that humanity was going 'on and on and up and up.' No five-power treaty could be signed, but the three-power treaty that emerged at last postponed the armaments race for another five years. The essential failure of the main Conference to achieve general agreement presaged a *débâcle* far more ignominious in 1936.

The United States Senate ratified the treaty, such as it was — the first post-war treaty negotiated in Europe in which America was anything but an observer. One may perhaps digress for a moment to ask what might have been the fate of that other treaty — eleven years before — if the American public could have 'listened in' to Versailles as it did to London in 1930.

Whatever value history may place on the Naval Conference of 1930, it cannot ignore the fact that with it came a new method of reporting the march of world events. Henceforth no conference of world importance is thinkable without the accompaniment — and aid — of broadcasting. In the history of broadcasting itself, the Naval Conference marked an important date, for it was the beginning of an international activity which has already had a profound influence on its development.

RADIO'S FIRST 'AMBASSADOR'

My own entry into broadcasting, as chance would have it, was closely connected with this stage of development. The details are indelibly impressed on my mind. As a member of the staff of correspondents covering the Naval Conference for a group of American newspapers [1] I came into contact with both 'Bill' Hard and 'Fred' Wile, the only two radio men at the Conference. Wile arrived in London with a letter of introduction from a mutual friend, which led to a drive into the country on the following Sunday. We had to return to London in time for Wile to 'go on the air' at the old B.B.C. studios in Savoy Hill.

I had never seen a broadcasting studio and asked to be taken along. We entered the ugly old building, a converted Victorian apartment house with its once proud façade on the Thames Embankment, a near neighbor of the Savoy Hotel. It was a fine March evening, and the chattering starlings in the Savoy Chapel graveyard presaged the coming of Spring. We were shown into a sound-proof chamber, decorated with a sham window (for the benefit of sufferers from claustrophobia), furnished with a reading-desk over which dangled, as from a miniature gallows, an old-fashioned carbon microphone. I had never even seen a microphone. A suave young man with the most perfect of Oxford accents spoke to us in subdued tones: 'Silence, please,' as a red light flicked over the door. Then, bending low over the microphone: 'Hello, America, London calling. And here is Mr. Frederic William Wile.' By the time Wile started to speak to the 'friends in America,' I was so fascinated that I thought it all a dream. Here we were, in this tiny room in an ordinary building, standing between an ancient churchyard and the river Thames, and over there, across three thousand miles of ocean, thousands — no, millions — could hear every word we said. A new world had opened to me . . .

---

[1] *New York Evening Post* and *Philadelphia Public Ledger*. My colleagues were Raymond Gram Swing and H. R. Knickerbocker, with the late-lamented Frank Simonds as 'star' commentator.

Wile must have read my thoughts, for on the way home he mumbled something about the Conference lasting too long, and himself having to leave with several things hanging fire — Secretary Stimson, Bernard Shaw, and others still to be 'aired.' Trying to sound unconcerned I offered to help, if necessary. About a fortnight later, on the eve of Wile's sailing, we had a farewell dinner. Before we went in, he handed me the copy of a cable he had just sent to New York. 'You may not know it,' he said, 'but until further notice you are our London representative.' While the Conference lingered on toward a probably inglorious end, I was to 'protect' the network — a mere 'dog-watch' service, to be fitted in 'after hours.'

A few days later the storm broke. Cables poured into my office, Columbia wanting everything from the Prince of Wales to the United States Secretary of State. If life was hectic before, it was frantic now. I was a newspaper correspondent and a radio reporter all at the same time.

But the Lord tempers the wind to the shorn lamb. I had the usual beginner's luck. My first guest speaker was that distinguished veteran of journalism, H. Wickham Steed, and within three weeks I was able to 'present' two of the principal American delegates, both at crucial moments in the Conference. Stimson himself announced to the American public the signing of the tripartite London Naval Treaty and expounded its meaning — a first-class scoop, which incidentally acquainted me with the uses of the still new transatlantic telephone, for it required a midnight argument across the ocean to convince program managers in New York of the importance of this speech!

By the end of April the Naval Conference was 'washed up.' Easter Sunday saw the delegates away, and his Lordship the Bishop of London had kindly consented to convey his blessings across the Atlantic under our auspices. Ancient St. James's Palace, which only a few hours ago had been a giant beehive swarming with politicians, diplomats, journalists, and hangers-on from the four corners of the world, became once more just a noble piece of Tudor architecture. The historic dull-red weathered brick building with its crenellated walls lapsed again into the drowsy dignity acquired in four centuries of serene contemplation. Outside, the red-coated bearskin-topped sentry marched as always across the open side of Friary Court (from whose central balcony Mrs. Wallis Warfield Simpson was later to watch the proclamation of her royal friend, Edward VIII).

Across and across, back and forth he marched, like a toy actor moving in a groove, executing those absurd rhythmic tramples at each end, by means of which alone he could manage, without sacrificing the illusion of a mechanism, to reverse and march the other way. For two solid months he and his alternates had to be in constant danger of treading upon dodging journalists as they hurried in and out of the palace, foreigners who did not always understand that a British guardsman is constitutionally unable to swerve — even in order to avoid a collision.

And now at last these sturdy guardsmen could again do their duty without mental qualms. Inside, the great Queen Anne's room, which had resounded to the fine Christian phrases of Ramsay MacDonald and the rich, mellow oratory of ageing Aristide Briand, was being swept out; below it, the long room reserved for the journalists and fitted up for all the world like a schoolroom, with a hundred individual desks and chairs, was all but deserted. Here and there a straggler was packing up; a grinning Jap was writing a 'round-up' for his Tokyo sheet. Scraps of paper, crumpled copies of the last mimeographed official communiqués were strewn about on the floor. Another event had passed into history; another newspaperman's job was done. What next?

As I sat at my typewriter, the last news message gone, it occurred to me that the one real experience of these two months had been that little microphone in Savoy Hill: the thrilling telephone conversation across the ocean, the frock-coated Secretary of State, his private abstract of the treaty in his hand, sitting at that little reading-desk and speaking to the millions of America. Here, for better or worse, was something new, something more direct, more speedy than this laborious reporting by written symbols. Had it come to stay? Or was it good only for extraordinary occasions like this? Sitting there, in the long, deserted room lit by the cold afternoon rays of the April sun, I visualized a new kind of activity — a permanent service of spoken messages across the Atlantic — not only of news, but opinions — the wisdom of the outstanding men of the age, scientists, economists, authors and poets, churchmen and teachers — statesmen, too, who could see in this service a great opportunity for Anglo-American understanding. My immediate broadcasting assignment was finished, but why not try a shot in the dark? I typed a message on a cable form:

> JUST GETTING INTO MY STRIDE.   WOULD YOU
> BE INTERESTED IN FORTNIGHTLY SERIES OF
> TALKS BY EMINENT SPECIALISTS.   HAVE PLAN
> TO SUBMIT.

When I walked home that evening, past the red-coated sentry up St. James's Street and across Piccadilly, I had a vague feeling that I was walking out of journalism as I had known it into something else. The answer to my cable asked for details. I cabled back a year's program for Sunday talks, bristling with great British names, with subjects assigned to each, and ending with the item 'Shaw on anything.'

Within three days I had my answer. It read: 'Your plan great. Who speaks next Sunday?' That was the beginning of the first regular transatlantic broadcast service, and a few weeks later I was the network's officially appointed European radio representative, the first permanent foreign emissary of radio.

ENTER, THE PRINCE OF WALES

Within the first four months America had heard thirty or more leading statesmen, writers, and preachers speaking from London. The newspapers had discovered a new source of material for news-hungry editors. The American radio audience had 'tasted blood.' It was obvious that second-hand reporting was no longer enough, even in the international field. If one could actually hear European statesmen while they were in the throes of shaping the fate of nations; if one could hear King George solemnly adjuring the statesmen to 'hasten the time of general disarmament,' there was no reason why one couldn't hear the voices of any of the generation's great men. This was, indeed, eavesdropping on history.

The public thinks of contemporary history in terms of the men who shape it. The personalities of those who are responsible for the work and thought of our time are subjects for universal curiosity, and the voice of a great man is an essential part of his personality. The two voices that the American public wanted most to hear from across the Atlantic were those of the Prince of Wales and George Bernard Shaw — the most popular Englishman and the most famous Irishman. It goes without saying that the efforts of an American radio representative in Europe would be concentrated on these two.

It was, of course, impossible to *ask* the Prince of Wales to broadcast to America. Royalty cannot be officially approached by foreigners except through diplomatic channels. Theoretically royalty does nothing by request; royalty takes the initiative in everything; royalty 'commands,' as prescribed by precedent. There was no precedent for international broadcasting.

In his own country the Prince had been heard by radio many times, opening Wembley, unveiling a monument, 'crowning the bard' at the Welsh Eisteddfod, and doing other royal chores. Once in fact his voice had been broadcast in Canada, opening the Peace Bridge across the Niagara River (1927), and as a hazardous experiment the speech was 'relayed' to England. Obviously the only way for Americans to hear their favorite playboy was to await another official occasion.

It came sooner than expected. In April, soon after the close of the Naval Conference, it was reported that the Prince was going to act as sponsor at the launching of the great new Canadian Pacific liner, the *Empress of Britain*, in

June. It was the largest vessel to be built in England since the war and would be the largest and fastest to act as a direct link of the Empire. Here was a great occasion; the country would want to hear the Prince's speech and, more particularly, Canada would want to hear it, for it was to be a proud day for the Dominion. But how?

The British Broadcasting Corporation's short-wave station at Chelmsford was not sufficiently reliable, and there were no corresponding facilities in Canada to insure a satisfactory rebroadcast. There was, on the other hand, the transatlantic radio-telephone service, linking Great Britain with the United States and indirectly with Canada; so if the speech was to be transmitted to Canada, it had to be done via the United States — an idea which somehow touched the pride of those in charge; and it was not thinkable that this event should be transmitted to the United States alone. In the end the B.B.C. decided to solve the difficulty by doing nothing, namely, by refusing permission to 'relay' the broadcast to anyone outside Great Britain. So neither Canada nor the United States would hear the Prince.

June 11 arrived and the Prince launched the ship. As he pulled the lever that released the vessel and smashed the traditional bottle of champagne on her bow, he spoke in a loud and clear voice, 'I name this ship *Empress of Britain* and may success attend her and all who sail in her.' Then followed one of those happy speeches which were increasing his popularity from day to day. I listened to it with mixed feelings: I had left no stone unturned; had argued and pleaded up to a few hours before the event. Yet all I could get was a polite and regretful 'no,' for reasons which seemed to me absurd.

Late that afternoon, as I sat in my office, a cable was handed to me. It was from the Columbia office in New York and it said that the Prince's speech was a great success, that we scored a great 'scoop,' and how had I done it? Next morning the American papers carried headlines reading 'Prince of Wales on Radio' and prominently recorded the fact that the Prince's speech was broadcast by the Columbia Broadcasting System. It was grand publicity.

I was dumbfounded. The B.B.C. telephoned to ask why we had disregarded their veto. We hadn't; but someone, in the excitement of the battle, and optimistic to the last moment, had failed to cancel transmission facilities previously ordered from transatlantic telephone service. When the time came for the speech, the London operator had simply 'cut through' to New York, and the New York operator had offered the transmission to Columbia. Columbia's 'master-control,' convinced that there had been a last-minute change, cleared the network and out went the speech, to be heard by thousands of lucky fans who happened to be listening at that hour.

Bird No. 1 was in the bag. And now for No. 2.

II. MEN OF GOOD WILL

WHAT next? Here I was, a little fellow with a Big Plan. Could I bring it off? I was not the conventional 'contact man': I had neither the impressive personality nor the advantages of social entrée or a well-known name. It was, moreover, a difficult one to remember and inordinately long; I had to spell out its eleven letters to all the skeptical secretaries of the eminent men who were to be my quarries. Moreover, the name Columbia meant nothing to any European; I had to explain that we did not manufacture phonographs.

I had tackled many famous men as a newspaper reporter in my time — from Charlie Chaplin to Field Marshal Ludendorff — but asking questions is one thing and breaking down prejudice is another. What I had to do now was to pit my wits against the cream of contemporary minds: had to argue with them, persuade them what they didn't want to do, or said they didn't want to do, plan with them, cajole them, criticize what they wanted to say and how to say it at the microphone. What is more, I had to make them say it in fifteen minutes or less. And I was a timid soul! The publicity blurbs called me the first 'ambassador of radio': the diplomatic metaphor wasn't altogether incompatible with the job.

In choosing my victims, two things had to be considered first — the trend of the news and international good will. 'Nation shall speak peace unto nation' was the motto of the British Broadcasting Corporation, and the B.B.C. was my most important contact in England. I soon found, however, that there were some obstacles in the way.

The British, having profited by the sad experience of pioneer America, had avoided the chaotic conditions which ensued after the early days of broadcasting in the United States. They had solved their problem in the British way, by putting their heads together and effecting a compromise. Their Government, having sensed the importance of the new medium, had temporarily licensed one single company, composed of all the chief radio manufacturing interests. After an experimental period of four years they decided definitely in favor of the monopoly principle and the original 'company' was converted into a 'corporation' chartered by the Crown.

The Corporation, licensed by the Government, would serve everybody — the public, by providing programs; the manufacturers, by creating a demand for radio sets; and the Government, by providing an effective, unified instrument for nation-wide communication, especially in a national emergency — not to mention a handsome revenue.[1]

So the B.B.C. fully represented Great Britain, so far as broadcasting was concerned, while neither of the two major American companies represented the whole United States. The N.B.C., as the senior American network, had been co-operating with the B.B.C. in technical experiments for years, and the two companies had exchanged programs experimentally from the very beginnings of shortwave transmission. Columbia had been granted temporary facilities only for the duration of the Naval Conference of 1930, on the presumption that the added 'circulation' for Conference reports would be good for anglo-American relations.

The snag about establishing a permanent relationship was that the American competitive system and the British

[1] The Government's share of the B.B.C.'s income during the first ten years of the Corporation's existence was £11,371,000 (approximately $56,000,000), leaving the B.B.C. £13,031,000 (approximately $65,000,000) for construction, maintenance and programs. In addition to its income from listeners' licenses the B.B.C. has a net revenue of about £442,000 (approximately $2,200,000) from its publications. The Corporation is non-profit-taking, hence all its net income goes to provide programs, service, and maintenance.

monopoly would not make an equal team. The equation 1:1 had to be converted into 2:1 and eventually (with other American companies coming into the field) into $x:1$, without sacrificing the obvious advantages of a tight little co-operative partnership between two single national concerns. British far-sightedness found a new formula, which in the end redounded to the benefit of all. The matter is of some importance, because the action of the B.B.C. in 'recognizing' more than one American company set the precedent for a general European policy with reference to United States broadcasting, and the credit was chiefly due to Sir John Reith, the Director-General, and his (then) Foreign Director, Major C. F. Atkinson.

THE 'AUTOCRAT' OF THE B.B.C.

Sir John, widely renowned as the 'autocrat' of British broadcasting, and by all odds the most commanding figure in the European radio world, first hove into my view in the summer of 1930, when with Henry A. Bellows, then vice-president of Columbia, I stepped into his office at the top of the old Savoy Hill studios for the final negotiations for a joint agreement. They were brief. Sir John, a towering, wide-shouldered figure of a Scotsman, with bony, war-scarred, youngish features, bushy eyebrows and a purposeful jaw, pushed a beautifully drawn-up document out to us to be read and — eventually — signed. It had been prepared with the care characteristic of the British civil-service mind, and it left very little to chance.

The conversation was equally brief. Sir John, looking at Bellows with a searching eye, said, 'What I'd like to know is how you Americans can successfully worship God and Mammon at the same time,' but didn't insist on getting the recipe, which was just as well. The bargain was made and Britain's radio relations with America fixed for a long time to come.

Sir John was nothing if not frank. The first time he met William S. Paley, the youthful president of Columbia, he told him he was just waiting for the day when the two great American companies would merge their interests and combine. Then, with a twinkle in his eyes, 'It's a nuisance to have to deal with two of ye.' But next time Paley arrived in London, the Stars and Stripes, hoisted in his honor, floated over Broadcasting House. As soon as we stepped into the room Sir John said: 'Did you see the flag?'

Whether he is the 'czar' he is reputed to be I don't know. He is, however, tremendously proud of his organization, and probably doesn't think the autocrat story does any harm. In any case, whenever there's a conversation in his presence he commands it, and whatever the circumstances he has never been known to lose his dignity.

The entrance to London's modernist Temple of Radio, modestly known as Broadcasting House, is adorned by a large statue of bearded Prospero holding Ariel. The most prominent thing inside the lobby is a bronze inscription beginning with 'Dominus omnipotentus' and perpetuating the name of 'Dominus Ioannes Reith' as the first 'rector' of British radio. When the erect form of Sir John walks through that lobby, the uniformed, bemedalled attendants stand respectfully to attention while he returns their salute. He is so tall that it is impossible not to single him out in a crowd. On the other hand he is able to pass even the man of average height on the street without seeing him, whether he worships Mammon or God. For anyone my size to keep countenance in his presence required self-possession or a sense of humor, or both. When, at the end of my incumbency, Sir John made a farewell speech, I was genuinely relieved when he asked the guests' permission to remain seated. . . . But this is jumping years ahead of my story.

'Nation shall speak peace unto nation.' The way to implement that motto was to find, in each nation, the 'men of good will' who were able and willing to speak. I wanted men with something to say, whose voice had the ring of authority, as well as those whose position of authority was sufficient reason for being heard. We didn't want the transatlantic glad-hander, the international yes-man, any more than the super-patriot who would lecture his 'American cousins' on the excellence of things British and the high-mindedness of British policy. Above all we wanted nobody with a private mission from Whitehall, or a political axe to grind.

It was not as easy as it looked. Yet one by one the lions came out of their lair, and it would now be easier to enumerate the really eminent men who have not had their say than those who have. Which does not mean that the 'say' was always worth saying.

LORD CECIL AND LORD GREY

The paramount subject in the world news in 1930 was Peace. The London Naval Treaty was signed and ratified; the French evacuated the Rhineland before the end of the legal occupation period; France signed the Optional Clause of the World Court; Italy and Soviet Russia concluded a commercial agreement; and Briand's plan for a United States of Europe was being circulated to the governments. There had been, it is true, a second Wall Street slump, but prosperity was rumored to be around that mythical corner, and recovery was in a vague way associated with the prospects of peace. The world, in the full tide of hope during that salubrious summer, was looking forward to the World Disarmament Conference of 1932, the greatest push for peace in the history of the world. The first person I turned to in these circumstances was Lord Cecil — Viscount Cecil of Chelwood — that most distinguished, most unswervingly idealistic, of British champions of peace.

Lord Cecil, scion of a family that had served British sovereigns since the days of Elizabeth, son of a great prime minister and himself holder of three successive portfolios, had resigned from the Conservative Government because of its attitude toward the United States in the abortive

Geneva Naval Conference of 1927. Politically unambitious, regarding public office only as a means to beneficent action, Cecil at sixty-six had gone into the 'wilderness' at home in order to continue to uphold at Geneva the principles of the League Covenant for which he, even more than Woodrow Wilson, was responsible. But now the Conservative Government had atoned for its previous sin by reaching agreement with America and Japan. A mere party politician might have been peeved; Cecil was happy over the propitious event. But would he talk to America? I proposed as a subject 'The Next Step Towards Disarmament.'

The greater task was still ahead — disarmament on land — and that was being prepared under League auspices. Might he, a world-renowned pro-Leaguer, not jeopardize the present treaty by talking about that next step? A passionate believer in the 'collective system,' Cecil's great dream was to see Britain and the United States within that system, leading the world to permanent peace. He hesitated; finally it was decided that he should consult his friends in the United States. Not till the Naval Treaty was ratified did he actually speak, and then — in August — he gave the most lucid, quintessential, convincing statement of the case for disarmament I have ever heard.

'No amount of treaties,' he argued, 'can be relied on to prevent war, so long as the nations continue to have and exercise the unrestricted right of arming themselves against one another.' Fear is the atmosphere that leads to war, and since 'it is the cry of invasion that creates the most dangerous panics,' land disarmament is for Continental nations the key to neutrality (since navies at any rate cannot *invade*). 'Be not weary of well-doing,' he said to his American listeners. 'We owe you a deep debt of gratitude for your initiative and tenacity in the promotion of naval disarmament, but there is still, from the peace point of view, everything to be done.'

Sixteen months later, on the eve of the Disarmament Conference, I organized a six-nation radio manifestation and once again it was Lord Cecil who made the issue clear. His three points were: 1) the abolition of five kinds of offensive weapons: tanks, war planes, heavy land artillery, battleships and submarines; 2) establishment of a permanent disarmament commission; 3) limitation of military and naval budgets by agreement. Even though the question of disarmament is now in abeyance, it is well to remember these points, for the world will some day have to return to them.[1]

At various times after that, Lord Cecil has — always unofficially — talked to American listeners, and always with the same mastery of the issue, the same clarity and classical perfection of phrase. Never an orator in the usual sense of the word, his style is peculiarly effective at the microphone, because unaffected yet personal. Of all the broadcasts on the abdication crisis Lord Cecil's put the case most succinctly. And when he said that 'next to a British subject we should welcome an American as queen,' he meant it — so far as he himself was concerned.

I look back on my interviews with Lord Cecil as a rare experience. He would receive me in his little ground-floor study, or, when time permitted, in the grander drawing-room upstairs, at the modest house on the borders of Kensington and Chelsea. With his tall, top-heavy body mounted on over-long legs, his bald, dome-shaped head with its coronet of gray wisps, and the huge hooked nose protruding beneath the deep-set, luminous eyes, he would swoop into the room like some great bird of prey; but soon he would slouch deep into an easy-chair, legs protruding far out into space, elbows supported and spread hands joined at the finger-tips, smiling with his small, deep-set eyes, and breathing kindliness, learning, and dignity as he administered a history lesson or expostulated on the 'situation' — always without rancor, however discouraging it might be.

When he arrived for his broadcasts — and once he arrived too late — the always black-clothed, hurrying figure crowned by an enormously round, wide-brimmed hat, would arouse the morbid curiosity of autograph hunters at the doors of

[1] This broadcast also comprised speeches by the Archbishop of York, a man of very liberal ideas; Baron Werner von Rheinbaben (for Germany); Don Salvador de Madariaga, Spanish liberal and a veteran leader in League affairs; Signor Augusto Rosso, afterward Italian Ambassador in Washington; and Mrs. Ben Hooper, of the American Federation of Women's Clubs.

Broadcasting House. Nobody recognized him. 'They take me for a film-star,' he laughed, the night he came to talk about the fate of Edward VIII. In Geneva, where his portrait adorns many a shop window, every child recognizes the man who personifies, to good Europeans, the ideal of World Peace, today, as winner of the Nobel Peace Prize, Lord Cecil is pre-eminent among Britain's men of good will; I shall always be proud to have induced him to use the transatlantic radio in the cause to which he dedicated his life.

In surveying the rapidly diminishing roster of Elder Statesmen surviving the World War generation my eye fell on the august name of Viscount Grey of Fallodon, the man to whom, as Sir Edward Grey, fell the fateful duty of declaring war on Germany in August, 1914. To the fact that Lord Grey was an admirer of George Washington and a deep student of his life I owe one of the unforgettable moments of my London quest. I wanted a Washington's Birthday oration by Lord Grey, a task which so appealed to him that he willingly emerged from the peace and quiet of his Northumberland estate, to journey to London and face the microphone for the first time in his life. It was the only broadcast he ever made; for he died not many months later.

I met Lord Grey on a bleak February day at Dartmouth House, near Berkeley Square. It gave me a queer feeling to be in the presence of the man whom many people held responsible for the tragic sequence of events that converted England into a house of mourning, and whom the Germans regarded as the personification of 'perfidious Albion.' But the sequel to that fateful turn of history was that the two great English-speaking peoples came together in armed conflict against a common adversary for the first time in history — the first time since General George Washington, the man to be celebrated, took up the sword against the Mother Country.

'How is it that an Englishman can enthuse about George Washington, who after all was responsible for the loss of England's American empire?' I asked Lord Grey.

'The present generation of Englishmen considers that

Viscount Cecil of Chelwood
In Geneva every child recognizes the man who personifies the ideal of
World Peace

English policy, and not the American colonists, was responsible,' he said. 'We think that Chatham and Burke were right, and that George III and his ministers failed in their statesmanship. It was, in fact, inevitable. A Frenchman, the elder Mirabeau, saw it coming. When he heard that France had lost its colonies to England he said: "Now they [the English] will lose their own." He meant that since the pressure of the French colonies was removed, the English colonies would not need the support of the Mother Country, and that all matters between them — like taxation — would have to be settled by consent. And this would need a complete change of attitude on the part of the British Government, which they would not accept.'

I watched Grey as he spoke. A grave, contemplative man — a scholar, not a politician, I thought. Would he tell his American listeners what he had told me?

'Ah, yes, if you like. But I also want to talk about Washington, the man. I love him, you know!'

This was said simply, almost naïvely; and then he proceeded to tell me why he thought Washington a *great* man, not just a man of genius, or a successful man. 'Success is apt to stimulate egotism,' he explained. 'A man wants to retain personal power; he fails to be great because he has ceased to care — or may never have cared — for anything greater than himself.'

In this brief analysis Grey, the man, seemed to reveal himself. He was anything but egotistical; he certainly had no desire to retain power, once he felt that his usefulness was gone; and he never ceased to care for things greater than himself. A profoundly religious man — a naturalist, a philosopher, a recluse in his northern sanctuary, where the mysteries of bird life held infinitely more charm for him than the affairs of men. A gentle, sensitive, high-principled person whom all perfidy and violence must have wounded to the depth of his soul. And it is with such people at their head, I reflected, that nations must face their crises and fight their wars.

Years ago, as a journalist, I had to interview General Ludendorff on the subject of the war. Sitting here, in a quiet

London room, opposite this tranquil, gracious, ageing figure, so deeply touched by tragedy, it would have seemed like a sacrilege to speak of anything so violent. Instead we spoke of Fallodon, and of Theodore Roosevelt, a brother-naturalist who had walked with him in its shady glades, observing water-fowl and musing on bird-life in general . . .

Grey asked if I were going his way — towards his club in St. James's Street; and together we walked to Piccadilly, which had to be crossed. I knew of his failing eyesight — he was almost blind. Should I guide him across, through the traffic? I held out a tentative arm. But he walked firmly on, picking his way through the dangerous street, unrecognized by the hurrying crowds as the man on whose words, seventeen years before, had hung the fate of their race.

Tall, erect, the embodiment of dignity, this septuagenarian of spiritual countenance walked on, an Englishman among Englishmen — almost an epitome of Englishness, in its most rarefied mood.

SCIENTIFIC PACIFIST; PACIFISTIC SCIENTIST

Both Grey and Cecil were, in the last analysis, pacifists, just as were Lincoln and Woodrow Wilson, whose names are forever associated with war. Both served in the British War Cabinet, one as Foreign Secretary, the other as 'Minister of Blockade' — a word that conjures up the most cruel of all the cruel aspects of the World War. Had they to make their decisions today, would they be the same? England was a peaceful country in 1914, after 1918 it was a *pacifistic* one. And out of the war generation has come another type of men of good will, the bitter-enders of peace, the Norman Angells, the Ponsonbys and Lansburys, and the Dick Sheppards — men whose fellows on the other side of the international fence are languishing in concentration camps, or in prison.

One of the outstanding figures of this type, who for clear

thinking and sheer intellectual honesty has few equals in the world, was a mousy little member of the House of Commons named Norman Angell — *Sir* Norman to people who need to be impressed before they will take a man seriously. Norman Angell is a scientist of peace. Others love peace, pray for it, suffer for it. He believes in it as the ultimate economic necessity. In his *Great Illusion*, written before the World War, he foretold all that people have since learned by bitter experience. Millions have read that book, in twenty-five languages; yet today the world is ablaze at three corners and it seems only a matter of time when the flames will merge. When they do, Norman Angell — like his more sentimental friends the religious pacifists — will probably find themselves in jail; and even while they are yet at large people see to it that their voices are muffled, for nothing is more dangerous to folly than the truth. Norman Angell, so far as I know, had never been asked to broadcast when I first approached him in 1931.

'It is not the facts which guide the conduct of men,' he said in his first talk to American listeners, 'but their opinions about facts; which may be entirely wrong. We can only make them right by discussion.' I should like to print that talk, word for word; for in it he destroyed so many false opinions about 'facts' — about nationality and empire and economics and trade — that no one who heard it would want to listen to the mouthings of the patrioteers and the apostles of 'national honor' again. Nobody, in fact, dares to say that Norman Angell is wrong; yet I do not hear his voice on the radio much oftener than before....

I cannot help thinking that this keen-eyed, unimpressive little man in tweeds did something for Anglo-American relations even in that one quiet little lecture across the Big Pond. 'Look me up sometime,' he said as we parted in the Strand, nearly six years ago. I never did, I am ashamed to confess. But I'm going to do it now.

To Americans, Norman Angell seemed too relentlessly rational, too dispassionate to stir people into sympathy. The American audience constantly clamors for 'human' qualities; Americans want their emotions to be engaged; their demand for 'personality' is insatiable. So I set about getting a man who combined high intellectual attainment with a genius for direct human appeal — a man whose greatness of mind was matched by his greatness of heart. Such a man was the venerable scientist, Sir Oliver Lodge, one of the pioneers not only in the discovery of radio, but also in its application to human needs — a man who could project his personality, by what he considered an occult force, more completely than anyone else I have known.

Sir Oliver Lodge, physicist, mathematician, inventor, philosopher, and researcher into the Unknown, was in his seventieth year when I first met him in his remote country house on Salisbury Plain — not far from Amesbury and Stonehenge, where the monuments of Europe's earliest known civilization stand like lonely stone sentinels against the uninterrupted expanse of windswept sky. For years a widower, he lived in the solitude of the gray stone house, served by an elderly housekeeper and assisted in his labors by a young woman secretary. I found him, on a burning hot afternoon, resting in a garden shelter, slowly waving a palmetto fan. His high, bald, dome-shaped skull, bulging into an enormous forehead, showed beads of sweat. But his manner was cordial despite the discomfort of the day. Looking straight ahead of him, out of deep-set eyes shaded by sensationally long and bushy eyebrows, he said:

'I should like to speak about the Destiny of America. Is that what you want?'

Secretly I had hoped for a talk on spiritualism, but I found that he wasn't ready for this. Did he mean a scientist's forecast of America's future?

'No,' he said, 'not that. I believe that America has a great world destiny — a political mission. Fifty years ago I heard your great historian, John Fiske, predicting the federation of the English-speaking race. Nothing we could do, he said, could stop it, and it would be a blessing to humanity. Now Anglo-American friendship is on the increase; the exclusive spirit of nationality is weakening, except among the small nations like South Ireland and Czechoslovakia, who have just acquired it. The United States probably hardly realize the part they are to play in human progress. They are developing into the mightiest nation; they are isolated from the jealousies of Europe; yet they have begun to realize that they must stand in with the rest of humanity....'

It all sounded a little too Utopian; but I realized he had meditated on that idea, and wanted to say what was on his mind. The tenor of his lay was that eventually we Americans would have to live up to the professions of our statesmen: that the world needed a police force to keep the peace, and that nobody else could be trusted to maintain it. America must become the policeman of the world.

'It may be too dangerous to suggest it...'

I said 'no' — for nothing is too 'dangerous' to the journalist when it issues from the mouths of men who are acknowledged to be great or wise. And there was something prophetic even about the appearance of this white-haired sage.

'Not yet,' he mused. 'Much to be done before this.... The mills of God grind slowly.... The destiny of nations is too big for haste. But like John Fiske, I feel that either that or something better will come....'

We were called for tea. Slowly he raised himself up and with much hard breathing got to the house. We agreed, around the tea-table, that he should do the talk.

It was a great success. So much so that in response to a cable I asked him to broadcast again a fortnight later. And this time it was spiritualism — 'The Reality of a Spiritual World' — the logical exposition of a tenet that is so difficult for agnostics to take seriously. Yet here was an accepted scientist, who had demonstrated in the physical world the existence of forces that the ignorant regard as a miracle — the very forces by which he was now, sitting in London, speaking to millions in America.

'The real fact,' he said, 'is that we are in the midst of a spiritual world, that it dominates the material. It constitutes the great and omnipresent reality, whose powers we are only beginning to realize.... Its forces are prodigious.' And he ended with the assurance that 'all will ultimately be well,' because he is one of the world's great optimists — with an optimism that the bitterest of life's sacrifices had not obscured.

As great as Lodge's optimism is his sincerity, and that is what made his broadcasting unique in its power. Every breath, every effort of speech 'came across' — the whole of this lovable old man was pictured in the sound of his voice.

DICK SHEPPARD OF ST. PAUL'S

If you were to ask anyone in the British Isles — a professor, a general, or a bishop, a Durham miner, a white-collar worker in Birmingham, an Oxford don, or a down-and-out in London's East End who Dick Sheppard was, he would look at you as though you were pulling his leg. For Dick Sheppard's name is known wherever in England men walk and talk, and wherever they listen to the radio — or listened, for his voice, too, was a discordant sound in the era of rearmament. Dick Sheppard was an Anglican priest — officially he was the Very Reverend Hugh Richard Laurie Sheppard, D.D., Companion of Honour, Canon of the Cathedral of St. Paul. He had even been Dean of Canterbury and 'priest-in-ordinary' to the King. But to the millions he was known as the 'broadcasting parson' (for he was the first to broadcast services in England — from his pulpit at St. Martin's-in-the-Fields) and as the leader of those who *will not fight*. He and a British brigadier-general, the late Frank Percy Crozier, C.B., C.M.G., who fought throughout the war and earned the D.S.O., the *Croix de Guerre*, and every conceivable distinction for bravery, organized a Peace Pledge Movement, in which are enrolled hundreds of thousands of young men (men only!) who have signed their names on open postcards under a pledge that in no circumstances will they take up arms, for King and Country or anything else. I think it is safe to say that nowhere except in Great Britain is such a thing possible today.[1]

[1] General Crozier, who was the author of a much-attacked book, *The Men I*

What does this mean? It means that next time Great Britain goes to war, many thousands of religious young men will either become guilty of moral perjury or the country will be dotted with concentration camps, filled with conscientious objectors, from end to end.

I wanted Dick Sheppard's appeal to be heard in America. I found him, a pudgy, middle-sized cleric with a winning smile — a 'practical' Christian to whom Christianity is a matter of works rather than faith — working like a business man in his office at St. Paul's chapter house, with a secretary taking letters, making appointments, arranging meetings. A tiny, inconspicuous advertisement in the daily papers announcing a mass meeting at which he would speak had filled the immense Albert Hall with fervent followers; postcard pledges had been pouring in ever since. Here he was, surrounded by the hard, lifeless symbols of ecclesiastical routine — advocating the Christian philosophy of non-resistance, as unperturbed by the relentless automatic workings of organized religion as by the hideous grinding of the traffic in the streets outside. He was the busiest man I ever saw; but no effort that might further the cause could be refused; so he came to Broadcasting House to 'tell America.' He was already ill, and he died in the midst of his campaign — while Britain was re-arming with all her might.

LORD SNOWDEN HITS OUT

A wide and tenuous arc connects the political rectitude of a Grey to the bitter-end pacifism of a Dick Sheppard. Between these two extremes I found many shades — many varieties of 'men of good will.' There was Sir Herbert (now Lord) Samuel, leader of the Liberals, whose sovereign remedy for war was Free Trade; and Major Attlee, leader of the

Killed, died in the summer of 1937, and Dick Sheppard preached a funeral oration. A special guard was required to prevent disorder, for patriotic citizens, as well as Fascists, had become infuriated by his frank confessions of barbarity in war.

Labour Party, a mild-mannered, Oxford-bred Socialist. There was Lord Ponsonby, one-time page to Queen Victoria, a hater of war who resigned his leadership in the House of Lords when George Lansbury resigned his in the Commons — because neither of them would countenance violence even in the homeopathic form of 'sanctions,' as advocated by the League. And there was old side-whiskered George Lansbury himself, like a photograph out of a Victorian family album, so full of the milk of human kindness that even his famous visits to Hitler and Mussolini could not sour it. Not to forget Lord Snowden, that hard-headed Yorkshireman who had the reputation of 'leaving no stone unflung' — even when talking about members of his own party. I asked him, as an honest, neutral expert, to sum up the 'tragedy of the Economic Conference for the American radio audience, and he placed the blame much nearer home than his countryman liked. Speaking of Franklin D. Roosevelt, accused both in England and America of 'dynamiting' the Conference, he said:

'It would not be fair, however, to attribute to Mr. Roosevelt the full responsibility for the breakdown of the Conference. The obvious differences amongst the delegates already manifest would certainly have brought the Conference to disruption later. The British Government must bear a large share of the responsibility for the tragic failures of the Conference. They went into the Conference without adequate preparation and with no policy beyond the statement of a few generalities. They favored a rise of prices, but they never contributed any plans to attain that object. They spoke eloquently about the evils of trade restrictions. They denounced excessive tariffs, not British tariffs, but those of other countries. They condemned quotas and embargoes, but insisted on maintaining their own quotas. They accepted a tariff truce, but reserved the right to go on meanwhile increasing their own tariffs. Though committed to the policy by the Roosevelt-MacDonald statement, Mr. Runciman announced to the Conference that the British Government will have nothing to do with public works, either national or international, as a means of providing employment. This was the second staggering blow!'

It would be impossible to name all our speakers, but even this list is varied enough to prove to the most rabid anti-British American that their talks were not dictated by the British Government or inspired by national prejudice. On the other hand, Anglo-American friendship did not suffer by anything they said — always assuming that this friendship of the English-speaking nations is a thing to be cherished and cultivated. Men like Lord Lothian and Sir Evelyn Wrench, economists like J. Maynard Keynes, Sir William Beveridge and Sir Josiah Stamp, speaking frankly on the problems that beset the two countries and the relations between them have, I believe, done a great deal more than all the 'hands-across-the-sea' orations that have been uttered since the war.[1]

PRESIDENT ROOSEVELT STIRS BRITAIN

It may be asked with some justice whether this principle doesn't work both ways. If Englishmen are to be encouraged to speak their minds freely to Americans, why not the other way about? It is perfectly true that for at least two years the voice of America, so far as England was concerned, was a 'melody unheard.' William Hard read a homily to England at Christmas, 1931; the president of Exeter Academy spoke on American education in 1932; a 'literary round table' comprising Theodore Dreiser, Ernest Boyd, and George Jean Nathan wise-cracked in the hearing of a none-too-amused British audience in 1933. That was all, until on March 4 of that year the clarion voice of Franklin Delano Roosevelt, making his first inauguration speech, floated across the Atlantic and electrified all England with ringing phrases of hope, such as 'we have nothing to fear but fear.' It was this speech — still remembered as a landmark in a

[1] Among the women the Duchess of Atholl, Lady Astor, Lady Rhondda, Miss Ishbel MacDonald, Miss Megan Lloyd George, Mrs. Mary Agnes Hamilton, and Miss Ellen Wilkinson contributed talks of genuine value.

country where public speaking is a fine art — that awakened British broadcasting officials to the possibilities of a west-to-east traffic in radio talks.

'Mr. Roosevelt's inaugural address thrilled the world,' said Lord Snowden, who never flattered anybody in his life. 'I heard it clearly at my own fireside, and I felt that at last a statesman had arisen to challenge the injustices and shame of the present and to wage a valiant fight against them. His bold policy since then is magnificent. It remains to be seen if it will succeed.'

When the following summer I made my periodic visit to America, the B.B.C. asked me to complete arrangements for a series of talks by prominent Americans, entitled 'American Points of View,' to be relayed to England alternately by Columbia and N.B.C. The first of these was made by Stuart Chase (on the economic situation), and the series included Madam Secretary Perkins, Governor John G. Winant of New Hampshire, and Pearl Buck. One would have thought that eminent Americans would have seized such an opportunity with avidity, but strange to relate it was not possible to enlist Senator Borah, nor Presidents Lowell and Conant of Harvard University, nor Owen Young, nor Sinclair Lewis and Willa Cather. Herbert Hoover was too far away and William Allen White was taken ill before his broadcast was to take place. But in 1935 the B.B.C. appointed a North American representative and an increasing amount of American material has crept into British programs since then.

'TRANSATLANTIC BULLETIN'

It was due to a request by William S. Paley for more good news interpretation that I was able to arrange an exchange series called Transatlantic Bulletin, which was inaugurated early in 1935 and has continued, with occasional interruptions and attenuations, to the present time. This consists of entirely uncensored, frank, and remarkably truthful commentaries on events and political trends in the two countries. Raymond Gram Swing, who proved himself one of the most masterful commentators in this field, has become the permanent and most highly accredited American interpreter known to England, and has created a following throughout Great Britain which rivals that of the most popular British commentators on their own ground. People of all classes, from the so-called intelligentsia to the working masses, listen to him with keen interest, and knowledge about American conditions and problems among the general public has in consequence grown to a remarkable degree.

The United States, in return, has heard a series of British journalists and commentators, of whom Vernon Bartlett, Sir Frederick Whyte, S. K. Ratcliffe, Stephen King-Hall, and Gerald Barry have been the most successful. Harold Nicolson, a first-class broadcaster but afflicted with an intensely English intonation, was — it is sad to relate — somewhat less successful, and on one occasion when he braved a heavy cold in order to do a broadcast at the inhuman hour of 3 A.M. (10 P.M. in New York), several ladies of the American audience had nothing better to do than write and upbraid him for his 'unmannerly' coughing and sneezing. His profuse apologies had been smothered by static, or just overheard.

These men, unfettered by any political or other consideration, describing and interpreting fairly the scene in their own country to the presumably interested spectator across the Atlantic, must be ranked, and honorably so, with the 'men of good will' to whom this chapter is devoted. I am proud to have been associated with an enterprise which is still fraught with incalculable possibilities for good.[1]

[1] A similar series of exchanges was subsequently arranged between France and the United States, and this has continued virtually without interruption. The leading French speaker of this weekly series is Pierre de Lanux, the American commentators (in French) included Percy Winner, now director of the N.B.C.'s short-wave service; Professor John B. Whitten of Princeton; and Pierre Bédard.

III. POETS, PROPHETS, AND BEST-SELLERS

POLITICS at its worst is a device for keeping people — and peoples — apart. At its best it is a means of bringing them together. But not the only means. So far as international radio was concerned, I always felt that literature could do as much, or more. England and America, despite Mr. Mencken and his followers, do speak more or less the same language, and that one fact has shaped their joint destinies and will continue to shape them, more than anything else. The poets and the prophets of the English-speaking races, irrespective of nationality, are read wherever the language is spoken, and the best-sellers, thanks to the publishers, even more. But they should also be heard; things can be said that cannot be written, and who would agree that politicians should have a monopoly of the air, other than hot air?

In the first summer of my radio quest I had a talk with John Masefield about this. He was then living on Boar's Hill, some miles outside Oxford — in a remote but comfortable house fronting on a leafy country lane. He had become poet-laureate not long before, and, as I was gradually closing in on his retreat after motoring wild circles around it, I had to think of one of his predecessors, whose behavior caused an American headline writer to announce that the 'King's Canary Won't Sing.' Would this 'king's canary' refuse to sing? Not likely. In fact, as we got talking — in one of the most cultivated and 'homey' interiors imaginable — about the poet in modern life, he developed a theory according to

which poets should be heard rather than seen — or read.
Not since ancient times had the 'canary' had such a good
chance to sing as now. Here is the burden of his theory, as he
afterward told it to the American audience, in the first overseas broadcast ever made by a poet.

THE POET SPEAKS

'In times past,' he said, 'poetry was the delight of every
member of the community. The poet sang or spoke to all
and was listened to with rapture by all. Then came the
printing press, which at first was thought to be of great
benefit to poets. I think it has become a detriment to
poetical art, though priceless as a distributor of knowledge.
It has had this result — it has put away the poet from his
public. Since the printing press came into being, poetry has
ceased to be the delight of the whole community of man; it
has become the amusement and delight of the few.'

Actually this idea was not a new one with him: he had
meditated on it for years, before broadcasting, and what is
more, had done something about it. In the garden of his
house he had built a barn-theatre and here, as a regular
event, took place the 'Oxford Recitations' — competitive
recitations of poetry by young men and women at which
Masefield, his wife, Laurence Binyon, and other poets were
the judges. It was an effort to raise a young generation of
people who would think of poetry in terms of sound; here,
too, the poet himself might speak to a limited but 'enrap-
tured' audience. Masefield showed me his little theatre with
the zest of a youngster showing his toys; play-acting was
evidently the great pastime of the family and its friends, for
heaps of gay costumes hung about 'back-stage,' and I had
heard exciting tales of dramatic house-parties from Oxford
students and young actors who had their first fling in Masefield's Thespian barn.

My coming had injected a new element into his theory.

'It may be that broadcasting may make *listening* to poetry a pleasure again. Though this,' he added pensively, 'can only come about with difficulty — with a great deal of hard work. . . .'

I wondered what he meant. Well, he meant that 'poets will work better at verse if they work before an audience they can see, so that they may know when their work fails and why.' Television had hardly been heard of, so that didn't enter our minds.

Masefield was speaking softly, as is his habit — thinking audibly rather than talking — and with a wistful air. He is an unobtrusive man, this 'people's poet' — anything but the robust and passionate creature you would suspect from the vigorous cuss-words of 'Nan' and the full-bodied tang of his sea-roving tales. His imagination was kindled by this new direction to his thoughts about the poet in modern life. But I thought he ought not merely to talk about it — he ought to illustrate it by reciting his own verse. It took some time for him to decide, then one day I got a note:

'Many thanks. Right. 5.15 P.M. the 14th, Sunday.'

It was about the usual length of his epistles. A few days later he was giving his unseen audience one of the simplest and best definitions of poetry. 'Poetry,' he said, 'is an art in which the artist by means of rhythm and great sincerity can convey to others the sentiment which he feels about life.' 'I speak to you this afternoon,' he concluded, 'in the hope that poetry will again become one of the main delights of life and really compete once again with the delights of the market place.'

'Sea Fever' is one of the poems he recited in his radio début, and the spoken version turned out to be slightly — ever so slightly — different from the printed one:

I must go down to the seas again, to the lonely sea and the sky,
And all I ask is a tall ship and a star to steer her by. . . .

But Masefield's example hasn't been followed — not even by himself. Except for the reading of his official 'Ode' on King George's Jubilee, he has, so far as I know, never broadcast again.

MIKE-SHY GENIUS

As for the rest of the poets, we didn't have much luck. Not that I didn't try. Take Kipling, for instance. I wrote the most seductive letters to the man whom Robert Graves has called 'the literary aspect of the British Empire.' I knew he hated the very idea of broadcasting and thought I might persuade him in an interview, but in a most extra-polite letter from his secretary, pleading the master's crowded schedule, I was asked to 'correspond.' That was six years before he died, but not long enough to make him change his mind. In his idyllic snuggery in a fold of the Sussex Downs he successfully fended off everything that smacked of publicity, and even his cousin Stanley Baldwin didn't often rouse him from his guarded seclusion, except on one or two really patriotic occasions. One of these came in July, 1933, when the Royal Society of Literature gave a luncheon in honor of the Canadian Authors' Association, and Kipling was persuaded to be one of the speakers. As all the proceedings were broadcast by the B.B.C. he could not prevent his voice from going to the outside world. I suggested an American rebroadcast, but just at this particular time the network was engaged and I had the chagrin of seeing my rivals walk off with the prize. The talk had nothing to do with poetry, but I remember one passage which revealed both the aristocrat of letters and the man. After speaking of 'our land's deep unconscious delight through all ages in her own strength and beauty and unjaded youth,' he said:

'That same headlong surplus of effort and desire goes forward along other paths today. But our eyes are held. Like the generations before us, we cannot perceive among what new births of new wonders we now move. And all these things, out of our past, in our present, and for our future, are yours by right.

'They are doubly yours, since the dominant strains of your blood draw from those twin races — French and English — which throughout their histories have been most resolute not to be decivilised on any pretext or for any gain.'

Once again, and once only, was Kipling's voice heard 'on the air,' a year before his death — at the St. George's Day dinner of the society which bears the name of England's patron saint. His words were less felicitous that time: rearmament was in the air and the British lion was in a mood to roar.

Then take Sir James Barrie, who, though not a poet in the literal sense, would be considered so by thousands of admirers. Barrie held a kind of monopoly for whimsicality at after-dinner speeches, but must have felt that his whimsies would evaporate in the ether waves, for he resisted all invitations to broadcast with savage stubbornness. At last, when he was 'caught' by the B.B.C. on an occasion he couldn't evade, he came to the microphone, coughed, excused himself for having a cold, made a quip about shattering ear-drums, coughed again, and announced that he was through. That was broadcast to America, and it cost a heap of money.

John Drinkwater, whose death robbed England of a very versatile man, broadcast to America not only his own poetic prose about Lincoln, but the verses of Keats, from Keats's Hampstead home; and T. S. Eliot, the American-born poet whom Englishmen rate above most of their own contemporaries, broadcast a talk on Dryden. I wish it had been his own poetry instead, but American radio as yet prefers great names to human values.

WELLS LOOKS AT THINGS TO COME

Masefield's hope that broadcasting might restore poetry to its original purpose might apply equally well to prose. In other words — through radio not only the minstrel but the soothsayer might be reborn.

This made me think of H. G. Wells, the greatest professional prophet of our time. *The Shape of Things to Come* was his latest work in 1930, and I was fascinated both by its

fantasy and its uncanny prescience. Would Wells broadcast
for me, as he had once done for the B.B.C. — but on the
world of tomorrow rather than the things of today? Wells
has always soft-pedaled the artistic side of his nature; he
wants to stress the social surgeon, the world-improver, the
pamphleteer. That has tended to dim the glamour of his
name; the public prefers the artist to the reformer, the
crooner to the moralist. But in the rôle of prophet he gives
himself away: his fantasy gets the better of his common sense.
Or is it because, in the future, Truth and Ideal become inter-
mingled? It takes both Wells's scientific speculation and his
fictional fantasy to build the Utopia of our dreams.

But when it comes to business, Wells is a very mundane,
practical man. Yes, he would speak, but the price is so-and-
so — take it or leave it. I don't blame him. American
broadcasting companies are not run by idealists; if you said
so their executives would resent being called names. Having
agreed on the fee and the subject, the next consideration was
Wells's voice. 'From November to April — in the English
climate — you can't hear me at all,' he laughed, 'that's why
I go to the Riviera for the winter. Better wait till I get back.'
Well, I didn't want to wait: 'that' war might have come
before spring (despite Wells, who put it at 1940), or the Big
Executives might prefer profits to prophets by then. So we
cleared the earliest possible date and just missed the first
London fog. Wells's voice at best is little better than a
wheeze, and my misgivings were pretty grave.

Wells talked about 'The World of Our Grandchildren' in
the first American broadcast of his career. It wasn't exactly
an inspired talk; it was intensely practical. It took only one
phase of our social life — economy — and showed where it
would have to go, not whole-hog socialism, but collectivism
from the angle of business. 'Mass consumption,' he said,
would have to complement mass production. And what is
the equivalent of mass production in terms of consumption?
Community buying. He was definitely talking to children —
'our grandchildren.' 'Even now we have community buying
for certain things. For instance, you buy battleships on a
community basis. If we can buy battleships and submarines

and airships as a community, I refuse to believe that we can't buy hotels, perfectly equipped houses, and boots and shoes for all the children in the world in the same way. Collectively we could buy everything which we collectively produce.'

And then he proceeded to predict the mass-production of houses and all sorts of things. Why do we insist on holding on to old and worn-out things, when there is surplus labor everywhere? We could, and should, change our houses and furniture as we change our cars and our clothes — newer and better and more comfortable all the time — which would of course be society's answer to the relentless fecundity of the machine.

'Well, how was it?' asked Wells, as I dropped him at the door of his huge block of flats built over Baker Street railway station — an example of our modern genius for the annihilation of the home atmosphere. 'Did I do my job all right?'

Actually he filled the assignment much better in a talk he made a year later for the B.B.C. It was a very short talk, but one of the most terrifying I have ever heard; it illustrated, moreover, what broadcasting can — and ought to — do, to awaken people's consciences to the most appalling possibilities of life. For once Wells was not concerned with Utopia, but with Pandemonium. It was the epilogue to a demonstration by sound-effects of the progress of Communication — our much-vaunted abolition of distance.

'In a little while,' he said, 'there will be no more distance left, and very little separation.... Let me ask you how long you suppose it is before it becomes possible for men to pack up a parcel of explosives or poison-gas or incendiary matter or any little thing of that sort and send it up into the air to travel to just any chosen spot in the world and drop its load?'

So what? The point of the talk was that there are in the world thousands and thousands of professors working on the records of the past, but not a single person who makes a whole-time job of estimating the consequences of new devices in the future. 'There is not a single Professor of Foresight in the world.' Unless there will be, we shall tumble into one frightful mess after another, created by our own cleverness and ingenuity. We shall be doing nothing but what we have been doing right along, in the case of the motor car, the aeroplane and — we shall probably find — the radio. 'We did nothing to our roads before they were choked' (with the result of an annual massacre of human life) — to take but one example.

'Let me draw a plain conclusion from tonight's audition,' he concluded. 'Either we must make peace throughout the world, make one world-state, one world-pax, with one money, one police, one speech and one brotherhood, however hard that task may seem, or we must prepare to live with the voice of the stranger in our ear, with the eyes of the stranger in our homes, with the knife of the stranger always at our throats, in fear and in danger of death, enemy neighbors with the rest of our species. Distance *was* protection, *was* safety, though it meant also ignorance and indifference and a narrow, unstimulated life. For good or for evil, distance has been done away with... Will there be no foresight until those bombs begin to rain upon us?'

Most people would say, of course, that this is sordid pessimism. Wells could almost prove scientifically that his pessimism is the plain rational truth.

There are few people outside my immediate circle whom I like better than H. G. Wells. There are few who have applied their brain power — and his brain power is prodigious — so exclusively to the service of mankind. And there are few more truly modest men that I have met. He has the humility that goes with greatness; the fine simplicity that is the attribute of the wise. And even he couldn't be sorrier than I would be to see him really grow old.

'Don't congratulate me,' he said, when I met him shortly after his seventieth birthday. 'It's a horrid feeling to be reminded that one's getting near to the end.' He was looking quite well, however; his sturdy, always well-groomed figure and his handsome purposeful face with the boyish smile were, as ever, a challenge to the Philistine on his own ground. A few days later, at the P.E.N. Club dinner in his honor I heard him make the most pathetic speech an anti-sentimentalist could be capable of. 'I feel as though I were still in the nursery, playing with my nicest toys, and Nurse opens the door to say: "Come now, George, it's bedtime — put those toys away." ... Well, it'll soon be time to put the toys away, and there's still so much to be done.' [1]

Last time I asked him to broadcast, he refused. But it was the wrong time of the year!

CHESTERTON ON CHRISTMAS

On Christmas Day, 1930 — my first broadcasting Christmas — I arrived at the old Savoy Hill studios of the B.B.C. and was told that my speaker was waiting for me in the drawing-room, a plain, square, modernized room whose sober walls were enlivened by vivid reproductions of masterpieces of Van Gogh, Cézanne, and Mattisse. There, on a low sofa, among the French modernists, squatted the incredible, flamboyantly anti-modern figure of Gilbert Keith Chesterton. This gigantic nineteenth-century Bacchus, with an English tension-spring pince-nez insecurely poised on his nose, and dressed in the loose garb of the literary Bohemian — a character out of Murger raised to Gargantuan proportions and adapted to the Dickensian scene — was an apparition so preposterous as to call for reassurance. And he hastened to reassure me, with a smile and an excuse for not rising, which indeed seemed an impossible exercise.

I had invited Chesterton to talk about Dickens, because, according to Chesterton himself, there was nothing else to talk about on Christmas Day. 'Christmas and Dickens remain the only things worth talking about,' he said, 'because modern religion, philosophy, and literature have produced no substitute for either.' At any rate they were a fit subject for this uncommon defender of the commonplace, this religious apostle of sensuality, this virtuoso of the paradox, this champion leg-puller of the highbrow 'humorists.'

He was in jolly mood; I had thrown him a bone, and here

[1] Wells's literary output consists of eighty-five volumes to date.

he was, licking his chops over the succulent slivers of satirical meat. An attendant came to show us to the studio.

'I suppose you think I can't get up?' he said. 'See how I do it!'

And with an astonishing, perfectly calculated movement he rolled over to kneel on the floor, then gradually raised himself up by his powerful arms, while his wife watched him with confident solicitude. There he stood, three-hundred-odd pounds of unashamed vitality, panting but triumphant — and we went forth to war. One of the party had to walk — to save the elevator.

Christmas and Dickens and Chesterton proved a perfect combination for sheer intellectual acrobatics. 'There is no occasion, no date, no day, that has been able to do what Christmas does; and there is no writer among all the brilliant modern writers who has been able to do what Dickens did.' That was his dictum, and for fifteen minutes he defended it by shooting deft arrows at unseen adversaries, never forgetting that he was talking to Americans:

'I deny,' he said, 'that Elmer Gantry is a Christmas present. I deny that anyone wants Theodore Dreiser thrust into his Christmas stocking.' The muck-rakers, the pessimists, the heretics, the atheists, the 'modern pagans' all came in for a dressing-down. Especially the last.

'It has been said that the modern pleasure-seekers are pagans and that all their life of jazz and cocktails is merely a life of pagans. This seems to me a harsh judgment. I mean, of course, that it is hard on the pagans.

'The pagan gods and goddesses of the past were never so tinselly as the fast sets and smart people of the present. Venus was never so vulgar as what they now call sex appeal. Cupid was never so coarse or common as a modern realistic novel. The old pagans were imaginative and creative. They made things and built things.... If we were pagans we should be content with nothing less than the worship of beauty. If we were pagans there would be a Temple of Venus in Hollywood. If we were pagans there would be a Temple of Bacchus in Milwaukee. There would be a Temple of Mercury at the end of Wall Street. I admit it is a curious coincidence that he was also the god of flight. But anyhow the point is that the pagans could mix things; they could make festivals, and if they were still alive they could make an alternative to Christmas.'

As I said, he kept it up for fifteen minutes and he had his fling at everybody that got in his way; just as he had tilted at Shaw and Wells in his writings before the war. But now the spoken word — his voice, his dryness, his quiet, half-disgusted drawl, his wheezes and his pauses, all heightened the effect; here at last was the radio satirist, the eighteenth-century wit transferred from the coffee house to the studio. Had he died fifteen years earlier than he did, radio would have missed a great pioneer.

The B.B.C. had, indeed, discovered him, and his sparkling polemics were to enliven their programs increasingly till the year of his death. Several times he was relayed to America. The last time he figured in a special American transmission was when we broadcast, from the heart of Soho, an 'initiation ceremony' of the Detection Club (so called because it consisted of detective story writers), of which he was president. In the rather dilapidated ancient house (once the residence of Lord Mansfield, chief justice of England), having been carried up the steep stairs on a chair by four stalwart members, he administered the oath with appropriate mock solemnity on the skull of 'Eric,' the mascot of the club. The ritual, with its weird procession, its bogus mystery and ridiculous mumbo-jumbo, filled him with childish delight and brought out unsuspected histrionic powers in the creator of 'Father Brown.' In the audience, whom he exhorted to 'honor the King's English' and abstain from sundry absurdities in the writing of detective stories, were Dorothy Sayers, Helen Simpson, Marjory Allingham, Anthony Berkeley, A. A. Milne, and other best-sellers whose combined circulation reached into millions. Anyone sneezing influenza germs in that crowded, smoky room could have cut down the world's output of the best detective fiction by fifty per cent.

When the grotesque figure of Chesterton, with flying cape and enormous, broad-brimmed hat, disappeared around the corner of Gerrard Street that Sunday evening, it was the last I ever saw of him. He loved living too well to grow old.

PRIESTLEY AND THE HIGHBROWS

Now, what about the best-sellers outside this charmed circle of mystery merchants? On the whole I have found that popular novelists are not particularly willing broadcasters. Mr. Noel Coward, for instance, is usually much too busy producing a play, or somewhere on the Riviera recovering from a success. Mr. Michael Arlen's valet is the nearest I have ever been able to get to him, so that was that. Aldous Huxley, highbrow among intellectuals, epicure among esthetes, is a perfectly charming man, but when I asked him to talk to mere Americans, he didn't reply. For John Galsworthy — quiet, shy man that he was — the microphone held unknown terrors. For five years or more I tried to lure him and he never really refused. The last time I saw him, when he was still presiding over the P.E.N. Club, although illness had been slowing him down for years, he

said meekly, 'Well, I shall have to do it for you one day.'
But he died before he took that hurdle, and his voice was
never heard by anyone but his colleagues and friends.

But even if willing, fiction writers are not always successful at the microphone. I know of two cases where a slight
impediment of speech made it impossible even to ask,
without hurting a man's feelings. And then — though it's
dangerous to generalize — the radio has taken less kindly to
fiction than to truth. Which does not mean that novelists
can't tell the truth, but they can't always make it as interesting as fiction, and — a man always wants to give of his
best.

But there are those that can. J. B. Priestley, for instance,
is so successful at telling people the truth, and in broad Yorkshire, too, that he got himself into a peck of trouble with the
newspaper reporters in New York. And only a week or so
earlier he had addressed a large section of the American
public by radio from London, to try to give them an idea of
how thrilled he was over the prospect of discovering the
'Unknown Continent.' That was the title of the talk; we
tried to think of something appropriate, and as he was about
to visit, for the first time, the country that was paying him
the largest part of his royalties, what could be better than
give his fancy free rein about the reputed wonders of New
York's 'ivory and rose and amethyst towers, like Babylon
piled on Babylon, like some starry capital of lost Atlantis'?
That was the way a poetic novelist imagined it; when he got
there he could always tell the truth as he *saw* it.

That's where he made his mistake. Sailing up New York
Bay on a murky morning, possibly with a hang-over from the
Captain's dinner, facing a platoon of 'tough guys' and a
battery of cameras taking unflattering snap-shots, was the
wrong time for a chunky, unimpressed, and unimpressive
Yorkshireman to tell the unvarnished truth. Also he didn't
know that the New York skyline is the ship reporter's
esthetic religion. The result was some rather disastrous
publicity.

However, publicity is publicity, and Priestley has a talent
for getting it. Next time he broadcast from London it was

for the B.B.C., but we in America were rebroadcasting the talk. It was called 'To a Highbrow,' and excelled in calling his particular *bête noire* all kinds of names. When he arrived at the studio he was minus his script, thinking that the B.B.C. staff, who always insist on having duplicates in advance, would be there with the goods. But they couldn't find a copy. He offered to improvise, or trust to memory, but that idea was too revolutionary. It wasn't done. So the minutes ticked by — twenty of them — and both England and America had a lovely silence, interrupted only by the announcer's casual words of hope — in beautiful highbrow's English.

The resultant publicity was so 'good' that I had to procure a copy of the script for the newspapers. Reading such phrases as, 'You're the Pharisee among the arts... You never fail to admire the gulf that lies between you and the common herd... You decide — God knows why — to overemphasize your sibilants... You pretend to understand and enjoy things you don't understand and enjoy' — I wondered if somebody hadn't lost that manuscript accidentally on purpose.

BEST-SELLERS AT WORK

Hugh Walpole, a best-seller in England and a super-best-seller in America, spoke for me twice in the early days. He, too, 'looked at America,' but with quite unexceptionable eyes. The son of a bishop, with a flat in Piccadilly and an estate in Cumberland, friend of Tenor Melchior and Pugilist Tunney, collector of Epstein sculptures and Beerbohm caricatures, as perfect an English gentleman as Hollywood has ever seen, could not be anything but kind-hearted and polite — but unfortunately I don't remember what he said.

Then there was the late-lamented Edgar Wallace, who wore the mantle of Conan Doyle with a rakish air. His output was fabulous and suggested the moving belt. One of the best-hearted men that ever lived, he started in Fleet Street and came to live in Portland Place, with a country estate on the river Thames, a string of racehorses and an income that was incalculable. His bets were sensational and he was a famous prophet of the turf. But he lost everything but his cockney accent, and died — though he didn't know it — heavily in debt. His ten-inch ivory cigarette holder, sticking upwards out of his mouth, was a landmark in the London hotels and sporting clubs. He couldn't ever deny a favor asked by a pal (and all newspapermen were his pals); so — busy as he was — he came along and spoke a piece for me on Daniel Defoe, the first best-seller in English fiction and the Father of them all. It was a good journalistic piece of literary criticism.

Another time I went to him for a short drama to be written especially for the radio. The price was ridiculously low — for Edgar Wallace — since radio drama hasn't the earning capacity of the stage. While we were talking, his mind began to work and he became interested. 'There should be three or four characters, not more,' he mused; 'the woman accused of the murder, her barrister, the Crown's attorney, and the Judge. She isn't guilty, of course, and the whole story unravels during her evidence and cross-examination. The man who was found shot...' And so he was off, composing the whole scenario in front of me. I realized that his detractors were wrong: Edgar Wallace wrote everything himself.

'All right,' he said, 'seeing it's you, my pal; when do you want it?'

A week or two later he delivered the manuscript. By the time his check came from America, he was dead. It didn't go far towards liquidating his debts.

Going farther afield we got Lion Feuchtwanger, German refugee author, to speak about his 'trade' — that of the historical novelist, and why people read him. And pink-faced, platinum-blonde Vicki Baum, author of *Grand Hotel*, pendulating between Berlin and Hollywood, gave a talk on America, reversing the process adopted by Priestley, and so playing safe. As she 'fell in love with America the very first week, and this kept on growing every day,' her job wasn't difficult. But she, too, had to tackle that 'skyline I had heard so much about.' Well:

'It was a chilly, misty morning. The statue of Liberty stood wrapped in fog and looked a little disappointing. Then came the reporters — boys and girls — and they were so nice — awfully nice — and they took me into the smoking-room and asked me questions and had so much patience and listened so kindly to my stammering answers. And when they were gone, the skyline was gone too — it had passed during the interviews. And I had to discover in the evening papers that I thought the famous skyline of New York was "not so hot!"'

And that's the way to handle *that* situation — Mr. Priestley (and others) please note!

It's a far cry from Masefield to Vicki Baum, and there is hardly a literary giant of this generation who wouldn't fit into that wide sweep. Most of them I managed to 'hook' in the first year of transatlantic broadcasting. Most of them, with one notable exception. And that was George Bernard Shaw.

IV. 'GET SHAW ON ANYTHING!'

THE FUNNIEST JOKE IN THE WORLD

NEVER shall I forget my first attempt to 'get Shaw.' I knew it would be a tough job, but the assignment left me plenty of scope. I was not to get him to talk on any particular subject, but 'on anything.' George Bernard Shaw might be the world's greatest living writer to his biographer;[1] to the American audience he was Public Jokester No. 1, and 'anything' would presumably raise the desired laugh. What most people didn't realize, however, is that he was very particular about his jokes. 'My way of joking,' he once said, 'is telling the truth. That is the funniest joke in the world.'

Another mistaken notion about Shaw was that he is just out for publicity. He may be out for it, but not 'just.' You can't eat publicity; and, anyway, an ascetic playwright nearing eighty doesn't eat very much. Nobody since Queen Victoria has reached that age with so much limelight playing about him, and there is a limit to the endurance of the human eye. When, years ago, he put down for *Who's Who* that his chief recreation was 'showing off,' he probably meant it, but it is *creation* — without the prefix — that has filled out most of his time.

When, on a chilly afternoon in the spring of 1930, I drove out to Shaw's modest country place in Hertfordshire, I knew that this supposedly cantankerous Irishman had never broadcast before, but I didn't know why. He had, it is true, read his little play, *O'Flaherty, V.C.*, from a B.B.C. studio

[1] Archibald Henderson: *Contemporary Immortals*, New York, 1930.

in the very earliest days of broadcasting nine years before. He had, as I found out later, presided at a public debate on 'The Menace of the Leisured Woman' between Lady Rhondda and G. K. Chesterton, and that debate had been broadcast, too. But he had never, in all the ten years of British broadcasting, done what you would expect Shaw to do — walk up to a microphone in a broadcasting studio and lecture the people of England, Ireland, and the world in general on the absurdity of their behavior, in the classic Shavian way. I didn't know why not; and although I didn't find out till years afterward, I must, for the purpose of this story, tell about it now.

HOW TO GET FREEDOM OF SPEECH

All of Shaw's utterances are somehow on the record, usually in the public prints. No man living or dead has been as eagerly quoted as he; no public character has been so persistently fertile as newspaper 'copy' for the last forty years. Yet, in looking up his case history with reference to broadcasting, I had not been able to find the text of his remarks in that debate. I finally looked up the back issues of Lady Rhondda's weekly, *Time and Tide*, where the debate was recorded, but very little was quoted from Shaw. I appealed to the editor for the complete text, but it couldn't be found. When I was on the point of sailing for New York, with the all-but completed manuscript of this book in my trunk, I received from Lady Rhondda's assistant editor a bunch of faded typescript which I hadn't time to look at till the *Queen Mary* was out at sea. And then I discovered that it was a complete, stenographic report of the debate, dug out of the archives of *Time and Tide*, and as I began to read it I discovered the key to Shaw's protracted silence on the air, as follows.

When broadcasting in England was first authorized by the Government, the conditions of operation specifically ex-

cluded all 'controversial' matter from the air. This edict
wasn't directed against anyone in particular, but it automatically excluded a man like Shaw, who refused ever to
submit anything he wanted to say to the scrutiny of any man
on earth. Imagine, therefore, what must have been the dis-
may of the B.B.C. officials when they discovered that the
above-mentioned public debate between two eminently 'safe'
people was to be refereed by Shaw, and that, instead of
confining his remarks to a mere introduction and summing-
up, this referee took the opportunity to explode a verbal
bomb. As might have been expected, he exploited the
situation with diabolical glee.

'Ladies and gentlemen,' he said (according to the verbatim report), 'I must ask you to be very specially on your
good behavior tonight because what is happening at present
is not merely Mr. Bernard Shaw addressing a crowded and
prematurely enthusiastic audience in the Kingsway Hall. It
is London calling the British Isles and the universe in
general.[1] . . . We are being broadcast, and the condition
under which broadcasting is conducted in this country is that
nothing of a controversial nature must be spoken from the
platform or anywhere else, except by members of the Government. (Laughter and cheers.) How an animated and possibly embittered controversy is to be carried on if neither of
the speakers is to become controversial, I cannot tell you.
I am sorry to say that I cannot undertake to keep order in
that respect because one of the conditions of broadcasting in
this country is that I myself, individually and personally, am
not to be allowed to broadcast under any terms whatever.
Therefore my task is somewhat difficult. My duty as chairman obliges me at all hazards to preserve the right of the
speakers to be as controversial as they please on any subject
whatever, in spite of all the Postmasters and Governments
in the world. (Laughter.) That duty I shall fulfill.

'But now observe what that will lead us to. Probably at
this moment the Postmaster-General is listening in. He is
realizing that I am speaking. His panic is probably growing
with every sentence that falls from my lips. How am I to be

[1] A slight Shavian exaggeration, in pre-short-wave days.

stopped? . . . I do not know, but it is evident to me that the Postmaster-General may call out the Guards. If you find, then, an energetic force of military and police breaking into this hall, destroying the microphone and leading me away in custody, I must ask you not to offer any resistance. (Laughter.) Your remedy is a constitutional one. *You must vote against the Government at the next election.* (Laughter and cheers.)

'Now some of you may reply that it is no remedy for you because you already intended to vote against the Government. Well, you have one more remedy. I believe it to be a strictly constitutional one. I am now speaking, not only to you, ladies and gentlemen assembled in this hall, but to the rest of the eight million persons who are listening in. I suggest to you that if every one of you writes a letter to the Postmaster-General telling him what you think of him, you will be strictly inside the letter of the law, you will contribute an enormous sum in three-halfpenny stamps to the revenue, and you will make it absolutely certain that no postmaster-general will ever attempt to interfere with freedom of speech in England again.' (Loud cheers.)

That, then, was Shaw's first broadcast and — for all one could tell — his last. No wonder he wasn't invited again. No wonder the *Times* — famous for its verbatim reports — didn't print his remarks. What must have happened behind the scenes between the Government and the B.B.C. is nobody's business, for no doubt hundreds, perhaps thousands, had taken Shaw's advice about writing to the Postmaster-General. A year or two later his prediction about free speech had come true: the lid was off, controversy was permitted on the British air.

But Shaw had not broadcast yet. On his seventieth birthday he had been asked to contribute some sage remarks appropriate to the occasion, if he would submit his manuscript in advance, but he told the authorities where they could go. That was the situation when I arrived with the proposal that Shaw should broadcast to the United States. The only certainty, at that date, was that you couldn't censor Shaw.

SHAW AND EINSTEIN AT DINNER

For me there were other difficulties, too. Shaw himself hadn't decided what broadcasting really was. Was it authorship? In that case who would pay his price? Was it public speaking? Since it was his principle only to speak when he had an axe to grind, and then gratuitously, he would have to make the broadcasting rajahs a valuable present, which surely they didn't deserve. But my trepidations were chiefly due to Shaw's reputation as a 'savage,' where intruders are concerned; the stories of his candid treatment of people he didn't happen to like were not reassuring in the least. He was a hard man to interview, the most elusive target for the lion-hunter, the most impossible man to enlist in the usual kind of 'good cause.' Nor could he be lured by flattery, however subtle; his shrewd eye would detect the purpose and force you to come to the point. And once his mind was made up, it was impossible to argue him out of his decision.

My previous acquaintance with the great man was slight. But my friend Albert Coates, orchestral conductor and Wagner specialist, was my sponsor, so we dropped in without warning and were given tea by that charming homebody, Mrs. Shaw, after she had sounded a shrill pea-whistle to summon her spouse from his garden haunt. Here, in a revolving sunshine hut, Shaw was correcting the proofs of his collected works, and he was glad of an excuse for interrupting a 'boresome' task. He didn't take tea, for he never does, but watched us tolerantly while discoursing on the relative merits of Wagner and Verdi. (I discovered that this one-time music critic was still the 'perfect Wagnerite,' who didn't share the moderns' high opinion of Verdi — Bülow's 'Italian hurdy-gurdy man').

How I injected politics and radio into that esthetic homily I can't remember, but presently he had poured scorn on the London Naval Treaty, which was about to be signed, and which was certainly not worth a broadcast from him. And what about another subject — in fact 'anything'?

'What will you pay me — a million dollars?' he said, in his still perceptible Dublin brogue. Then, after a moment, 'Don't bother about it.'

I knew he was having his little joke at the expense of Americans, and found that what he needed first of all was not anything but *something* to talk about. 'Whatever reputation I have,' he confided, 'is due to the fact that I never open my mouth unless I have something to say.' So we left it at that — until the desired subject should pop into his head — or mine.

I spent the summer holidays trying to think up subjects for Shaw. Nothing suitable turned up. But by keeping in touch I managed to get a broadcast — not a genuine one, but a public speech. That autumn a great dinner was given in London in honor of Professor Einstein, for the benefit of the suffering Jews in the Near East. Shaw was caught off his guard: he was persuaded to speak, and the minute I heard about it, I rang up the B.B.C. It was Shaw's re-entry into broadcasting — by the back door. The result was that the proceedings were not only broadcast, but 'relayed' to America.

Toasting the world's most famous Jew was just pie for Shaw. Sitting beside the Chief Rabbi of London, the fair, blue-eyed, white-bearded Irish free-thinker donned a black skull-cap in deference to the Orthodox Jews who were present in great numbers, and turned eastward while prayers were intoned. Then, with characteristic Shavian 'cheek,' he began by putting Isaac Newton in his place.

'Facts,' he said, 'will never stop an Englishman.' So Newton 'invented' the straight line and gravitation and the Newtonian universe, which lasted until a young man had a look at it and said: 'Newton did not know what happened to the apple and I can prove this when the next eclipse comes along. The heavenly bodies go in curves because it is the natural way for them to go.' And so 'the whole Newtonian Universe crumpled up and was succeeded by the Einstein Universe.'

This was Shaw 'on anything' with a vengeance — with a speech by Einstein thrown in for good measure. But still

Shaw hadn't 'broadcast' — that is, spoken into a microphone for the benefit of unseen listeners alone, nor had he
spoken at a time when all America could listen. Every few
weeks I rang him up. He would come to the telephone himself and try to put me off. Now and again he would ask me
to come along and see him, and next morning I would be
sitting in his London flat, high up overlooking the Thames,
with Shaw on one side of the fire, I on the other, and Miss
Patch, his faithful secretary, a few feet away. And in a
conversation that was usually two against one he would
knock down one idea after another.

'The Future of Kingship,' I suggested once. 'I've said all
I have to say on that in *The Apple-Cart;* let them go and see
that!'

'What about the talkies — are they the dramatist's
future vehicle?'

'Nonsense; talkies don't interest me.'

And so on. Next time another batch of subjects would
share the same fate. Nor could his interest be roused on the
centenary of Mark Twain — one of his great favorites and a
'kindred spirit.' Nobody with the sense of Mark Twain
would want any fuss made about him just because he would
be a hundred, had he lived. Still another time there was to be
a broadcast in America by the Irish poet George Russell
('A.E.') and I asked Shaw to 'introduce' him from London.
'Nothing could be sillier,' he wrote me on one of his famous
postcards, 'than this introduction business, wasting half the
speaker's time and dividing the interest. I have no patience
with such folly. Let the Announcer do it, in not more than
thirty words.' But these things were just outbursts of the
professional. My friends at the B.B.C. used to catch it
worse than that.

'You don't mind my bothering you like this?' I asked him
one day, returning to the charge with further suggestions.
'Not in the least,' he retorted; 'but I don't believe it's any
good — anyway, *your people wouldn't let me say what I
please.*'

I mustered all the outraged pride I could and told him that
there is no censorship of broadcasts in America.

THE MALVERN HOTEL.
MALVERN.
6. Sept. 1930

Nothing could be sillier than this introduction business; wasting half the speaker's time and dividing the interest. I have no patience with such folly. Let the announcer do it, in not more than thirty words.

G. Bernard Shaw.

6. SEP 1930

'Suppose, now, I wanted to talk about Russia?'

'Splendid!' I exclaimed; 'let's have a little talk about Russia.'

'Well,' he chuckled, 'we must see about that. . . . You've certainly advanced matters a bit today' was his good-bye.

'A LITTLE TALK ABOUT RUSSIA'

The following summer Shaw went to Russia, in the company of Lady Astor and some representative English people. It is more than likely that our last conversation was responsible for the trip. Soon after it he had seen Sokolnikoff, the

Soviet ambassador (who a few years later was to be tried
and 'convicted' as a Trotskyist), and Sokolnikoff in answer
to a request for information had suggested that Shaw go and
see for himself. Within a few months of his return he finally
succumbed to my blandishments and agreed to speak. I was
careful not to ask for a 'script.' His public speeches that had
been broadcast were *ex tempore;* this time he had written out
every word and rehearsed it; he knew he had just fourteen
minutes and he took no risks of overrunning. (My introduction was short!) I had no idea what was coming, though I
saw a wicked twinkle in his eye, and Mrs. Shaw whispered
to me as we entered the little B.B.C. studio: 'It's very cheeky,
you know.'

It was. Shaw is past-master at shocking people into taking
notice. And there is no surer way of doing that than by
calling them names. It may be a crude way, but it worked,
and proved Shaw right in calculating his audience. When he
sat down behind that microphone in old Savoy Hill and
addressed them as 'you dear old boobs,' he knew what he was
doing, for there wasn't a newspaper in the United States
next day that hadn't taken his bait. No radio speech had
ever been more widely quoted, none had drawn such volu-
minous and vituperative comment. If Shaw was indulging
in 'recreation,' he must have been having a marvellous
time; but he was only having his favorite joke — telling the
truth, as he saw it. A fellow-playwright of Shaw's, James
Bridie, says that some time ago Mr. Shaw became the
official Sage of the British Isles. Now, at seventy-five, he
may have had an ambition to be recognized as the Sage of
the English-speaking world. In any case, deep down he was
in dead earnest. Not even he would go to the trouble of
writing a little masterpiece of dialectics and delivering it
gratis, unless he were deeply concerned. Think of what it
must have cost him to be facetious about a matter which all
his life has been his religion!

No one — least of all Shaw — would pretend that the
'Little Talk about Russia' was a great political or economic
document. How long would an accurately thought-out study
of Russian state socialism have held the attention of millions

B. B. C.

Shaw's 'You dear old boobs,' the only talk, thus far, addressed
to America alone

G.P.O. Film Unit

Wells talked about 'The World of Our Grandchildren' in the
first American broadcast of his career

of 'boobs'? Shaw had sized up the American radio audience, and his verdict was not flattering. After all, if one must compete with the inanities of jazz and 'script acts,' he must produce something with the same amount of punch.

'Russia has the laugh on us. She has us fooled, beaten, shamed, shown up, outpointed, and all but knocked out.' True or not true, this made people sit up.

'Your President [Hoover], who became famous by feeding the starving millions of war-devastated Europe, cannot feed his own people in the time of peace.' If many of his listeners hadn't agreed with him, they wouldn't have voted for Roosevelt in such overwhelming numbers the next year.

'Our agriculture is ruined and our industries collapsing under the weight of their own productiveness because we have not found out how to distribute our wealth as well as to produce it.' No professor of economics nowadays would quarrel with that. Nor will any professor of history deny that Lenin and his friends 'took command of the Soviets and established the U.S.S.R. exactly as Washington and Jefferson and Hamilton and Franklin and Tom Paine had established the United States of America one hundred and forty-one years before.'

He then suggested an amusing Sunday game. 'Make a collection of the articles in the royalist newspapers and political pamphlets, American as well as British, issued during the last quarter of the eighteenth century. Strike out the dates, the name of the country, and the names of its leaders. The game is for your friends to fill up the blanks. What country is this, you will ask, which has broken every social bond and given itself over to anarchy and infamy at the bidding of a gang of atheists, drunkards, libertines, thieves and assassins? Your friends will guess wrong. When the right answer is America, they will guess Russia. When the right name is Washington, they will cry Trotsky. They will declare that ... Jefferson is Lenin, that Franklin is Litvinoff, that Paine is Lunacharsky, that Hamilton is Stalin. When you tell them the truth, they will probably never speak to you again; but you will have given them a valuable moral lesson, which ought to be the object of all Sunday games.'

Of course the gibing editorials didn't quote this. They cited some of Shaw's figures on Russia and dismissed them by saying 'bosh'; they seized upon his flights of enthusiasm and omitted his warning that Russia was not yet a paradise. 'Russia is too big a place,' he said, 'for any government to get rid in fourteen years of the frightful mess of poverty, ignorance, and dirt left by the Czardom. . . . I am afraid there is a good deal of the poverty, ignorance, and dirt we know so well at home, but there is hope everywhere in Russia because these evils are retreating there before the spread of communism as steadily as they are advancing upon us before the last desperate struggle of our bankrupt capitalism to stave off its inevitable goal by reducing wages, multiplying tariffs, and rallying all the latent savagery and greed in the world to its support in predatory warfare masquerading as patriotism.'

A jokester? America got what it asked for; but the trouble is that nobody likes a serious joke. So not only the papers but the politicians and the churchmen turned on him — the churchmen because of the religious fervor they detected in his words. (Churches don't attack infidels; they 'convert' them. But they *fight* rival religions.) And so the Columbia network had to give an eminent cleric a chance to answer Shaw on the air. Shaw's attackers couldn't have pleased him better if they tried.

RADIO SATIRIST NO. I

'Part showman, part schoolmaster,' the astute Mr. Bridie calls Shaw. He thoroughly lived up to it in this broadcast and those he has made since then. For this talk and the one he made that summer on Joan of Arc (for England, but rebroadcast in the United States) broke the ice. Largely, thanks to Shaw, 'controversial' broadcasting was now permitted in Great Britain, and if anybody accuses the British broadcasting authorities of muzzling anybody they need only point to Shaw. In the half-dozen talks he has made for them, at the rate of about one a year, he has lectured them without restraint — on morals, on politics, on economics, on education, and even religion — with the fearlessness of a Fox and the wit of a Swift.

He debunked every hero and every subject he touched. Joan of Arc had 'no sex appeal,' but was an inveterate soldier who wanted to go on fighting when there was no more fighting to do. Her career was, according to Shaw, the career of the Pankhursts and the Trotskys of our day. Concerning Freedom he told Englishmen to 'stop gassing about it,' because they didn't know what it was, 'never having had any.' Disarmament, as discussed in Geneva, didn't rouse his interest, because 'if I'm to be killed by a shell I prefer it to be as big as possible, as it will give the occasion importance and make a bigger noise.' And the pious effusions about the Empire he countered with this: 'If I were a stranger from another planet I should say that an attempt to combine England with India before England was combined with the United States on the one side and with all her Western neighbors on the other, is a crazy reversal of the natural order of things, and cannot possibly last.'

One of the most courageous things the B.B.C. ever did was to allow Shaw to speak about schools in a series designed 'for sixth forms' (which correspond to the top grade in an American high school). For if, as many people think, the average grown-up has got Shaw's number and knows that he's 'just a buffoon,' the young and impressionable, about to be graduated from school, cannot be trusted to have such superior judgment. Speaking to the schoolboys of England just about the time when the air vibrates with valedictories, when examinations are being struggled with and the Young Hopefuls are about to go out into the world, Shaw was permitted to tell them that 'school was to me a sentence of penal servitude'; and that 'I could not read schoolbooks, because they are written by people who do not know how to write.'

'Some of your schoolfellows,' he calmly warned his juvenile audience, 'may surprise you by getting hanged.

Others, of whom you have the lowest opinion, will turn out to be geniuses, and become of the great men of your time.'

Superficially it was just one joke after another, though once again, on closer examination, the jokes were all true. But equally true was the confession of the octogenarian: 'I am an old man before I have quite got the habit of thinking of myself as a boy.'

By virtue of these talks Shaw is, I think, to be rated — with Chesterton — as one of the world's first radio satirists. As a public speaker he was perhaps less effective than he would like to have been. His rather pugnacious attitude and his tendency to a kind of didactic bullying were apt to defeat their own object. At the microphone, however, his manner never irritates, though much of his rather brittle yet benevolent personality always 'registers.' With the intuition of the born showman he grasped from the beginning the essentials of the new medium — intimacy, simplicity, and naturalness — and its informality, which is very different from literary style.

He is, of course, a marvel of vitality. At eighty-one his rich, compact voice is as steady and vigorous as in middle age, and his exceptionally clear diction, with its shade of Irish, has just the tempo and inflection to give it buoyancy and point. The arresting picture of the lanky, quixotic figure of the white-bearded youth with the jaunty step and the devil-may-care look is so vividly before you that television seems superfluous.[1]

FACING THE 'BOOBS'

Practically all of Shaw's broadcasts, ever since I managed to break the ice, have been transmitted to America. Untold

[1] The first "curtain speech" in television drama was made by Bernard Shaw in July, 1937, when, after a televised version of *How He Lied to Her Husband*, he appeared on the B.B.C. television screen to say: 'You might not suppose it from my veteran appearance, but the truth is that I am the author of that ridiculous little play you have just heard.'

millions have heard the most famous literary genius of our
time, who had also become one of the must effective as well
as provocative broadcasters in the world. But the famous
'boobs' talk is the only one, thus far, that was addressed
to America alone. No offers of money ever tempted him: he
had to be convinced, not only that he had something to say,
but that it needed saying at the time. Simply 'lecturing'
America never attracted him as a sport and he has the utmost contempt for the horde of more or less educated
Englishmen who are 'telling America' year after year.

On the other hand, no trouble was too great for him when
it came to accommodating a friend. Once I discovered that
a talk that he was booked to make in a B.B.C. series had
been recorded in advance, because the date fell on the eve
of one of his long cruises. It would have meant cancelling
the American transmission, at the end of a series which
both American networks had taken almost solely for the
sake of the talk by G. B. S. We were in danger of playing
Hamlet without the Prince.

I told Shaw that American broadcasting chains couldn't
use recordings because of the existing laws. 'What do you
care about laws, anyway?' he chuckled. 'How about prohibition when you had it?' But a few minutes later he
agreed, not only to come to London on a Sunday night, but
to walk up five flights of stairs in a dormant office building
to make his talk — for American listeners — all over again.
He was almost indignant at the suggestion of getting the
elevator started for his sake. For a man nearing eighty this
was pretty generous, considering that there was no financial
or other consideration of any kind.

Those who say that Shaw is 'out for money' or 'out for
publicity' should think again.

Early in 1933 Shaw traversed the United States on a trip
around the world, and contrary to all expectations, agreed to
stop in New York. He had blustered again and again that
he wouldn't go to America because he didn't want to be
'mobbed' by his admirers. But somebody collared him, and
he allowed himself to be 'starred' at the Metropolitan Opera
House, whence his speech was to be broadcast on a National
network throughout the United States.

So here he was, facing the 'boobs,' three thousand of them, and most of them seem to have decided that, in Queen Victoria's phrase, they were not amused. The late Clarence Day, crippled and bedridden for years, who managed by an incredible effort to crawl into a dress suit and get himself transported to the Opera House for the purpose of 'seeing Shaw make a fool of himself,' said he was not disappointed. Most of the other members of the fashionable audience, however, were — probably because this time Shaw did not call them names.

The 'getting' of Shaw was not only my outstanding success to date, but one of the great experiences of an exciting career. When he had broadcast, the last of the available intellectual Big Game in the British Isles had been bagged. My eyes began to drift to wider fields.

V. PUTTING THE POPE ON THE AIR

O N THE first of January, 1931, Benito Mussolini made his first and only broadcast in English. Having taken daily lessons for months with an English lady resident in Rome, he was persuaded that he had mastered the language sufficiently to impress the waiting millions in America and could project the great message of Fascism to the New World direct from its fountainhead.

Sometime previous to this, a series of articles from the Duce's own hand had been commissioned by the Hearst newspapers to appear serially throughout the United States. It was a fat contract, and even measured by the sensational Hearst standards, the cost must have been terrific. So, in order to launch it with the requisite *éclat*, Hearst had arranged for the radio talk to America. This had required the intensive study of a language not hitherto in the great man's verbal arsenal. The optimism of his tutors was exaggerated, for the message, though carefully prepared and edited in idiomatic English, was probably understood better by Italo-Americans than Americans. By arrangement with Hearst it was broadcast by short wave from Rome and rebroadcast in the United States by the National Broadcasting Company's network. The plans were kept secret almost until the very day, in order to prevent the rival Columbia chain from 'horning in.' When Columbia heard about it, frantic efforts were made in Washington to get permission to 'relay,' but it was too late. Sitting in London, busily occupied in preparing to 'scoop' the Opposition in other fields,

I suddenly found myself 'scooped' instead. It was an awful blow. The polite ambassador and his minions in the London Embassy were sympathetic, but even their eleventh-hour intercession didn't do the trick. In my innocence I was determined that this sort of thing shouldn't happen again, but I realized that my virtual monopoly on broadcasts from Europe was at an end.

A few days later I was tipped that the Vatican's short-wave radio station was nearing completion and that something even more sensational might happen. Officially I was still only the London representative of the Columbia network, but as there was no other representative in Europe it soon became clear that my playground was the entire European continent. So I put 'European Director' on my letter-head and hoped for the best.

MARCONI BUILDS A SUPER-STATION

Ostensibly the projected Vatican station was for tele-graphic and possibly telephonic communication. The historic Lateran Treaty with the Italian Government — Mussolini's greatest master-stroke of statesmanship — had been signed two years before, and for the first time in sixty years the Vatican enjoyed a temporal, that is, political, existence. The Pope was no longer the 'prisoner of the Vatican,' and on February 12, 1929, had signified his new status by emerging to give the traditional blessing, *Urbi et Orbi*, from the balcony of St. Peter's in the presence of a great multitude.

The newly won 'sovereignty' of the Vatican State had been asserted by various visible signs. A Vatican coinage had been minted; Vatican postage stamps had been issued, to be sold by a tiny post office near the Vatican entrance; a showy new government building with an imposing Renaissance façade was nearing completion; and a Vatican court of justice set up for the benefit of four hundred and fifty

Vatican citizens. Moreover, a railroad siding had been constructed, leading by means of a tunnel through a spur of Vatican Hill to a small and rather pretentious-looking station. But no trains had ever run over it and the great portals shutting the tunnel on the Vatican side had not yet swung wide, although a royal train presented by Mussolini's Government stood ready to take the Holy Father and his retinue wherever they wanted to go. The world stood open to Pius XI.

All this had been done with the financial co-operation of the Italian Government under the treaty's provisions; now, with the same financial aid, the Vatican radio station was being built on the summit of the hill, and connected by telephone lines to the Palace, so that the Pontiff might communicate, directly and independently of any Italian or other 'foreign' aid, with his Nuncios throughout the world.

But the amount payable by the Italian State under this head had to be supplemented. What was wanted was not only a very modern and powerful station, such as the supreme pontiff should command, but a marble building and the most sumptuous accessories. The railroad might be just a symbol of sovereignty, but a radio station opened up practical possibilities. It was to be built by the Marconi Company under the personal supervision of Senator Marconi himself.

Senator Marconi, rated throughout the world as the leading inventor of wireless communication, had been raised to the rank of Marchese by the King of Italy, and although not a Fascist by inclination, had become one of the chief ornaments of the Fascist State, an elder statesman and president of the Italian Academy. But he was also a devout Catholic and a confidant of the Pope. His marriage with his Irish wife, the Honorable Beatrice O'Brien, had been annulled by the Sacred Rota in 1927 and he was now married to a beautiful young noblewoman, the Countess Maria Cristina Bezzi-Scala, member of an old family of papal aristocracy. He was reputed to be very wealthy. His cup of happiness, presumably, was full. Most of his time, when he was not engaged in business in London, was spent in his sumptuous apartment on the Via Condotti in Rome or on his luxurious yacht *Elettra*, conducting experiments.

The difference between the available funds and the actual cost of the proposed Vatican station was, it is said, contributed in part by donations from the Faithful (chiefly in America), and in part as a homage to the Holy Father by the generous Marchese himself. It was to be the last word in scientific perfection and efficiency. A neat and handsome little building, with the pontifical arms carved over the door, was to contain the machinery and the office of the director, Father Gianfranceschi, Jesuit savant and head of the Papal Academy of Sciences (housed in an idyllic pavilion which is said to have been a retreat for certain privileged ladies in days when popes were more worldly but less science-minded than now).

What use would be made of the new station? It would certainly not be as passively ornamental as the railroad station below. Great secrecy was preserved as to its mechanical details and characteristics. It could telegraph to anywhere, certainly; but it also had a speech panel and a duplex arrangement for two-way conversations with distant points. What about broadcasting? No one had even dared to suggest that the Holy Father himself would engage in anything so mundane as broadcasting, although the possibility of reaching the whole of the Christian world from the centre of the Catholic Faith was a fascinating prospect.

But fools rush in where clerics fear to tread. And we Americans have the imagination of fools. Busy with the problems of Austria and the League of Nations, I was oblivious to what was going on in Rome, when a cable from New York ordered me to go there and 'get' the Pope to broadcast to America! Had he signified any intention to broadcast at all? I asked. No, but he might. I was staggered by the very thought.

HEARST TAKES AN INTEREST

From Vienna, where Wilhelm Miklas, once a school-teacher, new president of the Austrian Republic, had to be introduced to American listeners, I went to Turin, the head-quarters of Italian broadcasting, to take counsel with the radio chiefs. The Pope to broadcast? Ludicrous! You can take it from us, on the inside, that he will not. So off I went to my next assignment, the meeting of the League Council in Geneva. German minorities in Poland were to be discussed, and other inflammable subjects. Doctor Curtius, Germany's liberal foreign minister, was going to address a tirade to American listeners, but at the last moment, scared by Nazi demonstrations, he had 'walked out.' In a half-hour conversation with him I got the first inkling of that rising storm in Germany which two years later was to sweep Hitler into power.

The Pope and his short-wave station were far from my mind as I fussed and fumed around the Hôtel Métropole, the cheerless headquarters of the German delegation. Further inquiries had confirmed me in the belief that a papal broadcast was music of the far distant future, and in my pocket was a cable ready to be sent to New York, recommending the cancellation of my trip to Rome, which would be a wasteful wild-goose chase.

In the lobby of the hotel were listless groups of secretaries, journalists, and hangers-on. Suddenly I saw an old friend, Karl von Wiegand, veteran Hearst correspondent, who said he had just come from — of all places — Rome. Somebody mentioned radio.

'You know I arranged that Mussolini broadcast for Hearst. And only yesterday I left Prince X down there, who's going to get us the Pope.'

'Great man, Hearst. He stops at nothing,' I said, mentally crumpling up my cablegram. 'Have you had dinner? Come along to the Bavaria!'

In that crowded and smoky gastronomic hang-out, whose

walls are covered with fantastic caricatures of the political
and journalistic Big Shots of Geneva, we talked of the good
old revolutionary days in Berlin, when the Wilhelmstrasse
bristled with barbed wire, and street battles were our diver-
sions between strangely concocted libations in the Adlon
Bar. Before midnight I left Geneva to make connections
with the Rome Express, in my pocket a nice note from Wiegand introducing an old colleague to Prince X at the Grand
Hôtel.

The Prince was one of those tall willowy Italians of the
north, whom you see either at fashionable hotel bars or
driving a flashy Bugatti to a rendezvous, those 'younger sons
of younger sons' who live by their wits, and whose chief
assets are elegant manners, aristocratic 'contacts' and a way
with the ladies. This particular Prince was, I was told, the
nephew of a Cardinal, high in the councils of the Vatican.
At the moment he was a Hearst correspondent in Rome. His
English was as elegant as his person and there was usually an
athletic-looking Swiss — a trooper of the famous Papal
Guard — in his room. Having just bowed out General
Nobile, that ill-starred explorer who had been thrown to the
lions for being an honest man but a poor 'hero' for the young
Fascist State, the Prince turned to me with that easy assurance which gets you into places and over problems at a
bound.

Sure, he was getting the Pope to broadcast — February
12 was the probable date. His uncle was a Cardinal, Marconi one of his pals. And Hearst was his boss. His interest in
broadcasting was platonic, and I doubt whether he knew
anything about the bitter rivalry of broadcasting companies
in America. Nevertheless, discretion was the better part of
valor and I decided to try and supplement my information
elsewhere.

THE MONSIGNORE WHO GETS THE NEWS

The newspapers knew as good as nothing. The other (non-Hearst) American correspondents were aware of the Vatican's broadcasting, but thought of it only in terms of communications. For Vatican news they relied almost exclusively on two sources, the *Osservatore Romano*, the official organ which usually conceals as much as it reveals, and a certain Monsignore who ran an unofficial one-man press service for the benefit of foreign correspondents, tolerated but not endorsed by the authorities.

The comings and goings of this dignitary — a swarthy and well-fed cleric who shaved on Sundays and feast-days, and seemed to live day and night in the same soutane, was one of the social oddities of Rome. He would be seen daily in and about the Vatican, where the tiny square of purple in the opening of his collar-band enforced obsequious respect from all attendants, courtesies from the Vatican police and military salutes from the medieval Swiss Guards. At night he could be observed in the Sala della Stampa working on 'copy,' or at the telegraph office filing messages with great assiduity — like any ordinary journalist. In off times and after hours he would join a convivial group of laymen in one of those restaurants that enjoy the reputation of a superior cuisine. (They say in Rome that a good rule to follow when in doubt about a restaurant is to see whether any clerics are among the clients. If there are just priests, the food is good; if there's a Monsignore, the food is excellent.)

But no matter how late he might be on his professional rounds, mornings at seven would find the Monsignore saying Mass in his little church somewhere beyond the seven hills of Rome. And an hour or so later one might have an appointment to meet him outside the bronze doors of St. Peter's. Nor would he neglect his meditations; punctual to the dot, one could see his broad-brimmed clerical felt hat and his flowing cassock approaching through the majestically sweeping colonnades that curve around the Plaza in front of St. Peter's, breviary in hand, his lips moving with great rapidity through the last of the rubrics, so perfectly timed that the last Amen would melt into his cheery 'Bon giorno!' or 'Bonjour!' as the case might be — for with the exception of English the Monsignore knew a language or two.

I have a notion that he knew more English than he admitted, too, but while his clients struggled through Italian or French, their hesitations gave him time to think.

In the difficult task of serving more masters than one the Monsignore performed miracles. Not a foreign correspondent in Rome would admit that this ubiquitous priest was on his payroll; yet all profited from his services in a particular way: everybody got all the news, but yet it wasn't quite the same news, and everyone had, or thought he had, something exclusive — in fact no one doubted that he, and he alone, enjoyed the Monsignore's confidence to an exceptional degree.

Despite his prodigious and ubiquitous labors the Monsignore was always reachable by telephone. If he wasn't home, his housekeeper was, and an hour or so later he would ring back from somewhere in or about Rome. And his voice was always reassuring; if there was no news in sight, one felt that it was just around the corner.

So it was with the rumor about the Big Broadcast. The Monsignore never denied it, never confirmed it. But in the long days of waiting, of secrecy, of sinister hearsay, it was a comfort to hear the soft, courteous, authoritative voice telling what could be and what could not be, but if the news should break, it would 'break right' — for you.

'CONTACT OLD GENTLEMAN DIRECT!'

Before I met the Monsignore, things looked black indeed. Against the claims of our Opposition, especially recommended by the Apostolic Delegate in Washington as well as an American Cardinal, I was to have the friendly offices of a lesser American prelate who was said to enjoy the special confidence of the Pope, and who was supposed to be somewhere on his way to Rome. Perhaps he was already there? I inquired at the headquarters of his Sacred Order — no news. I cabled my office in New York: 'When does Father W—— arrive and where will he stay?' — and waited for a reply.

While I was waiting I thought I'd take my first look at the Vatican. As I stood all alone in that vast, rectangular inner court, stretched to the full height of my five-foot-three, I looked up at the lofty walls of Pope Nicholas' fifteenth-century Palace of the Thousand Halls, rising canyon-like on either side of me, and the towering Appartamento Borgia straight ahead. I looked at the myriad windows, imagined the countless rooms and miles of corridors behind them, and I wondered — wondered just where in this awe-inspiring maze might be the Pope in solitary majesty; wondered, too, whether the whole idea of his broadcasting and my 'arranging' it for America's upstart radio chain wasn't too fantastic for thoughts, let alone words.

When I returned to my hotel, feeling rather blue, the answer to my cable awaited me: 'Father W—— unsailing. Contact old gentleman direct.' ('Old gentleman' was code for Pope!)

I looked again and it was like looking down an empty well for a pin. My mind went back to the Vatican, to the towering canyon, the thousand windows, the Papal guards, the closed doors of bronze that I had seen. 'Contact old gentleman direct!'

Well, there was still lots of time. It was near the end of January and the broadcast, if it happened, wouldn't happen before February 12. The date certainly sounded right, for not only was it the date of the Pope's enthronement, but in America it was a legal holiday, when millions could listen in — and would. Through diligent search I got to know a nephew of a brother-in-law of the Pope's chamberlain's brother — or some relationship even more remote, yet in Italy not too remote for a little personal favor for the sake of family ties. Within a week or so I had an appointment with the Chamberlain in his red plush and gold office in the

Vatican, which proved cordial but useless except for the offer of attendance at an audience, where one might kneel and receive the papal blessing from afar. Also I got an invitation to hear His Holiness say Mass in the Sistine Chapel.

It was a festive occasion. I donned my white tie and 'tails,' according to regulations, though it was morning, gave up hat and coat to silk-stockinged court flunkies, and sat on a back bench in that apotheosis of all interiors, staring at Michelangelo's ceiling, listening to the ethereal harmonies of Palestrina, breathing the incense-drenched atmosphere while the mitred Pius XI on his portable throne was carried shoulder-high through the central aisle, attended by the Noble Guards, a gigantic fan held over him like an Eastern potentate, attired in the rich, effulgent splendor of 'Christ's Vicar on Earth.' The spectators applauded with their hands — according to tradition — as the august figure approached. Two nuns next to me had opera-glasses, and as the ceremony proceeded they stood unabashed on the bench to peer through them over the heads of those in front.

The Byzantine pomp of the ceremony, the scintillating splendor of the altar, the age-old canticles intoned by the Pope's tenuous, quivering voice, the genuflexions of cardinals and bishops before the enthroned pontiff — all the accumulation of the mysticism of two thousand years, calculated to impress man with the humility of his being — these things were overpowering in their effect. And as these impressions crowded in upon me, my mind suddenly reverted to that classic cablegram: 'Contact old gentleman direct!'

My next approach was to the Papal Secretary of State, and there was officially referred to Father Gianfranceschi, Jesuit scientist, president of the Papal Academy and Vatican radio chief — the key-man in the story, as I shall relate.

Meantime things had begun to happen. In the night of January 30–31, speech tests from the Vatican station had been heard in New York and were acknowledged, worse luck, by our 'hated rivals,' the N.B.C.; and Senator Marconi was received in private audience by the Pope to report on the experiment. Special apparatus was to be installed in the

Pope's study for telephone communications with the overseas Nuncios. The American correspondents reported to
their papers that the station probably would be functioning
by February 12. Relying on the Monsignore's confidential
bulletins they said that a papal address would be read by a
cardinal, but seeing me around they added that at the last
minute the Pope himself might decide to speak. Nobody believed it; everybody around the Vatican stoutly denied the
possibility of anything so unprecedented.

Then the power house, already functioning for tests, was
to be formally 'opened' on February 6, the Pope's birthday,
by the Pontiff. The *Osservatore Romano*, in an obscurely
placed paragraph printed a statement that the station itself
would be opened on February 12 *con gran' solennità*. That,
said the nephew of the brother-in-law of the Chamberlain's
brother, means the personal presence of the Pope. It was
high time to see Father Gianfranceschi.

The upper regions of the Vatican City, where the station
was located, had been closed for weeks. Every bend in the
road was guarded by Vatican police. Now, armed with a
direct reference from the Papal Government, the Monsignore and I took a motor car; as he approached a policeman, he flashed his little purple square, the badge of clerical
nobility, whispered a few magic words, and we were waved
on. Up and up, along the medieval ramparts over which the
radio towers and antennae incongruously protruded toward
the sky, over newly made roads, we rolled up to the tiny
marble temple that housed the greatest of miracles that even
the Vatican had seen.

Father Gianfranceschi, an ascetic, slender intellectual in
cassock and skull-cap, received us. In his hand was an
English book of very recent date — Eddington's *Science and
the Unseen World*. His manner had a delightful blend of
fatherliness, urbanity, and simple charm. The childish
delight which he took in his great machine, his tubes and
rectifiers and indicators, broke through his reticence and we
soon became quite good friends. The idea that thousands of
the Faithful might be excluded from listening to the Vatican
unless both networks were given permission to rebroadcast

the opening ceremony, gradually softened his partiality. Armed with a document which not only certified Columbia's privilege to rebroadcast the 'entire ceremony,' but which also gave me free passage to the radio station, I became a daily visitor. Day by day, bit by bit, the details of that ceremony emerged in conversations with the suave padre, from the famous silver trumpets to herald the arrival of the Pope down to the proceedings of the Papal Academy, where Marconi was to be installed and decorated by the Holy Father himself.

Father Gianfranceschi, I found, visited the Pope every day, perfecting the elaborate program, instructing him in the use of the gold-mounted microphone, assisting in the articulation of his historic Message to the World. I was, in fact, as close to 'contacting old gentleman direct' as any lay mortal could hope to be. Without the slightest desire to supplant the busy Monsignore, I had, for the time being, become a valuable news source to the most excited group of newspaper correspondents I had ever seen, since they had been kept on tenter-hooks by the mystery-mongers about the Vatican for a fortnight or more.

The reason for this elaborate secrecy over an innocent matter, though of world-wide interest, I was never able to detect. Young Prince X, down at the Grand Hôtel, who was never seen in the sacred precincts at all, seemed to be the only one who all along 'knew.' Could it be that this epoch-making event in the history of the Church was being nursed as a scoop for one all-powerful newspaper magnate in New York? Not until four days before the great broadcast did the Monsignore release a communiqué to the effect that 'Senator Marconi and Father Gianfranceschi in audience with the Pope *this evening* have fixed the inauguration of the radio station for February 12.' The date and other details corresponded absolutely with what the Hearst man had confided to me three weeks before!

My only fear now, despite the Secretary of State, despite Father Gianfranceschi, despite Marconi (who at last, in the solitude of his Roman drawing-room, had avowed a benevolent neutrality), was that somehow we should be prevented in New York from 'picking up' HVJ.[1] An invisible struggle seemed to be going on behind the scenes to keep me from muscling in on this all-important event. If I succeeded, Columbia's claim to equality of status as one of the major chains would be established; if we failed — the blow to our prestige was too terrible to contemplate. Nowhere else in the world did a similar situation exist, for nowhere else was competition, if it existed, allowed to affect a broadcast of universal public interest.

Almost every night New York rang me on the telephone, only recently extended to Rome. Our own reception facilities were inadequate; the R.C.A. said there was no available 'channel.' Every day Gaston Matthieu, Marconi's construction chief, and one of the ablest engineers in Europe, would give me advice, which, without understanding it, I would shout into the receiver for our engineers in New York. 'Did I really have permission to pick up the transmission?' they would ask. 'Yes, in writing.' Again and again I had to reassure the administrative heads. Meantime, as the only American radio man on the spot, I fed them advance information on every detail of the transmission, and they passed it on to the press, getting due credit, while the Opposition was keeping close counsel, for fear of a 'leak' to us. Thus the public came to regard me, an outsider, as a leading instigator, the power behind the papal microphone!

Meantime, the fear that something would go wrong had reduced me to a bundle of ragged nerves. I came to suspect everybody of duplicity. With a bitter taste in my mouth, I eyed the Monsignore suspiciously through cheerless meals at the San Carlo or the Taverna Reale.

GOLDEN MICROPHONE AND SILVER TRUMPETS

At last the great day arrived. Shortly after four in the afternoon a procession of motor cars wound its way up the

[1] HVJ, call-letters of the Vatican station: H for Holy, V for Vatican, J for Jesus.

snaking motor road toward the summit of Vatican Hill.
Swiss Guards, in medieval doublet and hose lining part of
the way, stood at attention, holding tall halberds rigidly at
their side, Palatine Guards and Noble Guards saluted with
their swords. The white-and-yellow papal flag fluttered at
the masts of Palace and public buildings. It was the proud-
est day of the reborn Papal State.

When the papal car approached the station, everybody,
including the Chief of Police in white gloves, knelt. The
aged, white-garbed skull-capped Pius XI, peering through the
thick lenses of his spectacles, alighted, made his way between
cardinals and Palace dignitaries into the little marble building. The silver trumpets sounded; the ceremony had begun.
Inside, the proud inventor of radio led him between shining
rows of switching panels, generators and transmitting gear,
to a switch which the Pope himself was to throw, formally
starting the station's function. With Marconi and Father
Gianfranceschi standing near him, Pius XI, sitting at
draped desk in a tiny room, began his message with an
alloquy 'to all creation,' speaking in a clear firm voice:

*'Qui arcano Dei consilio succedimus loco Principis Aposto-
lorum ...'*

It was the first time in history that a pope's voice was
heard by the world at large. Beyond the borders of the
Vatican, in every country of Europe, in all of the five continents, a multitudinous audience, the greatest that had ever
listened to a single man, listened in devout silence to words
which only very few could understand. In many places
through the far-flung Christian world men and women knelt
in streets and public places, listening with feelings of bliss and
awe. A maze of radio circuits carried the words around the
earth.

Outside the station, on Vatican Hill, silence reigned. In
Rome, in the crowded city, people went about their daily
concerns. Few listened. 'We are so near the centre of
religion,' they said, 'we don't worry much about the Pope.' I
myself listened, for two hours, at a friend's house, but found
it hard to concentrate. Did our stations get it? Or had three
weeks' work and worry been in vain?

For the first time in history, a Pope's voice was heard by the
world at large

Behind His Holiness is Senator Marconi

At dinner, an hour after it was all over, a telegram was handed to me. It was from New York:

MAGNIFICENT WORK.   CONGRATULATIONS AND THANKS.

WILLIAM S. PALEY

The job was done; for the first time in three weeks I was able to relax. But not for long; for now I was expected to cover not merely England, but all of Europe single-handed, and to land every dictator, statesman, and 'stuffed shirt' making front-page headlines in the American press.

VI. DICTATORS AND DEMAGOGUES

MUSSOLINI THINKS IT OVER

THE first of the Dictators was close at hand. At the end of the long street where I had passed those uneasy weeks lay the Piazza Venezia, a beautiful Renaissance square, ruined by the brutally gleaming white marble of a monstrous monument to King Victor Emanuel I, and on its western side was the Venetian Palace, where Mussolini received his guests. From here he had made his first and only broadcast, in English, for the benefit of American listeners, as related in the preceding chapter. In it he had assured America that the modern world was unthinkable without it — a statement which did not surprise the average citizen of our optimistic land. Without America's aid, he said, the war could not have been won; and without America's aid prosperity could not be regained. This last, in the depression year of 1931, was rather less than might have been expected from a political miracle man. A pledge that Italy would never take the initiative in another war (four years before Abyssinia) and a firm advocacy of deflation (two years before the New Deal) were, to say the least, not prophetic utterances. It seemed to me that another speech — to offset the effect of the first one — would be a good thing.

So I began to haunt the Palazzo Chigi — the Italian Foreign Office — to try and argue the satellites into persuading the Duce to talk. Day after day I sat in the sumptuous Renaissance anteroom, admired the gilded carved-wood ceiling, the opulent tapestries and hangings — esthetic delights that comported very imperfectly with some of the unkempt loungers waiting at all times to see some *Segretario* or *Commendatore* on business that might be important but surely was never urgent.

Hours of waiting are nothing to the Italian, who is born to accept red tape, as he accepts sun and rain. In fact, the comparatively low unemployment figures of Italy might by some humorist be ascribed to the fact that one half of the population is always engaged in waiting for the other half. Fascism may have done away with delays on the railroads, but it has not altered the leisurely ways of Italian bureaucrats — nor their delightful operatic demeanor. One could not say that they didn't take my suggestions seriously, to judge from the agitated arguments that would ensue among themselves.

Everything, of course, depended on Mussolini, that man of iron will and quick, inflexible decisions; the pleasure of *Il Duce* was law — hence nobody could promise or prognosticate anything. Obviously the short cut would be to see the Duce himself. It took a long time, but at last — with the help of my friend Tom Morgan, of the United Press — I got my summons to the Palazzo Venezia, where the great man would receive me at six-fifteen one afternoon. I was told to be on time because the periods were exactly calculated, like an American radio schedule, on a quarter-hour basis. I arrived punctually and waited in a tiny antechamber, where another hopeful was already parked. He went in after the man before him came out; about ten minutes after I, according to schedule, should have gone in. I waited altogether about thirty minutes, which was anyhow a clear 100 per cent gain over the Palazzo Chigi, down the street.

The usual routine, which has been frequently described by others, now followed. The smiling flunky opens the door; you perceive the Duce at the other end of the enormously long, dusky room, sitting behind a massive, cornered desk, dressed in morning coat, gray trousers, and the conventional wing collar and gray tie — a stocky man of rather less than medium height, of swarthy complexion and earnest, almost weary mien. He rises, greets you with outstretched arm, and holds it till you are near enough to shake hands; then you sit down, opposite him at the desk.

After apologizing for not speaking Italian, I asked what he would prefer — English, German, or French.

'Let us speak . . . French — German — English!' he hesitatingly announced; so I was as wise as before and continued in English, with the usual compliments about Rome. And then, I found, I was through. He took the initiative and began to interview me, instead of the other way round.

'What is the situation in England?' he began.

Well, it was so-so. In 1932 there was the economic crisis and a lot of unemployed. Had he known slang he might have answered, 'You're telling me!' But apparently we had already crossed the English Channel, for he continued:

'What's the situation in France?'

I decided that this was just a technique, so we wouldn't have to talk about the weather — or the business in hand.

'What's the situation in Germany? Who is going to win the election? Von Epp?'

Here was a funny thing! Hindenburg was a candidate to succeed himself as President of the Reich; Hitler was his most likely opponent — yet Mussolini apparently hadn't thought of him. Von Epp was the general who 'recaptured' Munich from the Communists in 1919. He *might* be a candidate, but his chances were remote.

I gave the most obvious answer: 'Hindenburg.' It required no clairvoyance.

Down went the Duce's eyeballs in that peculiarly alarming manner, which might indicate anything from anger to surprise. As one might raise one's eyebrows. It's a special tic of Mussolini's; just as some people are double-jointed and others can wriggle their ears.[1] Well, I took refuge in some funny remark or other: he didn't even smile. But dictators do smile, so I suspected that my English wasn't as easily understood as I thought. After saying that Hindenburg was just a figurehead and too old to take any real part in things, I repeated it in French — and he quickly took it up.

'*Oui*,' he said. '*Trop vieux.*'

---

[1] My doctor tells me that this curious phenomenon is usually identified as one of the symptoms of Graves's disease (V. Graefe's sign), which causes the lids to lag behind the movement of the eyeball when looking down. Graves's disease is an affection of the thyroid gland.

There followed some more conversation about Germany and then a little lull. Perceiving that my time was nearly up, I said we hoped he would broadcast to America — on Washington's centenary, or whenever.

'You think that would have a good effect?' he asked, still speaking French. I assured him it would, and enlarged on the great influence of radio in America. He said he would think it over. As I got up, he came out from behind his desk and slipped his arm into mine as we began to stroll toward the door. It was all very leisurely and pleasant, and pretty soon I was out, thinking I had a new pal. But only for a few minutes. My last glimpse of him was strolling along the short wall near the door, and I figured out that by squaring the room he would reach his desk just after the flunky had helped me on with my coat. Sure enough, as I started to go, the buzzer rang for Number Next.

I never heard any more about that broadcast; according to the minions at the Palazzo Chigi he was still thinking it over the following year. In fact, America didn't hear Mussolini again till October, 1934, when the Italian elections had once more confirmed the power of the Fascist régime and the long-awaited Corporate State was about to be constituted. His speech, cheered to the echo by thousands of Italian throats, which we were privileged to relay throughout the United States, gave Americans a real taste of high-powered demagogic oratory. But after a while it palled. The excitement was provided by the background mob rather than the voice itself, though phrase after phrase of thunderous rhetoric rolled out upon the air.

'FOURTEEN YEARS OF SHAME'

To judge from the Duce's remarks one got the impression that he either had never heard of Hitler — in February, 1932! — or else did not consider him a serious factor in the situation. Or did he purposely avoid mention of his 'imitator,' who was destined to become his noble ally in the years to come? It is true that at the time he was not a candidate: he was not even a German citizen. Yet within a month this 'imitator' had polled over eleven million votes against the eighteen and a half million cast for Hindenburg, the idol of the German nation.

As soon as this happened I flew to Berlin to see Ernst Hanfstaengl, known from Munich to Harvard University as 'Putzi,' to get a line on this political prodigy. 'Putzi,' then a member of the innermost councils of the Nazi party and a close friend of the Führer, was in high feather. He was a grotesquely tall, broad-shouldered, lusty fellow with the nose and chin of 'Mr. Punch.' Waving his windmill arms in the direction of the Wilhelmstrasse, he predicted that 'those people over there' were practically on the rocks. Now, after reading the inside history of those harrowing months in John Wheeler-Bennett's admirable book (*Wooden Titan*, 1936), I realize how nearly right he was, but there was nothing in the manner of this clownish partisan that inspired confidence in his judgment.

Nor did my first look at Hitler himself, sitting in the lobby of the Kaiserhof, imbibing a soft drink in the company of some inconspicuous middle-class ladies, create any impression but that of sordid disillusionment. Life for him, at the moment, was at low ebb. The storm troops and the S.S. were still disbanded; the intrigues of Papen and Schleicher which were to bring Brüning to fall were still too nebulous to permit any definite hopes; old man Hindenburg was still contemptuous of the 'Bohemian sergeant' who dreamed of becoming master of the Third Reich. An ashen-faced, tired, depressed, altogether unprepossessing person, he sat hunched down in his chair, unrecognized and unimportant to the fashionable tea-drinking Berliners around him.

So this was the orator of the fiery tongue, who played on the wounded sensibilities of the German people, ringing all the changes from tearful lament to prophetic malediction — the modern Savonarola who had thrown millions under his mystical spell! A broadcast from him — as a sample of sheer rabble-rousing — should turn out to be a sensation even in America. But Nazi broadcasts in Germany were banned; Hitler himself had been kept from the microphone by the quaking authorities, who possibly might have done better by letting him talk...

This meant, too, that no technical facilities would be available for a transmission of his voice from Germany to a foreign country, that is, America. But Putzi, proud of his American connections, promised to sound the Führer anyway. I instructed my Berlin representative to 'follow through.' A few days later, in London, I had a telegram to say that 'Brillig' (our code-word for Hitler) was willing to speak from somewhere outside Germany — Salzburg, Bâle, The Hague, or Copenhagen — before April 1, and that his subject would be 'The German Struggle for Liberty,' in comparison with the American Fight for Independence. And the price would be fifteen hundred dollars — in other words, one thousand dollars per minute — pretty steep for a German harangue that couldn't be understood by most of our listeners. The widows and orphans of the Nazi martyrs, it seemed, had to be provided for by every possible means. But the deal didn't come off. The Führer's going to a foreign country appeared to present insuperable difficulties.

Suddenly, in the summer, the German authorities had a change of heart: they announced that the Nazi leaders would be permitted to broadcast, the same as other candidates, during the ensuing campaign for the Reichstag elections. I wired New York for new instructions, but the answer was 'Unwant Hitler any price.' Within five weeks Hitler went over the top as the leader of the largest party in Germany, winning 230 Reichstag seats — a world sensation. Exactly six months later — after a temporary setback — he was Chancellor of the Reich.

Hitler's stock as a radio attraction went skyrocketing in America. On February 1 the N.B.C., by virtue of its preferential agreement with the German broadcasting authorities, carried part of Hitler's victory speech, relayed by short wave to America. Listening to it at my loud-speaker in London, hearing the deafening acclamations of his followers — a continuous crescendo of *Heils*, brass bands, and roars

from a hundred thousand throats — for hours and hours, I
realized what was happening; an avalanche of pent-up mass
emotion, a tidal wave of political hysteria that would sweep
everything before it and crush anything that got in its way.
A real revolution, someone said to me. No — no genuine
revolution ever sounded like this; this 'people's victory' was
of 'superior' origin, staged by a master hand. Not in vain
had Max Reinhardt developed his art in Germany!

'Fourteen years have passed,' Hitler began, 'since the day
when, blinded by promises from within and without, the
German people lost honor and freedom...' His voice,
starting pianissimo, rose and swelled, dropped to liquid
whisper, dilated to a hysterical shout — climax after climax,
interminably. And each time the roar of applause and *Heils*
rose to meet him, giving him respite to recover his emotions
and resume the next cajoling strain. The sheer sound of it
riled one up; words no longer mattered: this was the Medicine
Man, healing souls and inflaming passions with the same
breath.

Again and again the German ether vibrated to this strain.
A new election campaign was on — the fifth within twelve
months — and the Voice that stirred the millions rose into
the air again, against the same background of obedient
throats shouting themselves hoarse. To appreciate the man,
to judge him dispassionately, it would be necessary to
separate him from this deceptive *coulisse*. What, really, did
he have to say? What was his appeal to cold reason?

I returned to Putzi, to see if we couldn't get a broadcast
talk by Hitler putting his case to the world — not shouting,
but talking. Hitler and a microphone, in the quiet of a small
room; nothing else. Putzi reopened negotiations. He was
now an important man, resplendent in his 'S.A.' officer's
uniform. His room in the Kaiserhof was part of a general
headquarters; the whole hôtel was alive with storm troopers
clicking their heels and giving the Nazi salute. Blustering as
ever, towering about two feet above me, he took to calling
me 'the giant,' laughing loudly at his own joke and putting
his arm about my shoulders.

A grand piano stood in the corner, and on it Putzi proudly

played me the latest Hitler march, composed by himself. A junior brown shirt came in to call for a phonograph record of it for someone. Putzi signed it proudly, putting the date and adding — in the style of the Italian Fascists — 'Year I' (of the new era!). Before our negotiations were over he was living with Göring in the Speaker's Palace, situated behind the Reichstag and connected with it by the famous underground passage which was to figure in the Reichstag fire trial later on.

Soon everything was 'arranged': Hitler was due to fly to Cologne, and there — from the seclusion of the Brown House — he would speak to America, his talk to be translated on the spot. But in the last stages this plan, too, collapsed: other and more important things intervened. The election campaign became virulent, then vicious; men were being killed in the streets; sinister plots were being 'discovered'; within a couple of weeks the Reichstag was gutted by flames.

So we waited until the end of the campaign, when Hitler, once again surrounded by the faithful mob, fired the last barrage of the campaign in Berlin's Sporthalle, cheered and supported by the usual roaring cheers. We rebroadcast an hour of it — then cut. Hitler has not made a 'genuine' broadcast — without a crowd — to this day.

One of the many stories they tell in Germany about the Nazi triumvirate is the one about Hitler in the dentist's chair. He was to have a tooth extracted, and the anesthetist asked him to count slowly, so he would know when the patient was 'under.' Hitler counted — 'one, two, three,' and so forth, his voice getting slower and fainter as he went on. At thirteen it was all but inaudible and the dentist got his forceps ready. Then suddenly came fourteen — and the voice swelled into full strength. 'Fourteen years have passed,' it shouted, and Hitler, instead of getting his tooth pulled, was making his usual harangue. That little story illustrates why the speeches of Hitler were not often rebroadcast abroad. To the finely attuned Nazi ear he may be saying something new; to the infidel he is making the same speech. To the foreigner, perceiving with his intelligence and not with his emotions, it conveys nothing that he does not already know.

DICTATORS NEED CROWDS

In a sort of way, the American listener's clamor for dictators had now been stilled. But strictly speaking I had failed — had failed to lure any of them to the lonely microphone, to tell what was on their minds. Why was this? Why were demagogues, usually so anxious to unbosom themselves to a crowd, reluctant to speak their minds in the quiet of a studio?

'The microphone,' says Bernard Shaw, 'is the most wonderful tell-tale in the world. If you speak insincerely to a political audience, the more insincere you are, the more hopelessly you are away from all the facts of life, the more they cheer you and the more they are delighted. But if you try that on the microphone it gives you away instantly. You hear the political ranter — you hear that his platitudes mean nothing and that he does not believe them.'

Can it be that the dictators, unlike most other politicians, have found out the microphone? Can it be that, since reasonable persuasion is not their *forte*, they eschew the dialectic or conversational style? In any case, the attitude of Europe's strong men showed a singular unanimity in this respect. Mussolini's first and only attempt would seem to have been an error of judgment; he has not repeated it in seven years. Joseph Stalin, sitting in his Kremlin, was as mike-shy as the rest. I never saw him, but I wrote him most seductive letters, and even went to Moscow to persuade his entourage. The argument that Hitler and Mussolini had, after all, been heard abroad caused a disdainful raising of eyebrows and holding of noses. Stalin does not allow even his public speeches to be broadcast except on rare occasions, and no foreign radio organization has yet been permitted to rebroadcast his voice.

The assumption that the radio has favored the growth of dictatorships does not, indeed, hold water, whatever effect it may have in keeping these men in power once they are there. The three great totalitarian systems of contemporary Europe

The excitement of a demagogue's speech is provided by the background mob. Dictators are not anxious to speak their lines in the quiet of a studio

grew to power without the aid of the radio; those of Russia and Italy in fact antedated the organization of radio as an effective instrument; in Germany the Nazis were deprived of its use until they were within a few months of reaching power, and even then they refused to use it, until Hitler was actually head of the government.

This is, in itself, no proof that the radio might not have helped the dictators to fasten their hold upon the nations they desired to rule. But we have at least one instance of an attempt to establish a Fascist or quasi-Fascist dictatorship by argument over the air, and that one attempt turned into a dismal failure. I refer to the sad case of Gaston Doumergue, one-time President, and more recently would-be dictator, of France.

PAPA DOUMERGUE TRIES IT ON

After the Stavisky scandal, the bloody Paris riots, and the parliamentary stalemate of 1934, conditions in France were, as never before, ripe for a Fascist coup — in fact, conditions for violent change were present in almost classic perfection. If only the opportunity could have been seized! Colonel de la Roque, leader of the Croix de Feu, failed to come up to scratch; Tardieu, who afterward admitted that as Premier he contributed government money to the war chest of the movement,[1] lacked the personal popularity to be anything more than the power behind the throne. But 'Papa' Doumergue, a veteran politician who enjoyed the prestige of the elder statesman, and the dignity of an ex-President of the Republic was induced to come out of his retirement to 'save the nation' from civil war. Papa Doumergue enjoyed the affection of the majority of the people of France; sick and tired of political trickery and corruption, Frenchmen put their faith in this venerable People's Friend. Though he had no black-shirt or brown-shirt army behind him, the armies of

[1] See the Paris dispatch in the *New York Times*, October 27, 1937.

the Croix de Feu and all the other militant leagues were ready to march to his support. And he had, as the first would-be dictator in European history, the radio at his command. He made the most of it.

Over the heads of his cabinet, from the security of his executive office, he appealed to the nation in a series of fatherly talks designed to rally the people behind the man who had sacrificed for their benefit the well-earned repose of old age. Then, in his fifth discourse, he not only attacked the socialists and communists according to the established Fascist pattern, but proposed certain constitutional changes which would strengthen the executive power, and allow him to crush the Red Ogre and establish order and progress along the familiar lines of national regeneration, regimentation, and economic reform.[1]

At first the people listened sympathetically; then they became suspicious; finally they got furious. The honeyed words and the silken voice lost their appeal. And in the end they rallied to the Opposition and drove Doumergue from office. The Left, instead of becoming bitter, used the weapon of ridicule. 'When is Monsieur Doumergue speaking?' asks a radio purchaser pictured as in a newspaper cartoon. 'On Wednesday night.' 'Then be sure to deliver my set on Thursday morning.'

Pretty soon the whole nation laughed; the dictatorship menace was over — perhaps for good. Had things turned otherwise, the whole course of European history would have been changed: as it is, France remains the bulwark of Western Democracy in the world.

Are we, then, to suppose that the radio is proof against Fascist arguments unless they are supported by the shouts of moron multitudes? I believe, with Bernard Shaw, that sincerity is the ultimate test. The microphone automatically eliminates most of the histrionic appeal, it vitiates the demagogue's animal magnetism, strips oratory of its trappings, and reduces it to the bare bones of reason and fact.

[1] The Doumergue scheme has been widely represented as an attempt to save democracy instead of wrecking it. The true facts are ably set forth in Alexander Werth's book, *The Destiny of France*, London, 1937.

Moreover, it allows the listener to think, to reflect without being swept off his feet by the wave of crowd hysteria and the terrifying compulsion of the mob.

THE GREATEST TELLTALE IN THE WORLD

Thus the old-fashioned demagogue, the political rabble-rouser of pre-war days, whose technique is that of the stump, has lost much of his power in political life. 'For some mysterious reason,' in the words of that shrewd observer, General Charles H. Dawes, 'that personal magnetism which sometimes deadens the intellectual perception of the crowd in the physical presence of the orator is not transmitted over the wireless.' And this applies, not only to dictators and would-be dictators, but to demagogues of all political faiths.

A case in point is David Lloyd George. This wizard of the silver tongue, whose oratory had carried the British nation through the hardships of the war and the Coalition Government over the top in the notorious khaki election of 1919, was — and still is — a comparative stranger to the microphone. I tried for years to get Lloyd George to make a radio talk to America; his reluctance was finally explained to me by people close to him, who said that he 'hates the wireless.' The reason is not far to seek. Unsurrounded by his admirers, with nothing but his voice to convey the workings of his agile mind, Lloyd George's eloquence simply does not come off. I have watched him addressing his supporters, have watched him speak in Parliament; age has not dimmed the glamour of his rhetoric, nor dulled the edge of his invective. Endowed with all the social graces and the superior gifts of showmanship, this dynamic white-haired Welshman, whether right or wrong, still gets the crowd. But on the ether, all his charm seems to evaporate: of all the speeches that woo the coy citizen sitting at his loud-speaker at election times, Lloyd George's are the dullest and least effective, because the histrionics — the winning smile, the half-closed eye, the clenched fist, and the hands toying with the golden spectacles — are simply of no use.

'The microphone is the most tell-tale instrument in the world.'

DEMOCRACY'S NEW INSTRUMENT

MY FIRST two years of broadcasting from Europe had convinced me that radio was an instrument of democracy. Despite the fact that populations were being regimented and intimidated by the broadcast blusterings of dictators and their henchmen, I could not help feeling that in the end the appeal to reason would be stronger than the assertion of force. Throughout history it has been easier to propagate ideas than to suppress them, and just as the printing press had become a mighty instrument of liberation, so enlightenment by radio would prove irresistible in the end.

Although the leaders of the European democracies had less attraction — even for America — as radio headliners, I was determined that America should take its measure of dictators and democrats alike, for no instrument so lends conviction to sincerity, none so easily exposes fraud. The cavalcade of Europe's statesmen, some of whom would one day loom to heroic stature in the history books, could, I thought, be given a new dimension in terms of sound. The words they would speak, however fragmentary, might help to heighten our sense of reality, help the ordinary man to form some sort of judgment of their worth.

The great democratic statesman of the early thirties was Ramsay MacDonald. Until Franklin Roosevelt loomed on the international horizon, he was the hope of the liberal world and the idol of those who believed in peace. No British statesman had so often filled the air with fine phrases; none had more often been listened to — and with more sympathy — beyond the British Isles. No other politician of his generation had more of what is vulgarly known as the gift of gab. His liquid, beguiling voice, his soft Scottish burr, his heart-warming appeals to 'my frrriends,' and his pious homilies on the moral progress of the world were consumed as eagerly as were, later on, the fireside chats of the American President. Indeed, they had much of the same qualities — the homely phrase, the happy metaphor, the apt hyperbole, and the clinching peroration.

I first met Ramsay MacDonald before he became Prime Minister a second time, at a luncheon of the American correspondents in London, where he spoke, simply and confidentially, without cant, confidently looking forward to his resumption of power and a great constructive work of reform. 'Revolution,' he said, 'as a method of progress, is out of date. We of the Labour Party don't believe in revolution because we have a better way.' It sounded convincing, especially from a man who had not yet taken on that fatal tinge of respectability and self-righteousness which were to make him one of the most despised of men among the British working-class later on. He still looked the old left-wing campaigner, too; his handsome face, his graying and still flowing locks, and his deep-set, honest eyes were the outer marks of the idealist.

THE TRAGEDY OF RAMSAY

When MacDonald first spoke to America — in 1930 — the one-time revolutionary had taken on the statesman's air; he fancied himself as settling the affairs of the world, and his personal vanity made him put the cart before the horse. But his attachment to Anglo-American friendship was passionately sincere, and when he spoke to an American radio audience he meant what he said. One such occasion was when Ambassador Robert Worth Bingham presented, on behalf of the American Council of Foreign Relations, a set of

B. B. C.

MacDonald liked broadcasting — it was a modern thing and
he fancied himself as a modern

B. B. C.

In Stanley Baldwin's broadcast, America got a sample of
quiet British oratory at its best

American state papers to Chatham House — once the home of Pitt, now the headquarters of the Royal Institute for Foreign Affairs. MacDonald presided, and made a graceful if platitudinous speech. I announced him and gave a running commentary of the proceedings. Afterward, in the private reception room, I thanked him on behalf of American listeners. Seeing Stephen King-Hall, the famous children's broadcaster, with me he quickly took his cue from the phrase, known to all English listeners, with which King-Hall always concluded his talks: 'Now be good, but not so frightfully good that someone will come along and say "What's he been up to now?"'

'Well,' said MacDonald, 'was I good, but not too frightfully good?' drawing a courteous laugh from the Ambassador and ourselves.

By the time the Economic Conference of 1934 was on, MacDonald had become so absorbed in the higher statesmanship that he was estranged from many of his old colleagues. Clad in immaculately fitting morning coat, his gray hair slicked and his moustache clipped in fashionable style, he looked every inch the royal butler as he conducted old King George to the speaker's dais. His sonorous phrases had become a distressing mixture of truth and humbug, optimism and eyewash, feeling and sentimentality. He was the sanctimonious preacher on the hustings, a schoolteacher scolding others for their lack of a knowledge he had only just imperfectly acquired. Standing at the death-bed of the Conference — that most humiliating of all pompous international failures — he had the nerve to call it (in words that were broadcast in Europe and America) 'a fulfilling prophecy of hope, a whisper of the imperturbable approach of world co-operation — an embodiment of the lilt — "It's coming for a' that."' It was no wonder that his followers were getting fed up.

So long as MacDonald had the truth on his side, so long as he was in Opposition, his phrases had the power of an evangel; when he became an apologist for principles contrary to his own, his words merely smote the empty air. It was his vanity that forced him into loneliness, that made him proof against disillusionment and robbed him of sincerity; and it was this lack of sincerity that stripped his broadcasting of its power.

'We have just crossed the dividing line of a new year,' he broadcast in mid-depression, 'and once again we look behind and before. Memory stands on one side of us and hope on the other. We ... have been going through a hard time.'

The prose was worthy of Dickens, but the sentiments had a disagreeably Pecksniffian taste. Like Pecksniff, MacDonald was convinced of his own virtue; he spoke his handsome phrases so often that he believed what he said. His Conservative colleagues let him talk — so long as he talked for the National Government. And the less he counted in that government, the more seriously he took his job.

One evening, after he had been suffering from nervous eye-strain, I had to go to 10, Downing Street and introduce him in an American broadcast. His physician, the eminent Lord Horder, came into the room, and leaned over him as we were passing the time in small talk. 'You must take care of yourself,' he whispered to the Prime Minister, 'and get some sleep.' MacDonald straightened up and said, melodramatically: 'Duty, my dear Horder. Remember duty!' This was probably not just for my benefit; it was sheer natural showmanship — and an important part of the audience was himself.

MacDonald liked broadcasting, as he liked flying — it was a modern thing, and he fancied himself as a modern. 'Knowledge is making us giants,' he said in one of his talks, and he liked to think himself a giant. But long before he gave up flying and broadcasting the country had given him up. He still came to the microphone to talk for the very things he had once fought against. His voice was still rich and vibrant, his rhetoric intact. But the power of conviction had gone out of it: if he fooled anybody at all, it was because he fooled himself. Listening to him over the air, one could imagine him posturing, bracing himself against an uncomprehending, unfeeling world. A democrat who had gone wrong — and the microphone was revealing the sad truth.

Yet, when all is said that must be said, it should not be forgotten that in his early days Ramsay MacDonald was the hero he later thought himself to be, and gave an example to his generation which few others had the courage to give. He alone among all his colleagues in Parliament opposed the World War; he alone faced the shout of 'Traitor!' and did not cringe. He went to prison and — worse still — he was expelled from his Scottish golf club, which no blandishments induced him to rejoin.

ENGLAND'S BALDWIN

Even while MacDonald was still in office, Stanley Baldwin was a power in the land. He represented the great conservative capitalist class which — under one name or another — has been responsible for British leadership for generations; yet he, rather than MacDonald, was to become the symbol of British middle-class democracy. For democracy, in England, is an attitude rather than a political creed, a method rather than an 'ideology.' And whatever others might think of Baldwin's democracy, he sincerely believed himself to be a democrat; it was this that made him one of the most effective broadcasters of his time.

When, in 1930, Stanley Baldwin was chosen by the Brotherhood Movement to make an address on democracy, I seized the opportunity to rebroadcast it to America, and America got a sample of quiet British oratory at its best. 'Democracy,' he said, 'is still an aspiration and not a fact.... It is still "an untravelled world, whose margin fades for ever and for ever as we move." What we have achieved is a democratic framework of government, which is not the same thing as a democratic society. We have perfected the machinery of popular government.... It is terribly easy for those in power to confuse justice with the interest of the strong, but oppression of the few by the many is just as ugly as its opposite.'

Baldwin's strength lay in two things: first, in the picture he conveyed of himself as a sound, average Englishman, a man whose mind worked slowly and who made mistakes, but who had the courage to do what he thought was right; and second, in a style so apparently simple, so improvisational that it always seemed to be the plainest kind of truth. Yet, while not rhetorical, his command of language gave evidence of a distinctly poetic turn of mind. Only half in jest, his brother-in-law and cousin, Rudyard Kipling, used to say that Stanley was the poet of the family. Whether he spoke of moral abstractions or political realities, he always seemed to be taking the hearer into his confidence. Even in election speeches he rarely resorted to attack; he gave an account of himself or his mental processes and let it go at that.

With these quiet methods he talked himself to the top. From complete political obscurity this member of the widely disliked industrial employer class, whose party colleagues questioned his abilities for leadership, who achieved office, as it were, by default, who made expensive mistakes and meekly admitted them — became the political prodigy of post-war England, rising to the highest office in the land and keeping himself there, supported by the free votes of the majority of the people — including millions of workmen — at a time when unemployment and industrial distress were at their worst. Here is a record that no dictator has equalled to date.

Shortly after the death of King George V and the fiasco of the Hoare-Laval dicker concerning Abyssinia, Baldwin's political fortunes were thought to be ebbing and there was rumor of serious revolt against him in his own party's ranks. The best he could hope for, it seemed, was to hang on till after the coronation of Edward VIII, when he and Mrs. Baldwin would play a transcendent rôle and he could retire in an orgy of festive celebration, with his political prestige unimpaired. A story went the rounds in 1936 according to which Baldwin had been speaking in a rather too fatherly way to King Edward about his private concerns. 'See here, Mr. Baldwin,' the King is supposed to have interrupted him, 'if you don't stop meddling with my personal affairs, I won't come to your d —— coronation' (the important word being the 'your').

In the light of subsequent events — then unsuspected by anyone — that story, however apocryphal, takes on a semblance of probability. To everybody's surprise, Edward made good the threat and, as if to spite him, Baldwin rose to as yet undreamed-of heights as the Warwick of his time. For whatever one might think of Baldwin the politician before the abdication, whatever sympathy one might feel for the luckless Royal Duke, the story of Baldwin's management of the historic crisis in British monarchy, told in the familiar, pedestrian, simple yet moving Baldwin manner, was a stupendous exhibition of political strategy and tact.

Baldwin passed into the somnolent shadows of the House of Lords with a sort of halo about his homely head, having triumphed where more brilliant men had failed. Many a time had his voice been heard in America, by means of the transatlantic ether waves — usually at official occasions, Lord Mayor's banquets and the like. His mastery of radio vindicated its claim as an instrument of democracy.

IRELAND'S 'DEV'

Since more Americans are personally interested in little Ireland than all the rest of the British Isles, I kept a watchful eye on 'Saorstat Eierann,' otherwise the Irish Free State, from the start. William Cosgrave, still President early in 1931, made his first St. Patrick's Day address to America on my invitation, but there was a fly in the ointment, as will be related anon. When less than a year later Eamon de Valera won his first national election I already had my foot in the door. On March 4, 1932, he spoke to America on 'The Future of Ireland' exclusively under our auspices, announcing his intention to abolish immediately the hated oath of allegiance to the British sovereign and his intention to repudiate the land annuities paid by Ireland to the British treasury under the treaty of 1921. Both promises he soon made good. It is a measure of De Valera's determination and of the faith of his adherents that even with the weapons of an economic war the British Government has been unable to make him retreat a single inch.

That American broadcast was the first broadcast 'Dev' ever made. He came to O'Connell Street — the scene of the barricade fights during the Irish Rebellion which had landed him in a British jail with the sentence of death hanging over him — and walked into the studio as though he were going to buy a stamp. Nobody recognized him, nor did he care a hoot. The director of the broadcasting station, a Cosgrave job-holder who could sing Irish folksongs in a mellifluous baritone and sign his name in Gaelic, thought he better come around personally, Sunday or no Sunday, 'because, after all, he [De Valera] will soon be my boss.' 'Dev' faced an incredibly primitive-looking microphone contraption and meekly took his instructions from this comic character.

His delivery, in his faint and attractive brogue, was quiet and matter of fact, almost casual, seeking to convince by the strength of argument alone. And the gist of the argument was economics. An old mathematics teacher, Dev is never at a loss for figures, and he produces them with an almost childlike faith that they will be understood. He was fully aware of the value of talking to America — the country which supplied him with the sinews of war when he and his friends were on the run — but he refused to make any emotional appeal, just as he refused to abandon that 'obligatory' opening paragraph in laboriously perfected Gaelic, no matter how many thousands of listeners, with American impatience, might tune out. That was characteristic of the whole man.

When I first met De Valera he was still only the leader of Fianna Fail — a party which the British fondly regarded as virtually outlawed and all but on the rocks. When I saw him in his office in the cheerless, abandoned-looking headquarters on lower Abbey Street, he seemed just an agitator in a hopeless cause. A few months later, as President of the Irish Free State, neither his manner nor his appearance had

changed — the rumpled homespun clothes and the old
slouch hat might have been the same he wore when he was
sniping at British soldiers in 1916. But there was no doubt
about the essential nobility and the fanatical ardor of the
man. His almost emaciated, weather-beaten, hawklike
face, the myopic yet piercing eyes, the deep lines descending
from his nostrils to his chin, suggested a terrible determination. Though he seemed to lack all the accepted graces,
including a sense of humor, his friendly and naturally democratic manner made me like him at once.

Eamon de Valera would hardly agree with Ramsay Mac-
Donald about the obsolescence of revolution. For he owes
everything he accomplished to revolutionary action, to
desperate and sanguinary revolt. It was he, foolhardy
enough to ambush a crack British regiment with a handful
of volunteers marching on the capitol from Kingstown quay,
to raise the banner of revolt and raise it again after each
escape from jail, and to abandon the safe haven of America to
walk into the very jaws of death; it was this 'crazy Irishman'
who finally won for an unwilling and lethargic people the
realization of a nationalist's dream — a merely 'poetic'
liberty if you like, and economic quasi-isolation (in a modern
interdependent world!).

But Dev is a man upheld by an inflexible faith. Today he
believes in the union of all Ireland in the same fanatical way
that before the war he believed in the quasi-independence of
the country that has now come to pass. Ireland and democracy are the synthesis of his religion. He keeps on and on,
if not by miles then by inches. Conscious of his debt to
America, he has not missed a single St. Patrick's Day since
he first came into office, to give an account by radio to
friends across the water. And he has always had something
to report. When Edward VIII abdicated he, alone among
the Dominion governments, completely ignored both the
abdication and the coronation of George VI, thus loosening
yet another tie with the Empire. Constitutional purists
maintain that legally Edward VIII, and not George VI, is
still King of Ireland. What matters to the Irish is that
foreign diplomats are received at Dublin Castle — not by a

royal governor, but by Eamon de Valera, the once out-lawed rebel, himself.[1]

LIBERATOR MASARYK QUOTES LIBERATOR WASHINGTON

My observation of De Valera made me turn to another democratic nationalist — one who might be regarded as his prototype, namely Thomas Garrigue Masaryk, liberator and President of Czechoslovakia, then nearing his seventy-third year. Both Masaryk and De Valera had derived inspiration as well as material support from the United States. 'Dev' was born in New York; Masaryk married an American wo-man and proudly adopted her family's as his middle name. Both men had been rebels and fugitives in America; Masaryk indeed had planned the liberation of Czechoslovakia in the shadow of the White House and declared his country's independence from Philadelphia's Independence Hall.

Masaryk, the son of a serf, blacksmith in his youth, pro-fessor of philosophy in early manhood, patriot-conspirator in middle age, political leader at sixty, father of his country at seventy, a fighter for moral, intellectual, and cultural ideals all his life, was now living in the Hračin, once the palace of the ancient Bohemian kings, elevated high over the Moldau River at Prague. No head of state was ever more beloved by a nation than this man, who never sacrificed his faith in democracy, and even as president lived the simple ascetic life of the scholar and political philosopher, preaching tolerance and peace.

His son Jan, raised in America, speaking more unmistak-able 'American' than some American diplomats, is Czecho-

[1] In September, 1932, this 'rebel' was representing the Irish Free State, as an independent national entity, on the Council of the League of Nations in Geneva. In a program which we organized he spoke to America together with Sir Eric Drummond (later Lord Perth), the British Secretary-General of the League. And in January 1938, in another broadcast speech relayed to America by my successor, he announced the new Constitution creating the State of 'Eire' (Ireland), sever-ing its last legal bonds between it and Great Britain.

slovakian Minister to the Court of St. James, a lively young
man who readily fell in with my plan to have his father
address the American people on Washington's birthday —
one *pater patriæ* about another. Strange to say, my New
York office saw nothing very significant in that, so I actually had to persuade them to accept one of the greatest
political figures of our time.

Here was a democratic statesman who had successfully
used the radio, if not in the establishment of a régime, then
in its consolidation. Without compulsion his people listened
to him, to his quiet words, preaching not hatred but reconciliation, with the federation of European states as his ultimate ideal. And lo! the people rallied to him more closely
than the peoples have rallied round the 'strong men' preaching self-assertion and force.

Sitting in the study of his castle on Washington's birthday
of 1932, Masaryk addressed an American audience for the
first time since the stormy days of the war. 'Washington
has taught us,' he said, 'that the fortunate outcome of a
revolution depends on the moral and political preparation
of the revolutionists.' The aim in this case was a federated
European continent. And he added significantly: 'Having
recovered our liberty we again follow the example of Washington in that we must no longer feel the old antagonism and
anger, which originated in the suppression of our liberty.'

I had the great privilege of introducing President Masaryk
in this, the only direct American broadcast he ever made —
and that by a curious fluke. I had invited the American
Minister to do the honors, from the studio, and my own
little speech was to precede that of the diplomat. But the
excited engineers (this after all was an event in Czecho-
slovak radio history) switched on the wrong signal, so the
President's voice burst forth while the astonished Minister
stared blankly into his script.

Another comic feature of this broadcast was barely
avoided, for the Czech orchestra rehearsing the Star-
Spangled Banner for the occasion made it sound like a
Slavic dance. With more valor than discretion I accepted
the proffered baton and 'rehearsed' one of the best radio

orchestras in the world — thus making my first and last appearance as a conductor on this planet.

Masaryk was a handsome old man, white-bearded, with remnants of white wisps on the top of his head, like late autumn leaves clinging to an oak. His life and character were pictured in his face — spirituality, probity, kindliness, steadfastness, hard work. 'Defeat is only a reason for exertion,' he quoted Washington as saying, and exertion had been his life-long lot. There was nothing that betrayed his lowly origin; I should have said he was an aristocrat, had I not known. And he lacked the assertiveness of the self-made man, because he had the humility of the truly great.

When Masaryk died, not only did the nation mourn for him, but millions — not only in Czechoslovakia — had a sense of personal loss. With him something rare vanished from the European soil, something that may never appear again.

FRENCHMEN SHOULD SPEAK ENGLISH

The greatest handicap in this business of presenting Europe's leaders to America was the problem of language. While radio had improved the premises for Anglo-American solidarity, the polyglotism of the European continent stood in the way of a more widely international program of radio talks. Now that I was to project not merely Britain but all of Europe to the American audience, I was disappointed to find how few of the outstanding men on the Continent commanded English to any serviceable degree. Americans are impatient listeners: a foreign language or even a difficult foreign accent is enough to reduce an audience to a mere fraction of itself.

The aged Masaryk and his successor, Eduard Beneš, were exceptions. They were the type of 'good Europeans' whose equipment was in line with their aims. Others, like Aristide Briand — the ace of good Europeans and one of the most

Masaryk was a democratic statesman who used the radio, not
in the establishment of a regime, but in its consolidation

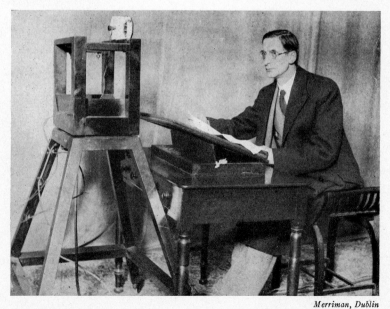

De Valera faced an incredibly primitive-looking microphone
contraption

appealing speakers I had ever heard — were, simply because of their lack of English, debarred from appealing to the unseen audience across the sea. Indeed, Frenchmen, being more insular than the reputedly insular English, rarely speak anything but French. Among those who did, Édouard Herriot was the nearest to Briand in human qualities, besides being a sincere democrat. Few people in America knew what he stood for, not many had even heard of him, yet the fact of his being the undisputed leader of the great French democratic party (the 'Radicals'), the virtually perpetual mayor of France's greatest industrial city, Lyon, and twice Prime Minister of France, were certainly enough to make him a world figure. To American newspaper readers and radio listeners he became 'news' when, after the Hoover Moratorium of 1932, he negotiated the Lausanne Treaty, which ended reparations, on behalf of France. I took my cue and caught him while he was still in the heat of his task; he agreed to do his first English broadcast, and thus in the hearing of America stretch out the hand of conciliation and friendship to Germany.

'We have shut the door in the face of passion,' said this corpulent incarnation of the well-intentioned French provincial. 'We, the French people, at the present time are preoccupied with our own affairs, but we are very deeply moved by the sufferings of the German people.... National policies have too long been keeping the nations apart; we must give them a new aim — that of coming together, both materially and spiritually. The new spirit must prevail.'

Phrases, you say? But in 1932 it needed courage to say these things. France was gripped by the panic of depression, and the Lausanne settlement was going to cost the French people billions of francs, and to rub out forever the mirage of Germany's hidden wealth. It was sensible, rational Herriot who had fought against repudiation of the American debt, who first advocated friendship with the new Russia, who preached Anglo-French solidarity, disarmament, and the strengthening of the League. It was this cultured and rather nostalgic politician who in the hate-filled post-war atmosphere was able to write a book on the German com-

poser Beethoven. And now, in the fierce hostile light of publicity, he braved French chauvinist sentiment with words
of friendship which, a little earlier, might have calmed the
fierce tempest of nationalism and rapacity that was to seer
the heart of Europe anew.

It is the fate of nations that such men are not heard in
time. No Frenchman had spoken words such as these in the
presence of German statesmen since the war. Here was good-
natured, square-headed Herriot with his funny, brushed-up
crop of graying hair, with the honest, tender eyes of the
romantic, saying things from his heart, things that Briand
might have said with more eloquence but not more sincerity,
to make people forget the harsh and brutal words that had
been spoken year in year out. But he was too late; after
six more months Adolf Hitler had been swept into power in
Germany, and Herriot was unseated by a *camarilla* of political patrioteers. The next time that French and German
delegates sat around the green table they had blood in their
eyes and the old anger in their hearts.

HERRIOT TO FLANDIN

That was in London, in 1936. Hitler's latest week-end
surprise, the reoccupation of the Rhineland, had been
sprung. According to the current British euphemism, the
Germans had just 'marched into their own back yard,' and
Anthony Eden was asking everybody to remain calm.
(Afterward some of his compatriots said that the French had
been 'bloody fools' to let the Germans get away with it.
'If they had mobilized, without our permission, we would
have come forward with a beautiful compromise proposal.
Hitler would have had to climb down.' [1]) But in France
people had a sinking feeling in the pit of their stomachs.
The Rhine was France's first line of defense. Across it the
old ogre of war had once again shown its face. The Locarno

[1] See Alexander Werth, *The Destiny of France*, London, 1937.

Pact, that 'most gilt-edged of all scraps of paper,' had been torn up, and Europe had 'entered a jungle of lawlessness' from which there is little prospect of escape.

The prime minister of France was Pierre-Étienne Flandin. A veritable giant of a man, he strode into St. James's Palace with a look of determination on his handsome, businesslike face, the straight, thin mouth tightly set and barely showing under the bristly moustache, his vaulting forehead accentuated by premature baldness. At forty-seven, Flandin was the youngest prime minister in modern French history. There was a tense feeling of pessimism as he faced the assembled statesmen of Europe, a new and comparatively youthful galaxy that had replaced the old embittered men of yesterday: dapper Anthony Eden; Dino Grandi, dark, wary, and intransigent; Litvinoff, shrewd and cynical, with the face of a Jewish impresario; tall and slender Paul Van Zeeland, the youngest of all, of serious ascetic mien, and — after a tense period of waiting — Joachim von Ribbentrop, the typical German Junker, brutally aggressive, speaking — in the tone of the Prussian lieutenant — as though not Germany but the rest of the world were on trial, to be judged by German standards of right.

It was the turning point of post-war history: that delicate moment when the scales might tip either way. Herded about the open door of the council chamber, veteran journalists indulged in flights of fantasy. What if Clemenceau, the 'Tiger,' were to rise from his grave to defy this hapless brood of waverers, once more to invoke the vengeance of 'victorious' France? Or again, if a somewhat glorified Briand were to speak with the tongues of men and angels, stretching out the hand of brotherhood to appease the rising devils of hate? But no miracle happened. Flandin, cold, legalistic, well-meaning but fearful of public opinion, with renowned French logic pleaded only the testimony of the bond. It was not good enough. The bankrupt statesmen of Europe crept home, hearing only the distant crack of the dictator's whip. Sick at heart we sat huddled in the Tudor armament chamber, hung with the shields and swords of ancient days, which served as antechamber to Queen

Anne's Room — the same room in which exactly five years before I had listened, with a catch at the throat, to the oily eloquence of Aristide Briand as he presented to Ramsay Mac-Donald the gold pen with which the London Naval Treaty had been signed . . .

I had had bad luck with Flandin. Ever since, in 1929, he had moved up into that motley political panel from which French ministers are chosen to make up the changing façade of French cabinets, he had moved in and out of governments in various capacities. Being the only minister with a real command of English he had, at the end of 1930, promised to explain his government's policy to American listeners. By the time the appointed day arrived, the cabinet had fallen and the policy had changed, so he was no longer entitled to speak. And so it went, time and again: if you want a French minister, get him quickly, for you never know how long he may last. Flandin held a near-record for brevity as minister of commerce — six days.

And now — at a crucial moment in France's history — he was at the top. I got him, in the heat of the crisis, to plead France's case at the microphone. It was excellent English: cool, dispassionate words that kindled no sympathy for a potentially bleeding France.

'France might have mobilized,' he said; 'she might have taken coercive measures against Germany; she might have occupied the Rhineland by force. She thought it her duty to abstain from such measures. She preferred to pin her faith to the inherent strength of international law and to the justice of the League of Nations. . . . She kept calm because she was sure of her strength and of her right. . . . France does not threaten any nation. She wishes peace for all people. This peace can be founded only on justice.'

Justice? 'Justice,' said Masaryk, 'is the arithmetic of love.'

We had travelled a long way from Lausanne and Herriot's sympathy for German suffering, three and a half years ago. It was March, 1936. Three months later Italian 'volunteers' were fighting in Spain; and a year after that women and children were being massacred by bombs in Shanghai — in breach of a solemn treaty signed by nine nations, including France.

But there was another new voice raised in London that gloomy spring. It was the voice of Paul Van Zeeland, Prime Minister of Belgium at thirty-eight. A tall, svelte thoroughbred, of calm, scholarly speech. His grave, softly spoken words were as profound as they were simple in meaning, and a fit answer to Ribbentrop, lecturing the world on the iniquity of keeping a good nation down. Belgium alone, it is true, could answer him with a spotless conscience. On the night before Van Zeeland made his moving appeal for Belgium, he accepted my invitation to speak to the United States from a London studio. Hardly raising his voice above a whisper, without a trace of meretricious oratory, he confided the case of war-ravished Belgium to the conscience of the world. By profession a banker, Van Zeeland's manner was that of a family trustee advising his client about prudent investment. Yet his apparently matter-of-fact words were the only ones spoken at that last abortive Conference which kindled the sympathies of those outside.

A new political star had risen. A year later Van Zeeland began his quiet campaign for economic disarmament, beginning with trips to London, Paris, and Washington. Soon Belgium, as the first Western nation, concluded a bilateral non-aggression pact with Germany. The pseudo-fascist machination of the Belgian 'Rexists' caused Van Zeeland's resignation from office in 1937, but his disappearance from the political scene was more formal than real. He is the sort of man of whom Europe stands in need.

Although this does not pretend to be an account of the Rhineland Conference, it seems proper to record that not only Flandin and Van Zeeland were invited to put their case to America. Through Councillor Dieckhoff, that high-minded German diplomat, I asked Ribbentrop to come to the microphone, but the invitation was not accepted. It is a pity that German statesmen are so reticent when they are abroad.

FRANCE'S 'NEW DEAL'

Léon Blum, unquestionably one of the outstanding democratic leaders of today, does not trust himself to address an English-speaking audience in English. It would have been interesting, especially to Americans, to hear him tell about the French 'New Deal,' that impressive set of reforms identified with the government of the Popular Front — the forty-hour week, the paid vacations for workingmen, the reform of the Bank of France, the nationalization of armament manufactures, the inauguration of large-scale national works and other measures against unemployment. The parallelism of social progress in the two great North Atlantic republics could not fail to strike even those people who are not usually given to comparison and analysis.

When Blum did speak to America in his high-pitched, rather feminine voice (for the N.B.C.), it was in French. Although the Popular Front Government had not yet taken office, he gave a succinct statement of its program and the implication of its advent. 'The recent French elections,' he said, 'mean three things. They mean, firstly, a victory for the republican form of government, of democratic institutions and of freedom, both civil and personal, over all forms of autocracy, oligarchy, and fascism. They mean, secondly, the stern resolution to seek a way out of economic depression and an alleviation of the ensuing misery of whatever sort, along an entirely new line. They mean, finally, the will on the part of France to keep the peace of Europe and throughout the world, a peace based on international law and the respect of contracts, on the effective solidarity of all the nations and on general disarmament.'

There was nothing startlingly new in this program; in ordinary circumstances these words might not mean much. But it has come to this in Europe — that a frank and unconditional avowal of democratic principles, without recourse to nationalistic or even patriotic shibboleths is an act of courage. France, at any rate, had travelled a long way since the days of the Stavisky riots, the Fascist leagues, and the threatened dictatorship of Doumergue — a longer way since the bad old days of Poincaré and Tardieu.

Radio had done its share, in France and elsewhere, in bringing about this change. Radio, by using the appeal of reason, by calming political passions and clarifying the issues, by its ability to focus national attention on the real problems, had given democracy a new chance.

NOT SAFE FOR STUFFED SHIRTS

But it has not made the air safe for 'stuffed shirts.' Contrary to supposition, invisibility has not helped those who, having no ideas of their own, obediently read off what is written down for them to say. Here, too, the microphone is 'the greatest tell-tale in the world.' Unless the speaker has thoughts of his own, or has at least made them his own, they will not convince anyone over the air. And no mere voice, however seductive, has ever won a man's opinion, though it may win a lady's heart.

That is why the radio speeches of high dignitaries are often just so much wind. More often than not they are prepared by that nameless crew of black-coated officials who, in every executive palace and every chancery in the world, produce with ant-like industry the substance, if not the spirit, of modern diplomacy. I wonder how many people realize, when they hear the voice of some ruling politician, some celebrity whose name figures in the world's headlines, that they are really listening to an obscure bureaucrat, a public relations expert, or a grandiloquent hack whose name never appears in print.

Those whose business it is to arrange for the broadcasting of speeches by public men often have no means of knowing who is the real author. It is not until the great man is in the studio that the category of the speech — genuine or ghosted — is revealed, and not always then. Introducing such men, however eminent, as the creators of what they are about to say has, to me, always seemed a pious but distasteful fraud.

I remember, for instance, a certain Lord Mayor who had been invited to talk about the great city of London to the American audience. Conceiving his job to be a bit of touting for the tourist trade, he had entrusted the composition to a travel catalogue writer, and when he arrived at the studio in his traditional horse and carriage he had no idea of what he was going to read. 'Won't you do it for me?' he said cynically. 'It's all the same.' He read the talk so badly that I almost blushed for him.

Another time the President of a European state, soliciting the friendship of the Great American People, read several pages of what newspapermen call 'blah' in the presence of the American Minister and several solemn-looking high officials, and his English reading showed that he didn't understand the meaning of the words. And an ambassador whose name is known all over the world came to the studio in great state, bedizened with glittering decorations, to read with pompous conviction a document on the issues of the World Economic Conference. It had been prepared by two young men who up to an hour before the broadcast couldn't agree on the text, and the ambassador had never seen it before.

None of this, of course, is of any use; and radio organizations should treat these prefabricated broadcasts as the newspapers treat so-called handouts — pick out the 'raisins' and look for the holes. The time has come, too, for the elimination of those world-wide engineering stunts by which statesmen in a dozen countries repeat, one after the other, sublime platitudes about peace — collections of phrases which lie ready-made in every foreign office, to be arranged and rearranged at will. In 1932 this was an impressive novelty; today it is a bore.

I have tried, in this chapter, to name only the real men, and speak anonymously of the stuffed shirts. There are, nevertheless, cases where stuffed-shirt broadcasts have made history, as will be seen anon.

VIII. WOODEN IDOL IN BERLIN
WOODCHOPPER IN DOORN

THE WOODEN FIELD MARSHAL AND THE REAL ONE

WHEN I first went to Germany as a newspaper correspondent, four months after the Armistice, a monstrous wooden statue stood, like a sinister reminder of the grim years, in the great open space near the Reichstag Building in Berlin. It was perhaps fifty feet high, and it represented in crude form the hulking figure of Field Marshal von Hindenburg, the hero of Tannenberg and the idol of the German Army — now raised to the status of a Teutonic deity in the patriotic mind. All over the statue were rough iron nails, which covered it so closely that the huge wooden body appeared to be covered with a rough, rusty skin. Each one of those thousands of nails had been bought by some patriotic citizen of the Fatherland, with money that went to prosecute the war. Similar wooden Hindenburgs were to be seen in other German cities all over the land, and millions of hard-earned nails were driven into them, while the nation gritted its teeth. And yet the war was lost.

In 1925 the real Hindenburg, nearing eighty, had become president of the German Republic, risen from the ashes of the Kaiser's Reich, and in March, 1932, this doughty octogenarian was to be put up for re-election against a former Austrian house-painter who had been an obscure corporal in the mighty army under Hindenburg's supreme command. That obscure corporal was — by 1931 — leading a brown-shirted army of malcontents which was threatening to boot the old Field Marshal out of his palace, where he was filling his slowly ebbing years with dreams of the glorious past.

Indeed, many people considered that the old gentleman was all but dead, though no one had thought it wise to tell him so.

Others, however, thought that he was just playing possum, and biding his time — when he would be as alive as he pleased. One thing only was certain: the palace *camarilla* which surrounded him, consisting of certain influential Junkers, including General von Schleicher, Doctor Meissner, his private secretary of state, and above all his son, Colonel Oskar von Hindenburg, kept him in very close seclusion and saw to it that his picture of the world outside was just what he could see through their eyes. His only watchword was Duty; and just now his duty was to sign emergency decree after emergency decree, which enabled a harassed government to rule without the interference of parliament. So many things were put before him to sign — too many for an old man to read! But he believed so implicitly in his personal advisers that whatever they approved he signed.

Many humorous tales went the rounds about the pathetic old man. According to one of them a certain civil servant came for an audience and was kept waiting in the anteroom. His sandwiches, spread with sausage meat, reposed — according to the German fashion — in his portfolio, and as the hands of the clock went past the time for his 'little lunch' he furtively munched his *Butterbrod* to sustain him against the interview, and smoothed out the sandwich paper carefully on a near-by table. Presently he was called out of the room, and when he came back he found that the paper bore Hindenburg's signature. The Field Marshal had passed through the room in the man's absence and, according to his habit, had signed whatever he found lying about.

HINDENBURG INVOKES THE DEITY

On New Year's Eve before his second election this venerable head of state was roused long enough to address the German nation — and the world — by radio. His voice was

still as firm as his signature, and he could be trusted to read
a speech in the good old soldier's way. Standing erect at a
microphone in the Chancellor's Palace in the Wilhelmstrasse,
he addressed to his countrymen 'a few but loyal words, to
help you bear the distress of the time,' namely by drawing
belts still tighter than before. It was the *annus terribilis* of
Germany, and hunger stood hollow-eyed at millions of doors.
'Let no one be faint of heart,' the old man said, 'but let each
of you cherish an unshakable faith in the future of the
Fatherland. God has many times saved Germany in deepest
need; He will not forsake us now.' It was a touching appeal,
and I was glad that the people of the English-speaking world,
of England and the United States, could hear it. Both
American networks carried it from coast to coast.

Midway in this little speech, which must have cost the
old man a great effort, a curious thing happened, though few
people outside Germany knew what it meant. A sudden
break occurred and the words '*Achtung! Rotfront!*' (Attention, Red Front!) were followed by the assertion that 'the
shadow of the Red Front is over Germany.' 'Let all pro-
letarians unite,' it went on before anything could be done
about it, 'against the emergency decrees and the dictatorship!' Whether it was done by communists, with the help
of a secret radio station (as was claimed), or by wire-tapping
Nazis somewhere on the inside (every government service
was swarming with them), it should have been a warning to
the world that Germany was on the eve of an upheaval. For
democratic Germany this was, indeed, the beginning of the
end.

Three months later, it is true, Hindenburg was duly
elected; but his opponent, Adolf Hitler, polled eleven million votes and the turbulent brown tide was threatening to
engulf the nation. Events began to move fast. Doctor
Brüning, the Chancellor, was battling against time, hoping
against hope to save Germany from the financial disaster
which would break the last remaining dam; rushing from
Berlin to Paris, from Paris to London, and from London to
Lausanne, bringing back the cancellation of reparations and
the echo of Herriot's fine words, but no loan. One more set

of emergency decrees and the battle would be won — perhaps.

The tension in the country was terrific; ministers were scared of their own shadows. I tried to get Doctor Curtius, the Foreign Minister, to broadcast to America; he agreed, but not from Berlin. I saw him in Geneva: the text was prepared, everything set. At the last minute he backed out, and in a significant interview he explained to me his difficulties. Some anti-international demonstrations had just taken place in Germany, the question of German minorities in Poland was being argued in Geneva, and the liberal Foreign Minister was terrified to speak — as he would have to, for America — in conciliatory tones! By the following September, Curtius and several other ministers were out, though Brüning still remained.

HINDENBURG'S DREAM

But mysterious moves were taking place behind his back. The Junkers had got his range; his credit with Hindenburg was being undermined; Franz von Papen, wartime military attaché at Washington (whence he had been deported for promoting acts of sabotage), now the old President's 'fair-haired boy,' was getting ready to sell the pass. Hypnotized by his *camarilla*, Hindenburg 'came to life' and refused to sign Brüning's decrees; on May 30, 1932 — ten weeks after Hindenburg's re-election — Brüning was forced to resign.

When this happened I was in Frankfort-on-Main, arranging to broadcast the national German *Sängerfest* to America. Crowds collected outside the newspaper offices to read the bulletins; something intangible was in the air, reminiscent of the old revolutionary days in Berlin. In a flash it came to me that this was 'it': it was the end of Germany as I had known it; the willing, democratic post-war Germany; the Germany alive with a new literature, a new art, and a new culture; the Germany that wanted to be a part of Europe and forget the past. A friend living in Frankfurt said to me:

'We've all been reading the wrong papers; if we'd read the *Völkische Beobachter* and the other Nazi papers we should have known what was happening. We were all fools.'

What was happening is this. In July, while hundreds of beer-drinking philistines from all over Germany were warbling about blue-eyed maidens and golden wine and the birds in spring at their annual orgy of song, the Nazis had just polled their highest vote; the Reichstag, with two hundred and thirty brown shirts in it, was dissolved the day it met; Papen was Chancellor, but soon had to give way to the sinister General Schleicher (the name means Creeper), and straightway opened the negotiations with Hitler which were to have such momentous results. Meantime the Wooden Idol, sitting in the mansion of his East Prussian estate, mourning the departure of his charming *Kamerad*, Papen, was thinking furiously and dreaming mighty dreams. Like unto that legendary dreamer, the Emperor Barbarossa of German pseudo-history, he saw himself awakening in a reborn German Reich.

The dream was not to become articulate until the day he penned his famous testament. 'From the eternally agitated scene of human life will emerge again that rock to which the hope of our fathers clung, that rock upon which ... we founded the German *Kaiserreich*' (Imperial monarchy). All his life the old man kept his counsel on his innermost thoughts. When I left the Emperor, in the afternoon of November 9 [1918],' he wrote, 'I was never to see him again.' His duty — the one duty which in the end invalidated every other vow — was to the Emperor alone.

'YOU STOLE OUR KAISER!'

It was sheer coincidence that my radio quest had led me that very spring in the direction of Doorn. The public has an almost morbid interest in the hapless creatures whom fate has singled out to wear a crown, and the interest becomes acute in the case of an exile from the throne. The fate of those who have wielded power in the quasi-sanctity of royal palaces appeals to the perfervid imaginations of romantic souls in a very particular way. As soon as the transatlantic radio was functioning, therefore, Americans wanted to hear the voice of the ex-Kaiser — the man who above all was thought to be responsible for the troubles of the world.

In a none too hopeful mood I attempted to supply this doubtful commodity to my 'customers.' I knew that dethroned monarchs are privileged but carefully guarded guests, who must not abuse the hospitality of the friendly country in which they reside. Politically they are severely restricted by their hosts. Still, the Dutch government officials whom I approached were not as uncompromising in their attitude as I had expected. A special civil officer — a sort of official watchdog of the diplomatic proprieties — had been appointed to look after the Kaiser's affairs; and this gentleman ruled that since in non-political matters the Kaiser was free, the Government's permission for a non-political broadcast to America was not required. The road was therefore clear, provided the Kaiser himself was willing. I applied to the chamberlain of the ex-Kaiser's 'court' at Doorn House, but soon found that the royal road led via Berlin. I went.

There, in one of the lesser palaces facing Unter den Linden, was concealed the headquarters of the Kaiser's estates, stewarded by a smart, dashing baron of the pre-war type — a trusted member of the imperial entourage. This gentleman not only supervised the administration of the ex-Emperor's extensive properties — which an accommodating Social Democratic government had first confiscated after the revolution and then legislated back into the Hohenzollern family — but he also kept close contact with his imperial master, reporting personally in Doorn every week or two on the general state of affairs.

The little palace, when I walked up to it by appointment, had the appearance of being shut. No one answered my knock on the stately front door. But a side entrance led through a littered maze of backyard passages to an open-air flight of steps, leading to an unobtrusive side door with a sign announcing it to be the office of the private estates of 'His Imperial and Royal Majesty, Wilhelm II.' An ordinary bell brought a servant to the door, who led me through a long corridor to the handsomer front part of the house, decorated in the neo-classical or pseudo-Empire style of early nineteenth century Prussia. Eventually I found myself in the cozy white-and-gilt waiting-room of the Herr Baron.

He was a very charming but temperamental person. When I told him that I was there on behalf of American interests he began to bristle. Suddenly, turning toward me in purple rage, he raised his forefinger and shouted: 'American — ha! Do you know what you have done?... *You — stole — our — Kaiser!*'

His attitude was terrifying, his face quivered as he waved me aside, before I could even voice my astonishment. In about ten minutes' harangue, delivered in tones of Nemesis, he went on: 'Yes, you stole our Kaiser.... Your Mr. Wilson did it, with his Fourteen Points.... Never, except for the lying promises he made to us, would His Majesty have consented to leave German soil. It was on the assurance of fair terms, in order to save the lives of our starving people, to avert needless bloodshed that he left, on the solemn promise of that famous 'peace without victory' (his voice had become a snarl).

'No! we were not beaten: never believe that the glorious German army was beaten in the field. We were *lured* into surrender after our Kaiser had left — to save the German people from more suffering...'

On and on went the flow of angry words, until the excited baron's voice gave out and I seemed to have wilted under the lash of his avenging tongue. At last, when I could be heard, I said that this was indeed an interesting version of history which I, of course, did not know. I thought that it ought to be told, and told by the Kaiser himself. The American public would no doubt be keenly interested to hear it. At this his angry countenance melted into a smile and he apologized.

'I ask your pardon,' he said, 'but you will understand. I had to get this off my chest. Now that I have said what I had to say, let us be friends.'

I was amazed at such naïveté — and almost touched. I seemed to have been the first American he had met to whom he could 'tell the truth.' Now he was satisfied and we talked business, quite amicably and intimately. He promised to put my proposal — about the broadcast — to His Majesty on his next trip to Doorn. But he wanted me to realize that the time was not yet ripe. And confidentially (the facts are now common property, so there is no question of violating his confidence) he told me that important political developments were about to take place — developments which would change the whole face of things — and then, presumably, the Kaiser might break his silence. In any case, my suggestion would have serious consideration, and I was definitely the first in the field. We shook hands cordially as he saw me out — through the front door.

HOHENZOLLERN OR HITLER?

I could not help pondering what he had said. 'Important developments!' Remember this was in the spring of 1932 — at least seven months before the Nazi coup, of which the world had no inkling then. But was that what he meant? It seems reasonable to believe that the Hohenzollerns knew what was in the wind. One of the Kaiser's sons was a prominent storm-troop leader; the Crown Prince himself was a benevolent friend of the movement. But if they did know, they must have had reason to hope for a different outcome of these 'important developments.' Who would have thought that utter oblivion was in store for them all?

But there was another story, of which I — as most people in and outside Germany — had no knowledge. The story has now been told on what I believe to be the unimpeachable authority of one of the actors in the shadowy drama that

was being enacted behind the scenes.[1] Speaking of Chancellor
Brüning, this authority says: 'Long hours of contemplation
had convinced him that one course, and one course only,
could prevent Hitler from ultimately obtaining supreme
power — the restoration of the monarchy.' In 1932 this
plan had, under cover, become practical politics. It was
known to a very select number of political leaders, it had been
broached to Hindenburg, whose re-election was the first step
in Brüning's well-considered plan. Step number 2 was the
end of reparations (accomplished in June); step number 3
the securing of a two-thirds majority in the Reichstag, which
could then change the Constitution and declare Hindenburg
regent for life. Finally, the old man would be succeeded by a
grandson of the Kaiser, who would become a constitutional
sovereign on the English model.

That's where the old gentleman baulked. He was outraged at the idea of anything less than a military absolutism
— a Greater Prussia, on the principles of the post-Napoleonic
era. And as for a grandson of the Kaiser — 'I am the trustee
of the Emperor,' he had said, 'and can never give my consent
to anyone's succeeding to the throne save the Emperor
himself.'

GOERING WAXES PIOUS

So that was it! The emotional Baron must have known —
or thought — that these differences of detail and personnel
were being smoothed out, and then — then the dream that
the Old Man was dreaming in the solitude of Neudeck would
come true. Few people shared that dream, but among them
were the Imperial Woodchopper, and the baron who shuttled
back and forth between Berlin and Doorn. Yet Germany
was within an ace of getting its Kaiser back. But the Junkers
overplayed their hand: Brüning was sent away; Papen and
Schleicher, trying to outsmart each other, got caught in the

[1] See John W. Wheeler-Bennett's *Wooden Titan*, London and New York, 1937.

meshes of their own nets. The very thing that should have helped the plan — the recession of the Nazi flood in November (they lost two million votes at the Reichstag elections) — sealed Wilhelm's fate; for Hitler, realizing that he had passed his peak, closed the deal with Papen and on January 30, 1933, Hitler's hordes marched through the Brandenburger Gate.

The Field Marshal's dream was dreamed out. From the very palace where barely a year before he had made his New Year's broadcast, he had to review the never-ending flood of marching 'S.A.' and 'S.S.' And another humorous tale went the rounds in Berlin. As the old soldier watched the brown shirts shuffling along rather sloppily, and then beheld the brisk, precise stepping of the Steel Helmet Corps (old front soldiers), his tired old mind carried him back to the great old days of the Battle of Tannenberg. Turning to Ludendorff he whispered (so the story goes): 'How magnificently your men march, General! But I didn't think they had made so many prisoners!'

'God has many times saved Germany in deepest need,' he had said in his broadcast. 'He will not forsake us now.'

Hermann Göring, seeing the old gentleman reviewing the Nazi triumph, said, 'How gloriously has the aged Field Marshal been used as an instrument in the hand of God!'

The dream was dreamed out. Adolf Hitler was Chancellor of Germany, and woodchopping was still the imperial occupation at Doorn.

IX. GANDHI EATS WHILE AMERICA WAITS

REVOLUTIONISTS ON THE MOVE

TWO of the most memorable events in the pioneer years of international broadcasting were the radio talks to America made by Mahatma Gandhi and by Leon Trotsky, the one from London in 1931, the other from Copenhagen in 1932. Neither of them had ever faced the microphone before; one had recently been released from prison; the other had just been granted a respite from isolation on a lonely Turkish island. Both were to proceed to further penance for their revolutionary activity — Gandhi to his Indian jail, Trotsky to perpetual exile. But in the interim the world had, by means of the new instrument of communication, been able to take an independent measure of these men.

Here were two revolutionary figures destined to live in history, yet as different in character and method as Jesus of Nazareth and Napoleon of Corsica. That two such leaders should leave their mark on the same generation of men is an indication of the curious contradiction of heterogeneous thought in a mechanically more than ever unified world. But there is a certain analogy to be drawn between these men's careers. Both are Orientals; both were members of a middle-class intelligentsia, destined to lead a revolt of the lowly against their oppressors. The differences in their philosophy and their technique were determined by the conditions confronting them in their struggles. They were intellectual leaders of the social revolution in the two largest politically integrated countries in the world, peopled between them by one quarter of the world's population and covering one fifth of the habitable globe. Coming into contact with these two dynamic personalities even for a brief space is an experience not easily forgotten.

Mohandas Karamchand Gandhi, styled by his followers Mahatma (the Great-Souled), had been the moving spirit of the Indian revolutionary movement for upwards of twenty years, but in England his personal power was thought to have been spent when he retired from active politics in 1924. But suddenly he emerged from his supposed retirement in 1930, to organize the civil disobedience campaign which was to result in violent disorder and much bloodshed just at the moment when Great Britain was tackling the thorny problem of Indian constitutional reform. 'Civil disobedience' was the practical expression of the doctrine of *Ahimsa* (non-violence) preached by Gandhi as the revolutionary creed and strategy of India. The campaign had reached its climax in the famous March to the Sea, the symbolical salt-making expedition which led to Gandhi's arrest and confinement in Yeravda jail in May, 1930. The whole country was once more aflame and a wave of sanguinary fanaticism swept the population toward revolt. Gandhi in prison — and this was not his first imprisonment — proved more dangerous to the British government than Gandhi at large; for his 'martyrdom' roused the Moderates to espouse his cause. Their venerable leader, Vithalbhai Patel, resigned the presidency of the Legislative Assembly to assume active leadership of the revolutionary Congress Party while Gandhi was in jail. Eventually, however, a truce was brought about which resulted in Gandhi's liberation and his journey to London to attend the second Round Table Conference.

By the time Gandhi was released and set to go to London, the Labor Cabinet had made way for the National Government. Sir Samuel Hoare was at the head of the India Office and the atmosphere of the dominant section of the British public was hostile to Gandhi. The ordinary uninformed man regarded him quite frankly as a political criminal, much as the average American business man regards even the mildest 'Red.' To that class of Englishman, fed by a ranting imperialistic press, even the personal integrity of a person like Gandhi was inconceivable. Yet even my own fleeting contact with this extraordinary man gave me convincing proof of the rarest kind of unselfish honesty — an example of that *satyagraha* which once enabled him to face a fanatical patriotic assembly and say that he would, if he had to, sacrifice even India to Truth.

HOW TO TALK TO A SAINT

The Round Table Conference, convened after elaborate preparation and tremendous preliminary touting, was to be opened with all possible pomp and solemnity by King George V on September 14, 1931. Gandhi, accompanied by his Indianized European secretary, and devotee, Madeline Slade, daughter of a British admiral, and several Congress leaders, sailed from Bombay on a P. and O. liner in August. In May his coming to England had still been doubtful, but I kept in touch with several groups of his disciples in London, who supplied me with a variety of advice, some of it curious. One of these disciples, who was stated to have spent some six months the previous year in close contact with the Mahatma, wrote that if we wanted the latter to broadcast it was advisable to:

(1) State clearly the object of the proposed address (he would fight shy of it if he thought it just a stunt of a 'scoop');
(2) Make no appeal to his vanity, as he has none;
(3) On no account offer him money;
(4) Not try to impress him; and
(5) Spell his name correctly — it means (in Hindustani) 'rubbish' or 'refuse.'

Despite the postscript which said that the letter was 'written under some difficulty in a pigsty,' I thought the advice very sound and determined to act on it. However, New York had already tried to 'impress' the Mahatma with long cablegrams

from Indian Congress representatives in America and heads
of organizations, and there was no reply to these grandiloquent invitations to follow in the footseps of Rabindranath
Tagore and address the American audience by radio.

Our Opposition had out-manœuvred us by sending a
personal emissary to Gandhi in India — an American newspaperman who knew the Mahatma and had orders to accom-
pany him all the way to England. He got a promise from him
to broadcast for the N.B.C., and kept silent on the existence
of any other network.

However, there were other factors to be considered.
One was the British Government; another was Gandhi's
hostess in London, for it had been arranged for him to live
privately in a settlement house in the East End of London,
namely Kingsley Hall at Bow, founded and administered by
Miss Muriel Lester, one of those angels of mercy whose
mission is to bring spiritual sunshine and a little material
warmth into the lives of the poor. I knew Miss Lester's sister
Doris, head of another settlement, the Children's House, just
around the corner from Kingsley Hall. It was a dismal part
of London — untidy streets lined with low and melancholy-
looking brick houses from whose narrow doorways swarmed
ill-clad, unwashed children. They would crowd around our
car with frightening familiarity when we arrived with bundles
of hand-me-down clothing for Miss Doris's waifs.

Kingsley Hall was a curious modern structure forming a
square around a courtyard, with a balcony running around
the inside walls, from which doors led to individual tiny
rooms or 'cells' in which to rest and meditate. In one of these
cells the Mahatma was to live on the simple, abstemious
scale to which he was accustomed, while the rest of the delegates to the great Conference lived at Dorchester House and
other fashionable West End hotels. The fact that this addic-
tion to lowliness involved daily trips of six miles in either
direction did not frighten Gandhi. He was to feel that he was
among his own people — the lowly and the poor.

I visited Miss Lester and got her permission to install
the special telephone lines and other equipment that would
be necessary to 'pipe' a talk by Gandhi to the Radio Termi-

nal of the General Post Office and thence to Rugby, where it
would be radiated to America. We also arranged that she, as
his hostess, should introduce the Mahatma to his American
audience, and should describe the surroundings in which he
was speaking — her own Kingsley Hall. And I gave the
requisite orders to the radio engineers of the Post Office
(with whom at that time we dealt direct, with the consent of
the B.B.C.).

SIR SAMUEL HOARE TAKES A CHANCE

As to the other factor — the Government — difficulties
were likely to ensue. A speech by Gandhi was considered
dynamite; a speech made direct to America, without the
possibly restraining influence of an English audience, might
be embarrassing to the British Government, which is rather
sensitive on the point of American opinion. (Katherine Mayo
had done too good a job to allow Gandhi to ruin it.) One may
judge the feelings of the Conservative press from a paragraph
in the *Morning Post* a few days before the broadcast: 'There
does not appear to be any relevant reason why Gandhi should
harangue the American public, but I suppose it is the natural
sequel to the immense flood of Gandhi propaganda in the
U.S.A.... Most American broadcast programs are sponsored by commercial firms, so perhaps it is an advertisement
for California lemon-growers.'

Luckily I had a slight but pleasant acquaintance with Sir
Samuel Hoare, the Secretary of State for India. I wrote him
a personal note, and although it is rare for a journalist or anyone of that order to be received privately by a Cabinet
Minister in office, I had a summons to the India Office by
return of post. It is not 'etiquette' to reveal ministerial con-
fidences, but I think it is permissible to say that I was not
deceived in my estimate of the Government's attitude. I laid
all my cards on the table and — rather rashly — assumed
the responsibility for the content of anything that Gandhi

might say. In other words, I guaranteed that it would contain nothing seditious, and this guarantee covered the entire enterprise, both for ourselves and any other American broadcasting organization! Sir Samuel, with one of those broad gestures of personal confidence, simply made me — a foreigner — Gandhi's sponsor, and on that basis gave permission to the Post Office (which at that psychological moment, as it happened, asked for his O.K.) to lay the lines.

Gandhi landed on one of those wet and hopelessly dreary autumn days that London excels in producing at all seasons of the year. He reached London on an ordinary train, arriving in a chilling, drenching rain. Wearing only his loincloth and a sort of white cotton sheet slung over his shoulder, with the usual crude sandals on his feet, he was hustled by a band of admirers, white and brown, to the Friends' Meeting House for an official welcome. The Quakers had taken it upon themselves to be the first hosts to the World's Non-Resister Number One. He told his audience he had come on a mission of peace, simply because he had promised the Viceroy he would come. Laurence Housman, the English poet, in introducing him said that 'no man loses by keeping his word of honor.'

GANDHI 'UNITES' THE U.S.A.

I got my first glimpse of the Indian saint a couple of hours later, at Kingsley Hall, where some twenty of us, mostly representatives of local organizations led by the Mayor of Bow, waited for him in a large empty room through which he had to pass on his way to the 'cell.' It was a long wait, for a melancholy Saturday afternoon, and outside the rain came down in sheets. At last we heard a cheer. None the worse for the wet, the Mahatma arrived, hatless and bald, his thin brown legs and arms bare, greeted us with a smile exposing the gaping vacancies between his teeth, and regarded us through his tin-framed spectacles. A more puny, homely,

and unimpressive human being I have never seen. Miss
Lester introduced us all, with an astonishing virtuosity of
memory. The Mahatma looked at each one in turn, patiently
smiled again and said, 'I don't think you'll expect me to remember your names.' And that was that. No well-meaning
mendacities. As he disappeared into the corridor I realized
that a Gandhi couldn't tell even a 'white' lie for the sake of
being polite.

A group of dusky turbaned gentlemen followed — the
white-bearded Pandit Malvya among them — and were
ushered into the 'cell' for a political conference. The picture
had something biblical about it: a council of high-browed
elders, crouching on the floor, listening to the wisdom of the
Master...

Hovering outside, on the long narrow balcony, the women,
swathed in homespun *sharis* draped over their heads — with
Sarojini Naida, the Indian poetess, and Madeline Slade
looking dark and Oriental despite her long English face —
completed the illusion. There was no interrupting the conclave; the fate of a nation was being discussed, while all mundane business waited. At long last I was ushered into the
Mahatma's presence. He was affable and came to the point
at once. He listened to my explanation of the American
broadcasting system and the existence of two major competitive 'chains.' He said he was not willing to make two
broadcasts, but would like the one to be shared by all; the
time I proposed, six in the evening on the next day, a Sunday,
was acceptable; it fitted in with his rigid program of meals
and silences and conferences. It also happened to be our
regular Sunday hour for European programs, to which a vast
audience was accustomed. He proposed a miniature 'round
table conference' with the two American competitors and
himself.

An hour or so later the 'Opposition,' hastily summoned,
arrived, two men strong. Once again we were ushered in. It
was Gandhi's mealtime. Crouching on the floor, with an
appetizing ensemble of fruit and a jug of goat's milk before
him he laughingly bade us be seated, and as there were no
chairs we all squatted in a circle on the floor. Gandhi spoke.

'Mr. M——,' he began, 'I have promised to broadcast for you, and I am prepared to do it. Now here is another broadcasting company, and you did not tell me there was more than one. Nevertheless, *a promise is a promise* and I must fulfill it. I want to accommodate everyone, but I am a busy man just now and prefer not to make two speeches. I suggest (with a gesture meant for all of us) you get together and arrange to help me save time.'

He looked at me questioningly and I signified my agreement. The Opposition, represented by the European Manager of Mr. M——'s press association, spoke up and said:

'We have heard your wishes, Mahatma, and I am sure we'll now be able to straighten the matter out among ourselves.'

'Hurrah!' cried the Mahatma. 'America is at peace. That's splendid,' and shook hands all round. Once again we confirmed the time, and we left the little old man to his bananas and dates. Outside, on the stairs, my rival calmly announced that the broadcast was 'exclusive' and could be given to us only if his New York office agreed. I was dumbfounded. I reminded him that his office had omitted to do anything about telephone lines and broadcasting equipment, and that I was not prepared to let him use mine.

'Oh, I'm glad you mentioned this,' he said. 'In that case I'll just take the Mahatma in a taxicab to Radio Terminal (the point of distribution for all transoceanic talks), and make the broadcast from there.'

The mental picture of this struck me as comical and I heartily agreed to this proposed arrangement — if he could carry it out.

Meantime tremendous and completely useless struggles were carried out between the rival organizations in New York. The press agency whose representative had been acting for the N.B.C. was bombarded with telegrams from client newspapers who also owned stations on the Columbia network. Long-distance telephone wires hummed with pleadings and recriminations; the transatlantic telephone did a rushing business. Both networks announced 'exclusive' broadcasts in the press. I sat tight, knowing the Mahatma's mind, and feeling armed against all eventualities by my government permission and my lines.

Next morning, the morning of the broadcast, a radio telephone official called me at my house to say that N.B.C. had applied for lines to Kingsley Hall. It was impossible to get permission for another installation at such short notice; was I willing for them to be used by our Opposition? 'Yes,' I said, 'provided they are not used earlier than our broadcast.' That being reasonable, orders were given accordingly.

'DO I TALK INTO THIS THING?'

The time for the broadcast arrived. In my excitement I had forgotten that I had to introduce another speaker at the B.B.C.'s studios in Savoy Hill a half hour before Gandhi's talk. I kept my appointment and had my car ready outside. Checking by telephone with Miss Lester and the engineers, I heard that all was going according to plan. Realizing that I could not reach Bow in time I stopped near St. Paul's Cathedral and turned into the Radio Terminal building — the very place where my competitor had so confidently threatened to take the Mahatma. Here I could listen not only to the broadcast but to the tests and all the preliminary conversations going on in the room. The engineers were there, Miss Lester was there, my competitors were there. The Mahatma was late. Calm and unconcerned, he was finishing his meal of fruit and goat's milk upstairs. The clock ticked on; zero hour came and passed. Someone said he was coming soon; as all America was waiting with bated breath, some speaker had to fill the empty air. The redoubtable press association chief produced a lengthy script — an 'introduction' prepared in advance on behalf of the Opposition and mentioning that company by name, which he was to read.

I held my breath; would my absentee diplomacy work?

The radio engineer in charge spoke up; asked whether I wasn't present. No, I was delayed, Miss Lester informed him; but I had invited her to announce the distinguished guest. General approval around the room. Miss Lester began. As she described the place, the voices of slum children playing in the street floated in through the windows. Then the Mahatma entered. He had never seen a microphone.

'Do I talk into this thing?' he inquired audibly — a stage whisper heard by millions.

Sitting at the table prepared for him, opposite a statuette of Saint Francis discreetly set into the wall, he folded his hands and closed his eyes. He had no manuscript. After a few seconds silence he began, simply, without any attempt at oratory, in beautiful English which hardly showed a trace of an Indian accent:

'In my opinion the Indian struggle bears in itself consequences not merely affecting India but the whole world.'

In simple, clear-cut, moderate phrases, unadorned by hyperbole, he stated the Indian problem, in its historical perspective, in its social aspects, and as a revolutionary challenge. He had no manuscript; yet there was not an instant's hesitation. Would he stick to the bargain I had made without his consent? I knew that government officials would listen on monitor lines; knew that shorthand transcripts were being made. For nearly a half hour he went on, slowly and every word distinct, his thin, high-pitched voice automatically lowered through transmission, but clear and unwavering, explaining his 'non-violent' revolution:

'I feel in the innermost recesses of my heart that the world is sick unto death of blood-spilling. The world is seeking a way out, and I flatter myself with the belief that perhaps it will be the privilege of the ancient land of India to show that way out to the hungering world.'

A PLEA FOR INDIA'S MILLIONS

But the climax of the speech was his plea for the 'semi-starved millions scattered throughout the seven hundred thousand villages dotted over a surface nineteen hundred miles long and fifteen hundred miles broad.'

'It is a painful phenomenon that those simple villages, through no fault of their own, have nearly six months in the year idle upon their hands. Time was not long ago when every village was self-sufficient in regard to the two primary human wants — food and clothing. Unfortunately for us, when the East India Company, by means which I would prefer not to describe, destroyed that supplementary village industry and the millions of spinners — who had become famed through the cunning of their deft fingers for drawing the finest thread, such as has never been yet drawn by any modern machinery — these village spinners found themselves one fine morning with their noble occupation gone, and from that day forward India has become progressively poor, no matter what may be said to the contrary.' This was the only note of criticism in the twenty-minute talk. Gandhi was in England on a mission of peace. I knew he would not abuse the hospitality of his hosts.

But most eloquent was his plea for the Untouchables — the outcast millions of India whose fate lay in the hands of his own countrymen and for whom he himself was not long afterwards to undertake a 'fast unto death,' stopped only when — near his extremity — he was assured of their salvation by a pledge of reform.

'It is a matter of still deeper humiliation to me that we Hindus regard several million of our kith and kin as too degraded even for our touch. I refer to the so-called Untouchables. These are no small weaknesses in a nation struggling to be free, and hence you find that in this struggle through self-purification we have assigned a foremost place to the removal of this curse of untouchability and the attainment of unity among all the different classes and communities of India representing the different creeds. It is along the same lines that we seek to rid our land of the curse of drink.'

The room was hushed; everybody seemed under a spell. Outside in the twilight, the children were still at their play; their voices could be heard wherever people listened to Gandhi, as a reminder that he was speaking from an English slum. It was heard by millions; it was printed in full by newspapers in three continents. Nothing Gandhi ever said reached so many people; it was the largest audience he had ever had.

He had risen, as usual, at four that morning; had meditated, prayed, and worked. After his broadcast he — the one public figure in the world who lives completely by the Golden Rule — preached a sermon in a Christian service held in Kingsley Hall, then left for a surprise conference — on neutral ground — with the Prime Minister, which lasted till nearly midnight. Next day, the Round Table Conference opened — on a Monday, Gandhi's 'day of silence.' He sat at the Conference table, listened, and spoke no word. Even his dumb presence electrified some who were there. Here, at any rate, was a man; here, for once, they were confronted with the inflexible power of Truth. The compromise announced by Ramsay MacDonald at the end of the Conference he met with an openly announced resolve that he would resist it with his life.

He left England as he had come — with empty hands and a pure heart. Six days after his arrival in India he was imprisoned and returned to Yeravda jail, where nine months later he began his historic fast.

X. TROTSKY'S WEEK OUT

THE LION IS AT LARGE!

ONE fine Monday morning in November, 1932, I picked up my paper and read a report that Leon Trotsky, the Russian revolutionist, had escaped from Prinkipo, the island in the Sea of Marmora on which he had been confined for the past four years. The lion was at large, and the world pricked up its ears. Ever since, after years of exile in eastern Siberia, the Trotsky family had been deported at the orders of Joseph Stalin, the undisputed master of the Soviets, the Turkish Government — as the only one in Europe or Asia — had given him this refuge, where, like Napoleon at Elba, he was isolated yet under convenient surveillance. Here — unlike Napoleon — this restless rebel had developed a prodigious literary activity, the proceeds of which helped to finance a new world-wide revolutionary movement, the Left Opposition, and to promote the organization of the Fourth International.

For most people of literary bent this exile might have entailed no hardships: Trotsky's writings were in fair demand in 'bourgeois' countries, and the intervals of intellectual work were filled out by fishing and sailing adventures which provided excitement of a kind. Faithful disciples had gathered around him, and he was in a fair way to becoming a revolutionary sage. But physically the old fighter was cut off from the world; and his autobiography, closing with a sardonic chapter on 'The World without Visa,' revealed the exile's grief. Here was the man of action; the revolutionist who had tasted power; once the War Commissar of the world's largest country, who had negotiated the Peace of Brest-Litovsk, who had fought the 'white' forces of Europe to a standstill; sterilized, cut off from active strife in the midst of a world in turmoil.

Sickness, the hardships of exile and deportation, and personal bereavement had done little to break this man's spirit; the untimely death of a son and the suicide of a daughter were mere episodes in an embattled rebel's life. None of these things, nor his professed need for medical attention, had induced the European statesmen — some of them his former Socialist 'comrades' — to relax the political quarantine which held him prisoner.

And now, all of a sudden, he was to have a week out — a trip to northern Europe, not for rest but for political work. It seemed incredible. It seemed incredible that a socialist students' organization in Denmark, which desired to hear him speak, could secure not only a week's permit for him to stay, but free passage through Italy and France — countries in which two former Socialist comrades, Mussolini and Laval, were in command.

The newspapers were none too certain in their first reports. A man named Lubinsky, supposed to be Trotsky, had embarked in the Italian steamer *Praga*, bound for Naples and now at sea. The news was both interesting and disquieting to a radio man in London. Here was one of the actors in the greatest human mass drama of our time; a man who had one of the most thrilling inside stories in history to tell. Europe might be afraid to hear it; but what about America, where a violent Red scare had made him an object of the fascinated admiration accorded to first-class gangsters? It was from America that Trotsky had sailed to Petrograd to play his rôle in the 'ten days that shook the world.' I myself remembered the rather shabby, studious-looking Bohemian as he came to visit an editorial colleague in the office of a very bourgeois New York magazine (*Current Opinion*) in 1916, of whom no one suspected that a few months later he would help to 'shake the world.'

A broadcast by Trotsky, aside from all other considerations, would be a 'scoop.'

A BOLSHEVIK'S ODYSSEY

Taking an off chance, I addressed a radiogram to 'Lubinsky,' aboard the S.S. *Praga*. To my surprise, back came a reply signed 'Lubinsky-Trotsky,' thus disposing of any doubts as to the passenger's identity. Beyond this the precious telegram didn't help much, for it deferred everything to Trotsky's arrival in Copenhagen, which — what with meddlesome governments and an active competition — might be too late. So I 'parked' at the telephone for the rest of that day and the next; frequented Communist acquaintances; ferreted out connections in Paris, London, and Copenhagen itself. Max Eastman, the translator of Trotsky's 'history,' happened to be in London and was helpful with advice. In Copenhagen the Socialist students were duly excited and ready to take matters in hand, incidentally hoping to recoup some of the expenses of Trotsky's trip, which they had guaranteed; ready, too, to exploit the well-known American spirit of competition. Everything considered, I thought it better to go to bat myself — on the ground.

Meantime Trotsky's ship had touched Athens, where he was not allowed to land, while wife and daughter were given a police escort to help them look at antiques, and at Naples, where Fascist press men, darting from ambush, clicked cameras at the sight-seeing revolutionist. By this time the Trotsky Odyssey had become a world sensation and his secretaries had been promoted — in the newspapers — to bodyguards. At Marseilles the police were prepared with an elaborate strategy which infuriated the cheated press. Taking the 'dangerous' party off on a police boat they landed them outside the city, motored them to Avignon, and put them on board a sealed carriage attached to the Paris train. (In 1917 Lenin was sent in a sealed carriage through Germany to start the revolution in Russia.) The carriage was later switched on to another train which would reach Dunkerque on Tuesday, just eight days after the Trotskys had left Prinkipo. The news that they were to embark on the regular Dunkerque-Esbjerg steamer *Bernstorff* made me reserve a cabin on the ship in the hope of clinching the business en route.

When I arrived at Dunkerque Harbor on that gray November morning, there was not a newspaper reporter in sight. Foiled at Marseilles, the world's press had given up the hunt!

For extra security the train was run right onto the quai. Trotsky, his small, blonde, and rather tousled-looking wife, and three youngish disciples were trailed all the way by two French secret-service men, who seemed to have stepped straight out of the funnies, unmistakable by the large, round, black slouch hats favored by their kind — with slight indentations to break the monotony. The whole group was marshalled by a sectional chief of the Sureté Nationale. I never saw a police officer who was such a perfect gentleman. His clothes, speech, and manner were those of a rising diplomat, and he treated the reputed firebrand with an old-world courtesy that bordered on deference, viséing the party's papers, looking after their tickets and accommodations, and bidding them good-bye with affable charm, but leaving the two detectives on board.

The harbor police, who were looking after mere folks like myself, weren't half so pleasant. I had gone ashore in order to meet the train, and it took quite a lot of explaining and showing of credentials before I managed to get back. Besides the Trotskyites I was almost the only passenger; at any rate, if there were others I don't remember them.

POPE OF THE WORLD REVOLUTION

Trotsky and family disappeared into their compartment as soon as we cast off, and for the duration of the twenty-four-hour journey were not seen again. At the entrance to their corridor, day and night, stood a hefty detective; in the hall, just beyond, day and night, sat a secretary — or bodyguard. The three young men who accompanied him — one

German, one French, one Czech — were animated by fanatical devotion to a worshipped chief, like paladins to a cru-
sading prince.   Indeed, a pope in transit through infidel land
could not have been more reverently guarded.

Only once, in the middle of the night, did I see the great
man emerge halfway down the corridor, in shirtsleeves, pen
in hand, to call in one of his aides. He was evidently hard
at work. An interview with him was a hopeless quest. One
of the paladins, who afterwards turned out to be his personal
secretary, eyed me with suspicion from the start, and evinced
a strange curiosity as to my purposes and designs. After
hours of small-talk fencing we came to grips. It was a question of money; Trotsky's man was not in a hurry to close the
deal. After all, I might be a spy!

When we arrived at Copenhagen the dock was crowded
with a mob of hooting, whistling, jeering men. They carried
immense red banners inscribed 'Long live the Soviet!' and
'Down with Trotsky, the Traitor!' in Danish and German.
When they saw Trotsky himself, standing on the narrow
upper deck, near the rail, flanked by his family and friends,
they shouted what must have been ugly threats. Trotsky,
calm and undisturbed, peered at them with the professional
curiosity of an entomologist examining a new specimen. We
went down the gangplank; police held back the crowd and
nothing happened.

There was no sealed train this time: the party travelled in
a compartment not far from mine; the rest were filled
with Danish newspaper men. Trotsky, quite alone, stood
in the passage, on the off-side of the train, as it stood at the
station. Suddenly a grease-blacked face appeared in the
doorway and looked furtively around. My heart stood still.
I expected to see the man whip out a revolver. But it was
only a slip of paper. He was an oiler or a brakeman and evidently a left-wing Communist, who had been sent as emissary by the local comrades. Presently a couple of other
workmen appeared outside the window and handed up bits
of paper for Trotsky to autograph. Trotsky signed them,
smiled, and shook hands.

At Copenhagen that evening a terrific crowd met the train.

In the rush I couldn't see what happened, and I barely captured a taxicab to take me and belongings to the Palace Hotel. There, not long after me, appeared the two French secret-service men, sheepishly inquiring whether I had Monsieur Trotsky concealed — presumably in a cupboard or under the bed. Evidently the porter had sent them to the newest arrival, as the most likely man. They had tried to connect with their charge at the station, but he had eluded them. They looked helpless and worried as they sat on the edge of my plush chairs and twirled their black hats to hide their embarrassment. They spoke nothing but French and here they were, lost — lost in a strange, unfeeling world!

I offered to telephone around, and — sure enough — I got hold of the head of the Socialist students, who revealed that Comrade Trotsky was at the suburban house of a trusted party chief. What had happened was that the Danish police, unmindful of their French confrères, had stopped the train at a suburb and quietly taken the Trotskys off, while the retinue went on to Copenhagen.

The French detectives were profuse in their thanks, but they wouldn't stay for a drink. Full of fresh hope, they bowed themselves out.

PRIME MINISTER STAUNING CLEARS THE LINES

My own 'detectives,' who had been taking local soundings, had bad news. The Danish State Radio Administration could not give us facilities for a talk by Trotsky, evidently by reason of orders from higher up. The state telephone people, who could — if they would — 'pipe' the talk to England for transmission to New York, were uncommunicative in the absence of government orders. A young Danish university lecturer, husband of a charming and radio-minded American girl of my acquaintance, came to the rescue, took me to the government offices, and engineered an interview with the Prime Minister, Thorvald Stauning, in person.

This gentle, fatherly statesman, a Social-Democrat of the solid pre-war type, who has maintained himself as the trusted head of a coalition government for eight consecutive years, was especially friendly because I had invited him some months before to address Americans on an all-Scandinavian occasion (with the Prime Ministers of Sweden and Norway) by way of the transatlantic radio. This had brought him hundreds of fan letters from former compatriots now citizens of America. He agreed that a talk by a Russian radical, via the same route, could not be interpreted as an act unfriendly to the Soviet Government. The Danish telephone, though a government department, would in fact only act as a 'common carrier' of what was really a private message until it reached New York. He smiled and stroked his enormous, graying Victorian beard. No, he had no objection, but it was for the Foreign Minister to decide (who probably had vetoed the plan in the first place). Might I go to the Foreign Minister and tell him the Prime Minister's view? I certainly might. I hustled back to the Foreign Ministry, and in a few minutes the deadlock was broken; the red tape was cut and the state telephone chief was at our service.

Moreover, this had been a blessing in disguise. For the Trotsky camp, which had held out for an astronomical fee, saw their prospects fade when I betrayed no desire to break through the official barriers. An amiable American Leftist intellectual named Gould (one of the growing band of the faithful surrounding the great man) had, I learned, already been working on the translation of the proposed talk and coaching Trotsky, whose English was rusty from lack of use. Late on Friday night, two days before the projected broadcast, we came to terms — a fee which any first-class American crooner would consider low. We were all set. Trotsky was to speak from the Telephone Building on Sunday evening, two hours before his great lecture to the mass meeting assembled by the Socialist students.

TROTSKY TAKES HIS COAT OFF

Meantime the newspapers had got wind of the negotiations, and were on our trail. Trotsky's one condition was that there should be no local publicity. So when the day arrived we calmly referred all reporters to the broadcasting studios, while Trotsky was spirited in a closed cab to the main telephone exchange in another part of town. When he arrived, accompanied only by his Czech secretary, and was ushered with all ceremony into a room full of people, with the frock-coated telephone chief playing host, he thought he had been betrayed.

'What are these? Journalists?' he burst out.

We reassured him. There wasn't a journalist in the room, though every newspaper had been hounding the man of the hour for five days. The dignified telephone chief deferentially asked for an autograph (like the greasy workman the day before) and got it. An improvised studio had been prepared next door, and no one was admitted except myself. Here I was, alone with the world's most dreaded Red, one of the acknowledged military geniuses of the century and one of the greatest orators of all time. And I perceived that he was nervous. He had never spoken into a microphone: radio had not been developed in the Russia he had known.

He spoke of his 'bad English' and tried it out on me. We went over phrase after phrase, he — like a good student — marking every wrong accent and inflection as I corrected him.

Halfway through he asked, politely, might he remove his coat? He sat down before the 'mike' and tried his voice; was it all right like that? I suggested his natural, conversational tone. 'You speak to millions, but to each man separately.' He agreed that oratory was not called for; he would try to keep subdued.

He started quietly, without gestures. But as he warmed up — and this was his first public speech in five years or more! — he was like a warhorse smelling powder. He raised

Trotsky's Copenhagen Broadcast, November, 1932
'Here I was, alone with the world's most dreaded Red, one of the acknowledged
military geniuses of the century and one of the greatest orators of all time'

his voice; he gesticulated; oblivious of me and the empty
room, he thumped the table with his forefinger, clenched his
fist under the table, swung his arms as best he could. He
was in a visionary's world: a Savonarola, a Danton, talking
to imagined multitudes, as 'present' in that tiny room as
they would be in a crowded hall.

I heard him again that night in an immense auditorium,
crowded to the doors. This time he spoke in perfect, almost
accentless German. His manner at that distance seemed
singularly simple, unrhetorical, almost didactic; yet the
accumulated logic of the facts was compelling. 'An aristocrat and an actor,' Stalin once called him in derision. A professor and a hypnotist would describe him more truly. His
speech, like the broadcast, was a historical analysis of the
Russian revolution, nothing more. Pure theory; but it was
the theorizing of a *clairvoyeur*. I thought of the shabby
Bohemian I once saw in New York; I thought of the news-
paper-reading lounger familiar to the café waiters of Central
Europe before the war. I tried to think through the story
of the twenty intervening years. Had history ever been
made so fast before?

Less than a week later, this man — one of the three or
four who more than any others have made the history of our
time — was on his way back to his island exile, guarded as
before by the two comic men with black hats and stubbly
chins, rushed through France in another sealed train, to
spend another two years preparing that mythical Fourth
International. How, like a political werewolf, he was to be
hounded from country to country — France, Norway, Mexico — still frightening timid souls; how, in the country he
helped to build, his name — rightly or wrongly — became
the symbol for political heresy and the 'treason' that sent
thousands to their deaths — all this is too recent to need
repeating. Trotsky, at sixty, is still a young man. Has the
world drawn his sting?

XI. NEW KINGDOMS FOR OLD

I'M SURE I cannot understand it,' said George V to the Archbishop of Canterbury, as they were walking in the garden of Buckingham Palace, in the spring of 1935, 'for after all I am only a very ordinary fellow.'

They had been talking about the Royal Jubilee and the overwhelming acclamations of the populace on that resounding occasion. The Archbishop silently agreed with the King's estimate of himself, as later on he confessed — in the same speech by which he revealed this rather intimate conversation. For he told his audience that the late British Sovereign was 'not endowed with any conspicuous gifts of body or mind' and had 'no fuller education than that which was given to a sailor voyaging the sea.' And in the same strain Stanley Baldwin, His Majesty's minister and friend, spoke of George V as a modest man, 'diffident as to his own powers, often wondering what his people thought of what he had done and tried to do for them.'

Yet this 'simple and truly humble' man, whose personal horizon was bounded by the daily routine of a dutiful civil servant and the recreations of a country squire inordinately fond of shooting, whose chief hobby was collecting the postage stamps of his own country, and whose literary and musical tastes hardly went beyond Sherlock Holmes and Balfe's *Bohemian Girl*, came to fill the throne more completely than it had been filled in centuries. George V was the first British king who was obliged to call a Socialist to power, and early in his reign he had surrendered the Sovereign's most highly prized social prerogative to the designs of politicians. Never before had monarchy been so stripped of even the vestiges of power. Yet at the end of his reign an American commentator was moved to reflect: 'How much wider is the influence of a British monarch today — how much more pervading his personality — than ever before in the history of kings!' [1] King George, in truth, had given a new and wider meaning to kingship, in an age when thrones were toppling as never before, and only a bare remnant of reigning royalty was left in the world.

In explaining this paradox it is of course necessary to consider the radical changes in the social fabric that had followed the Industrial Revolution and the World War, the depreciation of aristocratic values, and the enthronement of the bourgeois ideals of which King George and Queen Mary were the most perfect protagonists. George V was the kind of person that every genuine middle-class Briton would like to be — a family man with a love for children and animals, a devotee of country life, simple in taste and suspicious of intellectual pretensions, a hater of everything foreign and sophisticated. It is because the King didn't try to be more, because he was so obviously one of themselves, that the people came to respect and admire him as they did.

GEORGE V DISCOVERS A NEW POWER

But that is not the whole story. Real affection does not thrive on hearsay and symbols alone. If King George had not been able to establish a *direct* contact with vast numbers of his subjects, they could not have grown to love him like a near relative and friend. As the first monarch in history he came to be on 'speaking terms' with virtually the whole English-speaking population of his realm and Dominions — by means of the all-pervading ether waves. It was the radio that enabled him to make his nation into 'one great family,'

[1] Raymond Gram Swing, in a transatlantic broadcast, January 1936.

with himself as the father; it was by means of the radio that he established that sense of confidence which created a real feeling of identity with the people. To the radio was largely due the *aura popularis* which no previous constitutional ruler ever enjoyed and which allowed him to practise by sheer personal influence a statecraft which his earlier predecessors exercised through power.

Perhaps even more than his predecessors King George in his earliest approaches to his subjects was hindered by the aloofness and formality which isolates all royalty from the masses. Gradually he lowered these barriers, but especially during the last decade of his life, when through quasi-direct communion with the people he came to know and love them. When, as Duke of York, he faced the cheering crowds he spoke to them as his future subjects, and of the Duchess as his 'royal consort.' When, near the end of his reign, he addressed them by radio they had become his 'very dear people' and the Queen his 'dear wife.'

King George did not, like his more talented son Edward, enjoy a long training as orator and after-dinner speaker. He was thirty-six before he became heir apparent, and nine years later he was King — 'sucked into the swirl of political controversy' within five years of the outbreak of the war.[1] During the short years of his apprenticeship he hardly did more than read out the state speeches prepared for him by sagacious but tradition-bound advisers. Even after his accession the King's few speeches, formal and prescribed, only indirectly reached more than a small number of people.

The first time the whole nation heard his voice was in 1924, when, clad in the uniform of an admiral, he opened the British Empire Exhibition at Wembley, near London. Almost a hundred thousand people were present in the flesh; but millions everywhere listened to the speech of their King, for it was the first time that radio had come to their aid. It was probably the first king's speech ever to be broadcast anywhere. It was a plain speech, with 'the Empire' for its keynote, and there was only a passing reference to the 'difficult conditions which still surround life in many parts.' The

[1] Sir George Arthur: *King George V* (London, 1929).

following year he reopened the Exhibition for a second spell, and then his voice was not heard again by the nation at large until 1927.

He himself, though he had begun to get tempting fan mail, discouraged too many repetitions of the experiment, having a shrewd idea that a monarch must be heard and seen by his people only on rare and important occasions. But the B.B.C. officials persisted, and during the next two years he was heard five times, opening new educational buildings, docks, and bridges in various parts of the country. Late in 1928 King George fell seriously ill and his life was despaired of. The astonishing demonstrations of genuine anxiety, the long vigils outside the Palace gates, and the pious gratitude which followed his recovery were a revelation to the aging monarch, and there can be little doubt that broadcasting had had a considerable share in creating that immense wave of popular sympathy.

'THIS GREAT FAMILY'

By the time he was again able to speak in public, radio had become world-wide, and the speech with which he opened the Five-Power Naval Conference in 1930 was the first to be heard throughout the world. A somewhat less formal tone could be detected in the next two addresses, and when he opened the King George V Dock in Glasgow the following year he referred to 'my dear son, the Prince of Wales' in unwonted accents of affection.

But the really personal note that was to knit his ties with the people more and more closely came into his utterances with the first Christmas Message in 1932. It had required a good deal of persuasion to get him to do anything so unconventional and unprecedented as to address his people without some particular public function to justify his 'appearance.' But he finally agreed, and the necessary installations were made in his favorite palace of Sandringham, where the royal family spent its holidays. Sitting in one of the smaller rooms of that immense country residence — a room chosen by the engineers as being the most convenient for the purpose — he allowed himself to be instructed in the intimate art of the microphone. Settling himself down at the desk — all he wanted was to be 'comfortable' in his chair — he obediently read a few lines of his talk by way of voice test, as indeed he did on every similar occasion after that. The broadcasting official who remained with him (no one else being present) explained the electric light signals that had been arranged, and when the red light came on he conscientiously started the speech, which so far as it is possible to ascertain he had written virtually alone, and which — as always — he was anxious to hide until he had delivered it.

'I take it as a good omen,' he began prophetically, 'that wireless should have reached its present perfection at a time when the Empire has been linked in closer union, for it offers us immense possibilities to make that union closer still.' He then spoke of the great purpose in hand — 'to regain prosperity without self-seeking and to carry with us those whom the burden of past years has disheartened or overborne.' None of his previous speeches had been so full of sincere solicitude, nor so intimate (the royal 'we' had been abandoned long ago). The 'very ordinary fellow' felt that at last he was talking not to bigwigs but to 'just ordinary fellows,' like himself. And he didn't mind revealing his inmost thoughts.

'I speak now from my own home and from my heart to you all; to men and women so cut off by the snows, the desert, or the sea that only voices out of the air can reach them; to those cut off from fuller life by blindness, sickness, or infirmity, and to those who are celebrating this day with their children and their grandchildren — to all, to each, I wish a happy Christmas.'

The Christmas Message, which by virtue of the newly inaugurated Empire station of the B.B.C. had been heard in all parts of the Empire, was an overwhelming success. Thousands upon thousands of messages were received from

all over the world. Yet it took even more persuasion than
before to make the King repeat it the following year. The
resourceful young men at the B.B.C. had to think up something new. So for Christmas, 1933, they 'built' the most
elaborate intercontinental program that had ever been attempted. It was called 'Absent Friends,' and it consisted
of a chain of messages which girdled the world, by means
of the various short-wave 'beam' services established between the different parts of the British Empire. London
would begin by calling Dublin; Dublin would reply, ending
with a Christmas wish, and would then call Bermuda.
Bermuda would repeat the process, with variations, and
so on through Canada, Australia, New Zealand, India,
South Africa, and back to England, where a Voice would
pass all the Empire's wishes on to the King. Who could
resist the temptation to reply to such an elaborate homage?
When King George finally spoke again from Sandringham,
to be heard by the whole Empire and indeed most of the
world, emotion was audible in his voice.

The response was such that, as a matter of course, the
Christmas Message became an annual event. So twice more
in his lifetime George V was able to speak to his peoples
direct. 'I should like to think,' he said in 1934, 'that you
who are listening to me, in whatever part of the world you
may be ... are bound to me and to one another by the spirit
of one great family.... May I add very simply and sincerely
that if I may be regarded as in some true sense the head
of this great and widespread family, sharing its life and sus-
tained by its affection, this will be a full reward for the long
and sometimes anxious labors of my reign of well-nigh five
and twenty years.' And this led up to his Jubilee Messages
a few months later, which in their genuine feeling and overflowing gratitude stand alone in the utterances of kings and
potentates.

'At the close of this memorable day I must speak to my
people everywhere,' he began his first Jubilee broadcast from
Buckingham Palace. 'Yet how can I express what is in my
heart? As I passed this morning through cheering multitudes, ... as I thought of all that these twenty-five years

have brought to me and to my country and my Empire, how could I fail to be most deeply moved? Words cannot express my thoughts and feelings. I can only say to you, *my very dear people*, that the Queen and I thank you from the depths of our hearts for all the loyalty and — may I say? — the love with which this day and always you have surrounded us.' It was at this point that his heart overflowed and the 'ordinary fellow' spoke to the Archbishop as above.

He never forgot the children, and in this Jubilee Message he said: 'To the children I should like to send a special message. Let me say this to each of them whom my words may reach: The King is speaking to *you*. I ask you to remember that in days to come you will be the citizens of a great empire. As you grow up always keep this thought before you; and when the time comes be ready and proud to give to your country the service of your work, your mind, and your heart.'

It was perhaps his longest speech; yet the last one, within a month of his death, was the most moving of all, because there was in it an unmistakable premonition of the end. He had now arrived at complete freedom of communion with the great Unseen Family of which he felt himself a part — an 'ordinary fellow' among millions of his kind. That was the new kingdom he had built for himself.

'My words will be very simple, but spoken from the heart, this family festival of Christmas,' he began. 'How could I fail to notice in all the rejoicings not merely respect for the Throne, but a warm and generous remembrance of the man himself who, may God help him, has been placed upon it?' This was indubitably his very own speech — no official scrivener would have dared to prescribe these self-revealing words. And this time, too, he thought 'not so much of the Empire itself as of the individual men, women and children who live within it,' as for the last time he sent his 'truest Christmas wishes and those of my dear wife, my children and grandchildren who are with me today.'

It had been the climax of the most magnificent and truly moving demonstration of unity of spirit that science and showmanship had ever made possible. Every nation of the Empire contributed its share — individual messages from grown-ups and children, from men in cities and in lonely places, men and women at the farthest corners of the earth projecting their thoughts to one point, to be flung out again for millions everywhere to hear. Then the National Anthem was sung by unseen choirs — invisible to each other because stationed thousands of miles apart — but all melting into one and to be heard by all. And then the quiet voice of the King, an old man mellowed by life and at peace with his God, saying words so simple and moving that every child could feel their weight. No wonder men everywhere wiped tears from their eyes and for a brief hour felt that the world after all held better things — things of which one had despaired. Be that as it may, a new kind of kingship was born — or a very old one revived — a conception of majesty fused with paternity, in a world of human beings that are very much alike.

Personally there was nothing so distinctive about King George as his simplicity and his humanness. A gray-bearded man well below average height, none too robust, with an expression that betrayed no profound preoccupations or speculations, and eyes that suggested a rather grumpy kindliness and a quiet sense of humor. He was meticulously attired, but always in the unfashionable yet rather dressy style that he had adopted long ago — the Prince Albert coat, the four-in-hand tie drawn through a signet ring, the white carnation in his buttonhole.

Thus attired he came to the World Economic Conference of 1932 to deliver the speech addressed to all the peoples of the world and heard by most of them, for short-wave voice communication by then was girdling the earth. For all his sixty-eight years he stepped briskly to the raised platform, flanked by his Prime Minister, Ramsay MacDonald and M. Avenol, the Secretary-General of the League of Nations. The representatives of sixty nations stood, while he delivered his speech from a manuscript before him in a clear, resonant, well-modulated voice. He bowed to them with a comic little bow before he began; he bowed again at the end, and walked off as briskly as he had come. It was a set ceremony, allowing for no emotional display, yet a touch of the quaint dignity of the little man was somehow touching. Here was a king, not by any quality of superiority but because he represented the average man — a man who as any man of good average attributes could and did grow into and beyond his job. A sympathetic figure, a gentle man, not merely a 'gentleman.'

He had the simple delicacies of the ordinary well-bred citizen. An official who usually supervised his broadcasts and saw to his comfort on those occasions would be allowed to sit and chat with him before and after — to pass the time of day and talk about the current events. On one of those occasions the King proffered what looked like a cigarette case, but didn't open it. The official didn't know what to do — smoking wasn't the 'done thing' at these times. The King proffered it again, and when again nothing happened, a third time, probably enjoying an inward laugh. Finally he explained the mystery: 'I want to give you my personal Order, because you've always looked after me so well.' It was the Victorian Order — a much-coveted distinction, given as you would give a boutonnière out of your garden to a friend.

That, so far as I know, was his only 'personal' recognition — except for the more or less official knighthoods — of the great new force that had given royalty a new function and possibly a fresh lease of life.

The new kingdom that George V had created for himself — to use a trite but nevertheless fitting phrase — in the people's hearts, had every prospect of being held by his successor, the first royal broadcaster in the world. But Fate decreed otherwise: the most potent medium of communication between a ruler and his subjects was to be all but barred from the next in line, namely George VI. An early malady had impaired the new monarch's speech, and much of his life had been spent in overcoming a difficulty which imposed a degree of reticence unusual even for an Englishman. Yet George VI as prince had with great fortitude fulfilled his formal duties, and his voice had been broadcast a number of times in connection with public functions of one kind or another.

What he did on the evening of his coronation, however —
but a short time after his brother's amazing Farewell — was
nothing short of heroism. Sitting at a microphone in Buckingham Palace, fatigued by the ceremonial ordeals of the day,
he addressed the waiting millions in England and overseas,
many of whom must have listened with trepidation in their
hearts, for ten minutes or so, carefully pronouncing each word
and overcoming each obstacle by sheer mental effort, with
the psychological aids by which he had learned to conquer
emotional stress. Millions heaved a grateful sigh of relief
when it was over; and it is not likely that this astonishing
performance will be repeated except on exceptional occasions.
The Christmas message of 1938, though brief, was a flawless
performance.

The personalities of George and his consort are being projected to his peoples by every possible means of publicity,
and by subtle comparison with his father, whom he resem-
bles in many ways. Will he, a virtually silent king, be able
to retain what his father created by means of a voice?

THREE KINGS PLEAD FOR SANITY

Curious as it may seem, no other European monarchs
have made any extensive use of the radio, and certainly not
with a conscious purpose of cultivating a new relationship
with their peoples. There are eleven kingdoms left in Europe in place of the pre-war seventeen (not counting the
petty states of the old federal Germany). There is also
Hungary, a titular kingdom but not likely soon to have a
king, and the Grand Duchy of Luxemburg. All of the remaining rulers are constitutional monarchs, although a kind of
semi-absolutism, or quasi-royal dictatorship, has raised its
head in the Balkan countries. The only real dictator-king,
Alexander of Yugoslavia, fell victim to political assassination, leaving a regency in his place. It is a mere coincidence,
perhaps, that broadcasting is all but non-existent in the

Balkans, except for Rumania. Neither King Carol nor King Boris, so far as I know, has yet been lured to the radio.

Nor has the King of Italy ever been heard by his subjects, except for the one time (1934) that the conventional reading of the speech from the throne was broadcast from the Chamber of Deputies, although Mussolini has allowed the Crown Prince to help raise enthusiasm for the Abyssinian adventure. There is an old joke about poor King Victor Emmanuel's saying that his handkerchief is the only thing he is allowed to put his nose into, and there seems to be no exception in favor of the microphone.

That narrows our inquiry down to the 'democratic' monarchies of the North and West. If none of the three Scandinavian kings has made much use of the radio, it is probably because there is not much need for it. These three are the most democratic countries in Europe, accepting the monarchial form as a symbol and safeguard of their independence — as a part of the mechanics of government: the King being little more than a royal hat-peg for outgoing and incoming prime ministers. Their thrones are safe, not despite but *because* of their lack of power; too much self-assertion on their part would only be likely to raise distrust. As it is, an unobtrusive monarch on the throne is worth more than the loudest dictator beside it. In Scandinavia the Crown would almost certainly become the rallying-cry of the democrats against any threat of a Fascist surge.

A concession to nationalism, the King is on a par with the national flag, and just as the flags of the Scandinavian countries have the same design, varying only in color, so their Kings are made of very much the same stuff (two of them are brothers), and vary only in name. When they do speak to the people, it is not so much to identify themselves with their subjects as to identify the three countries with one another, in the peaceful policy which has kept them out of the European turmoil and their kings on the throne.

This was the underlying motive of one of the most remarkable transmissions that have taken place since the beginning of radio, namely the joint broadcast of the three Scandinavian Kings and the President of Finland, to assert the com-

mon interests and proclaim the unified policy of all the
countries of Scandinavia. The broadcast was simultaneously
radiated throughout the four countries, was listened to in
many parts of Europe, and was rebroadcast in the United
States by the two largest networks. Coming when it did, in
October, 1936, this combined Nordic declaration was a
counterblast to the aggressively nationalistic and autarch-
ical policies of other European countries, as well as an
answer to the pretensions of pseudo-Nordics further south.

Sitting in his sprawling palace overlooking the harbor of
Stockholm, lanky, seventy-eight-year-old Gustaf V, in whose
veins the blood of Napoleon's General Bernadotte is mixed
with that of the redoubtable Vasas of medieval Swedish
history, affirmed that the solidarity of the North is a vital
condition for its future happiness. 'In their common ancestry and language and their similar outlook on life and
culture, the Nordic peoples belong together.'

In any other country of Europe such language used by
the head of the State would signify an aggressive boast, and
a militant warning of irredentist claims to come. In these
happier northern lands it meant just the opposite; it meant
a prospect for peaceful economic union and political collaboration. 'Our governments deliberate the same questions,'
announced King Gustaf, 'and solve legislative problems together; social and industrial groups with practical or idealistic aims co-operate with corresponding groups of the sister
nations' — the very essence of that internationalism so
detested and feared by governments claiming a divine mission to order the welfare of their peoples! Echoing these
sentiments, King Christian X, sixty-six years old and every
inch a soldier, called for even stronger co-operation in the
future. His slightly younger brother, Haakon V of Norway,
expressed the wish that the hitherto largely cultural collaboration of the Scandinavian peoples be now extended to the
economic field.

Significant, too, was the inclusion of the Finnish republic
in this manifestation. Its President, Professor Svinhufvud,
in accordance with his age, spoke in second place, a recognition of the equality of status between kings and presidents.

He spoke of the Scandinavian co-operation 'in defense of the common peace and neutrality of the North ... which is of double importance in these turbulent times' — words of prophecy and warning to Europe as a whole. The foundations of Scandinavian neutrality were laid under the shadow of the World War at the famous Malmö Conference of the three Kings in 1914; now Finland, having gained her independence, has joined the pact, and it was a sign of the times that the second northern 'conference' took place not in Malmö but in the air — a reaffirmation of common interest in the hearing of the entire world.

For the sake of completeness let me mention that the first time — in 1933 — that King Christian of Denmark (and Iceland) was heard by radio he spoke to the United States. Invited to address Dano-Americans, he spoke from his Castle of Amalienborg, in a program of Danish music and poetry arranged by Statsradiofonien at my request.

KING ALBERT'S LITTLE JOKE

The late King of the Belgians, Albert I, perhaps the most familiarly democratic of modern monarchs, made no conscious effort to capture public sympathies by way of the new medium, which indeed had its very first tryout in his little country before the War. Albert was, it is true, in no need of popularity after the experiences of that war; a more sympathetic figure could hardly be found among the hereditary rulers of the war-torn Continent. Albert was, moreover, intimately known to masses of the common people, whose ordinary pleasures he shared. No lover of pomp, ceremony, and ostentation, he could be seen chugging along roads of his country on a motorcycle, unattended, or clambering up the modest mountain sides of his favorite Ardennes. It was on one of these lonely climbs that he lost his life in February, 1934. Any ambition to claim for himself more than the ordinary man's stint of comradeship or popular affection was foreign to his shy and hesitant nature. If his advisers refrained from urging him, it was probably because they realized that after the War, when Flemish nationalism had become very sensitive, any speech that was not made — or repeated — in Flemish would only detract from the pleasant fiction that Albert was a representative national Belgian monarch. (Albert's son has the advantage of his father in this respect, for he speaks French and Flemish equally well.)

It therefore required an outside initiative to bring about a broadcast by King Albert. Both the leading American companies laid siege to the Belgian authorities, with the benevolent acquiescence of the American Embassy, my own efforts having begun in the summer of 1930. It took two years for the project to mature. At last the Belgian Broadcasting Institute prevailed upon the King to speak for five minutes in a special program for America on the Belgian Independence Day (Fête Nationale, July 21), consisting of music by Belgian composers, both Flemish and Walloon, and songs in both national languages. The King's language problem was solved by the fact that he spoke excellent English. In simple words he talked about his little country and its gratitude to the American people who fed its population during the War. It was this genuine feeling which at last persuaded gallant Albert to speak to a foreign audience.

On the evening of the National Festival, microphone and the usual gear had been installed at the summer palace of Laeken, and the Director-General of Belgian broadcasting, as well as a very distinguished radio engineer were in attendance. It was all very simple; the King, in ordinary attire, came in and had everything explained to him, while the company stood rather stiffly about. He asked how loud and how fast he should speak, so the engineer picked up the manuscript and began to read the English text in an almost unintelligible French pronunciation to demonstrate the volume of sound. The King listened attentively. When the engineer finished he turned to him with a very faint twinkle in his eye. '*Ah, comme ça,*' he said, '*et avec le même accent?*' (So that's the way! And must I speak with that accent, too?')

Everybody laughed, and all stiffness had gone. The King, however, was so nervous that his paper shook like the proverbial aspen leaf, and he was obviously relieved when it was over. It is not likely that it had given the King a taste for broadcasting; at any rate, he was never heard again. Sixteen months later, when microphones were once again installed at Laeken, it was for Albert's funeral.

King Albert's successor, Leopold III, a gifted and purposeful young man, has only been heard once — when he took his oath as sovereign in Parliament, and made an excellent speech in French and Flemish, without the suggestion of a foreign accent. I had the fun of translating that speech as he was delivering it, phrase by phrase, for the benefit of American listeners, but unknown to the King, for I was sitting in a London studio, listening on earphones to the incoming telephone circuit from Brussels and speaking into a microphone connected to the transatlantic radio circuit carrying his voice to New York. In other words, the translation was being filtered into the speech, using the natural intervals between phrases that every deliberate speaker makes. (This, by the way, was one of the rare occasions when both rival networks carried my voice, despite competition, simply because there was nothing else to do.)

Tragedy was to overtake the headstrong young monarch when a year and a half later his car overturned and his beautiful Swedish consort, Astrid, was killed. He has the reputation of being rather autocratic in his manner, and the world has already had an indication of his active interest in international politics.

WILHELMINA SPEAKS; JULIANA MAKES RADIO HISTORY

His near neighbor, the portly Queen Wilhelmina of the Netherlands, discovered the radio as a means of reaching her distant subjects in the East Indies a few years ago (1931), when she sent them Christmas greetings via the short-wave

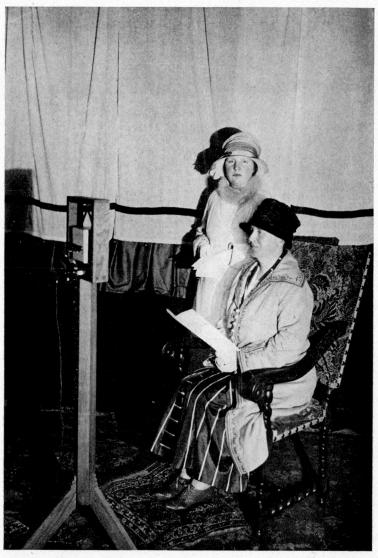

Queen Wilhelmina of the Netherlands discovered the radio as
a means of reaching her distant East Indian subjects
Princess Juliana accompanied her mother

station in Huizen. Dutchmen at home did not all relish her speech to the same extent, for poverty was widespread at the time and the Queen was a strong supporter of the de-flationist policies of her Prime Minister, Doctor Colijn, a very orthodox economist.[1] She was, however, heard again on subsequent Christmases and on several occasions of personal import to the royal family. In 1934 the twice bereaved Queen thanked the Dutch people for their sympathy on the death of the Queen Mother and the Prince Consort; two years later she announced the betrothal of Princess Juliana, and she was again heard, throughout the world, in the summer of 1937, when she addressed the Boy Scouts at their Jamboree in Amsterdam — in excellent English as well as Dutch.

Her daughter, Juliana, has since her betrothal and marriage to Prince Bernard repeatedly addressed her future subjects by radio; she even made history by choosing this unconventional manner of taking them into her confidence on a very personal matter, namely, the prospect of giving birth to an heir.

'I should have been happy to attend all the festivities,' she said to the citizens of Amsterdam who had given her and the Prince a cordial official welcome after their return from abroad; 'but for joyful reasons of health — which you will all understand and approve — I am prevented from doing so.' And she was followed by the proud prospective father, who also spoke his thanks for the great welcome. This undoubtedly was the first time that any person, royal or otherwise, has used broadcasting for the announcement of a 'happy event,' and it points to the fact that in Holland, at any rate, the efficacy of the radio in building up popularity for the ruling family is well understood.

[1] Queen Wilhelmina's speeches from the throne, at the traditional opening of Parliament, by the way, have been broadcast annually since 1932, and have on occasion been rebroadcast in America.

XII. ROYAL BROADCASTER NUMBER ONE

THE 'PRINCE'S OWN' STUDIO

IN ONE of the small talks studios on the third floor of
London's handsome Broadcasting House, a bronze portrait plaque of Edward VIII adorned an otherwise empty
wall, ever since, as Prince of Wales, he began coming to these
studios to speak in aid of good causes.

It was from here that Edward's voice went forth to the
largest English-speaking audience which had ever listened to
a royal heir. It was here — and in an even smaller studio at
the earlier B.B.C. in Savoy Hill — rather than in the great
halls and the ornate public banqueting rooms, that he mastered the peculiarly friendly manner with which he beguiled
the millions. It was here that he stirred up sympathy for
Britain's unemployed, appealed for playing fields for the
children, exhorted the country to care for its poor and distressed. And it was here that he was to introduce himself
to the Kingdom as its King and to the Empire as its Emperor.

The decorations of these rooms proclaim the strenuous
simplicity of the modernist — plain fawn walls of sound-
absorbing celotex, a false window with cream and brown
curtains of severe design, soft woollen carpets to harmonize,
a table and chair for the speaker, two other easy chairs,
modern diffused lighting, the usual electric clock, thermostat,
and signal lights over the sound-proof door. A strictly
'functional' interior, after the radio engineer's heart. Edward liked coming to it quietly and simply — 'no top-hats,
no fuss,' as he said — for he preferred the businesslike broad-

casting machine to the sumptuous Victorian interiors of the royal palaces, where his father had sat when addressing the nation in lonely state.

But his radio experience did not begin at Broadcasting House. It started with the very inception of broadcasting in England, before there was any B.B.C. Edward VIII was, in fact, the first royal broadcaster in the world. And the story of his broadcasts is interesting because it reflects with remarkable fidelity his extraordinary and, in the end, soul-stirring career.

THE FIRST ROYAL BROADCAST IN HISTORY

He was still in his late twenties when broadcasting began. In 1922 he had only recently returned from his eventful journey to India when, as Chief Scout for Wales, he addressed nearly sixty thousand youngsters — Boy Scouts and 'Wolf Cubs' — by radio from St. James's Palace. The idea was proposed to him by Lord Baden-Powell. Interested, as always, in new and adventurous things, he accepted with alacrity. It was a highly experimental and very informal affair.

The Marconi Company had erected the first London station, 2LO, whose aerial was swung along the Strand, from Marconi House to Bush House, where it aroused the curiosity of passing crowds. Elaborate tests were necessary the day before, and the Prince was exceedingly painstaking — under the supervision of the engineers — in adjusting his voice to the primitive and rather insensitive carbon granule microphone. He entered into the adventure with zest, and his brothers, later the Dukes of Gloucester and Kent, who came to the Prince's study in York House, were fascinated spectators. Everybody present felt that this was an historic occasion, as indeed it was.[1]

[1] I am indebted for these details to Mr. A. E. Burrows, now secretary-general of the International Broadcasting Union, who announced the Prince, and whose book *The Story of Broadcasting*, (London, 1934) is dedicated to 'the first royal broadcaster.'

The Prince did not make another studio broadcast for three years. But many of his public speeches at dinners and official solemnities were broadcast after 1924, and something was happening to him that had not happened to any Prince of Wales before: he was becoming genuinely popular — not so much in high society as with the common people over whom he was destined one day to rule. He was, in fact, one of the first public men to discover the power of the new medium; he became one of the first to master its technique. In any future history of broadcasting, the engaging figure of Edward VIII must appear as that of an amateur who handled the instrument with the skill of the professional. He applied to it the free and easy manner of the after-dinner speech, eschewed all oratory and high rhetoric, and as time went on acquired the intimate and improvisational manner which distinguishes the microphone speaker from the ordinary speech-maker. Allowing for the difference in temperament and nationality, his radio style became effective in much the same way as that of Franklin D. Roosevelt.

His diction differed decidedly from that of the average cultured Englishman and reflected the influence of all sorts and conditions of people with whom he mixed — as a cadet, as a midshipman afloat, and in the War. Oxford left no impression on his speech; it was too transitory an experience. But during the War he talked, day in day out, with common soldiers — British, Canadians, New Zealanders, cockneys, yokels, all sorts — for here he shed his shyness and became an easy conversationalist. And so his speech became not so much the 'King's' English as the English of the common-wealth citizen.

If Edward was quick to grasp the power of the radio, those in charge of his career as national spokesman were not far behind. The politicians who had been glad to exploit his ability as 'good-will ambassador' and 'empire salesman' now found a new method of widening the radius of his influence — and they made the most of it. His speeches got more and more publicity: after 1930 they were often heard in America; soon after, in the whole empire as well. Up to 1933 he made an average of eight broadcasts a year. Then sud-

denly the number dropped to two in 1934 and one in 1935 —
for reasons which were then known only to his intimates.
Many of these speeches were made, of course, on formal occasions to which the appearance of royalty lends dignity; there
were bridges to be opened, new public buildings to be dedicated, ships to be launched. These occasions fall to every
public man's lot; as often as not the speeches are prepared by
others. They would hardly be worth mentioning were it not
for the fact that in the Prince's case one could even here
detect a personal touch — a happy informal phrase that
betrayed his humanness — and a capacity to turn any
occasion to good account.

WAR, EMPIRE, REMEMBRANCE

It is at any rate remarkable how few of his speeches were
merely perfunctory. Like many other things in his career,
they indicated a certain insistence to decide things for himself, a 'wilfulness' which those in authority were to find so
inconvenient later on. A post-facto examination of his
utterances certainly reveal purpose and character, as well as
a real ability for felicitous expression. Equally illuminating,
perhaps, would be a list of the speeches he refused to make.
Through all those post-war years when Allied statesmen and
generals were unveiling monument after monument and
spouting eloquently of victory, this young scion of the House
of Windsor was going about the world speaking of the War
not in terms of glory but of reconciliation, compassion and
hope. The War, in fact, became less and less important, and
its memories receded before the impact of a new emotional
urge — sympathy with the victims, and pity for the poor and
distressed.

However cynically sophisticated people might regard
public demonstrations of charity by royalty, there was, until
recently, no doubt in the common man's mind that the
Prince of Wales's preoccupation with the underdog was

genuine, and his efforts to alleviate suffering sincere. It was different from the usual salving of the rich man's conscience because it had its roots in real experience. The Prince was a mere youth when he went, like thousands of other youngsters, to satisfy his craving for adventure on the battle-fields of France. He was twenty, but both in looks and in character he was nearer eighteen. His eagerness to be 'in it' was probably that of any average youngster, and he gave those who were responsible for his safety some sleepless nights.

On one of his private excursions during the battle of Loos he motored into a village near the front, left his car to go up to the lines for a few minutes, and came back to find both car and chauffeur blown to bits. The chauffeur was almost a pal; he had been his servant at college in Oxford. The Prince picked up the remnants of the man's belongings, carried them back to headquarters tied in a handkerchief, kept them, and on his next trip home restored them personally to the chauffeur's family.

In the same year — 1916 — and probably with this tragic incident in mind, he started a fund for the relief of the families of those killed in action. By reason of his title he had already acted as chairman of the first committee under the War Pensions Act; and from the beginning had come to realize that State aid would not suffice. 'Our special duties will be,' he said to the committee, 'to initiate schemes for training and of finding active employment, and thus enable the men to feel that they are still active members of the community.'

When he returned home at the end of the War, and the mad whirl of his first empire tour was over, he had plenty of opportunity to see what was happening to the men who fought for the 'war to end war' and had come back to a country 'fit for heroes to live in.' He had become patron of the British Legion and he had heard the stories of the men. In a broadcast appeal for the British Legion Fund (there are no soldiers' 'bonuses' in Great Britain) he said:

'It is not only of those who laid down their lives that we must think; we must never forget, at any time, both their dependents and those others who, without losing life, lost health and strength in the great struggle. There can surely be no more sincere act of remembrance of the dead than an act of service to those of their comrades who are today in need. . . .'

The word 'remembrance' had a special significance. At Christmas time during the second year of the War, two English clergymen founded a soldiers' club behind the lines at Poperinghe, in Flanders. One of the two was the Reverend Neville Talbot, whom the Prince had known at Oxford, and the name of the club became 'Toc H,' the Morse version of Talbot's initials. The Prince's division came into the Poperinghe sector in 1916, and ever since then he has been identified with the movement which from a private work of two kindly men, without funds, has largely through the Prince's efforts become nation-wide, with clubs throughout the country and in many parts of the Empire.

The movement is based on the idea of fellowship, and its symbol is the lighted lamp. It caught the imagination of England's young men. Every Armistice Day there are Toc H 'festivals of remembrance' all over the country. In London, where thousands gather in Albert Hall, the leader of every new branch gets his lamp lighted from a central light — which year after year was held by the Prince of Wales. The Festival of Remembrance was first broadcast from the Albert Hall in 1927, and the Prince made a speech that changed the meaning and tenor of Armistice Day celebrations throughout the Empire.

'This Armistice Day,' he said, 'was once a day of rejoicing. It is now a day of remembrance. The full sum of that remembrance not I nor anyone can express in words. . . . In the actual day of battle, every man who fought by our side was our comrade and our friend. For nine difficult years we have endured the inevitable consequences of war, and whether he who fought by our side has fared better or worse than ourselves, or whatever his luck may be, he is no less our comrade and friend today.'

The Festival of Remembrance broadcast has become one of the great occasions for reverent listening throughout England and the Empire. The Prince, when he has not spoken words of his own, has recited Laurence Binyon's verses, 'To the

Fallen,' with deeply moving effect. They begin like this:

> 'They shall not grow old, as we that are left grow old,
> Age shall not weary them, nor the years condemn,
> At the going down of the sun and in the morning,
> We will remember them.'

On November 11, 1936, he read them for the last time in that great assembly, but this time they were not broadcast. In 1937 he was no longer there.

But his presence at these gatherings, year after year, had created a faith — semi-religious, semi-chivalrous — among the war veterans and the millions whom the War had robbed of all that was nearest and dearest to them — a faith that will not die while this generation lives. These people, whatever else they may think about Edward, have no doubt that what he said he meant.

DISCOVERING MISERY

Outside that charmed circle there has been a rising tide of skepticism and resentment. More and more frequently the question has been asked whether the great human note in the Prince's career was not just part of a policy adjusted to the needs of the time, was in any case induced by outside suggestions of a more or less specious kind. The question has, I think, been most convincingly answered by a dramatic incident related to in Hector Bolitho's recent biography, *Edward VIII*. It took place, not many years after the War, in the poor section of a northern English industrial town, where the Prince came face to face with stark misery and destitution, such as he had never seen before.

After a day of depressing experiences he was taken to a soup kitchen, and there, at close quarters, he saw how hundreds of hungry men were fed. He watched silently, spellbound by what he saw. Then, pointing to a young man standing in line he said to his companion, in a shocked whisper, 'That man

has no shirt under his coat!' Later that night, returned to
his quarters, he was seen alone, walking up and down in great
agitation, pressing his hands together and saying, 'What can
I do? What can be done?'

That, in his biographer's words, was the real awakening of
the Prince's social conscience, although the suffering he had
seen in Flanders and in the hospitals and homes for crippled
veterans had already mobilized his sense of compassion. Now
he discovered that 'sympathy is not enough'; so instead of
merely acting as the patron of a great charity, the Lord
Mayor's Fund for distressed miners, he also insisted on going
to the mining areas 'to see for himself.' He mixed with the
people, talked to the men, asked questions, and tried to find
answers to their problems with the help of expert advisers.
More than that, he saw how the families lived, on the edge of
starvation, spoke to the children, comforted the wives. On
one occasion he asked a man about his wife and heard that
she was in the throes of death in the tiny bedroom upstairs.
'If you would hold her hand for a minute, sir, I think she
would never forget it,' said the man. Edward went up and
held the emaciated hand — till a contented, almost happy
look came into the sick woman's eyes. There were many
incidents like that.

All this was in 1928 — eight years before that fateful trip
to South Wales which was to be his last. Henceforth a new
direction was given to his broadcasting career.

Only twice before had he gone to the old B.B.C. studios to
make his charitable appeals; this time, with a cause he had
made peculiarly his own, he went to Savoy Hill on Christmas
night, to speak as he had never spoken before. The British
miners' leader at that time was Arthur Cook, a tough fighter
whose name was anathema to the upper classes and who had
led the bitterest strike in British history two years before.
'Never have I been so impressed,' said this doughty revolutionary years afterwards, addressing the Prince at a public
gathering. 'I was with two Communist friends, and when
your name was announced... they undoubtedly scoffed.
But they listened to what you had to say, and when you
finished, with tears in their eyes, they put their hands in their
pockets and gave what they had on them to the fund.'

UNEMPLOYMENT AND SOCIAL SERVICE

The miners of Wales and Durham are Britain's permanent post-war calamity; but soon their tragedy was to spread its shadow over the whole land. Depression, starting in America in 1929, reached England in full force the following year: unemployment rose to three millions, and a quarter of the working population was idle for years. Under the stress of this crisis, social service among the unemployed became Edward's chief concern. To alleviate distress — not only by raising funds, but by organizing a Voluntary Service movement which would save the out-of-work's self-respect and keep him from becoming a human derelict, he gave unsparingly of his time and energy, becoming more than ever the acknowledged champion of the underdog. No royal heir in British history had ever done anything like it before.

Broadcasting came to his aid. The B.B.C., to help the movement, put on a series of talks entitled 'S. O. S.' by a nationally popular broadcaster, S. P. B. Mais, and the Prince went to 'his' studio in Broadcasting House to launch the series with an eloquent appeal. There were, of course, many difficulties. In the midst of the Depression — in January, 1932 — he made a now historic appeal for a reform of the movement by 'splitting it up into small parts,' so that it could relieve enforced idleness in villages and poor neighborhoods by co-operative action. This remarkable speech, made before a huge audience in Albert Hall and broadcast to the nation, contained passages that are akin in spirit to those uttered by another famous broadcaster raising his voice a year or so later on behalf of the Forgotten Man in the United States.

'There is,' he said, 'a certain doubt whether the social progress of recent years has not, perhaps, been rather superficial — a feeling that, just as many a fine-looking house may conceal a load of hire-purchase debt, so the better material conditions that have been won may not represent a very solid gain.... There is an enormous call at the present time for *personal* service. . . . The tasks are there, and every one of us can play a part, for the race is not necessarily to the swift nor the battle to the strong!'

That speech had the force of religious revivalism in it, and the result was a nation-wide activity which went far toward lifting the 'other half' out of the slough of despond into which it had been thrust. The Prince himself travelled up and down the country, giving the lead to workers in many localities, mixing with the people as one of them and spreading good cheer. At the end of two years he was able to 'report' to the country in another speech — one of the last important utterances of his that were heard in America as well as in England. Two thousand occupational centres had been organized, over a quarter million pounds had been subscribed, $150,000 by the unemployed themselves in pennies and tuppences; clubs and camps had been set up and a new fabric of social life had taken root, bringing sunshine into the lowliest circles of the land. That new fabric is the Duke of Windsor's living monument in the land he was born to rule.

The fellowship idea ran like a *leit-motif* through all his activities. He was the Prince of good mixers, and that saved his social work from the by-taste of condescension. He had seen these men in the trenches in France; he saw them now with their families crowded into wretched hovels and tenements that passed for homes. Like no other social worker of his time, he could compare the utmost luxury with the utmost squalor, and while with the gilded youth of his generation he partook of the giddiest social whirl, he didn't shrink from the squalor when he saw it. 'We stand and talk,' said George Lansbury, a Socialist leader who all his life has lived in London's East End; '*he* goes into the houses.'

Housing became a particular fetish with him. With the impatience of youth he wanted to sweep away the slums, and inevitably found many obstacles in his way. But, as with other things, he sought expert knowledge (a sort of brain trust had grown up about the Prince's staff) and then he brought his revivalist's methods to bear on the problem. He harangued the architects to devote themselves to the problem of mass production in housing; to build for the many instead of the 'favored few.' He promoted the fund to build homes near the big towns for ex-soldiers in memory of Marshal Haig. When he opened the first London group of one hundred and twenty-three houses, his words once again were broadcast and new support enlisted.

The practical results of his broadcast appeals for these movements was, of course, immeasurable; the returns to charity, in cold cash alone, must have been tremendous. Nor could the Government of the ruling classes quarrel with him, for his activities raised the morale of the unemployed, and eased the constant pressure for more doles; it gave new hope to the sorely tried working classes and the disillusioned ex-service man. On the other hand, the cause of the disinherited part of the nation became almost an obsession with the Prince, and must have been unwelcome to the 'hard-boiled' industrialist by focussing too much attention on bad working conditions, wretched housing and the like.

He visited area after area in the most depressed sections of the country — in Durham, in Scotland, in Wales — and his words after a thorough investigation of actual conditions contrasted sometimes inconveniently with the complacent remarks of parliamentarians. Before each visit he would prepare himself by study and consult people with special knowledge of the subject. He would address proud mayors and self-satisfied citizens and tell them always to look forward to the 'great occasion when the whole country is clear of slums.' He would have awkward impulses to vary official programs by insisting on seeing the seamy side. When his speech opening the new Severn Bridge was broadcast in 1932 he calmly announced that there was one place he would visit that was not on the program — the centre for the unemployed. When he was taken to see the great ship *Queen Mary* just before she left her Tyneside berth, he told his top-hatted reception committee that he also wanted to see the Glasgow slums — said to be some of the worst in the world. And when he had seen them he asked how a civilization that could produce this great ship could tolerate such squalor.

'LECTURING' BIG BUSINESS

Another phase of what Basil Maine [1] calls the Prince's 'crusade' was his drive for more modern methods in industry and commerce, which got world-wide publicity and applause, and earned him the epithet the 'Empire's chief salesman.' Indeed, the commercial Pooh-Bahs had every reason to be delighted with some of the results of his crusade. When he launched the 'Buy British' campaign, or when, during his trip to South America, the city of Buenos Aires signed a British contract for the materials of a $50,000,000 underground railroad, they applauded, and took a little advice into the bargain. When in the hearing of the entire country he told the cream of the British business world at the British Industries Fair dinner in London that they must learn to 'adopt, adapt, and improve,' a great chorus of bravos went up in the press, while the Prince was being quoted and toasted in the clubs. They even put up with his flattering references to the methods of American business!

But when he took his job too seriously and told the assembled sales managers of Great Britain that 'all is not well with our salesmanship,' they applauded with less enthusiasm, and some members of the older generation certainly felt the sting when he asked: 'Has Britain taken any steps to make good the promise of the men who would today be organizing business but for the fact that they are lying beneath the sod of many countries?'

Whooping up business was all very well, but this was a different note, which didn't fit into the go-getter's tune. For the thought of the 'comrades' the Prince met in France, the chaps who first made him come out of his shell, was never very far from his mind. The big manufacturers and managing directors were being lectured not merely for their own good ...

When the whole story of Edward's estrangement from his countrymen comes to be written, this feature of his develop-

[1] Basil Maine, *Our Ambassador King*, London, 1936. ,

ment must not be overlooked. At any rate, it is a fact that
after 1931 he dropped the rôle of business counselor, and,
except for his favorite charities, confined himself to that of
good-will ambassador. His 'Americanism,' moreover, was
finding an outlet in a more private and social sphere. . . .

Most of the Prince's broadcast speeches, beginning with a
relay of a Clydebank launching in 1930, have been rebroadcast in the United States. No foreign broadcaster, public or
private, professional or amateur, had the ear of the American
public as consistently as this perennially youthful and
attractive 'star.' His famous curtain lecture to the sales
managers; his gingering-up talk to the British manufacturers;
his opening of the Shakespeare Memorial Theatre, with its
graceful acknowledgment of American generosity; his unveiling of the Somme Memorial in France; his S.O.S. talk on
unemployment; and finally his appeal for 'voluntary service'
in January, 1934, were a few of those that were heard by even
more American than British listeners.

Then, suddenly, something happened. After that last
'voluntary service' talk came a strange silence; he was not
heard again, except for one routine appeal, until 1936, after
his father's death, when once again he went to Broadcasting
House — this time to introduce himself to his peoples as King
and Emperor. Except for one other brief obligatory talk, this
was his one and only microphone appearance in over two
years. What had happened in these two years to his public-
spirited activities? What had become of his ardent preoccupation with social service, with the unemployed? Distress in Durham and Wales was still severe; had Edward's
sympathy waned?

If it had, the doubters and the skeptics had perhaps been
right after all; for nothing but a mental aberration — or a
cataclysmic emotional experience — could blot out the
memory of two decades of genuinely vital activity. But we
now know that a matter of great personal urgency had
supervened. We know, too, that things happen to people
which change the whole course and purpose of their lives —
things which shatter the very mainsprings of human volition,
and turn perfectly rational men and women into psycho-

March, 1936, when for the first time a reigning British king
came to Broadcasting House to speak

'Although I now speak to you as the King, I am still the same man...'

physiological phenomena of the strangest kind. And that is the kind of thing that had happened to Edward. He had fallen victim to a passion that blotted every other interest out of his life.

Nothing but such an experience could explain the change that had come over Britain's favorite son. Report had it that during his father's last illness he had got completely out of hand, that is, unapproachable by those who had the most valid claims of friendship and loyalty. King George's death brought to a head a crisis of which only the vaguest reports gave an inkling to the outer world. It was nearly two months before Edward VIII could be persuaded to declare himself, in the hearing of all the world, as a sovereign who intended to reign.

KING EDWARD CALLS THE EMPIRE

It was a pleasant though chilly Sunday afternoon in March, 1936, when for the first time a reigning British king came to Broadcasting House to speak. He arrived in an ordinary motor car — unguarded. With his usual brisk step and the same nervous, jerky gestures as always, he walked into the little studio which had become recognized as his own. The speech he made — heard by many millions throughout the world — was short and singularly detached. The only significant thing in it was his assurance that 'although I now speak to you as the King, I am still the same man...' It might have given some people pause. Many others, moreover, detected a new and strange note in his voice. The use of the phrase 'over the radio' was definitely an Americanism, almost unknown in the British Isles; and the short 'American' *a* in the word 'broadcast' gave the English purists a shock.

Outside, on the street, a few hundred people had collected to see him off. A handful of policemen good-naturedly pushed them back to make a lane for the royal car. The

King bowed, doffed his hat to acknowledge the cheers. No one could have guessed that it was for the last time. The following July he went to France to unveil the Canadian monument at Vimy Ridge; a few days later he was on his way to that blissful Adriatic cruise with the woman he loved.

In the autumn, after his return to England, he suddenly bethought himself of his one-time charges, the Welsh miners, forgotten these two years or more. Someone had jogged his memory, perhaps. But his old advisers — official and private — had not had his ear for months, it was complained, though matters of state were crowding in upon him with ever increasing urgency. Who, then, persuaded him to make that sudden, unprecedented, and — according to some — 'unconstitutional' dash to South Wales, to promise his undernourished friends that 'something will be done'? In other circumstances such a trip, by the reigning monarch, might have caused Britain's toiling millions to rise to him like one man. Was that the purpose behind the trip? If it had 'worked,' a great national appeal, a new clarion call by radio, was the next indicated move.

But it was not to be. The effort, mildly applauded by the Opposition press, raised a vaguely discordant chorus of comment. The workers, for some reason, were not impressed. The radio remained silent, while Edward waited at Fort Belvedere and Mrs. Simpson in her mansion at Regent's Park. The 'clarion call' would have fallen on empty air. The royal broadcaster remained silent.

* * * * * * * * * * *

The portrait plaque which adorned the little broadcasting studio is gone.

PART TWO

Events

XIII. RADIO GETS THE NEWS

ENTERTAINMENT VERSUS NEWS

INFORMATION, instruction, and entertainment are acknowledged to be the principal functions of radio; but the greatest of these, by common consent, is entertainment. This at once sums up radio's similarity to journalism, and a vital difference between the two.

The newspaper, through centuries of evolution and development, has achieved a certain balance between these three main departments, but there is no doubt that here information takes precedence over the other two. No merely instructive article or entertainment feature would in ordinary circumstances replace information; that is, news. In broadcasting, however, none but the most urgent or important news would even displace temporarily a program designed to entertain. This distinction determines the present place of broadcasting in the social scheme. It limits its function as a carrier of news, the more so since its basis of measurement is Time, while that of the newspaper is Space. The newspaper can expand in size, according to necessity; radio is forever bound by the twenty-four hours of the clock. It cannot, like the newspaper, add time to its schedule; it must defer news until, in some cases, it is — no longer news.

Radio is by far the faster medium, and it has much the greater scope; yet it surrenders to the newspaper its right of priority in news distribution, except in sensational cases — when the demand so outruns supply that competition is suspended for the time.

In the field of foreign news the handicap imposed on radio

is even greater, partly by reason of the censorship to which most of the world supinely submits, partly because of mechanical limitations, and the lack of adequate facilities at the present stage of development. Hence international broadcasting hitherto has mostly been content to supplement, rather than originate, the news. Actual news-beats by radio are rare and therefore thrilling occurrences, of which broadcasters are inordinately proud.

An early instance of such a beat was the transatlantic radio talk by J. Ramsay MacDonald, then British Prime Minister, from Chequers, the week-end retreat of British premiers, in March, 1930, in which he finally killed France's hopes of collective security based on military guarantees. This talk was one of the series on the London Naval Conference, arranged by Frederick William Wile. Another momentous pronouncement by radio was that made by Henry L. Stimson, the American Secretary of State, from London the following month, already noted in Chapter I.

Great hopes were set on the World Disarmament Conference of 1932 — by broadcasters as well as by the world at large. By this time both American companies had permanent representatives in Europe, and there was assembled at Geneva a group of six radio people representing the two principal American chains. Yet so little real news emerged that after five weeks activities were suspended by all. The radio commentators competed with each other but not with the newspapers, and were content to parade the voices of eminent statesmen — Tardieu, Simon, Grandi, Beneš, Cecil, Madariaga, etc. — pouring forth more or less wishful platitudes. The opening speech of honest 'Uncle Arthur' Henderson, an aging, red-faced British ex-workingman, who had risen to be foreign minister without ever travelling far beyond his favorite Brighton, raised hopes of peace in millions of American hearts, but spread boredom among the cynical delegates and journalists of the fifty-odd nations in the hall of Geneva's Bâtiment Electoral.

DOCTOR YEN ARRAIGNS JAPAN

A real scoop, however, was scored by radio a fortnight later, when Doctor W. W. Yen, the Chinese Foreign Minister, made his famous indictment of Japan at the extraordinary session of the League of Nations Assembly to adjudicate the Manchurian dispute. Indignation over Japan's aggression at the very time when the nations were supposed to be trying to outlaw war was such that the Disarmament Conference was shouldered out of the limelight for a time. The session opened on March 3 in an atmosphere of tense expectation suffused with almost universal hatred of Japan. The assembly room of the old 'Palais Wilson' was packed; the press of the entire world was there with pencils sharpened to needle-point, when M. Paul Hymans, Belgian Foreign Minister, opened proceedings at 4.40 P.M.

Special significance attaches to the hour, which was considerably later than that originally scheduled. Never before in the history of the League had its proceedings been broadcast, and it was important to consider the time difference between the continents. Frederick William Wile, then in charge of Columbia's interests at Geneva, had reserved the hour of five to six for the transatlantic transmission, and had persuaded both Hymans and Yen to delay proceedings so that America would lose nothing essential. The elderly Doctor Yen, handsome even according to European conceptions and the very personification of dignity, rose, looked at the clock, and began to read a sheaf of telegrams about the situation in Shanghai. He then asked the translator to re-read them in French, while the clock crept up to 5 P.M. and past. Wile, in a broadcasting booth near the platform, described the historic scene to the American audience: for the first time a great nation was being brought to the bar of a world parliament for aggression. Then, for fifty minutes or so, grave, Harvard-bred Doctor Yen pilloried Japan in impeccable 'American,' piling evidence upon evidence with relentless logic. Thus, for once, the text of an important public document was known to American listeners before it could be printed anywhere in the world.

The further sequence of events, leading from calamity to calamity, and one of the greatest human tragedies of history, is only too well known to require comment here: that afternoon, however, the mantle of virtue hitherto assumed by the Japanese Government dropped from them for good and all, and their collaboration with the world's civilized nations was — for the time being — at an end. Broadcasting had given the world a glimpse of Woodrow Wilson's open diplomacy which even its exponent could not have foreseen.

THE 'KIDNAPPING' OF AMELIA EARHART

While the Disarmament Conference at Geneva was still news, while republican Germany was swaying to its death, perilously poised between the alternatives of restoration and Nazism, and I was still in Berlin pondering the mysterious words of the Kaiser's confidential Baron (as told in Chapter VIII), news reached me of the sudden take-off of Amelia Earhart from Floyd Bennett Field near New York on the first solo transatlantic flight since Lindbergh's spectacular exploit five years before. Fascinating as the stewing of the political cauldron was at this time, this daredevil adventure at once focussed public attention on an adventure which, if successful, would make history of a more cheerful kind. Here was an opportunity for the transatlantic radio to catch news 'on the wing.'

When Charles A. Lindbergh made his historic flight in 1927, radio was still in its infancy and international broadcasting played no part in spreading news of the event. When four years later Wiley Post and Harold Gatty flew from New York to Berlin, the N.B.C. was able to interview the fliers on their arrival at Tempelhof Field, and soon such transatlantic news-casting was bound to become a commonplace, whenever the aviator was lucky enough to land where he intended to land. But here was a case where the chances of disaster were so high that a happy landing would be big news. And the human interest element was as great as the element of chance. It was as daring an exploit as was ever undertaken by a member of the 'weaker' sex.

As Earhart's announced objective was Paris, I telephoned an order for transmission facilities to be installed at Le Bourget, took a fast Farman plane, and arrived at the French airport after a bumpy ride, only to find that the gallant Amelia had been forced down in a remote spot in northern Ireland, out of reach of any respectable telephone line. Thence she was trying to reach Croydon, the great London airport, as soon as her machine could be repaired. My resourceful secretary actually got into personal touch with her through Londonderry, while I took off again, on a dismally foggy morning, from Le Bourget to join a helpful friend, Raymond Gram Swing, already keeping watch at Croydon. Once again microphones and transmission gear were in place.

Meantime the 'Lady Lindy' had taken off again, not in her own damaged plane but that of an enterprising news-reel company which had flown to her aid in the hope of getting exclusive pictures. We hurriedly made an alliance with the newsreelers and were promised co-operation.

At Croydon the greatest confusion reigned. Newspaper reporters, sound-film operators, and a miscellaneous lot of official and unofficial welcomers crowded the airport. Our engineers were ready; we were in touch with New York; American listeners were waiting. But no sign of the heroine. A rumor began to buzz that she would come down — or be set down, since she was no longer her own pilot — somewhere else. We queried the operators of the news-reel company which owned the eagerly awaited plane about this; to convince us they calmly pointed to their own sound-truck, standing there ready to 'shoot.' We had no reason to doubt their word; yet the rumor persisted and the Croydon officials were at their wits' ends. When the crews of the competitive news-reel trucks were getting restive, we began to see light.

Knowing that the American Ambassador would have to receive Miss Earhart officially, we telephoned to the Embassy, and here an official revealed that the Ambassador had left not for Croydon but for Hanworth, a private club air field to the northwest of London, where the aviatrix was expected to arrive at any moment! Not a newspaper, not an official knew this; in fact not even Miss Earhart knew it; she had, in fact, been temporarily 'kidnapped' by the clever news-reel people, in order to score a beat.

By a lucky chance we found a top-hatted gentleman who was personally commissioned to receive her, with a fast car and a good chauffeur. He was in a panic. In return for our sensational information he took us aboard and we drove hell-for-leather around the outskirts of London, minding no speed limits and arriving at the club gates just as Earhart was sighted. We found them closed and guarded; the news-reel people had done a thorough job. Almost literally crashing the gate, we ran onto the field as the plane appeared in the west, against the rays of the setting sun. The Ambassador's car was waiting in front of the clubhouse, ready to rush the distinguished lady in her flying kit to a 'welcome dinner' at the Embassy, for it was getting near to eight o'clock. But the Ambassador, old Andrew Mellon, was a radio-minded man, having permitted his almost inaudible dulcet voice to be transmitted across the Atlantic on various patriotic occasions. I told him that for once Broadcasting House would have to take precedence over the American Embassy, and that listeners throughout the length and breadth of the United States were all agog to hear the 'Lady Lindy's' voice.

The aged Ambassador submitted meekly, and his chauffeur drove us to town in the Embassy car. So for the second time that day the intrepid lady was kidnapped — this time to make a radio fans' holiday.

The diplomatic flag helped us to make speed, and we reached Broadcasting House by eight o'clock — four hours later than the scheduled broadcast. All day long the wires had hummed between London and New York, as the arrival was postponed and postponed. But no amount of engineering magic would have made it possible to set up facilities at

Broadcasting House opened its portals to receive Amelia
Earhart, heroine of the year, and let her speak to America

Hanworth in time for the arrival; all our beautiful equipment in Croydon had to be sent home, as had been done at Le Bourget the day before — an illustration of the hurdles radio must take in order to get real news.

As it happened, the delay — with frequent bulletins issued to listeners through the day — increased the tension and made the broadcast more valuable. It was a Sunday, too, and many millions of people must have been listening in their homes. Only once before had the Atlantic been flown solo, and never had anything comparable been accomplished by a woman. It was a chance for the eagle-hens to scream.

The bareheaded 'Lady Lindy' in her breeches and leather blouse was cool and self-possessed. Boyish, yet graceful in her movements, she fairly jumped out of the car and into the lift. Her resemblance to Colonel Lindbergh was arresting. The slender figure, the long, rather rugged face with the deep-set, poetic eyes, the large, full-lipped mouth, and the tousled crop of blond curls made her as engaging a figure as I have ever seen.

Owing to the news-reel company's 'hoax' there wasn't a soul to receive us, not a newspaper person in sight. Broadcasting House, being all but asleep on Sunday, opened its portals to receive the heroine of the year, let her speak to America — but no one even thought of seizing the chance for British listeners. [1]

The experience of interviewing her at the microphone gave me one of my real thrills. She answered impromptu questions simply and without hesitation, told of her difficulties with the engine manifold, the leak in her petrol gauge, the failure of the altimeter, the ice forming on her wings, her flying 'by trial and error' all night, and hitting Ireland by guess. 'I realize that this flight means nothing to aviation,' she said. 'Such crossings will become commonplace — though possibly not solo ones.'

Earhart's candid modesty, her charm, and the smile which lighted up her handsome features were irresistible. As I write this the search for her in the watery wastes of the

[1] Two nights later she was persuaded to talk a few minutes in the 'news' broadcast period. Everything in its time is the British motto.

Pacific is still going on but hope is practically abandoned.
She was of the stuff of which heroes are made.

LA COUPE DAVÍS

There is just one department of news in which broadcasting is supreme, and that is sport. By no possible means
can any other method of reporting beat the 'news-caster'
when, opposite a goal, or in the grandstand at a football
game, he gives the result with hardly a second's delay, and
at the same moment a million fans are in possession of the
facts. The broadcasting of sporting events has become,
wherever radio exists, a boon to the stay-at-home.

Transatlantic broadcasting entered this field as soon as
short-wave transmission had reached the practical stage.
The Derby, run on Epsom Downs in June, 1930, was the
start. Then came the Grand National at Aintree; the
Oxford-Cambridge Boat Race on the Thames; tennis at
Wimbledon; and finally St. Andrews and the other battle-
grounds of championship golf. Tennis and golf presented
the most difficult problems, because it was obviously impossible to keep a transoceanic channel open for hours. So
we had to guess, as shrewdly as possible, when the decision
might come, and reserve 'strategic' quarter-hours on a
chance. The first time we did this from the Continent was
for the famous Challenge Round of the Davis Cup matches
at the Stade Roland Garros near Paris, in the summer of
1932. The United States, with Ellsworth Vines, Frank
Shields, Wilmer Allison, and John Van Ryn, faced France,
the holder of the Cup. On the last day the score stood two
matches to one in favor of France, with two more to be played.
The decision might come either in the fourth or fifth match,
and anywhere within the space of two hours. A half-hour
period was all we could get for broadcasting to America.

The French radio men whom we asked for 'facilities'
probably thought it was a harebrained scheme. At any rate

they couldn't have taken it very seriously, to judge from
the place they assigned to us, on top of the uppermost roof
of the stadium — a mere parapet, crowded with news-reel
men and press photographers. Anyone with the slightest
tendency to giddiness might have fallen to his death. However, we considered ourselves lucky to have been admitted
at all when we heard that Mr. Davis, the donor of the Cup,
who had either forgotten his badge or couldn't pronounce
Davis in French, was turned back by the stern guardians of
the gate!

Our case was much more serious; we were just radio men
with nothing to prove it. The American sporting expert who
had been appointed to cover the match for Columbia had
suddenly disappeared, complete with admission tickets,
broadcasting permit, and all, and wasn't discovered till days
after the match, recovering from something or other, in the
American Hospital. The stadium was jammed and tickets
were rarer than hens' teeth. Luckily I found John R. Tunis,
one of America's leading tennis writers, in Paris; to help me
out, he took over at a few hours' notice, and that was, so far
as I know, his entrance into radio. Tunis and I literally
fought our way to our perch (for there is no one more skeptical
than a Frenchman guarding a gate); found our microphone,
and, flanked by noisy chatterers, did a quick-fire commentary through cupped hands.

But luck was with us. Our half-hour period began in the
fourth set of what turned out to be the decisive match, between the two veterans, Borotra and Allison. Allison, at
5–3, appeared to be winning, but Borotra (who had un-
expectedly beaten Vines on the first day) was the hero of the
crowd, who were shouting 'Borocco! Borocco!' with savage
enthusiasm. Twice Allison had been within a point of
victory. In the tenth game, within a point of drawing level,
Borotra split a tennis shoe but was obliged to fight on, losing
three points and making it deuce. Then he appealed to the
umpire and was allowed to change his shoes, which he did
very leisurely, sitting on a ball-boy's back. Both men were
highly wrought up, the crowd in an ugly mood, while
thunder clouds darkened the sultry sky.

Despite his rest, Borotra lost the vantage point to Allison, who was for the third time within an inch of victory. Borotra then served what looked like a double fault. We broadcast America's 'victory,' and Allison gleefully threw his racket in the air. But the linesmen kept ominous silence: the ball was declared good. The crowd cheered — and jeered — and Allison began to lose his nerve. Borotra summoned his remaining strength — it was the last great chance of his career — winning game, set, and Davis Cup for France.

A terrific roar went up: it was the last flare-up of France's tennis supremacy. We were so excited that we lost track of the time; so we kept right on, hoping that America was hearing us somehow. Our half hour was up — it was a matter of minutes: had we been cut off, according to the inexorable broadcasting schedule?

Twenty minutes later a cable was handed up the vertical iron ladder. New York, too, had listened with bated breath, had allowed the program to run over. So they had everything, including the sad news. America had taken a licking, but we had made radio history.

Soon transatlantic tennis commentaries became obligatory; today they are regular features of the summer schedule both in England and America.

OLYMPIC GAMES ON THE AIR

But it was the Olympic Games of 1936, in Germany, that provided the biggest sporting event to date. No such elaborate broadcasting arrangements had ever been made before. Not only were the games being broadcast nationally, but they were being transmitted to some forty other nations of the world. It was not just a case of 'feeding' one commentary to all: each country had to be served in its own language, by its own sports commentators; each country had its particular pet events, in which its own athletes excelled. Thus America concentrated on track events, and the diving of its girls;

the Japanese on running and swimming; the Finns on Marathon; the French on bicycling and boxing; the British on rowing. Only the Germans were interested in practically everything, but particularly in javelins, weights, and anything that could be thrown.

Great organizers that they are, the Germans in charge of the Games made a great point of efficiency, and everything went practically without a hitch. As for broadcasting, they built five additional short-wave transmitters, bringing the number up to eight, working on eighteen frequencies directed to every part of the world, thus providing the most magnificent service to the nations concerned and, incidentally, the biggest propaganda machine in the world for themselves. The Olympic Games were not only the Nazis' greatest 'circus' to date, but the prestige to be derived from it was regarded as a matter of life and death.

Radio provided not only the instrument for news-distribution and the gingering up of morale, but for the marshalling of crowds. This regimentation by means of the ubiquitous loud-speaker — especially in Garmisch, where arc-light standards and flagpoles were endowed with a mechanical voice — gave one an idea of the uses to which this new gift to man might be put in time of war.

One night, when the Winter Olympics were in the first stage, I witnessed a weird and sinister scene; thousands of workmen were hurriedly completing the immense Nazi amusement hall, the *Kraft durch Freude* headquarters, put up in eighty-eight days for the entertainment of the German proletariat during the two weeks of the Games. It was dark, except for the piercing shafts of light from the projectors at the four corners of the field, and the snow was falling thickly. The men moved silently, in long files, carrying beams and materials; others, like giant ants, were swarming to their tasks. And from a loud-speaker somewhere came the bellowing voice of the invisible overseer urging them on... It gave me the creeps; it was Wagner's Nibelheim scene enlarged to gigantic proportions and transposed to the surface of the earth.

But there were things of beauty, too. A kindly nature had

provided the much-needed snow at the eleventh hour; and Garmisch, gay with the colors and costumes of all the nations, was turned into fairyland. The great ski stadium, a white arena built against a steep wooded mountain side, with its giant ski-jumps, its flags and its Olympic fire, was a never-to-be-forgotten sight. During the closing ceremony, timed with unerring showmanship at the fall of night, a team of eight skiers, at the word of command, gathered in the giant Olympic flag — white, with the five colored rings representing the continents of the earth. Spread horizontally between them, they rushed it at breakneck speed down the mountain side, while a moving floodlight made it the one luminous object in the vast natural arena. To the playing of the Olympic Hymn, the tolling of bells and the gradual dying down of the Olympic fire, the immense crowd stood, electrified. That was one of the most beautiful spectacles it has been my fortune to see from a broadcasting booth or anywhere else.

The summer games in Berlin, though more gigantic in scope, were an emotional anticlimax after this poignant close, but for two weeks they kept at least a half-dozen American broadcasters in one mad whirl. I can remember only a few sensational and some absurdly funny things. I remember Ted Husing's *tour de force* in describing, for American and British listeners, that incredible 200-meter dash won by the American negro, Jesse Owens (who also won the 100 meters and the long jump and was in fact the hero of the Olympics, but was not invited to shake Hitler's hand). Ted, in reporting that race while it was being run way down in the bottom of that immense bowl, not only described the runners and their style, but every change of relative position, spotted changes of pace, forecast the result, and told his listeners the timing before the official watcher could get it out. He spoke faster than Owens ran; every word was distinct and the drama complete.

These direct commentaries had to be made through 'bottle' microphones, which were held close up to the lips, from an open platform, with the speaker flanked by polyglot colleagues on either side and completely surrounded by a sport-frenzied mob.

I remember, too, how the half-prostrated winners of these mad spurts of physical power came up to the microphone to say pleasant platitudes with their remaining breath; and how in the evening we had to lure them out of their 'Olympic Village' to come to the cubbyhole studios atop the grandstand to speak with calculated modesty to the folks at home. Among them were Helen Stephens, that amazingly masculine woman who won the 100 meters, brainy little Jim Lovelock, Australia's 1500-meter world champion, A. F. Williams, the hero of the 400-meter race, and many more.

I remember the weird scene at that woodland colony (whose builder preferred suicide to political ignominy soon after the Games), when bands of hefty athletes of different nationalities stood around in the moonlight and sang their songs into our microphone, the Germans with determined precision, the Italians with gay abandon, the Canadians — wearing enormous scarlet maple leaves on their white sweaters — with a lustiness that nearly shattered our eardrums. And I remember the terrific excitement at the swimming tank when Jack Medica won the 400-meter swim for the United States; and also that other American 'victory' — in the same place — when a California woman, hunting autographs, kissed Adolf Hitler on his moustache in front of a gaping crowd.

But above all I remember that rainy afternoon at Grünau on the river Havel, when two middle-aged Englishmen, J. Beresford and L. F. Southwood, won the double-skulls, and eight mere college boys from Washington State University walked away with the 'eights' — both against the supertrained rowing stars picked from all Germany who were winning every decisive race that day. We had had to stand up for the German anthem and the 'Horst Wessel' song after every event, until we were nauseated.

America was interested only in the eights, though her chances seemed slim, and we had reserved a transatlantic circuit for the period of that race alone. Suddenly I discovered that the time had been changed — retarded by fifty minutes — and our broadcast would fall into an empty space. I blanched, harangued the officials: nothing could be done. I jumped over seats, shouldered my way past Nazi guards into the clubhouse, grabbed a telephone, and asked for — New York. The bystanders thought I was mad. In twenty minutes, just before the original timing, I got the New York control-room to change the program: by a great stroke of luck it could still be done. Then Bill Henry, my greatest standby in these frantic weeks, and I climbed to the roof of the grandstand and waited at our microphone.

The starting shot rang out; the Italians jumped ahead, then the Germans — would they win again? The Americans were fifth, with only England trailing them, for three-quarters of the 2000-meter course. Then they pulled up to third place and 300 yards from the finish it was neck and neck. They spurted, Italy keeping up with them; but less than twenty yards from the finish Washington shot forward, winning by a mere six feet, the most important water race of the Olympic Games. And what a chance! We were the only American radio commentators to catch that race, with millions of Americans listening to us.

A shout went up, and some groans. Then the Star-Spangled Banner was played, which almost nobody in that predominantly German crowd could sing. So four of us — two men, two women — yelled and sang it into the microphone, thus making our musical radio début....

Competition between American broadcasters was keener than ever. Both networks jockeyed for the first broadcast from the Games. What would it be? The American team's arrival at Hamburg? We both tried for it; it fell through. So Columbia arranged to take a short-wave transmitter on to the special boat-train, and for a half hour Bill Henry interviewed America's athletic stars while that train sped at sixty miles an hour toward Berlin, where our competitors were waiting for them to arrive. So we won the first round. Needless to say, the Opposition won others; but for once we were both too busy to notice what was happening in the other camp.[1] In 1940 the fight will start over again, unless...

[1] In justice to our friends of the N.B.C., let me add that for a week or so before the Games they relayed the Olympic torch-runner's arrival at various points on his way from Olympia to Berlin.

Seeing us broadcast to America from a position in the stadium grandstand, a pudgy little Japanese squeezed up to the microphone and asked if he might say a few words to the American public. He was a member of the Japanese Parliament, and a graduate of Harvard. Japan having just been selected for the Games of 1940, he wanted to invite all his friends to come to Japan. Will they be in a mood to go?

ELECTIONS: RADIO'S BIG CHANCE

Elections are of all news events the most suitable for broadcasting, outside of sport, both being prearranged yet speculative; certain in time, but uncertain in outcome. Election returns by radio can reach more people and by a more direct route than through any other medium. The first election to be broadcast anywhere was the United States presidential contest of 1920 (Warren G. Harding), when the Westinghouse Company's station KDKA at Pittsburgh sent out the returns. This, however, reached only a small section of the public, and the first nation-wide broadcasting of election returns could not take place in America until 1928, a year after the National Broadcasting Company had been established. Meantime the B.B.C. had broadcast the British General Elections of 1923 and 1924.

Since international broadcasting did not start with any degree of regularity till 1930, the first opportunity to transmit the results of a European election to America was in 1931, when a sensational landslide swept the first British National Government into office. Although the matter received no newspaper notice at the time, it may be worth mentioning that two people, one sitting in the garden room of my house in St. John's Wood, London, the other in a broadcasting studio in New York, were responsible for stealing a march on the entire American press by broadcasting an analysis of results at an hour (3 A.M. in London; five hours earlier, namely 10 P.M., in New York) when the decisive returns were already in, and radio listening was at a peak hour in America.

The man in London was Raymond Gram Swing, then London correspondent of the New York *Evening Post*, his partner in New York was myself. The process was simple: after sketching the political background of the election in a five-minute talk I simply gave a cue to the transatlantic telephone operator to switch me to London, an open circuit being held in readiness for Swing, and by a series of questions elicited the outstanding facts — the unprecedented *débâcle* of the Labor Party, the defeat of ex-ministers, the altogether surprising revulsion in public feeling as recorded at the polls.[1]

Since this pioneer job every European election of real importance has been broadcast to America, notably the German elections of 1932–33 — three within a year! — which prepared the way for Hitler, and the British elections of November, 1935, when S. K. Ratcliffe and myself broadcast 'rival' resumés from London.

But the most exciting and amusing broadcast of this category was the commentary on the Saar plebiscite in January, 1935, which is a story worth telling in detail.

---

[1] For the sake of technical accuracy: the telephone transmitter at either end was of course equipped with microphone and amplifier.

XIV. RADIO FIGHTS ITS FIRST WAR

IN THE spring of 1933, following the exciting events which swept Hitler first into office and then — after the burning of the Reichstag — into power, I was travelling through Germany into Austria. It was the centenary year of Johannes Brahms, the great German composer who some fifty-five years before had travelled over the same route, to spend the rest of his life in Vienna. Both Germany and Austria claim him as their 'son'; both Berlin and Vienna had planned great celebrations for the month of May. Turning my back on the brutalities of the Nazi revolution, I was glad to follow the great master's footsteps and enjoy his music in the city of his choice.

Vienna, poor and down at the heel, was nevertheless enjoying its Brahms. The multi-colored kiosks on the Ringstrasse, where the trees were breaking into feathery green, announced the concerts; the newspapers were full of comment on the superlative performances of Furtwängler and Schnabel, Huberman and Casals. But they were also full of other, more sinister things. One day they reported how two Germans of official rank, including a Doctor Frank, Minister of Justice in the State of Bavaria, had arrived at the Vienna air field for a speech-making tour of Austria; they were in Nazi uniform and their manner was that of conquerors. They were met by representatives of the Austrian Government and told in so many words that they were not welcome. Nevertheless they stayed. They were given a police escort, which accompanied them until the end of their much-curtailed tour, and were soon delivered across the German border into the hands of their compatriots, in good order but rather ugly mood.

For many months the Austrian Nazis, aided and abetted by their German comrades, had spread terror through the Austrian countryside. Their growing legions had been trained with advice and help from more experienced Germans; arms had been smuggled across the frontier; a German 'Inspector-General for Austria' was in charge of the movement that was to bring Austria into Hitler's *Reich*. Now that Hitler was in power, his agents stalked up and down the land more arrogantly than before, dangling visions of German fleshpots before hungry Austrian eyes.

But the worm turned at last. A little man named Engelbert Dollfuss, barely five feet high, had made himself dictator of Austria two months back, almost on the very day that Hitler's power was confirmed by an overwhelming if not wholly voluntary vote. He had been in office ten months before that, but had ruled by virtue of a precarious balance of numbers in Parliament. But now Parliament had conveniently voted itself out of existence, and Dollfuss, with aid of a private army of green-hatted peasant lads, the *Heimwehr*, was in control. It was the chief of the Vienna *Heimwehr* detachment, a tough and able operator named Major Fey, who had provided such a sour welcome for the flying Nazi missionaries at the Vienna air field.

But people about the Government were worried. The Nazi battalions in the country grew by leaps and bounds; violence — shooting, burning, hooliganism of an expert viciousness — increased daily. Vienna, except for its hangdog look, seemed pretty normal: the cafés were full, as always; pianists banged their stale Mitropa jazz on tinny night-bar pianos; people cracked jokes about their 'Millimetternich' chancellor. Paraphrasing a famous Austrian general in the war, they opined that the situation was 'hopeless, but not serious.' But they knew little of what went on beyond the range of their own vision; like their German cousins in the years just passed, they read only the papers that printed what they liked to read, not what they ought to have learned.[1]

The German Nazis were furious over the treatment of their emissaries; their papers dripped venom; their radio stations, just getting reorganized under a Nazi head, cried havoc through the land; retaliatory measures were planned, resulting in the famous tourist boycott and — the radio war.

My presence in Vienna, though accidental, seemed providential. I felt that the world should think more about Austria than it did — its economic plight, the threat to its independence, its apparent helplessness before the coming avalanche. Peace in Europe was at that moment poised on a delicate arch, and Austria was the keystone of the arch. A Nazified Austria would mean a solid wall of Fascism from the Baltic to the Mediterranean, with peaceful democracies on one side and Stalinism on the other — a situation that was bound to lead to war.

DOLLFUSS TELLS AMERICA

People I talked to felt that Chancellor Dollfuss should be heard by the world. At that time he was not the internationally popular figure he was to become: his diminutive stature was the only thing that got him friendly foreign publicity. I delayed my departure; before I left I was summoned to the Ballhausplatz — that great baroque government building in which the map of nineteenth-century Europe had been drawn after the Napoleonic wars, and which a year hence was to be the scene of the most melodramatic chapter of post-war history. Before these sanguinary

---

[1] The situation at this time is well illustrated by one of the many jokes that passed from lip to lip. A poor Viennese on the edge of starvation asks a friend what on earth he can do to keep body and soul together. 'Go up to a policeman and shout "*Heil Hitler!*"' says the friend. 'That will get you to jail and there you'll be fed.' The desperate man takes the advice and picks a policeman at a busy corner: 'Heil Hitler!' '*Heil Hitler!*' answers the policeman in a whisper, 'but get along with you quick or they'll put us both in the jug.'

events, however, the access to the historic chancellory was easy, and the hall porter as *gemütlich* as only a Viennese can be. I mounted the long flights of stone steps in the rambling palace; a labyrinth of corridors guarded by slouching, bearded attendants — relics of Emperor Franz Josef's time — led me to the anteroom of the Government's press chief — a very important official close to the Chancellor and Foreign Minister, namely, Dollfuss himself.

The attendant in charge of the waiting-room, after considerable head-shaking, finally agreed that I might possibly see the *Herr Gesandter* (a title indicating a certain rank in the Austrian diplomatic service) but doubted whether it would be today. The fact that I had an appointment failed to shake his pessimism: they were all *so* busy — not excluding himself, it seemed, for as quickly as possible he turned his back on the waiting visitors and applied himself most assiduously to some important-looking papers. Long, boresome waiting, broken only by the arrival of further visitors (none of whom got more than fleeting and grudging attention from the busy official), finally made me curious, and I spied over his shoulder. The supposed document was *music* — band parts being copied out in government office hours and obviously with official sanction! I looked again to read the title of the opus; it was 'Weaner Mad'ln' — 'Viennese Girls,' a waltz! I had heard of Viennese police inspectors writing string quartets in their spare time, but that was before the war. Now, with the country in danger, it was a waltz. 'Desperate, but not serious'...

Let me hasten to add, however, that there was seriousness within the guarded doors. The gesture to put Doctor Dollfuss on the air was appreciated, and the matter was quickly arranged for the following Sunday afternoon.

I first saw the diminutive statesman in a large, high-ceilinged state chamber of the Chancellor's palace — the very room in which eventually he was to meet his fate. He came through one of the gigantic doors, followed by his press chief and an attaché, both of more than average height. His tiny stature was thereby greatly accentuated: at least two chancellors his size, standing on top of each other, could have walked through that door. Everything in the room was on the grand scale, in line with the sprawling elephantism of the Austrian Empire that was no more. But though small, Dollfuss made a 'complete' impression — a finely proportioned, good-looking, well-groomed man with very simple, disarmingly direct manners.

'I am delighted to meet you,' he said. 'Why, you're not much taller than I!' And he made me stand back to back with him so that the rest of the company could see there wasn't *much* difference. He seemed pleased for once not to have to look up in order to talk with a stranger. While engineers made final adjustments to the microphone on the table, and press photographers clicked their cameras from various angles, Dollfuss discussed his broadcast to America.

It had been agreed that it should not be aggressive. It was to attack nobody, but was to assert Austria's individuality, its right of self-determination — 'Austria for the Austrians,' in short. Ever since the war the Austrians had been talking *Anschluss*, emphasizing their Germanness. Whatever a party's policies, whether Pan-German, Christian-social, or Socialist, *Anschluss* — union with Germany — had to be one of its planks. Yet every Austrian hated the 'Prussians' — which meant every German north of Bavaria. I once asked an Austrian how the politicians reconciled these two ideas. 'You know what the Germans of the eighteenth century,' he said, 'oppressed by petty tyrants, but dreaming of liberty and unity, used to whisper to each other? "Never speak of it, but always think of it!" Well, it's the reverse with *Anschluss*. The slogan is: "Always speak of it, but never think of it!" — in other words, don't take it seriously.'

So now the sacred dream of 'union with our German brethren' had given way to Austria's struggle to 'maintain its Austrian character in the interest of Germanism as a whole,' to quote Dollfuss's words. Was that, I thought, what Mussolini was spending his money for? For it was he that financed the *Heimwehr*, while Germany poured millions into the Austrian Nazis' till.

The speech was, in fact, a string of political euphemisms. It explained the 'elimination' of the Austrian Parliament as an epoch in the country's organic development, though it affirmed the equality of all Austrians before the law and asserted that all kinds of racial hatred were contrary to the national character. It eulogized that redoubtable Monsignor Seipel, the deceased Catholic leader, as the only post-war Austrian statesman, and ignored the existence of the largest party in Austria, the Socialists. And it ended on the seductive note of Vienna's charm (an approved formula of all Austrian post-war politicians for the attraction of tourists), but remained silent on the most remarkable achievement of the Viennese people, the municipal workers' tenements, erected by opponents of his régime.

This was hardly the stuff I had hoped for; still, it was Dollfuss, and Americans might as well hear what he stood for. But, as I heard afterwards, the speech wasn't heard, because somewhere between Vienna and the Swiss border (transmission was via the League of Nations' short-wave station at Prangins) some telephone engineers, either Nazi or Socialist, recognizing Dollfuss's voice, stopped working the 'repeaters,' without which the volume of sound is insufficient for retransmission. It was another typically Austrian maneuver. Comically enough, however, the English translation of the speech did go through, evidently because of the engineers' blissful ignorance of what it was!

The day before this, a jolly company was lunching in an old-fashioned Viennese *Keller* when one of those quaint Viennese characters, a sixty-year-old flower 'girl,' came in to sell us little bunches of spring flowers. Having done good business she shouted 'Heil Dollfuss!' by way of good-bye. We thought that it was a common and spontaneous greeting and concluded that the little Chancellor was popular among at least a section of the people. But we never heard it again, and next day I had quite a different impression. Dollfuss, having accomplished his broadcast to America, had to go to the air field to congratulate the winners in the great Race around the Alps (*Alpenflug*). He invited me to come along, and we rode, side by side, in his official car, accompanied by two high officials. When we reached the field a crowd had collected at the entrance, marshalled by a couple of police-

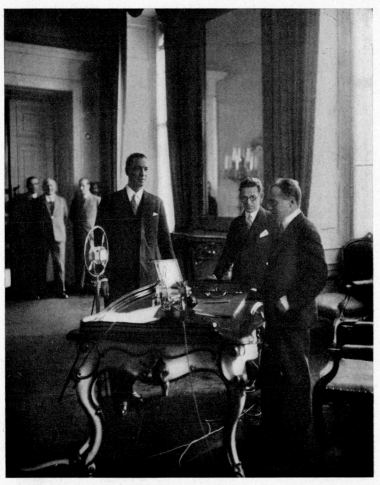

Chancellor Dollfuss spoke from the very room in which
eventually he was to meet his fate

men, who saluted, as did some soldiers further on. The sullenly curious crowd stared silently at the Chancellor, whose face and figure are unmistakable. There wasn't a cheer, there wasn't a greeting; only one or two people rather furtively took off their hats. On the other hand, there were no gestures of hostility, and there was no detective or bodyguard in attendance. This didn't strike me as noteworthy at the time, but I thought of it when Dollfuss's name was on the front pages of the world press a few months later.

Dollfuss's conversation showed him to be even more naïve than I had thought. Or was he merely feigning simplicity? We talked about his plans for Austria, and he said that the crux of the country's prosperity was farming. (He himself was an expert agriculturist.) It was his plan to make Austria as nearly self-supporting as possible by organizing the 'peasant front' and planning the perfect exploitation of the soil. This, in view of the fact that two fifths of the country is forest and that nine tenths is mountainous, seemed rather a large contract. Of industry he had little to say, and of the workingman not a word. This may all have been political eyewash, but it seemed to show where his sympathies lay. Dollfuss, beset by enemies on the Right and Left, had more than one chance to compromise with the Socialists, the moderate Austrian democratic workingman's party, but his completely rural sympathies and his rigid piety made it impossible for him to cross that bridge.

Against the Nazis his feelings were, if anything, less bitter. It was they who were threatening him openly; to them his life was forfeit. Yet when someone in the car said that from now on 'they would be paid back with their own coin,' Dollfuss was eloquently silent.

THE WAR BEGINS — IN MUNICH

The Nazis across the border, however, were going strong. They had been blocked in carrying the torch of revolt to the enemy's camp; very well, they would find another way. Early in July the Munich broadcasting station issued an official announcement that from then on they would pay more attention to the situation in Austria, would broadcast regular talks revealing the 'true position' to listeners in Germany *and Austria.* Refugees from Austria would come to the microphone and tell Germans on both sides of the frontier about 'the brutal fight which is being fought by a small separatist clique in Austria against all things German.' The Austrian Government, preaching 'Austria for the Austrians, in the interest of Germanism as a whole,' were thus branded as just a clique of separatists, on whom war had to be declared.

The 'war' started on July 5, when the notorious State-Leader Habicht, formerly Nazi 'Inspector-General for Austria,' began his series of harangues against Dollfuss and his government. Habicht had been expelled from Austria after preaching disobedience to his followers; he had thousands of partisans, spoke their language, knew their troubles. He now followed the same tactics from afar, exploiting these troubles, systematically bringing discontent and revolt to fever heat. The Munich transmitter could be heard practically throughout Austria, as well or better than the Austrian stations, and the Austrians were helpless. Day after day, night after night, the attacks went on, interspersed with cleverly produced 'cultural' offerings attractive to the Austrian peasant and mountaineer.

The Austrian broadcasting authorities, realizing that retaliation would be useless, appealed to the International Broadcasting Union, on the basis of some mild resolutions against hostile broadcasting that had been adopted. It had little effect. The Germans boycotted Austria economically, and that summer in hundreds of Tyrolese hotels — empty because the German customers couldn't come — hungry natives listened to broadcasts which blamed the Government for their country's plight. Little did it matter that at last the outside world was waking up; little did it matter that little Dollfuss was the hero of the World Economic Conference in London that summer, while Doctor Schacht, as

German delegate, coolly laid down the law to the world's statesmen who showed no enthusiasm for throwing good money after bad. Doctor Dollfuss went home a Parthian hero, while his native Austrian countryside bristled with Nazis, more and more enraged.

Some three months after his return, on October 3, he was shot by one of them, but was wounded only in the arm.

Radio, the instrument which had in all likelihood been the cause of his being laid low, now came to his rescue and made him popular at last. From his bedside on the day of the attempted assassination he spoke to millions of listening Austrians, for even his enemies must have had a morbid interest in hearing a man who had just by inches escaped death.

At last the European Powers were aroused. They made representations to Germany, and a kind of truce ensued while Dollfuss recovered and succeeded in buttressing his position within Austria and without. But the worst was yet to come. The truce, so far as the Nazis were concerned, was only a lull — the quiet before the storm. Dollfuss, who even back in May seemed to me very polite about them, was by January ready to dicker with the very Habicht who had been thundering imprecations across the frontier by radio.[1] But Major Fey, whose Heimwehr derived its sinews of war from Italy, found another solution in the nick of time, and the thunderer returned to his Munich microphone.

The Austrians, having obtained no satisfaction from their correspondence with the Broadcasting Union (whose German vice-president, Doctor Giesecke, was by this time in a Nazi concentration camp), now proposed to take the matter of the Munich attacks to the League of Nations. Dollfuss himself was to go to Geneva to appeal to the January session of the Council. This, it seemed to me, was a peculiarly interesting and apposite occasion for international broadcasting, so once again I invited Dollfuss to tell his tale to America and the world by means of the short-wave channel. My offer was accepted and the date provisionally set for the first convenient Sunday in February. But fate decided

[1] See John Gunther, *Inside Europe*, p. 295.

otherwise: momentous events were in preparation; Doctor Dollfuss never went to Geneva, he went to Hungary on a 'state visit' instead, while Major Fey was left in charge at Vienna. Yet the broadcast was not cancelled; it was fixed for February 18.

DOLLFUSS 'EXPLAINS' THE BLOODSHED

On the twelfth — the previous Monday — the world was shaken out of its complacence by one of the most appalling tragedies of recent times — the Austrian civil war. Instead of counterattacking the Nazis, the Government's troops and Heimwehr volunteers attacked the quiescent Socialists at the very moment that their leaders were pleading for peace. For four days the military poured fire and lead into the model workers' tenements, which had been the pride of Vienna and an object of envy to the social-minded of all nations. My friend John Gunther, who saw this ghastly massacre with his own eyes, has recorded it vividly in his *Inside Europe.* And here he records, too, how Dollfuss — returned from his state visit — was at Mass in St. Stephen's church when the lights went out, and at tea with the Papal Nuncio while innocent women and children were being bombed in their homes. Unaware of the inside facts but fully alive to the importance of these cruel events, I arranged, by long-distance telephone from Paris (where I had gone to report on the Stavisky riots), that Doctor Dollfuss should broadcast as agreed, but instead of the original subject his talk was to be an explanation, from the Government's point of view, of what had happened in this bloody week.

By Friday the fighting had died down, except for cleaning-up actions in the provinces, and by Sunday all calmness was restored, while victims of the correct political color were given state funerals. I asked John Gunther to take charge of the broadcast for me, to introduce the Chancellor at the microphone, and to 'set the scene.' I realized that the Government would use the opportunity for an interpretation which might minimize its own responsibility, but like the rest of the world I was prepared to accept the theory of a simple revolt, summarily crushed. I knew Dollfuss, and thought him incapable of wanton cruelty.

The broadcast, in any case, would make headlines, for it is not often that the head of a government is heard at the crucial moment of a revolutionary struggle. The Austrian Government asked me whether we would extend to the 'other chain' in America permission to relay the Chancellor's talk, and in the circumstances I felt we should not refuse. Austria was entitled to a 100 per cent coverage.

But John Gunther, whose emotions had been stirred by the events of the previous days, refused to introduce the Chancellor when he was shown Dollfuss's text. In it the socialists were represented to be the attackers — an irresponsible group of enemies of the state. Now, knowing what I do, I can't blame him; though it would have been quite permissible for him simply to tell listeners that he disclaimed responsibility. In the end the matter was settled by having a government spokesman, in impeccable English, introduce the Chancellor, whose speech had been read to me in full, for my approval, over the telephone. I suggested some vital alterations, and they were made. This may have been the only time that a mere radio representative censored a prime minister's speech — and a dictator's at that!

This time no sabotage interfered with the broadcast. The little Chancellor's voice went out to the world with a steadiness that seemed, if anything, too calm. Almost a thousand of his compatriots — men, women, and children — lay dead, and here he was explaining it was just an 'attack by a small group of fanatics against state and society' and boasting that 'full order had been restored.' There was no word of reconciliation, only a promise that all citizens who 'felt nationally' would be protected; the Chancellor himself assumed the guardianship of all the dependents of the dead in 'our' forces, leaving general relief to the Archbishop of Vienna.

I thought of the simple, little man talking about the Austrian farmer, about Austrian scenery and Austrian music on that short motor trip a year ago, and felt that this was not good enough.

Nothing more was said about the radio attacks from the Munich station, which, however, went on unabated. Largely thanks to them, the Nazi organization within Austria grew and grew, while on the German side of the border the Austrian Legion, made up of Nazi refugees, was being armed and drilled. Habicht and Frauenfeld, the fugitive leaders of the Austrian Nazi Party, were in charge. The Austrian Government, having disposed of the Socialists, were more than ever in the hands of the victorious Heimwehr, and now looked only to Mussolini for support. Dollfuss was planning to go to Italy to seal the pact.

Attention had, indeed, been diverted from Austria by the Nazi blood purge of June 30, and we were busy getting some sort of a report from inside Germany, an eye-witness account being out of the question. On July 13 Hitler made his radio speech on these hair-raising events, and we rebroadcast it in America. On July 25, between twelve noon and one o'clock, Nazi conspirators attacked, almost simultaneously, the Federal chancellery (with Dollfuss inside) and the Austrian broadcasting building ('Ravag') — the two places which I knew more intimately than any others in Vienna. The story of the Ravag attack has again been told most vividly by John Gunther, one of the very few outsiders who happened to witness it; among the five victims were the Director-General's chauffeur, who on more than one occasion had driven me on my errands in Vienna, and a favorite radio comedian. Director-General Czeija himself escaped, by virtue of his *sang-froid*: a Nazi attacker entered his private office, but was tackled by the jovial and hefty *Herr Direktor*, and held tightly till the police arrived.

The important fact, however, is that in this attempted revolution the broadcasting headquarters was deemed a primary point of attack — and so it will be in all revolutions from now on. These conspirators had been radio-minded ever since the Munich radio calumnies started, a year before.

If now they did not wholly succeed, it was due to lack of technical precautions. They rushed into a studio, covered the announcer with their revolvers, and made him say: 'The government of Doctor Dollfuss has resigned; Doctor Rintelen has assumed power.' That was the agreed signal for revolt all over Austria. But they were unable to repeat it every ten minutes, as they had planned to do, because a Ravag engineer had the presence of mind to sever the cable connection with the actual broadcasting transmitter, situated outside Vienna, on the Bisamberg. Had they seized this station as well, they would have had the entire country by the ears. Even to this day both the studio building and the station are guarded day and night with truly Austrian precaution — by one lone soldier.

A DICTATOR'S DEATH

But if the 'revolt in the ether' failed, the attack on the chancellery was pursued to a ghastly, sanguinary end. There Dollfuss, ignorant of approaching danger, was holding a cabinet meeting to decide, among other things, the fate of a theatre devoted to Viennese operetta. A warning reached him shortly before noon and the cabinet was dismissed; but Dollfuss and the redoubtable Major Fey (who had sent the Nazi emissaries packing, as related above) stayed in the building. A few minutes later, 140 rebels disguised in the uniforms of the crack Deutschmeister regiment, arrived in three huge motor-trucks at the Chancellery, guarded only by two policemen and a small guard of honor, who were quickly disarmed. They entered through the main gates, sped through the corridors and arrested all the officials in their offices. A small detachment burst into the oyster-white room — the same in which, only a few months before Dollfuss had broadcast his message to America — and there they found him, trapped at the crucial moment because his valet couldn't unlock the door!

At that moment Otto Planetta, the Nazi ex-corporal, shot the little man down, stepped nearer and shot him again through the throat. The little man shouted weakly for help. He was carried to a little rose-colored divan — the very divan on which I had sat correcting my broadcast introduction of him in 1933 — and there he slowly, miserably bled to death. An hour and a half later, still dying, he meekly whimpered: 'Children, you are so good to me.'

Meantime the *Putsch* was fought out and lost in the streets. While the fate of Austria was in the balance, the whole country — because the Vienna station had been wrecked — was being entertained with Viennese waltzes transmitted from Linz. The Munich transmitter, however, announced that Dollfuss had been killed and the government overturned.

After that the hostile broadcasts ceased. It was the end of radio's first 'war.'

XV. GERMAN IS THE SAAR

HOW NAZIS HANDLE A PLEBISCITE

NOT long after this the political efficacy of radio was to be demonstrated in even more convincing if less predatory manner. For months, throughout the summer and autumn of 1934, the broadcasting stations of western Germany aimed their blandishments at the little German territory of the Saar, which was being governed by the League of Nations, but under one of the clauses of the Treaty of Versailles was to decide its future status by means of a plebiscite the following year.

Previous plebiscites under the Treaty — in Slesvig, in Silesia, and in Memel — had been held without benefit of radio. They had gone more or less against Germany. The case of the Saar territory was different; Germany in the course of fifteen years had learned many a lesson, and had acquired a new national status. The Saarlanders, moreover, had lived for fifteen years in close proximity with French officials and had evidently made up their minds to belong to Germany. Nevertheless the Nazis in Germany were not disposed to take any chances; so aside from the other effective methods of political penetration they loosed an evangelical barrage of edification, instruction, and enlightenment upon the Saarlanders, bathing them in a flood of patriotic sounds.

Except for outward appearances the Saar was as Nazified as it would ever be; the prohibition of uniforms and flags simply added fuel to the nostalgic flames and persuaded the good people that they were the victims of an international oppression, as they were being told by their compatriots across the Rhine. It was later admitted, with some pride, by Doctor Josef Goebbels, Nazi minister for 'propaganda and public enlightenment,' that small secret Nazi broadcast transmitters were also functioning in the Saar before the plebiscite; but what with Cologne and Stuttgart and the other great German stations, and what with so many willing ears, this seems rather like painting the lily, unless these transmitters were used for more definitely strategic ends. Neither the League, which governed the Saar, nor France, which ran the technical services, had thought fit to provide local broadcasting, thus throwing the population into the arms of the German propaganda machine. The Strasbourg station, though partly using the German language, made no effort to offset this influence, and Luxemburg, for business reasons, observed the strictest neutrality.

Officially, then, there was no broadcasting of any kind in the Saar. Yet I realized that the January plebiscite would be one of the big stories of the year. The one way to get a radio commentary out of the Saar would be by telephone lines to Paris and London, whence it could be short-waved to America. I applied to the League Commissioner, and at his behest the Frenchmen in charge of the Saar Telephone Administration were willing to permit the use of their lines, if we could provide microphones, amplifiers, and a technical crew to work them. We therefore got a commercial concern, the Standard Electric, to supply the material and an engineer for importation to the region, at our risk. Shipping the gear would have meant confiscation by the customs authorities or at least fatal delay, so we took it along as travellers' luggage, in huge trunks. Crossing the French and Saar borders in the early hours of the morning we had no trouble in convincing the sleepy customs officials that the goods were 'official,' being consigned to the P.T.T. (Posts and Telegraphs), without saying for which. It was a case of 'white' smuggling, but it had to be done. Our engineer, a hefty Briton who had been a top-sergeant in the World War but spoke no word of French, was an impressive and formidable-looking guardian of the precious goods.

GEOFFREY KNOX'S 'TERROR'

Saarbrücken was in turmoil when we arrived. The population was in a state of suppressed excitement, and the atmosphere was tense. Evergreens and swastikas were everywhere. Any house that did not show its patriotic sentiment was a potential target for the violence that officials expected at any moment to break out. They, and especially the French, were as nervous as witches; the Germans, on the other hand, though living in perfect peace under the benevolent and neutral government of the League commissioner, an upright Scotsman named Geoffrey Knox, had hypnotized themselves into believing that they were sorely oppressed by the 'Knox terror' (pronounced 'K-nucks terrohr'). Luckily for us, however, the League had entrusted the military occupation to neutrals, mostly British, and khaki-clad Tommies were to be seen everywhere, providing the one element of stability.

The broadcast had been arranged to take place at an improvised studio — the furnished flat of the American member of the plebiscite committee, Miss Sarah Wambaugh, in a residential district on the Saar River. Her presence was our greatest piece of luck, and saved the whole enterprise. The B.B.C., who also wanted to broadcast from the region but had no facilities of their own, made common cause with us, and that increased our staff by two. Once we got our equipment transported to the 'studio' (no simple matter, with nothing on wheels available and even taxis scarce) we thought we were 'set,' and while I fell asleep, exhausted from the all-night journey, my top-sergeant engineer disappeared in the crowded town. Worried about his safety, I was about to send out an S.O.S. when he wandered in, late at night, having made whoopee with Tommies who had recognized a pal.

Meantime my troubles had started. The French official who had promised the telephone lines calmly denied all knowledge of the affair, and said that the permission of the

Department of the Interior was necessary. This sent me scurrying back and forth all next morning between the Government and Telephone Buildings — at opposite ends of town — in a frantic attempt to get action. Knox, the High Commissioner, who had sanctioned the broadcast in the first place, was invisible. The department head (a German) was absent in a mysterious conference somewhere, while long queues of citizens clogged up the passages, trying to get passes or certificates of origin (45,000 former Saarlanders came into the town from across the border to vote). The plebiscite was to be held the next day, and our first broadcast was scheduled for that evening. But next day was a Sunday; miles of telephone lines had to be laid, and there might be no workmen available. Hours — even minutes — counted. I had visions of our broadcast melting, like the snow in the streets, into mush.

A stern feminine secretary refused to admit me and hear my case, since the *Herr Minister* was 'unreachable.' The uniformed watchdog outside shrugged his shoulders. In desperation I sat down and wrote the lady what was virtually a love-letter, in my most poetic German — an appeal that must have melted her heart, or, more likely, made her laugh.

It did the trick. Violating instructions not to disturb the *Herr Minister* on any circumstances, she got him on the telephone. Orders began to be given, down and down the line, till they reached our forgetful French friend at the telephone department, who was suffering from jangled nerves. From his window this petty tyrant in an occupied country could see hordes of stalwart Nazis arriving on every train; if the plebiscite went as everyone expected, a French official's life wouldn't be worth two *Heils* — or so he thought. In this jittery state it was difficult for him to remember anything, and even more difficult to handle a German engineering crew.

Not till noon next day, within six hours of the first broadcast, did a couple of jolly-faced German linesmen appear at Miss Wambaugh's flat, with coils of wire and the familiar telephone tackle. My top-sergeant shot a mouthful of rich

Cockney at them by way of instructions, to which they answered '*Ja, ja.*' Years of listening to orders in a foreign language had accustomed them to cheerful acquiescence, whatever was said. I had the greatest misgivings, but somehow the technicans of different nations soon find the magic key of understanding. By midafternoon the studio had been rigged and our British engineer was calling gadgets by their German names, pronounced as in Bromley or Bow.

HITLER DECREES SILENCE

All that day the voting went on, in schoolhouses, assembly rooms, and municipal buildings. Five hundred and twenty-eight thousand Saarlanders, men and women, trudged through slush and snow; over ninety per cent of them cast their vote for Hitler's Third Reich, while only a miserable 8.87 per cent dared to vote for the continuance of League government. France didn't get even a decent handful of votes (0.44 per cent). Absolute order was maintained; the voting machinery was as perfect and fraud-proof as anything can be. Englishmen, Dutchmen, Americans — solid citizens of all neutral countries — acted as watchers and tellers, the most complete example of international collaboration in a critical task I had ever seen. I hustled from polling place to polling place to see how it worked. Old and young, rich and poor, male and female — one by one they got their ballots, disappeared silently in the booth to make their cross, and as silently walked off — mouths tightly shut — in obedience to orders broadcast from distant Berlin. Feeble old people tottered up the steps, helped by Red Cross nurses stationed at every entrance; invalids were rolled in on wheeled chairs — not a German able to crawl stayed indoors that day. The vote was ninety-eight per cent of the electorate — probably an all-time record.

The result was a foregone conclusion, but the extent of Hitler's victory was a surprise; and the story was full of human interest. The snowclad, spired city astride the lovely river made a fascinating picture. Frederick Voigt, the diplomatic correspondent of the *Manchester Guardian*, described it for the English, I for the American audience; Miss Wambaugh, world authority on plebiscites, explained the technical procedure. Both broadcasts were successful. Elated, we went forth to gather more atmosphere for the next day's stint.

Returns were not to be declared till the day after that, but the public counting of votes conducted by men of many nationalities made a story. Then there was a threat of violence to Separatists and Socialists; the leaders of the anti-Nazi parties were marked men; some had already fled. Afraid that the electricity supply might be cut off, we scoured the garages of the town for batteries that might supply sufficient emergency 'juice.' The top-sergeant was in his element, presiding over rows of accumulators and a system of alternate switches for all eventualities.

Once more we assembled in the 'studio,' ready to perform. Ralph Murray, a handsome young B.B.C. news-caster speaking Oxford English, excellent Viennese German, and Swiss boarding-school French, manned the control circuit and shouted his 'Hello's' to reach the telephone exchange and ask to have the broadcast channel set up. No answer came. He shouted and shouted, and still no answer came. We tried the private telephone, but the 'international' operators of the day before were gone, and no line to Paris and London was on tap. We phoned around town to locate officials: our French friends had left; their German deputies were celebrating the victory in places unknown. The clock ticked on to zero hour, our broadcast time elapsed. We knew that at the other end, in London, people were likewise shouting 'Hello!' trying to reach us; and here we were, with our own batteries, our own crew, bursting with information and nothing but a dead 'mike.' We went home crushed.

Next day the results were to be announced. I awoke to the sound of church bells and human voices singing in harmony. It was the most extraordinary sound I had ever heard. Unseen thousands, afar off, singing, singing, singing without stop, a wave of sound rising and falling as new groups, now near now far, joined in. It was the Saarland song, being sung that day by uncounted multitudes on both sides of the Rhine; and it went on all day, almost without break, like continuous round.

> 'German is the Saar,
> German evermore!
> And German is our River's shore —
> My Fathers' Land.'

Windows were thrown open and the same song issued from loud-speakers, tuned to stations across the Rhine; the bells of Cologne Cathedral, of churches all over the land, mixed into this strange kaleidoscope of sound; it was the German people rejoicing over their first triumph since Versailles.

The streets were alive with people, for a national holiday had been declared. Enormous flags burst from the windows of every house; the town was a sea of waving scarlet set against a background of snow. There were parades and parades, triple shouts of 'Heil!' as group met group. Here was a sound-picture such as had never been and perhaps would never be again: it was the picture I wanted to convey to listeners across the sea. But would our circuits work this time? Once again there had to be pilgrimages of protest to Government and Telephone Department.

A FRENCHMAN GETS DISGUSTED

This time, despite the universal whoopee, we reached the top. The French telephone chief and *de facto* Postmaster-General of the Saar, was in a curiously nostalgic mood. A middle-aged, grizzly-moustached Parisian of easy-going pre-war mentality, he had spent fifteen years bossing German civil servants in this artificial miniature state. He had done his job, but had done it without learning German in all those years — a triumph of French culture among the 'bar-

barians.' Now, within days of his inevitable abdication, the vision of a peaceful apéritif on the Boulevard des Capucines began to mollify his inward rage:

'*Quinze ans!*' he cried. '*Quinze ans dans ce sal pays! C'est beaucoup, vous savez, pour un Parisien.*' Fifteen years of bother with the 'boches,' and now he would go home to his slippers and his good French food. 'When I came here, how they all professed to love the French! How they came to me, saying their great-great-grandfather had fought under the Emperor Napoleon: anything to get promotion. And now — now I, who have helped them, been a father to them for years, no longer exist. They're going to be their own bosses in their own fatherland, they say, and everything's going to be fine!

'*Mais!*' he cried, holding up a wagging forefinger. '*Écoutez!* I'm coming back. In two years I'm coming back on a visit, and I'm going to ask these chaps: "*Eh bien? Comment ça va?* How do you like your 'freedom' now?" They'll learn a thing or two after standing at attention and marching and shouting *Heil* while there's not enough to eat. They'll find out how well off they were when *I* was here!'

We sympathized with him, and he promised to help. The boys of the telephone service, he explained, had been out celebrating last night, but they'd be on the job tonight. Whether they'd be sober was another question, for the beer saloons and *Kneipen* were doing a roaring trade.

HEIL! HEIL! HEIL!

We went into one of these emporia of liquid patriotism, one which was also the headquarters of the secret S.A. troop. At last these brownshirts would be able to cut loose; hitherto they had been kept quiet by the 'K-nucks terrohr.' Now they'd show these Reds to whom the country belonged. The beer flowed freely, washing down dozens of the local breed of hot dogs. The atmosphere was thick with smoke, the noise of celebration deafening. A little girl of five was being taught the Nazi salute. We explained to the troop leader that we were broadcasting to England and America, and wanted to be sure to catch the atmosphere of the Big Day. Would there be celebrations in the vicinity of our studio tonight?

Well, they'd see to it. In fact there was a beer hall just down the street, where a detachment would meet, and they would time their homeward march to pass our house while the broadcast was on. We compared watches, and sealed the bargain with another pint. The time of the broadcast arrived; the town went on Carnaval. Festoons of multi-colored lights turned the streets into fairyland. Church bells rang and searchlights swept the river; bands of singing celebrants marched up and down, interspersing their songs with '*Heil! Heil! Heil!*'

Again we were all set, but just as luck would have it there was a lull in our remote part of town. I started to talk; Murray opened the window — no sign of the revellers. Then, remembering the Nazi's beer saloon, he leapt down-stairs, raced down the street, stormed into the celebration to ask, in the richest South-German dialect ever spoken by an English Public School man, why in blazes they weren't marching home as agreed? Being blond and tall, more Aryan-looking than the native 'Aryans,' he got his orders obeyed by the men and — especially — the women. The crowd poured out into the street and marched past our windows singing and yelling as only Nazis can, just five minutes before our time was up.

We shouted down to them to sing the Saarland song, opened our windows wide, and placed a microphone on the windowsill. And so we gave America — and England — an earful of patriotic singing and '*heil*-ing' as background to the plebiscite returns. When it was all over we too felt like celebrating, for we had transmitted the first plebiscite ever broadcast, and the first program from a place that had never been on the air. By the skin of our teeth.

XVI. A MIKESIDE SEAT FOR THE WAR

FLOYD GIBBONS: FIRST WAR BROADCASTER

THE human tragicomedy enacted in Europe through the spring and summer of 1935 will live as one of the most curious ironies of modern history. Two months after the successful Saar plebiscite, universally hailed as a great League achievement, Germany began officially to rearm. On Easter Day five Roman Catholic cardinals — American, Irish, French, Austrian, Italian — joined in a transoceanic broadcast for world peace. In June, eleven and a half million people in Great Britain voluntarily voted against war on Lord Cecil's famous Peace Ballot, and over ten millions of them voted for sanctions, thus unwittingly helping to bring Great Britain and Italy to the verge of war.

In July and August the British fleet assembled in the Mediterranean in unprecedented strength, while Mussolini was massing troops in Eritrea and in Libya. In September the war clouds gathered in Geneva and drifted over most of Europe, while further east the guns were actually beginning to growl. The Empress Menen of Ethiopia broadcast a pathetic appeal to the women of the world from the little station outside Addis Ababa, and on October 2 the Duce roared his warlike challenge from the balcony of the Palazzo Venezia in Rome, while baffled humanity listened at its loud-speakers in three continents. Then the storm broke in full force over the hapless people of Abyssinia, and since then the world has not known a single peaceful month.

Radio was to bring these hideous events closer to peaceful people's homes than they had ever been brought before, for competitive radio cannot ignore the morbid demands of its listeners; and while people moralize about war they listen as eagerly as ever to tales of strife. The radio commentator, in uniform and gas-mask, may well become a permanent adjunct of future wars, although his activity will be even more restricted than that of the newspaper correspondent, because his reports can be picked up by the enemy.

The first attempt in radio history to convey war news plus war atmosphere direct from the scene of conflict must be credited to Floyd Gibbons, veteran war correspondent, who transmitted a commentary from the Manchurian war zone in January, 1932, for the N.B.C., which was punctuated by the sound of Japanese big guns, much to the delight of the accommodating Japs. Now, in Ethiopia, this high-speed, battle-scarred radio newshawk was once again in the field, beating his nearest competitor (John T. Whitaker, acting on my behalf) by three days. I heard him give a graphic account of Italian road-building operations near the Eritrean frontier which, full of breathless excitement, was an amazing performance, considering that it took place at an altitude of six thousand feet above the sea.

Whitaker, however, had already surveyed the Italian war zone from the air a month before and had given a gripping account of it to our listeners from Rome, where I bade him Godspeed on his perilous journey across the Mediterranean, up the Nile, and over the mountains of Ethiopia into Asmara, undertaken under the auspices of the *New York Herald-Tribune*. Young, impetuous, and adventurous, he was the first foreign correspondent to reach the war zone, and was privileged to survey it by mule-back, camel-back, motor-car and an aeroplane piloted by Mussolini's son-in-law, young Count Ciano, whom he described as a daredevil youth and 'one of the most likeable men' he had ever known. 'He used to fly me out over the Red Sea and drop petrol tins so that we could have target practice with machine guns.' [1] After making his report from Rome late in September, Whitaker was back in Asmara on October 25 to transmit a description of the operations, and the obliging Count Ciano broadcast some

[1] See John T. Whitaker, *Fear Came on Europe*, London, 1937.

rather obvious propaganda both for Gibbons and for Whitaker. It was short-waved to Rome and retransmitted to America, but owing to static the results were none too good.

HAILE SELASSIE CALLING

Meantime, however, the Abyssinians' little short-wave station near Addis Ababa — at an altitude of some nine thousand feet — operating on the ridiculously low power of one kilowatt, had made itself heard throughout the western world. Here was a romance of engineering, indeed. The Italians, who years ago built this station for the Abyssinians merely as a commercial telegraph terminus, little suspected that it would one day be used against them by their dusky enemies. It had no speech panel and no speech-input amplifier, though for some remote contingency there was an old-fashioned carbon microphone lying about. With this meagre equipment a Swedish engineer named Ernst Hammar, employed as director of communications by Emperor Haile Selassie, managed to rig up something that could actually make itself heard, first in London and then in New York. Early in the conflict the engineers of the Radio Corporation of America tried to get into contact with Hammar, whose name — discovered by my friend Max Jordan working at Geneva for the N.B.C. — proved the ethereal password to the Ethiopian stronghold. After picking up a talk by Doctor Malaku Bayan, a nephew of Haile Selassie, early in September, and the Empress's appeal three days later, the R.C.A. managed to present the Emperor himself in their 'Magic Key' program on September 13, after which they made Abyssinian facilities available to American broadcasters in general.

The first white commentator to report from the station was Robinson McLean, correspondent of the Toronto *Evening Telegram*, who spoke for Columbia three days after the Emperor; but like that remarkable potentate, he was only partially heard. Nevertheless the account of conditions, apparently uncensored, was as graphic as it was revealing, and I cannot resist the temptation of reproducing what I, sitting at an ordinary set in London, and others sitting at their sets all over America, heard on October 16, 1935.

'On the plains outside of Addis Ababa hundreds of *tukuls* are pitched when the feudal dukes of Ethiopia gather to their Emperor. Right now, two miles from this radio station, there are thirty-five thousand men under the Dejasmatch of Kambata Province. His men are the toughest babies you would ever want to see. Though most of them have rifles, even the ones with only spears are not the sort of men you would like to meet on a dark night on a lonely African hilltop.

'Tomorrow fifty thousand more brown warriors will pace through the streets of Addis Ababa, singing their war songs. They are the men of Dejasmatch Gabre Mariam of Walago Province, fifteen days' ride from Addis Ababa, and this afternoon the Minister of War of Ethiopia put on four European uniforms and drove around the city. Soon he will be headed for the front with his men — two hundred and fifty thousand of them. . . . So, tomorrow morning when thousands of brown-faced men gather at the foot of the Throne of Judgment in the palace in Addis Ababa, in front of the tired little Emperor, and sing their war songs, it will be impressive. To see men of sixty wearing spears and swords and guns and acting out in pantomime the way in which they will kill their enemies is something that sometimes makes little cold shivers run up and down your spine. And you don't feel much better when you learn that the Government has ordered all liquor stores closed to prevent any accident to the newspapermen.

'The warriors yell their hate at us whenever they pass us in the street. Personally, I don't blame them. So far, all the whitefaces have brought to Ethiopia is the sewing machine, the radio station, the phonograph, and a war, although they don't call it a war — as yet. So that when someone — we will say, for example, Private Waldo Mariam from Kambata — shakes his spear in my face because civilization wouldn't give him a gun, and yells that he would like to break me up and feed me to the birds, I don't blame Private Waldo Mariam. On the other hand, Private Waldo Mariam won't hurt me if I duck back when he shakes his spear. He just laughs all over his big brown face and then goes on singing his song — the war song of Ethiopia. It goes something like this: "*Ee ya saparack! Ee ya saparack! Asst da lambarack!*" — meaning "Break it up and feed it to the birds!" That is the closest I can come to the words. It doesn't sound like much when I sing it, but when you hear seventy-five thousand men pouring out their voices in their howl of hate, it makes you think that perhaps the Italians are not going to have the pushover they expected.

'Of course it's just a little tin-pot kingdom, lost in the African mountains. Of course it's not a real war, because these brown men haven't got tanks and airplanes and because nobody has declared war. Of course, getting excited over a little Italian skirmish in the African mountains is rather childish. But I want to tell you a story about a newspaper correspondent.

'He had gone down into the Ogaden Desert and written that Italy was going to have a tough time battling across the burning sands and through the malaria-filled swamps. His newspaper, after a few days, sent him back a cable telling him that their readers, who had seen a real war, did not share his excitement. Maybe it isn't real war, but the forts he visited had been bombed. Maybe it isn't a real war, but when he got that cable from his office he was in hospital with malaria, and ten days ago he died.

'So maybe it's not a real war, and maybe you will pardon me for my childish excitement about it. But so far as I can see, it doesn't really matter much when men, women, and children die whether they are killed in a real war or merely a glorious little expedition to bring civilization to a savage tin-pot kingdom lost in the African hills. Maybe it's not a real war, but this may be the last broadcast from Ethiopia. I wouldn't want to have the job the operator of this station has, and wake up wondering each morning whether or not civilization was going to explode on the roof.'

While the quality of the transmissions, owing to the poor

Emperor Hailie Selassie's address to America, seventy-five hundred miles away. With him are Josef Israels II and the Negus' youngest son

equipment, was imperfect, the sensational nature of these broadcasts made people strain their ears for every word.

Conditions were absurdly difficult. There was no 'talk-back' arrangement, of course, no radio telephone, and instructions had to be given by radiograms, which would sometimes arrive too late. A broadcast might begin several minutes late or early, and night after night I would sit at a receiver in London, anxiously waiting for the words to come through over the noisy carrier-wave. But Abyssinian clocks rarely corresponded with ours; probably they reacted to atmospheric conditions at excessive altitudes. And there were no means of checking with Greenwich or New York.

The problem of quality was finally solved by getting the co-operation of the Paramount news-reel people, who eventually sent their own up-to-date equipment to Addis Ababa. Josef Israels 2nd had been placed in charge of our interests, while McLean was off somewhere trying to rescue his mule caravan in the wilds of Tigré Province; and when Haile Selassie was about to leave for the front, Israels induced him to make a direct talk to the American people in which he appealed to them 'unofficially' to boycott the aggressor. With the help of Paramount's dynamic microphone, the ingenious engineer, Hammar, managed to transmit the Emperor's speech (in Amharic) and Israels's translation with such excellent quality that they arrived in New York, seventy-five hundred miles away, without a blemish, and were heard perfectly throughout America. This was later followed by a speech, in good English, from the Emperor's son, the Crown Prince, and further commentaries from Israels and McLean, which gave American listeners a sense of the more and more hard-pressed Abyssinian people and their ultimate doom. The Addis Ababa broadcasts altogether covered a period of two months; thanks to Israels, more than anyone else, they were a landmark in transatlantic broadcasting.

THE IMPERIAL BAND ON THE RUN

By way of comic relief to their otherwise unrelieved gloom, Israels managed to organize two concerts by Ethiopian musicians with native instruments, and the 'Imperial Guards Band' playing European martial music by ear. His account of the adventure is worthy of perpetuation. Ethiopian musicians were modest as to financial emolument, but they required generous libations of the native brandy called *tej* to help them face an audience, seen or unseen. The amateur extras, being more cultivated, needed whiskey. Both beverages were provided and a first-class ensemble turned up at Israels's hotel early in the evening, to be entertained and then transported six miles to the outlying station — for rehearsal and the midnight broadcast (5 P.M. in New York).

As they seemed unresponsive in the Europeanized surroundings of the hotel rooms, they were invited to make themselves comfortable on the hotel lawn, where a caravan had pitched a large tent. Here they squatted, tuned up their instruments, took plenty of *tej*, and were soon singing their interminable sagas of love and war and heroism that make up the native repertoire by the light of a single candle. According to European ideas they were making the night hideous with noise. Suddenly, while Israels was at dinner, the native police arrived and started to arrest the musicians. It was after curfew, when the natives were to be indoors; and they had no permits to break the regulations of martial law.

The radio man, warned, rushed out; it was too late. The *balambaras* ordered a bâton charge, and the frightened musicians scurried to the four winds. By the time matters could be explained to the *balambaras*, the sixteen musicians had fled to sixteen parts of the scattered town. Finally, an appeal to the Emperor's chief aide resulted in an order to the police to round them up. Not till eleven o'clock that night did the official cars begin to arrive, bearing one or two musicians at a time, still frightened and in need of further applications of strong spirits. Three quarters of an hour before the broadcast the cavalcade started for the station, bumping over deserted roads and frightening hyenas and owls from their midnight repasts...

After a twenty-minute rehearsal under the native conductor, the musicians were properly placed around the floor of the little workshop with the microphone. The testing calls and English announcements elicited loud guffaws, and silence was with difficulty restored. The show started at last, but each piece had to be forcibly suppressed when the time was up, as Ethiopian musicians, once started, never want to stop. When the 'program' was over they were just warming up, and went on and on, drifting into the generator room and continuing their weird entertainment against the incongruous background of motors, radio tubes, amplifiers, and control panels — playing, singing and dancing, black men and women, in ever wilder convolutions, through to the early hours of the morning. Finally the cavalcade started back through the deserted streets of Addis Ababa, past startled sentries and packs of roaming dogs, under the tremendously brilliant stars of the equatorial sky.

After two months of broadcasting from Eritrea and Ethiopia, American listeners were tired of the subject. 'Consider we have exhausted broadcastable material,' wired my New York office, and we quit. The rainy season set in and held up the Italian steam roller for a while. Then, in February, it thundered on. In April the advance on Addis Ababa began; Emperor Haile Selassie fled, first to Jerusalem, then to Geneva, whence in the following June — eight months after the war began in earnest — we broadcast his pathetic appeal against the removal of sanctions. Seven weeks earlier, Mussolini, once again addressing a full-throated crowd on the Piazza Venezia, had proclaimed tiny King Victor Emanuel Emperor of little Haile Selassie's empire...

One evening the following winter, while we were rushing in and out of Broadcasting House reporting on the abdication crisis, I almost bumped into a small, dark-complexioned, bearded man of arresting countenance, very finely chiselled features, and high forehead, wearing a long black cape with a silver clasp. It was Haile Selassie I, Emperor of Ethiopia, King of Kings, Lion of Judah, etc., etc., who had just broadcast an appeal to America for funds for destitute Abyssinians. He was attended by one young Ethiopian and drove off in a common taxi, through the murky London night.

IN THE SPANISH FIRING LINE

Within a few weeks of Haile Selassie's personal appeal before the League of Nations Assembly, when Italian journalists distinguished themselves by hooting and whistling, Hell broke loose in Spain. Franco's troops, in their first formidable offensive, were being held at bay near San Sebastian by ragged militiamen and undisciplined miners from Asturias, who were expert at throwing sticks of dynamite. Old men, women, and children were streaming across the frontier into France, welcomed on the French side of the international bridge by cheering crowds of Basques and Frenchmen of the newly constituted Popular Front. Immersed in the — for America — far more important intricacies of broadcasting the Olympic Games, I sent my Paris man, Didier van Ackère, scurrying down to refugee-crowded Hendaye, where he managed to interview a few of them before the microphone, thus starting the second series of war broadcasts within considerably less than a year.

By the grace of geography and the friendly French officials it was possible, for the first time, to report a war actually in progress from the safe vantage-ground of neutral territory. As luck would have it, one of Columbia's most experienced political commentators, H. V. Kaltenborn, a microphone veteran with an astonishingly fluent technique, was available, and a few days after the initial Hendaye broadcast he made his headquarters in the little French town, dashing now

into loyal, now into insurgent, territory for eye-witness
material and interviews with the leaders of the most brutal of
all civil wars.

As the battle-front approached the frontier town of Irun
he was able to observe, from the roof of an advantageously
placed hotel, the actual progress of the fighting, even while
speaking to the peaceful millions at home. Here was an
unprecedented chance for the radio reporter — literally an
armchair view of the war. Speaking from his rooftop,
Kaltenborn reported that two Englishmen had their tea while
watching the bombardment that afternoon. The idea of
broadcasting a 'running commentary' on the cruelest kind
of war, just as you do with a football game, was grotesque
but perfectly feasible, though the opportunity is not very
likely to occur again. Kaltenborn and his successor kept it
up for five weeks, with daily fifteen-minute reports at the
most critical time. He was able to describe the bombardment
of Fort Guadalupe by two insurgent men-of-war, while it was
in progress, and to report attack and counterattack near the
frontier to the sinister sound effects of machine-gun fire and
the whirring of fighting aeroplanes.

'We who report the battle,' Americans from New York to
San Francisco could hear, 'sit in plain view of both forces on
the terrace of a little village café some hundred yards across
the valley from the combatants. It is so real and yet so
fantastic that it seems like a battle set up for the moving
pictures.'

And again: 'In a moment or two, when the machine gun
which has been barking intermittently all evening sounds
again, I will stop talking for a moment in order that you
may get something of the sound of this civil war as it con-
tinues through the night. This farm is the one most near to
the fighting scene... located some three hundred yards
from the lines where rebels and government soldiers are
fighting it out tonight. [Sound of rifle fire.] Those are
isolated shots which are being exchanged by the front-line
sentinels on both sides.'

'We happen to be straight in the line of fire. Fortunately
for us the bullets are going high. Four times this afternoon,

while we were waiting for an opportunity to link up with New York our wires were cut. And now finally we have put the radio machinery inside of a house and I'm standing around the corner of the house with the microphone in the open, but with a good thick mortar wall between me and the bullets that are constantly whizzing past.'

And so it went on, while the slow and bloody tragedy was being enacted to its end. Irun fell on September 4, three days before the last talk from Hendaye.

MADRID BROADCASTS FROM A BOMB-PROOF CELLAR

Soon after this, Franco's Moors were fighting their way through the Guadalajara mountain passes and threatening the plain of Madrid. Long before, almost simultaneously with Hendaye, we started operations in the capital. Conditions there were indescribable, with a provisional government trying to organize an army out of revolutionary elements bent on hunting down the enemy within the gates rather than obeying military leaders charged with the country's defence. No one knew where anybody stood, and the people on whom we tried to rely — wearing bourgeois clothes — were in constant danger of their lives.

Telegraph and telephone were disorganized; censorship was brutally and none too discriminatingly enforced. On July 28 — long before the Madrid offensive began — we managed to transmit, from EAQ, the only powerful short-wave station in Spain, a talk by Ogier Preteceille, a Spanish journalist in British employ, who had the confidence of the Defense Junta and the trade unions. Señor Preteceille gave a talk on the conflict, but it had been so severely censored that its only value lay in the fact that it actually came out of embattled Madrid. Getting a direct broadcast at all was indeed an achievement, as can be judged from the fact that no one else duplicated it till over a month later, when the intrepid Floyd Gibbons managed to get himself heard.

Here is just one aspect of the tragic inefficiency imposed by circumstances on a revolutionary leadership relying on the untutored elements of the population. Distrust of the intellectual, hostility to the middle class, suspicion of the foreigner, all combine to paralyze potential instruments of success. Throughout the two first years the Government had the advantage in the ether; it had the most powerful medium-wave broadcasting stations, at Madrid and Barcelona; it had the only efficient short-wave station at Aranjuez near Madrid. The insurgents had only lesser stations, chiefly at Saragossa and Seville, and — evidently in expectation of capturing EAQ — had not thought it worth while to build a short-wave station which could reach distant and oversea lands.

Yet the Madrid authorities, while using every spare minute to broadcast inspired 'bulletins' (which, true or untrue, are taken with a large grain of salt), put every possible obstacle in the way of neutral reports by friendly foreigners. Such reports, especially at the time of Madrid's savage bombardment, would have turned a great deal of sympathy in the right direction; but an inefficient and unimaginative censorship make it impossible for the outside world to get a reliable account of events. Since radio reporters, like journalists, would obviously resort to 'deferred' eye-witness accounts, given over neutral channels outside Spain, the only result was that such reports, entirely beyond the Government's control, lacked the dramatic quality which might arouse more than casual interest.

On both sides the broadcast stations were commandeered by the authorities for propaganda purposes, while each side did its best to 'jam' the other, with minor success. The second Madrid station, for instance, tuned its own transmissions to the hostile wave-length of Seville, yet the fantastic broadcasts of the notorious General Queipo de Llano, of the southern rebel army, were picked up almost anywhere, except in Madrid, without any trouble.

As the insurgent armies closed in on Madrid, our problem became more difficult. The authorities were, if anything, both more inflexible and more dilatory: by the time a broadcast could be written, censored, and the lines cleared for transmission, it would be out of date. The studio building, within easy range of bombing planes, became a dangerous place; the station itself was within six to eight miles of the front, and was probably spared only because the insurgents expected to make use of it later. Finally, the lives of the journalists and potential broadcasters were in constant peril. During the siege of Madrid they worked in the Telefónica, the central telegraph exchange, which is the loftiest building in Spain. It was struck by shells again and again, and bombs fell all around it. Every morning they would drive to the front, roam perilously among indistinguishable battle lines, and return in the evening to sleep in their embassies. Lester Ziffren, of the United Press, records how three journalists and two diplomats were captured in one week and he himself narrowly escaped being taken, having been warned by a lone and straggling militiaman that he was walking into enemy lines.[1] No less than six foreign journalists were killed in Spain, and several were wounded.

Yet I managed to speak with Lester Ziffren by telephone from London, thanks to the patience and help of the American diplomatic staffs in both cities, and it was he who finally broadcast for us, late in December, when the city was under fierce bombardment. To escape a terrific aerial attack such as had taken place the previous night, the broadcast had to be made from a bomb-proof cellar whose locality could not be revealed.

When Ziffren left Madrid, his place was taken by Philip Jordan of the London *News Chronicle*, who tried again and again to broadcast to America from the cellar studio, only to find that the technical quality of the transmissions did not satisfy the engineers in New York. To me, monitoring the tests from London, they were perfectly intelligible; what spoiled them for America I am not able to say.

On the other hand, not only Philip Jordan but Vernon Bartlett and Jay Allen were able to give graphic and sometimes startling accounts of conditions in Spain after personal observation, immediately after they reached the safety of

[1] See *Political Opinion Quarterly*, Princeton, New Jersey, 1937.

Paris, London, or New York. And Bartlett's story of the Government's attack on the Alcazar is something he would probably not have been allowed to broadcast from Madrid:

'It certainly is an odd war. The first time I went to Toledo, while the Alcazar was being besieged, I met a girl with a lot of hand grenades hung around her belt. She took me, much against my will, through two smouldering houses and up a steep bank into the garden of Alcazar. There was only a wall between us and the followers of General Franco, who were being besieged inside. She was a Communist and talked to me a lot about Karl Marx. I protested she had never read anything that gentleman had written. She just lugged a hand grenade over the wall and came back to tell me that, if I looked on such and such a page of the Spanish translation, I should find such and such a statement. Then she threw another hand grenade, then she talked about Karl Marx again. This went on until, in her excitement about politics, one of her grenades came down on our side of the wall. After which I decided I wasn't really very interested in Karl Marx and left, rather in a hurry.'

And that may be one explanation why the Government was not winning the war in 1936.

Broadcasting has become an important feature of war; the radio reporter, as I remarked at the beginning of this chapter, has evidently come to stay. At the time of writing the predominating scene of the gradually spreading Second World War is China, and already the broadcasting organizations have been engaged in jockeying for vantage-points from which to describe the horrors to their listeners. Short-wave transmitters may be set up near battlefields, where the authorities with cynical complacency will in all probability grant the necessary privilege to broadcast the operations.

What, we may ask, is the value of all this? Will people hearing first-hand accounts of brutal conflict, with the noises of battle for realistic effect, grasp the real horror and so have their sensibilities roused against war? Or will war, benefiting by this new instrument, thrive on the added publicity, as other 'human' manifestations do? No description can equal the realities of organized human slaughter, and it does not seem to me that greater familiarity with it will breed anything but a dangerous contempt.

With the actual use of radio in war we are not here concerned, except to point out that, as in all other methods of expression and communication, any remaining radio freedom in the warring country is immediately suppressed.

XVII. TEN NIGHTS THAT SHOOK
THE ETHER

THE ROYAL ROMANCE

IN THE summer of 1936, when rival forces were spreading carnage and terror through Northern Spain, when the first miserable contingents of refugees were pouring into France, and frightened people everywhere saw rising before them the spectre of another European holocaust, two good-looking, apparently care-free people in fashionable sports attire were romping in the sunshine of the Adriatic Sea. One of them was the new King of England and the other an American woman, just under middle age, whose name was being whispered all over Europe, while her picture was prominently displayed in the international press. Famous Paris dressmakers competed for the privilege of preparing their latest masterpieces for her, and advance copies of their designs were being syndicated to Sunday supplements for the edification of American girls.

It was known in the fashionable circles and newspaper offices of European capitals that Mrs. Ernest Simpson of Baltimore had been the King's favorite for some time. Although a divorcée, she had 'officially' dined at Buckingham Palace — a radical break with the rigid rules of the British Court under King George V, and a virtual affront to the widowed Queen Mary, matriarch of the British royal family. To Europeans this seemed to indicate that the rigidly Victorian days — so incompatible with the freer post-war moral concepts — were over. To Americans, more naïve and more imaginative, it opened up romantic vistas that brought far-away looks into the eyes of shop-girls and débutantes, and heavy returns to popular newspapers in search of additional circulation.

The public in general passed over this seemingly trivial subject to the more diverting events on the international scene — such as the Olympic Games at Berlin, which were being broadcast throughout the world for the first time in their history, and the preparations for the Inter-American Conference, which was expected to fill the American front pages for many weeks of the following fall. Nevertheless, one or two of the pictures which made their way into the European papers, showing a radiantly happy couple rowing ashore from their luxurious chartered yacht, or disembarking hand in hand, gave thinking people a jolt.

In Great Britain, however, none of this aroused any general attention, for the simple reason that matters concerning the royal family are sacrosanct and not susceptible of the usual treatment by the press — a voluntary censorship maintained in the interest of royal prestige, which is considered to be a national asset and a thing above party politics and controversy. Moreover, in this particular case the entire British press had imposed silence upon itself by virtue of a decision of the Newspaper Proprietors' Association, a powerful body controlling all the organs of printed publicity in Great Britain. Thus a grotesque situation was brought about: the press of the United States and any country that might be interested could publish all the details of the incipient 'royal romance,' while the one country most concerned was kept in utter ignorance of the story that was being built up. American papers containing references to the affair arrived in England with pages removed or passages blacked out by distributors who obeyed the N.P.A. ban. No broadcasting organizations in the British Isles or the European Continent so much as mentioned the matter in their spoken news; nor was it possible, in the circumstances, for any American radio reporter to mention it in any transatlantic broadcast.

About the middle of October the story had developed to a point where scandal in high places was hinted at, and British politicians and statesmen — especially the Prime Minister —

were being bombarded with letters enclosing cuttings from American papers and magazines. William Randolph Hearst, always more adventurous than his rivals, came out with the startling story that the King contemplated marriage with Mrs. Simpson — a lady still married to another man.

Thus it happened that the news of Mrs. Simpson's application for divorce, in the middle of October, came as a bombshell, especially to those who knew what had gone before. The English papers printed no details, and when a decree *nisi* was granted on October 27, the bare announcement of it in the legal columns escaped the casual reader's notice. Once again the B.B.C.'s news department ignored the occurrence, as a matter of course, for no divorce is ever mentioned over the British radio, which takes careful account of its juvenile listeners.

But the stream of letters and cuttings sent to government people and members of Parliament from abroad increased, reaching flood tide in early November. An apparently innocent question asked in Parliament about the 'scrutiny' of publications imported from the United States was ambiguously answered by the President of the Board of Trade; but a supplementary question from that fiery atom, Miss Ellen Wilkinson, M.P. for Jarrow, startled the usually complacent House. 'What is this thing,' Miss Wilkinson asked, 'that the British public are not allowed to see?'

Still the newspaper ban continued to operate, and the general public dismissed the matter from its mind. Even the sophisticated Londoners contemplated nothing more than a discreet court affair, such as the histories of all monarchies have recorded through the ages. To continental Europeans, used to royal intrigues, and also to morganatic marriages, the matter even in its worst aspects had no political importance.

'NOT A MATTER FOR BROADCASTING'

If, in the meantime, momentous conversations were taking place behind the scenes, no one in either England or America was aware of these portentous developments. The world had plenty of other things to think about: Italy and Germany were defying the League and the Covenant; the three Kings of Scandinavia were declaring their solidarity and appealing for European peace; President Roosevelt was on his way to South America to open the great conference that was to establish permanent peace in the western hemisphere. He arrived in Buenos Aires on November 30. My New York office was cabling me to 'hold down' on European material, as all available foreign broadcasting periods would be blanketed by South American reports.

On the day of the opening of the Inter-American Conference, another and very different conference was taking place in Bradford, in the English midlands. It was a conference of churchmen; and the Bishop of Bradford, Doctor Frank Blunt, made a speech which bore out both his names. Speaking of King Edward VIII — 'a man like ourselves' — he commended him to God's grace, which he would abundantly need if he was to do his duty faithfully. 'We hope that he is aware of this need,' added the good Bishop. 'Some of us wish that he gave more positive signs of his awareness.'

No churchman had spoken thus about an English king in centuries, for no church is more subservient to royalty than the Church of England, of which the King is the titular head. Nor was this all: the British press almost without exception reprinted his words, and many commended him for speaking out. It seemed more than likely that the bishop's reprimand was inspired. In fact, the hunt was up and at last the British press threw reticence to the winds. Only the B.B.C. remained silent, and still most people in England didn't know what it was all about. The working classes only remembered that but a fortnight ago the King had made a sensational visit to the distressed areas of South Wales, flouting the Conservative Government and taking with him the former Commissioner for the Special (*anglice* Distressed) Areas, Mr. Malcolm Stewart, who had resigned because his report proved too radical. They had still ringing in their ears his words after seeing the destitution in the dead town of Dowlais, to the effect that 'something must be done to find these people employment,' and his confident promise that 'something *will* be done.' To them he was a hero; a king who would champion the cause of the poor, even against Conservative politicians.

Some of them may have remembered how, after an all-night parliamentary debate on the eve of that journey, the Cabinet had met at six in the morning, an extraordinary event, obviously occasioned by the action of the King. What they did not know was that on the day before Mr. Baldwin, the Prime Minister, had seen the King and learned from him his intention to marry Mrs. Simpson as soon as she should be free. Nor did they know that another Cabinet session, only four days before the Blunt pronouncement, had dealt, not — as was supposed — with the war in Spain, but with the crisis arising out of the King's matrimonial plans.

In fact, the crisis was already coming to a head, although the papers were still speaking cryptically of a 'constitutional issue' rather than an affair of the heart. Only in America the headlines screamed that an American woman was fighting for a British crown. On Thursday, December 3, the British papers mentioned Mrs. Simpson's name for the first time in connection with the crisis, and on that day Mr. Baldwin admitted to Parliament that a situation had arisen on which he would make a statement as soon as possible. Also, two 'King's men' had raised their voices in Parliament, namely, Colonel Wedgwood and Mr. Winston Churchill, to ask ominous questions which hinted that grave decisions were imminent.

The issue from now on was to be fought out openly in the newspapers, while weighty but invisible moves were going on between the Government, the Church, and the King. Broadcasting, it was tacitly understood, was not a fit medium to deal with a situation so delicate — so far as England was concerned; but the question now arose whether American broadcasting should, like the newspapers, go 'all out.' In Great Britain broadcasting was a monopoly chartered by the Crown and licensed by the Government. Any statement made concerning a controversy between these two arms of the State might give rise to serious difficulties. In America the broadcasting companies were giving out brief bulletins under their restrictive agreement with the press, while the press was free to indulge in an orgy of prophecy and conjecture, controversy and sensationalism, without let or hindrance.

There was just one way in which the radio could counter the advantage of the press, and that was to get material from the spot, from England direct. It could do this only with the concurrence of the B.B.C. and the British Post Office, which controls the European end of the transatlantic telephone. Hitherto it had tacitly deferred to the policy of the B.B.C.; on the crucial Thursday, when the crisis reached Parliament and Mrs. Simpson's name was mentioned in the British press, both of the major American chains approached the heads of the B.B.C., obtained permission to transmit fair comment on the crisis, and within fifteen minutes of each other their first broadcasts reached America that afternoon.

Radio had caught the big story at its flood, and from now on millions of eager people in the United States and Canada literally hung on their sets with bated breath as it unravelled, chapter by chapter, a story which raced with increasing momentum to its dramatic close. Nothing else mattered; the great Conference in America, the war in Spain, the Pope's illness, some of the worst airplane disasters in years — only the love story of a King and an American woman and their struggle for happiness, against the effulgent background of the greatest throne and the oldest tradition in the world.

For the next ten days and nights three American radio chains (for the Mutual Broadcasting Company had recently entered the international field) sent an aggregate of about eighty fifteen-minute commentaries — an average of eight a day — from London, occupying a total air time of over twenty hours, an all-time record for any single subject or event since international broadcasting began. Most of these talks, in order to reach American listeners at convenient evening times, had to be made during the night and early morning, London time; and the pressure on the technical and service staff of the B.B.C. was terrific. Broadcasting House,

on account of the B.B.C.'s service to Britain's world-encir-
cling empire, is never asleep; at this time it was a beehive of
activity all night.

As for the American broadcasters — we practically stood
on our heads. I have worked in newspaper offices at times of
crisis, when the strain and confusion seemed unbearable; but
the downright torture of nervous tension and physical
fatigue of these ten days and nights had a character of their
own. Against the sheer labor of persuasion to get the 'big
shots' to speak at such a time and on such a subject, our
much-vaunted high-pressure salesmanship was a mere
parlor game. Some of our 'prospects' would figuratively bite
our heads off in their anger or wither us with their righteous
indignation. The higher they were in the social scale (with a
few sensible exceptions), the more sacrosanct were the issues
involved. Fifty telephone calls might be required before one
speaker was booked. One of them, though in London all the
time, actually had to be tracked by telephone via Hollywood!

Yet New York was never satisfied. When we offered a
prominent M.P., they wanted Winston Churchill; when we
proposed Lord Beaverbrook they wanted Lord Rothermere
as well; when we delivered a viscount they wanted an earl, or
a duke. Lady Astor, on the ocean, was bombarded with
radio messages. Hardly had we given the latest available
news in a midnight talk, when they wanted another one at
4 A.M. — even if there was nothing new! The public was wild
and we were going mad. New York rang up to confirm every
wild rumor; conservative but reliable information merely
aroused a suspicion that I was 'slow.' Day after day, night
after night we kept it up — with almost no sleep — hunting
news, hounding speakers, sometimes telling them what to
say and how to say it; and dickering about terms. A noble
earl, having settled the business before tea, raised the stakes
during dinner (*my* dinner), throwing confusion into the
night's work. For a week my bed was used not for sleep but
as a reference shelf, and two telephones were at my elbows
during meals.

Each of us (my rivals and myself) were a one-man team
with a harassed secretary at our elbow, watching the Opposi-

tion as a cat watches a mouse. If we booked a transatlantic
circuit at 11.30, the Opposition would counter with 11.15,
scooping us on time if not on facts. The New York–London
telephone rang and rang — finally it just rang to make sure I
was still awake — or alive.

EXPLAINING TO AMERICA

In telling the story itself, radio could of course do no more
than duplicate the press, and it wisely confined itself to the
bare outward facts. In the matter of interpretation, however,
its limitations proved its strength. To mere speculation and
sensation-mongering it opposed authoritative analyses of the
points at issue. It gave the historical background of the
crisis; interpreted the traditional aspects and the political
implications; presented the trend of public opinion from day
to day. It was soon clear which way this opinion was going:
from ordinary human sympathy with a genuinely beloved
monarch it passed to condemnation on the basis of moral
principles and stern judgment on constitutional grounds;
for, whatever the merits of the sentimental considerations,
no Englishman could contemplate with equanimity another
conflict between Parliament and King — a conflict won
after centuries of strife in the fight against James II in 1688.
Lawyers and historians, sociologists and statesmen, nobles
and commoners, men and women, parliamentarians of every
shade were drafted to this task of explanations and interpretation. It was a job worthy of their mettle; for here was
an unprecedented situation involving two people belonging
to two countries whose nationals might well have been at
verbal loggerheads through a misunderstanding that lay so
plausibly at hand.[1]

[1] Those who assisted in this process of clarification for the American networks
included the Duchess of Atholl, the Marquis of Lothian, the Marquis of Donegall,
the Earl of Birkenhead, Lady Reading, Lady Astor, Lady Rhondda, Viscount Cecil
of Chelwood, Lord Elton, Lord Ponsonby, Lord Strabolgi, Sir Josiah Stamp,
Sir Frederick Whyte, Sir Alfred Zimmern, Professor Harold Laski, Ellen Wilkinson,

One and all these speakers assured their American listeners that there was nothing repugnant in the idea of an American woman and a commoner on the British throne. Most people may have taken this with a large grain of salt; but the fact remained that this romantic possibility never entered into the argument, for there were other, more weighty, reasons in the way. As the case developed through the days, three simple points emerged: (1) Mrs. Simpson was not acceptable to the British people as their queen; (2) the idea of a morganatic marriage was repugnant to Anglo-Saxon moral and social concepts; and (3) in any conflict between King and Parliament, Parliament must prevail.

The crux of the whole matter lay in point 3, that a constitutional monarch must be guided by the will of the people, as expressed in the advice of his ministers, in all public concerns — and in the case of a king even his marriage is a public concern. 'The will of Parliament must prevail,' said Lord Ponsonby, a convinced monarchist whose father for a quarter of a century had been Queen Victoria's private secretary. Harold Laski, Professor of Political Science in London University, in saying that 'no precedent must be created that makes royal authority once more a source of political power in the State' merely voiced the opinion of the masses throughout Great Britain, as represented by the Labor Party in Parliament, whose leaders would have been only too glad to condemn the Government.

It was true that King Edward had shown more sympathy with the working classes than that Government; he might have been a powerful aid in securing a greater measure of social justice for them. But all personal and class considerations had to be sacrificed for the greater principles of democracy. 'It is but a minor cruelty of history that the lives of two people should be bruised in the preservation of the democratic tradition,' said Philip Jordan in his broadcast shortly before the abdication. 'In a world seething with less

M.P., Vernon Bartlett, Gerald Barry, Hector Bolitho, Alistair Cooke, Frank Darvall, John Drinkwater, Joseph Driscoll, Philip Jordan, Commander Stephen King-Hall, J. B. Priestley, César Saerchinger, H. Wickham Steed, John Steele, and Frederick Voigt.

amiable forms of government we can ill spare a jot or tittle of our heritage, and that is the sad truth.'

In the light of these main points of the controversy the question for the King was clear: was he or was he not willing to sacrifice his own happiness for the throne, in other words his duty, or as the plain man put it, his 'job'? The fact that he was not, settled his fate with his subjects, high and low. 'When we went to war,' said a mob orator in Hyde Park, 'we were told to leave our homes, our wives, our sweethearts, everything we had, for the country's good. We did it, millions of us. He, the first citizen of the country, isn't willing to do even less.'

As these broadcast talks went across, some voices of dissent were raised. A Representative asked in Congress — of all places — why the Columbia speakers represented only one side, and why the King's side wasn't heard. It was heard; but if it wasn't heard more insistently it is simply because his side had nothing to say. I myself invited his leading champions, Lords Rothermere and Beaverbrook and Mr. Winston Churchill, to speak; they one and all refused — more or less politely. John Drinkwater and J. B. Priestley, both professed partisans of the King, had their say. Abdication was abhorrent to almost every man who spoke.

Yet, when the controversy was three or four days old, it was almost impossible to find a King's man in London, or in the country, and least of all in the streets.

'What's going to happen?' I asked a laboring man on the Sunday of the critical week.

'He's going to get the sack.'

'And you think that's just?'

'Yes, because he's let us down. He ought to be an example to the rest of us, and he's let us down.'

The day after this typical pronouncement by the man in the street, the word 'abdication' was heard for the first time in Parliament. It was spoken by Colonel Wedgwood, whose words were lost in the uproar they provoked. From then on events galloped to their conclusion. Mr. Baldwin made his fateful report in the House; Mr. Churchill, warning against irrevocable steps, was shouted down; Mrs. Simpson made

her equivocal statement in Cannes. On Tuesday the die
was cast, though Mr. Baldwin's staying for dinner with the
King and his brothers at Fort Belvedere threw the newspapers off their scent.

On Wednesday the royal family, including Queen Mary,
assembled at the Royal Lodge in Windsor Great Park to
meet the King, while Cabinet meetings and the comings and
goings of palace officials indicated that a decision was imminent. The Prime Minister promised a statement for next
day. According to rumor, only slightly premature, the King
had already abdicated, and Lord Strabolgi, broadcasting
to America, forecast the terms of the Act of Parliament,
conferring the succession on the Duke of York. 'The bill,'
he added, 'is now ready.' He also forecast its passage by a
large majority and predicted the King's virtual exile abroad.
As far as it was permissible, the American public had been
told.

SETTING THE STAGE

Yet there was an element of doubt, which would not be
dispelled till Parliament met. Elaborate arrangements —
the most elaborate machinery ever provided for a single
event — were set up for the flashing of the fateful news.
The leading American press associations leased open telephone circuits from London to New York; all cable and wireless telegraphic services were virtually commandeered by
the press; all other business was suspended for the essential
part of the day. Wires between Parliament and the newspaper offices were doubled and trebled; every great newspaper had its own system of signals and messengers, its own
private tricks in an unprecedented effort to score a beat.
Presses in New York and all the big cities of America stood
ready to rush extras to the street. It was the climax to the
biggest news story since the Armistice in 1918.

But since the Armistice a new factor had come into the

business of distributing news. Broadcasting companies in America had two channels through which the decisive news of the abdication could come — the Press-Radio news bureau, which was limited to flashes and brief bulletins, and its own representatives on the spot. The rapidity of modern news transmission at moments of crisis is almost incredible; relays from Parliament to newspaper offices in this instance was virtually instantaneous. Yet radio could conceivably take this a stage further, for a speaker in London would be heard by listeners all over America. However, the speaker could not be stationed in Parliament itself, and there were several possibilities of delay between that point and the radio circuit across the Atlantic. Moreover, it was obviously impossible to maintain an open circuit indefinitely; and much depended, therefore, upon calculating the correct moment when the news would break. The clue was given by Ellen Wilkinson, M.P., in her talk on the fateful morning, which set the stage for the American audience.

'What will happen today?' she said. 'The Country is on tiptoe, but the House will meet at 2.45 as usual. The Speaker, tall, slender and dignified, will go with his Chaplain through the lobby. The Chaplain will lead the assembled members in prayer, as he does every day. As always, we shall pray for our sovereign lord, King Edward, and for the safety and welfare of the realm.

'The Empire is on tiptoe, but the all-important statement from the Premier will not be made first thing. In the words of the hymn, "Crowns and thrones may perish, kingdoms rise and fall" — but it is the inalienable right of the members of the House of Commons to question the Ministers about their departments before any other business is taken up.

'The world is on tiptoe, but Mr. Gibson, M.P. for Greenwich, will ask Mr. Brown, Minister of Labor, why the unemployment benefit of Neal Tonnett, of 160 Ranken Street, Greenwich, has been reduced from seventeen shillings to nine shillings per week. There are fifty-three questions on the paper. All these will be asked before we get to the business which is in everyone's mind.'

That, I figured, would be not earlier than 3.30 P.M. Actually a few minutes later, Mr. Baldwin, pale and haggard, a sealed document in his hand, amid a tense silence, rose from his seat, bowed to the Speaker and said: 'A Message from His Majesty the King, signed by His Majesty's own hand.' At the same moment, approximately, Lord Halifax made the same announcement in the House of Lords.[1] *That was the news.*

WE SCOOP THE WORLD

How could I get that news and get it the moment it happened — before the big agencies streaked it like lightning to all the world? Obviously there must be some indication — some unfailing sign as to which way the cat would jump — even before the Prime Minister opened his mouth. I obviously can't reveal just what happened — in fact I hardly know myself, except that I had my scouts at three strategic points, and one of them 'came through.' The essential fact is that at precisely 3.32 P.M. in London my telephone outside our Broadcasting House studio rang, and a voice, having identified mine, announced the fact of abdication. The terminus of the open circuit to America was but three yards away, and I shouted for 'the air.' My colleague in New York asked me to stand by, and while the connection with master-control, the heart of the broadcasting network, was made in New York, I rushed to the microphone, ready to shoot. Bulletins on the crisis were being read to the American audience at the time, and the announcer in his studio gaily went on reading, unconscious of being cut off. In the excitement no one thought of telling him. The moment I got my signal, I was able to announce to the waiting millions

[1] By a curious coincidence, another Lord Halifax, in the seventeenth century, played a leading part in the forced abdication (correctly: flight) of James II. And chance would have it that Edward VIII left England on December 11, the day that James II, the only other exiled king in English history, fled the country.

that King Edward VIII had abdicated, announce it from the very studio from which he had introduced himself to the Empire as King.

In the meantime, over another telephone in Broadcasting House, the bulletins giving the actual text of the King's message had begun to come in. This, and Mr. Baldwin's moving recital of the whole story leading up to this tragic end, we read direct to the American listener at the very moment that the story was barely arriving in the newspaper offices in New York. Listening to the open return circuit from New York I heard the announcer reading the Press-Radio bulletin announcing the King's abdication twenty minutes after I had announced it to the listeners direct. For twenty minutes the world outside knew through my words alone that King Edward was King no longer. For once, radio had 'scooped the world.'

That night, limp with the reaction from effort and excitement, I listened at my radio to the sensational burning of the Crystal Palace—the last gaudy survival from Queen Victoria's Jubilee...

King Edward VIII, the only English king in history to abdicate voluntarily, had sacrificed his throne for 'the woman I love,' and that woman was an American, born in a modest Baltimore house, where her mother—like thousands of American mothers with daughters to support—had kept boarders in less prosperous years. The story was almost unbelievably romantic to the simple American schoolgirl's mind. Next day the King himself was to confirm it in his own words, broadcast to the four corners of the world. Millions in all the continents listened with strangely mixed feelings, as the voice of Sir John Reith announced in the simplest formula: 'This is Windsor Castle. His Royal Highness, Prince Edward...' Stripped of his kingly dignity, 'Prince Edward' once again became the perpetual adolescent whose eager, youthful figure had flitted through the illustrated papers for two decades.

EDWARD'S FAREWELL

Future generations of visitors to Windsor Castle will be shown the room in the Augusta Tower where lovelorn Edward bared his heart to the peoples of his Empire. Kings had ruled from here through nine centuries — conquerors, despots, murderers, scholars, saints — but none had taken his subjects into his confidence before all the world to show that he was but a man like the rest of us.

Three miles away lay Fort Belvedere, that pastoral bower where Edward's idyll had ripened into drama. He had left the fort in the darkness, shortly before ten, to make probably the last broadcast of his career from the ancestral castle home whose name was henceforth to be his title. Taking a few loose typewritten sheets from his breast pocket, he laid them on the table with the microphone and started to make last-minute corrections. Attendants, engineers — everybody — left the room; in this historic moment he wanted to be alone.

'You all know the reason which has impelled me to renounce the throne. . . . You must believe me when I tell you that I found it impossible to carry the heavy burden . . . without the woman I love. . . . The other person most nearly concerned has tried to the last to persuade me to take a different course. . . .

'And now we all have a new king. . . . God bless you all. *God save the King!*'

It was all over. Someone opened the door. Smiling in his usual cheery manner Edward, a Prince once again, shook hands with the broadcasting officials and started to go. Turning back for a moment, he saw the crumpled leaves of his manuscript lying on the floor. Stooping quickly, he gathered them up, stuck them in his breast pocket and left. A few minutes later a car with three male passengers sped through the night toward the south coast — to Portsmouth. After midnight he was there. In the darkness, deepened by an English fog, the grim Destroyer which was to carry King

Edward into exile crept across to France. Her name was *Fury*.

The last words spoken to America, before Prince Edward's own, were those of a woman. 'In a world,' said the Duchess of Atholl, 'where only too often a woman has been sacrificed to a man's passing fancy, here is a man who has renounced the greatest throne in the world for the woman he loves.'

The story of the crisis started with the words of a bishop; it ended with those of an archbishop. What rôle the Church of England played in all this may never be known, but that it was not without importance we may be sure. Would the Archbishop of Canterbury ever have crowned Mrs. Simpson Queen? As the chief spiritual adviser of the royal family he was known to have been charged by aging King George to admonish the Prince; what was the charge the dying monarch confided to the kingdom's chief priest? How far was the future of Church and State involved in the crisis, and what was the meaning of that strangely timed 'Call to Religion,' launched after Edward's departure?

With the farewell speech Edward had had his say; no one felt that it called for a reply. It was the end of a sad story. 'Let the past bury the past' — that is what people thought. Not so the Archbishop. Using the same medium as the King, he broadcast to the world these bitter words:

'From God he had received a high and sacred trust. Yet, by his own will, he has abdicated — he has surrendered the trust. With characteristic frankness he has told us his motive. It was a craving for private happiness. Strange and sad it must be that for such a motive, however strongly it pressed upon his heart, he should have disappointed hopes so high, and abandoned a trust so great.'

No stranger message, surely, had ever been broadcast; no words, however true, that had better have been left unsaid.

XVIII. 'COMPETITION IS THE LIFE OF RADIO'

THE 'AMERICAN SYSTEM' IN EUROPE

ONE of the grimmer aspects of a radio representative's life is competition, still widely credited with being the life of trade. Newspaper correspondents take competition in their stride; it adds zest to their activity. When they compete on the same story it is a competition for quality, since the same story can be told in a hundred ways; when they fight for 'exclusives' it is a battle of wits. Rarely, in the process, does anyone get hurt. In radio, the first kind of competition is exhilarating and in the long run results in better programs. The second kind, however, often deteriorates in a ruthless exploitation of advantage or the most gruelling kind of battle against invisible odds. At worst this kind of rivalry ends in hard feelings, at best it results in a duplication of stunts. In newspaper work the fight is general; in radio it is a single combat to the death. It is also more bitter than in journalism because the objects are fewer and the defeats more spectacular. The battle of wits often becomes a battle of tempers — a cock-fight in which the victims are normally friends. I never had much use for that kind of work, for it stultifies the imagination and sharpens one's strategy at the expense of creative thinking. But it does from time to time result in amusing episodes, and if I recount some of them here it is because I thought them amusing and not because I approve of the motives and methods which lay behind.

I first ran up against competition when I heard about the Mussolini New Year's broadcast in 1931. Competition gave me a few bad nights during the battle for the Pope's first broadcast a month later. It made me see red the month after that in Ireland, where I went for the 'wearin' of the green.'

I had had the bright idea to broadcast a Saint Patrick's Day speech by President Cosgrave, and after some complicated negotiations the matter was arranged. Just two months before the great day, I received an official letter from the Irish Foreign Minister telling me that 'the President has much pleasure in accepting the invitation to broadcast.' I was elated until, some ten days before Saint Patrick's Day, New York warned me that our rivals had suddenly announced a Saint Patrick's Day broadcast — also from Dublin and also with Cosgrave — for the fifteenth — two days *before* Saint Patrick's Day! But due protests were made through Washington and on the tenth I received a reassuring cable from New York:

IRISH MINISTER CABLES COSGRAVE POSTPONED TALK ON FIFTEENTH UNTIL AFTER OUR PRO-GRAMME.

Imagine my feelings when, on a chill and foggy March 16, I arrived in Kingstown Harbor, and on my way up to Dublin in a decrepit boat train saw spread all over the Irish *Independent*: 'President's Radio Message to America — Full Text of Yesterday's Speech.' So he'd made it after all! My tongue stuck to the roof of my mouth; my breakfast in the newly swabbed, wet-smelling dining-room of the Gresham Hotel tasted like gall. Swearing vengeance, I drove in a rickety taxi to the Government Buildings to learn — what? That the President was very, very sorry, but had been told that the talk he had made was just an internal affair — a 'greeting to the Chicago World's Fair and the Chicago *Tribune*,' and so he thought it wouldn't pre-empt my undoubted claim to the President's first message to the American *people*. Moreover, my competitor had arrived in the company of the American Minister, and how could an Irish President refuse anything to the American Minister (then the only foreign diplomat in Dublin)? I saw it all — it was just Ireland — and, worst of all, my 'competitor' was no other than dear old John Steele, correspondent of the Chicago *Tribune*, acting under orders and entirely innocent of the mess.[1]

What's done is done, and there was nothing for it but to grin and let the President talk again, on this fine Saint Patrick's Day, for the sun had now begun to make a feeble effort to pierce the gray sky. I bought myself a Shamrock from a ragged colleen on O'Connell Street and watched the entire Irish Army parade across College Green, which made me long for a *real* Saint Patrick's Day parade — on Fifth Avenue, New York. Cosgrave, a colorless little man who looked rather like a dry-goods clerk, except for a sign reading 'President' in Gaelic and English on his office partition, made an inconsequential speech, calmly ignoring his previous one and saying that this was 'the first time in history that the head of an independent Irish government could have the privilege on Saint Patrick's Day of addressing you from the Government Buildings in Dublin' — which was of course the letter of the truth. And he ended up by 'evoking memories' in the accepted manner, not forgetting the Battle of the Boyne, Saint Patrick, and the rest. If it wasn't his first broadcast, it was certainly his last, for a few months later Eámon de Valera swept him out of power. Needless to say, I booked the redoubtable revolutionary for the following Saint Patrick's Day, with due precautions against 'horners-in.'

LAVAL SAILS FOR THE U.S.A.

That autumn Pierre Laval, Prime Minister of France and one of the wiliest politicians that ever walked, was to make his famous 'buccaneering trip' (in Stephen King-Hall's phrase) to Washington. I felt I ought to try to get a broadcast from him on the eve of sailing with his attractive olive-skinned daughter José. I flew to Paris and began the usual

[1] John Steele is now the London representative of the Mutual Broadcasting System.

round of harangues in official quarters, to set the machinery in motion. Politicians of all shades, from Marin to Chautemps, were buzzing back and forth, and going into tail spins in the vicinity of Laval's office, the Ministry of the Interior. No special broadcast could be made, *Monsieur le Président* was much too busy getting ready for President Hoover, and in the end it was arranged to broadcast a speech which he would make to the world's press, whose representatives he was receiving at the Ministry on the eve of his tour. That, being in the nature of an official occasion, had to be shared by the two American radio companies, and 'neutral' Ralph Heinzen, of the United Press, was to read a translation, since Laval didn't speak anything but French. *Faute de mieux*, we acquiesced. I was assured that the technical arrangements would be made.

Thursday evening arrived; the entrance halls of the Ministry were a human anthill. Chattering journalists, newsreel people, politicians, and a nondescript mob of hangers-on made it impossible to move. Nobody to take a message, and the broadcast only half an hour away. At last I spied a French radio man; apparently there would be a broadcast, but he didn't know when. Time was nothing to him; a speech by the Premier would be taken when it happened, like a shower of rain. American broadcasting was run differently; they would 'take' the Premier at thirty seconds after half-past six, or not at all.

I finally charged through the crowd and into the office of the *chef de cabinet*. Oh, everything would be ready, he opined. There was the gentleman making the translation now! So even the translation wasn't done; and Monsieur Rueff, an economic expert with some knowledge of English, was working on page one. 'Ah!' he said when he spied me. 'An American. Perhaps Monsieur will help?' We set to, working a mile a minute, on alternate pages. Meantime Laval had arrived; I rushed in, translation in hand, while cameras clicked and Kleig lights were trained on the swarthy and perspiring statesman. The noise and confusion were awful; I ducked through the crowd, reached Laval's desk, raised my hand to stop the talking, and announced His Excellency, the French Prime Minister. Everything happened in the nick of time, or just after. '*Comme toujours*,' coolly remarked a Frenchman, standing near-by. And after all that heroic effort, not even an 'exclusive!'

Well, next day, I was sailing with Laval and a group of American and French journalists in the *Île de France*. I determined to make one more try — from aboard ship. An exclusive mid-ocean radio talk would be 'something.' Watching my chances, I sat in on the daily press conferences which the wily French politician used to hold in his presidential suite, always wearing his white lawn necktie and grinning at us through his gnarled, tobacco-stained teeth. There was something strangely oriental about this son of the South.

'What earthly connection is there between the war debts and disarmament?' he used to ask, with an ingenuous air. 'I'll tell you what,' he said one day. 'I'll get France to pay the American debt, if you'll get Mr. Hoover to abolish prohibition.' (Laval hailed from a wine region, so this was a good joke.) And then he would pour us champagne from a magnum, but never take any himself. Meantime I was exchanging messages with New York and getting chummy with the wireless operators up on the hurricane deck. These optimistic Frenchmen were sure their radio-telephone equipment could transmit the proposed broadcast to New York when we were within a day of the American shore. But they forgot to mention that their 'microphone' was just an adapted telephone mouthpiece.

Laval was ready to talk — to greet the American people as a 'messenger of peace,' come to help 'ward off the dangers which menace civilization.' We set the broadcast for ten o'clock at night, ship's time, and started to make tests. Up in the wireless room I shouted into the mouthpiece, trying to get myself heard by the American engineers: 'This is the *Île de France* calling WABC, New York.' 'Hello WABC, hello W2XE, hello WLA and the rest!' No answer. They put on all their 'juice'; so did I. Finally I had none left; I was too hoarse to talk. It was a heartbreak. Morse messages came in to say New York couldn't hear us. I gave it up.

Meantime Old Man Competition had raised his head. Half way across, the Opposition, knowing I was aboard, had appointed the press agent of the line — also aboard — their representative. He told me so himself. Realizing that the ship's wireless outfit was too weak, the Opposition had loaded a short-wave transmitter on a seagoing tug, and while I was up in the wireless room we picked up their messages — to the ship and to the shore. To the captain of the ship they wirelessed their intention to come aboard and transmit the Premier's speech; to their home office they sent dramatic reports like 'Plowing through heavy seas' (the weather was calm and the moon bright) — 'Going strong, now in touch with *Île*' — 'All well, ought to reach *Île* at 11 P.M.' — and so on. I raced up to the bridge and found the Captain, Commandant Blancart, a large, full-bearded Frenchman, in a great state. 'That tug,' I said, 'is going to cause a lot of trouble, I'm afraid. When do you think they'll reach us?'

He went over to his map and showed me the position of the enemy; then, calculating for a minute, he said: 'They can't be here much before midnight, and I'm not going to wait up. We have to dock early in the morning — I want some sleep.' Finally he said, categorically, that he would let no one come aboard. I sent a message to Laval that the broadcast was off. He was relieved; his minions closed in on him and put him to bed.

About midnight, the ship slowed down; we looked over the side and there was the tug. 'Throw us a ladder!' they cried. 'Nothing doing,' we shouted back. 'Captain's orders, no one on board.' And so they steamed away. I don't know what it cost to send that tug, but it wasn't worth two cents.

Next morning we were all taken off by the government tug *Macon*, had a microphone shoved up to our faces at the Battery, and then watched Laval's reception at City Hall, where the Honorable Hector Fuller, the mayor's official glad-hander, announced him as 'Paul Laval' and the French Ambassador as 'Pierre Claudel,' thus giving Mayor Jimmie Walker a wise-cracking chance to put things right. From the gallery of the City Hall chamber, an excruciatingly funny brass band played 'See the Conquering Hero Comes,' while Laval with his daughter, looking like a gangster at his wedding, marched up the aisle. It was my first taste of America in seven years, and I was dazed.

The principle of competition having now been firmly established in transatlantic broadcasting, the Opposition got ready to swing out. When Fred Wile and myself arrived in Geneva for the Disarmament Conference the following January, we found them on the battle-ground, three strong. Doctor Max Jordan, former German newspaperman in Washington, a tremendously informed, hard-working, polyglot globe trotter, had been assigned to the Central European field by the N.B.C., while an equally formidable competitor, the suave and convivial Fred Bate, was being put in charge at London, where he was accredited in the highest social circles.

This was good news; as a friend of mine put it, it meant a 'job insurance' for me. It also kept me from putting on unnecessary fat. In Geneva Max proved a cheery soul and a good sport, and we had great fun gunning for exclusives among the world's eminent statesmen then assembled in the League capital. One of them, André Tardieu, we actually had to share, because he wouldn't talk for less than *all* of America, which took the joy out of it for Max. Since Tardieu was springing his famous idea for a League air force, it was just as well that all America heard what the French had in store for us (but they couldn't see the tongue in his cheek).

HOW KING CAROL DID NOT BROADCAST

Max and I were both resting from our labors at Montreux, where the International Broadcasting Union was holding its summer conference, when the genius of Competition played one of his most absurd tricks. 'Exclusivity' had become a fetish by then: a broadcast, however important or interesting, was only half a trick if it was not exclusive. We had both done a bit of excluding, and to the European broadcasting officials we had become a standing joke. At Montreux they eyed us with amused astonishment when they saw us eating lunch — actually — at the same table. I was just gloating over having landed the first exclusive broadcast by President Masaryk, one of the grand old men of Europe, on Washington's Birthday (see Chapter VII), when I was handed this cable from New York:

EXCLUSIVE AGREEMENT COMPLETED FOR KING CAROL OF RUMANIA BROADCAST FROM PALACE BUCHAREST HIS ACCESSION DAY JUNE EIGHTH YOUR INTRODUCTION TO START PRECISELY 6.05 PM NEW YORK TIME ADVISE EXACT TIME YOUR ARRIVAL BUCHAREST

I assumed my best poker face and pocketed the cable with affected nonchalance. This was Thursday. The next Orient Express passed through Montreux about 6 A.M. Saturday; that would give me time to get a 'pinch-hitter' to Montreux to attend meetings and watch Max. I sent the wire giving my schedule and went about the business of booking transportation. The florid-faced hall porter of the Montreux Palace Hotel yanked out timetables and began to think out loud, and his stentorian thoughts echoed from the marble slabs and mirrors of the hall. 'For the holy cause of Swiss tourism, shut up!' I said. 'I'm not anxious for the world to know where I'm going.'

'*Pardon, monsieur!*' he cried, and turning around to a huge blackboard, he chalked 5 A.M. next to my name and the number of my room. Discretion was clearly not his specialty; I made him rub out that tell-tale memo just in time. Max was swinging through the doors for the afternoon meeting. I tried not to leave him out of my sight; I knew of course that we had an exclusive agreement, but the question was, did the Rumanians know it, and if so, did they know the meaning of the word? I also knew that as soon as C.B.S.

publicized the proposed broadcast, N.B.C. would tip off Max.

Next morning, at the meeting of the program commission I suddenly noticed that Max wasn't there. Remembering that the only Rumanian at the Conference was an engineer, I strolled over into the Technical Section and there — ye gods and little fishes! — was Max in earnest conclave with that Rumanian! After lunch I walked over to the post office to book a call to Bucharest, and casually asked whether the other gentleman's call had come through all right. Yes, said the official, the gentleman talked to the Palace.

That was a lovely afternoon . . .

We sat up late. Max didn't go to his room till after midnight, so I didn't either. I winked at the porter as I went upstairs — four and a half hours to train time. And then I packed. It seemed as though I had just dropped to sleep when a terrific commotion in my room awoke me: I thought there was a fire. But it was only the night porter in a panic, shouting that it was ten minutes to six. Never before or since have I seen an individual so steamed up. I *would* insist on having that chalked memorandum rubbed out. How can a Swiss night porter remember to wake anybody without seeing the order in chalk?

He threw my night clothes into the bag as I took them off. I raced downstairs after him as I tied my tie. He was spluttering excuses all the way and had a taxi at the door. 'Don't pay him, don't pay him!' he shouted. 'It's my fault!' Only then did I realize *how* distressed he was.

The taxi crossed the railway track just before the bars went down, and raced alongside the incoming train as it pulled up to the platform. The sleeping-car porter pulled me aboard while my bags were thrown after me. In another minute I was speeding along toward the Simplon Pass; I tied my shoe-lace, felt myself all over, and found I was intact. Anyhow, it would be hours before Max found out I'd gone.

Italy was hot, but the Italian breakfast was a comfort: Milan, Venice, Udine — then next day a bit of Yugoslavia (where the frontier police liked my cigarettes so much they decided to take a ride to the next town — in my compartment). Then came Belgrade, where they murdered a king and queen in their beds before the war, and then Rumania, where the former Boy King was now the Crown Prince, and his father — after having been chucked out of England — the King. And America wanted to hear him broadcast: a crazy world!

Bucharest was hot and dusty — a half-finished southern metropolis, with white *art nouveau* buildings and shabby palms in the littered parks. Its nickname, the Paris of the Balkans, was hard on Paris — or the Balkans. The royal palace was having a new wing added to it, and the scaffoldings looked very ugly. The town's best hotel, the Athénée Palace, was a cheerless, jerry-built place, but its women were definitely handsome. They say that the porters usually ask you whether you want a room with or without. But I was arriving too early in the morning.

My first call was on the Director of Broadcasting, who had gone out for a long shave; he came back at last, looking as though he needed another. He professed complete ignorance about the King's broadcast, having received some warning cables, as it developed later. The Foreign Office was more encouraging, but there was a ministerial crisis on, and things were hectic. Nevertheless, the King *would speak;* of course, he hadn't had time to prepare a speech — as yet. They were charming people, those under-secretaries, but they hadn't the faintest idea how a broadcast was engineered. Nor could they control the broadcasting head.

So I went to the head of the telephone company, a hearty and hefty American named Ogilvie, who was fighting a great battle to make Rumanian telephones work; hitherto they had been an expensive but dubious ornament. Now the King had granted Ogilvie's company a private concession, which was anything but popular with the local grafters. Ogilvie had actually been ordered to run lines from the broadcasting station to the Palace, but didn't know for whom, as he had had a wire to say that Max Jordan was on his way.

So my worst fears were realized. Max, as soon as he discovered I had left Montreux had jumped on the next train

for the 24-hour journey to Bucharest. It pulled into the
station six hours after mine!

I raced back to the Foreign Office. 'Is this an exclusive
broadcast or isn't it?' I asked. It was, so Under-Secretary
Filotti informed me, and he would stand by it. But my suspicions were right; they didn't know the meaning of the
word! He called the King's private secretary, the chief of
the palace, everybody who counted — except the broadcasting director. But — there was that crisis; the King was
fighting the ministers, Queen Marie was fighting the King,
Madame Lupescu was fighting Queen Marie, and the politicians were fighting each other. Nobody was any surer of
his job than I was of my broadcast; in fact, next day the
cabinet was 'reconstructed' and I saw the amusing spectacle of one foreign minister taking over, with polite speeches
and elaborate bows, from his predecessor, whom no doubt
he had been knifing until a few hours ago. Meantime, in the
Athénée Palace the porter rubbed his hands as usual and
the beauteous denizens would ride down in the lift, casting
handsome looks at you over a rakishly dipped cigarette.
They were the most aristocratic *cocottes* in Europe, with
plausible hopes of making good in a big way. I was in the
Balkans.

Max, as soon as he arrived, concentrated his efforts on
the broadcasting director, while I stuck to the dapper diplomats at the Foreign Office. Finally I got an interview with
the King's secretary at the palace. That was quite a procedure. You gave up your card to a sentry at the postern gate.
The sentry handed it to a gatekeeper. The gatekeeper telephoned to a flunky at the palace entrance, who checked with
the secretaries inside. Finally word came back, you got a
pass, and then traversed the long courtyards where, whenever challenged, you showed your pass.

I waited in an ornate waiting-room, where two officials
were ahead of me. They were talking excitedly, but my
Rumanian was too sketchy to catch anything, so I looked
out of the palace window onto the square. There were
plenty of soldiers; I had never felt so royal before. Suddenly my two companions stood up, muttering '*Regele*,' and

I saw King Carol, in a white uniform, passing our door. He looked sullen and determined; I somehow felt he wasn't thinking about that broadcast speech. But his secretary was courteous, as royal secretaries are, actually showed me a draft of the speech, and said that if I'd come back at six he would have definite word for me. At six, when I got back, he was gone — had been gone for an hour and had no thought of returning. Rumania!

At the Foreign Office things looked very quiet indeed. My friend the Under-Secretary, considerably perturbed, said the King had left. 'Left? For where?' For the country. I guessed the right answer. But next day — the anniversary day, *the* day — I saw Carol come out on the balcony to acknowledge the cheers of a crowd, assembled, with plenty of military and flags, to celebrate his accession day. He was 'gone,' however, so far as we were concerned, and that day he rode out of the palace to Sinaia, his country residence, where Madame Lupescu was said to be awaiting him. It was about 98 in the shade.

TWO NETWORKS THAT BEAT AS ONE

When I got back to the hotel for dinner I found Max in the dining-room, and we ate together. On the advice of the honest Ogilvie I had already proposed to him a united front. 'I hate to see two perfectly good Americans being given the run-around by these dagoes,' Ogilvie had said in good American slang. 'Can't you see they're just playing you for a pair of suckers? Why don't you make a truce and end the agony?'

I saw that he was right; but Max, who among other advantages had special lines to Queen Marie, was undecided. He was getting daily cables and telephone calls from New York. So was I, incidentally, and the night porter would get them mixed up, so we had to pass the lines to each other. Even then we could almost hear each other's conversations, what with the prehistoric telephones and the lath-and-plaster partitions.

Now, at dinner, I returned to the subject of the truce. 'Do you know,' I said, 'that Carol has left for the country?'

'Stop your fooling,' he said; but on my advice he went out to check up with his contact, the broadcasting director. Only an hour before, this worthy had been telling him that I had offered him a price for the broadcast, and asked whether he was inclined to raise the bid! Max came back crestfallen, and ready to sign. The American Minister wouldn't be party to the contract, but procured the American secretary of the Y.M.C.A. I worded the truce to the effect that if and when King Carol should broadcast, it should be for both American networks, with neither's name mentioned. We also wrote an introduction which the Y.M.C.A. man should use *verbatim*, in case the broadcast ever came off. It never did.

Next day we invited the Director of Broadcasting out to lunch, in a luxurious open-air restaurant, where the food was Bucharest's best and the champagne French.... He hasn't got over this sample of American competition yet. Then we booked a joint sleeper on the northern route of the Orient and left Bucharest in glee. We crossed the border into Hungary in the middle of the night, but Rumania was still with us, as I shall now relate.

When I came to dress, I found my shirt gone, with a fine pair of specially made cuff links; it had hung next to the open window through the torrid Balkan night. If my shirt was gone my coat must be gone, thought I, for I had hung it on top. It was; and everything inside it. Only the trousers were there, securely fastened by their suspenders. In them — thank Heaven — was my wallet. And the porter had our passports.

'What on earth has happened to my clothes?' I stormed at him.

'Excuse me, gentleman,' he said, 'but it must be thieves. It happens all the time on this line.' I vaguely remembered about train burglars, with their long hooks reaching into windows from the roofs.

'Then why on earth don't you put up a sign? — "Beware of thieves"?'

'Oh we couldn't do that,' he said, shuddering at the thought. 'You see — the Rumanians, they are so touchy!'

We had learned many things about the Rumanians, but this was a new one. So I arrived in Budapest in a variegated costume, which, as it turned out, was quite the *dernier cri* in the Hungarian capital.

As we pulled out of the station, Max and I leaned out of the window and saw a man selling hot dogs. On his tank hung the name of his firm — 'Picar.' We both started to speak, and we both stopped ourselves at the same time. From that moment I knew that he was after a broadcast of Professor Picard, the stratosphere man who was about to make his first ascent. So was I. Well, Max won, largely because we wouldn't beat the N.B.C. bid. The result was that that broadcast cost hundreds more than it should. Competition still kept the pots (other people's) boiling.

Our next king in the line of popularity was Albert of Belgium, but once again Max and I had to share. We tossed as to how we should divide the work; he drew the introduction, I the epilogue. It was unexciting. Then, five months later, when he wasn't looking, I walked away with King Christian of Denmark (and Iceland), and I felt we were square. But I had forgotten about Max's pal, who was covering England and France.

The wine harvest in the Bordeaux region was plentiful that year; and the end of American prohibition was in sight. So we braved the Anti-Saloon League and staged a half-hour show from the wine harvest festival at the little town of St. Julien. The mayor was master of ceremonies, and Americans could hear the rushing of the fresh-pressed wine from the great vat. This was so successful that other wine broadcasts were in demand.

So the Marquis de Polignac agreed to do a broadcast on champagne, his family being the hereditary producers of a famous brand of 'bubbly.' At the last minute, however, he decided in favor of the Opposition, for reasons best known to himself. Nothing daunted, our Paris man, Percy Noel, enlisted the Prince Caramay de Chimay, another scion of the champagne aristocracy; so they both talked to America — in English — about the joys of drinking, and on the very same day. It was a great day for competition — and for France.

NEW YORK WELCOMES THE 'QUEEN'

In May, 1936, the great liner *Queen Mary* made her maiden trip. All the three leading American companies had *carte blanche* to broadcast, by means of her very efficient transmitter, of course. Each of us had our own crew aboard, and there were broadcasts every day — several of them. The B.B.C. was in full charge and gave everybody first-class service, without favoritism, and with great good will.

My program was fixed long before the ship sailed; it consisted of a daily broadcast, always at the same hour by American time, but each day a different hour by the ship's clock. So we could have programs at bedtime, just before the 'night-cap,' at dancing time, at lounging time (during the auction pool), and finally at dinner — with a daily change of scene. Everything was known; only one trick we kept up our sleeve — a broadcast on the morning of arrival, when two American air liners would circle over the ship with American notables aboard, who would talk to their colleagues or 'opposite numbers' on the ship, while the whole show was being stage-managed from the shore. So Lily Pons talked to a singer aboard the ship, a United States Government representative exchanged greetings with a British M.P., an American boy scout conversed with a British boy scout, Captain Rickenbacker spoke with a brother aviator, and the Honorable Grover Whalen on behalf of the City of New York welcomed Sir Edgar Britain, the Captain, to the port. (When the announcer on the bridge, having heard this welcome speech, asked Sir Edgar to reply, the Captain whispered audibly, 'And who is Grover Whalen?') It was a show after the stunt broadcaster's heart.

But the climax was to come a few hours later, as the ship
was majestically steaming up the bay. It was to be a really
royal welcome, such as no new ship had ever received in
New York or anywhere else. Moreover, the British public
was to hear America's enthusiasm — something so wild that
no Englishman could imagine it. For the first time in British maritime history would it be possible to let the people on
both sides of the Atlantic in on this picturesque triumph of
Anglo-American good will. The B.B.C., alive to its responsibility, sent along George Blake, one of its star commentators, who had known the *Queen Mary* from her birth and had
broadcast her launching. Blake had never seen New
York, but had dreamed of the fabled beauty of its skyline
and the riotous scene that awaited the *Queen*. He brushed
up his vocabulary and braced himself for the greatest
descriptive improvisation of his career.

The two leading American networks were to share this
program with the B.B.C., while each was to contribute
something from the shore — from airplanes and skyscraper-
tops and other vantage-points. Then, after a half hour or
so, each was to continue with its own supplementary show.

While we were slowly gliding through the sun-bathed
waters of the harbor, bedlam was let loose. Sirens shrieked,
guns fired salutes, jets of water shot up from fireboats, airplanes circled, swooped, and dived, thousands of flags and
multicolored bunting broke from hundreds of masts — a
truly unforgettable sight. High up on the hurricane deck
stood Blake, and one of England's crack announcers, John
Snagge. The great moment of the broadcast arrived, and
Snagge shouted his hello's to the A.T. & T. engineers, just as
I had done from the *Ile* three years before — and with as
much effect. No answer. Blake, like a thoroughbred, was
rearing to go. No answer — and panic came into the burly
Scotsman's eyes. At last Snagge's earphones came to life,
but only to say that the circuit he was speaking on had
been cancelled. No one knew why, or by whom.

Wild-eyed, we scouted around the decks, and discovered
that there was indeed another microphone, one deck below,
which was connected up to a small short-wave transmitter,

brought aboard at Quarantine by one of the rival networks. And this short-wave circuit was working beautifully. But instead of Blake's inspired first impression, British and American listeners were having read to them a prefabricated script describing a scene which couldn't fail to be true to prediction.

I have never seen such furious indignation as the faces of those frustrated Britons showed. Knowing our American propensities for stealing marches on each other, they suspected that they — the neutrals — had been outflanked. Well, George Blake was given a few minutes, by way of consolation prize, to vent his remaining eloquence on the Hudson River front, but of course he hadn't come all those three thousand miles for that! I don't know exactly what happened to this day, nor what anybody gained. But Old Man Competition was somewhere on the side-lines, no doubt, playing his tricks.

I have a notion that that particular line of competitive horse-play is practically played out. American radio has more important things to think about. There are times when co-operation is worth more than competition, and in any case the public is better served when broadcasters get together for the good of the job.

My mind goes back to 1934 and the funeral of King Albert of the Belgians. The broadcasting authorities at Brussels were using all the available equipment for French and Flemish commentaries along the lengthy route; no facilities for an English commentary were available. Nevertheless the broadcast was being 'piped' to London and thence to America, for the benefit of England and the two American chains. I listened to the preliminaries, the solemn music, the muffled drums, the booming of the guns, the commentary of the French announcer describing a very moving, impressive scene. I realized how much more impressive it would be to American listeners if we could insert an English translation in the intervals, against the background of the music and the marching feet.

I appealed to officials, got the consent of both American networks, and had an additional speech circuit, originating in a London studio, inserted so as to feed into the circuit from Brussels. Then, for nearly two hours, listening to the Brussels commentator on earphones, I gave American listeners a detailed English description of what was going on, until the King's body had been lowered into the crypt. The trick worked perfectly — even the newspapers wanted to know how the 'miracle' happened. Our rivals cabled their thanks. For once, two networks had beaten as one — for the benefit of all. To me that broadcast gave more satisfaction than all the 'scoops' of my career.

PART THREE

Atmospheres

———————————————

XIX. IN SEARCH OF ENGLAND

PRO AND CON

WHAT is it about England that makes people either love it or hate it? There are no halfway opinions about it, no compromises about the Land of Compromise. You are either crazy about it or crazy to get away. Nor are these sentiments confined to any one aspect — the people, the scenery, the life, or the climate. You like all these things, with the exception of the climate (which you must be born to), or you like none. As for the climate, I have heard people curse it year in and year out for years, and never leave it except for a short spell when it is at its best; others to revel in it at its worst; and still others to revel in the fact that they can stand it, no matter how bad.

I have known tourists to land for the first time, intending to 'do' England, and then getting away to Paris on the first train or plane. I have seen others come here *en passant* and stay a lifetime. I myself came to England on a visit during one of those rare early springs when the almond blooms peeped over the hedges in March, with the air so mild and the countryside so ravishing that I determined to come back for good. I have never experienced another such spring (which turned out to be nothing short of a hoax), but I stayed in England for fourteen years.

I have never done England as a tourist, but in the course of those years I have discovered a great many things by accident, and then tried to explain them as phenomena. 'To know all is to understand all': you can know all of England, I have discovered, and understand nothing.

Some people can spend a Sunday in London or a week-end in the country and find both of them insufferably dull. Others will think both of them enchanting, and not know why. One visitor will consider London one of the ugliest cities on earth; another will fall in love with it at first sight. A first-time visitor can be made to boil with rage over the 'superior' casualness of the natives; another will discover that the English are the politest people in the world, and the only ones who know how to leave one alone. To some, their clinging to tradition, to custom and 'form,' is just a slow-witted inflexibility; to others it is the charm that gives its peculiar spice to English life. To some, the apparent contradictions in English habits and nomenclature are boresome affectations; to others, gifted with a sense of the past, they supply an inexhaustible subject for inquiry and fanciful speculation.

Why is a chalky upland a 'down,' why do you go 'up' to London and 'down' to anywhere else, no matter how high? And why, though you travel down to Oxford, does a student go 'up,' and why if he doesn't behave himself is he sent 'down'? Why is Manchester a city and London just 'town' (with a 'City' as its heart)? You might as well ask why there are twelve pence in a shilling instead of a rational ten, and why some things are paid in guineas instead of pounds. Other European countries humor the tourist by making things easy; Englishmen manage to survive by making them hard.

I soon discovered, in speaking with these visitors, that their different attitudes are determined by a difference of approach. Many things, irritating or bewildering at first, will turn out to be acceptable, because inevitable. Some things, on the other hand, though beguiling at first, will make you impatient in the end, for they turn out to be unnecessary and unnatural. But the first thing to realize is that Britain is one of the oldest countries in the world, and that the continuity of its civilization is the longest. And nearly everything can be explained by reference to history or the predestination of nature herself.

As for England's landscape, its charm is the most difficult

to convey, which largely accounts for the wealth of English poetry. It is rarely startling, never sensational; in describing it, superlatives are out of place. Switzerland has higher mountains, Germany more romantic woods. Italy has brighter colors and contrasts, France lovelier rivers and plains. America has all of these, and more. But England, within its restricted gamut, has greater variety, finer gradations, more infinite charm. And nowhere has nature been so happily nurtured by the hand of man (even though the commercial vandal is pursuing his nefarious game). The greatest 'art' of England, as one very discerning critic has pointed out, is not to be sought on canvases, but in the landscape and the gardens of its manors. And the great virtue of English architecture is that it conforms to the spirit of the land.

Now, the fascination of English life and the abiding beauties of the country began to dawn upon me after six or seven years. Would it be possible to convey some of these things to an audience across the ocean — an audience of people who trace their culture and to some extent their ancestry to this island, a people whose language is similar and whose literature is the same, people more receptive than any other to the message of England's past? Thousands of American visitors came to England every summer; hundreds of thousands were planning to come one day; millions would never be able to. Could broadcasting, even without television, convey something, by way of indemnity, to these?

I wanted to give them the feel of English life — the simple charm and the elaborate pompousness of it; the old customs and the surviving pageantry; the relics of history and the abiding beauties that inspired the poets; the atmosphere of the village church — and the village pub; the spirit of the race as it lives in the folk-music and the madrigals of Tudor times; the spirit of the crowd at sport and at play; the sanctity of the cathedral service and the vulgar jollity of Blackpool. These things have their parallel in both countries — in any country — but how different their manifestations! Men prate about the 'common heritage,' about similarity and cousinship; to aid understanding, you must explain not so much the similarities as the differences between peoples. To supplement the talks that had gone across the Atlantic in the first two years of my activity, a few actual scenes would not be out of place. The movies have done a great deal but, it seemed to me, they had missed a great chance.

TOASTMASTER, SPORTS, AND THE NIGHTINGALE

The first occasion on which American listeners were in touch, as it were, with an English crowd was early in 1929, when a Queens Hall concert was picked up experimentally by the N.B.C. (the first short-wave program on record), and a few months later, in July, they were able to participate in the Thanksgiving Service for the recovery of King George V, which was held in Westminster Abbey. A banquet, given in January, 1930, at the Guildhall in London, to the delegates to the Naval Conference, must have been the first time Americans heard an English toastmaster — that flamboyant flunky unknown outside the British Empire — shout his stentorian 'Your Royal Highness, Your Grace, Your Excellencies, my Lords, Ladies and Gentlemen, pray silence for your Chairman, the Right Honorable the Lord Mayor of London.' It always creates a sensation among American visitors in England, and it must have made a great and possibly hilarious impression on thousands of listeners in the United States — their first taste of real English swank.

Then came a rebroadcast of a football match — the national Cup Final at Wembley, and that gave America the measure of a British sporting mob. The Derby, broadcast from Epsom Downs, was relayed that year by the two leading American networks, and has not missed a single year since then, nor has the Oxford-Cambridge boat race, which was first relayed to America in 1931. Since then America has listened in to tennis at Wimbledon, golf at St. Andrews and elsewhere, the Grand National at Aintree, as regularly as they listen to their own baseball games and

The 'ceremony of the keys' at the Tower of London
A bit of English pageantry which, to the American, is fairyland

major sporting events. Sport was the radio listeners' first step in the discovery of England.

Then came something else. The B.B.C. regularly broadcast the 'ceremony of the keys' from the Tower of London, and in 1932 this was relayed to America. For six centuries in unbroken daily routine a keeper has gone the rounds of William the Conqueror's fortress after sunset, to lock the ancient gates of the various keeps and walls with old-fashioned keys. The burglar who would be baffled by any of these cumbersome precautions has yet to be discovered; yet nightly the solemn top-hatted key man goes on his prescribed round, flanked by two yeoman warders, is challenged at each gate, while a detachment of guards salutes and performs some intricate evolutions.

'Who goes there?'

'The keys!'

'Whose keys?'

'King George's keys.'

'God preserve King George!'

When it's all over the band plays 'God save our gracious King,' the keys go to bed, and anybody entering the Tower must give the password, as confided to the Lord Mayor over the sign-manual of the King. It's one of those marvellous games of make-believe that make Britons feel secure by binding them to their past — and a compliment to their histrionic ability, outstanding since the days of Elizabeth.

To the American this is fairyland; it shows him a side of English life that he has seen in picture-books, and which is not 'real.' It is difficult for him to accept it as such, but it does indicate an ingredient in the national character, the love of pageantry and ritual and rural customs that nothing on earth would persuade an Englishman to abandon. One such custom is the famous Dunmow Flitch trial, which takes place each year in the village of Dunmow in Essex, where with mock solemnity the gentry 'try' by the rules of evidence the claims of married couples to have attained conjugal bliss. The prize, if won, is a flitch of bacon. This, too, was relayed to America, for it is a true picture of English rural life; and so was a scene in a village public house, not more than forty-five miles from London, where the characters assemble each Saturday night to listen to the wisdom of 'Uppy' Andrews, who has never seen a city but can cure warts by faith.

It may have been rhetorical extravagance, and certainly an exaggeration, when an American broadcasting executive said that the greatest thing his company had ever done for Anglo-American relations was to broadcast the song of an English nightingale, but it certainly gave some Americans a touch of the magic stillness of an English night in spring. At any rate, American radio editors felt justified in voting this the most interesting broadcast of the year (1932). The B.B.C. began trapping the nightingale's song back in 1926, in a Surrey garden, where a well-known lady 'cellist with romantic turn of mind had succeeded in stimulating the nightingales' ardor with the seductive tones of her instrument. The bird concert, in turn, lured motorists to the locality, whose raucous horns spoilt the fun. The following year the B.B.C. engineers chose a secluded wood in Berkshire, where a gramophone proved just as good a decoy. Shattering more poetic notions, the birds appeared to like jazz as well as Beethoven, and penny whistles as well as jazz. The method was to place microphones in the trees, take the leads to an amplifier some hundred yards away, and connect this via a telephone line to the studio. Then, when the luring noises awakened response, the operator would warn the control engineer in London, who would 'fade down' a dance band and 'fade in' the nightingale.

It occurred to me one day that America has no nightingale, and as every English poet from Shakespeare to Shelley celebrates its song, Americans might like to hear how it sounds. Alas! An amplified nightingale rather exceeds expectations — the quality of its liquid dulcet tones, as I have heard them for many springs outside my cottage window, eludes the skill of the engineer.

WORDSWORTH'S BIRDS AND SHAKESPEARE'S FLOWERS

We were rather more successful with the birds of Wordsworth's cottage garden in Grasmere, by the side of a lovely
lake in romantic Westmoreland. It was on the poet's birthday, on April 7, when the flowers in his hillside garden were
bursting into glory, while the birds that sing in his poems
intoned the first polyphony of spring.

The Lake District is distinguished by the fact that it produces even more rain than the rest of England; but when the
sun does break through its mysterious drifting mists, its
rays are like the laughter of a happy child. It was a perilous
experiment — to transmit the rhapsody of nature herself as
a background to the nature poet's verse, for nature herself
was as capricious as the combination of Lakeland and April
could contrive.

When I arrived at that delectable hamlet, with its Gothic
church, its whitewashed inn, and its stone cottages nestling
against the sweeping moorland slopes, the rain was drenching
everything and the engineers with their coils of wire and a
truckful of gear were looking wistfully at the sky. The
kitchen of eighteenth-century Dove Cottage was our control-
room, and a fire in the antiquated range the one cheerful
thing in it. But 'outside' radio engineers are a unique race
of optimists. Pretty soon they had microphones in three
rooms of the house, and in various parts of the garden as well;
and bubbling over with excitement they dropped a pair of
earphones over my head. 'Do you hear it?' gasped Harvey.
'Do you hear the bubbling brook?' By placing a microphone
in a tree — for the birds — they had discovered the rustle
of a garden brook, which to bare human ears was shut off by
a stone wall. They were as thrilled as children, but the problem was: would the rustle sound as poetic as we heard it,
or would listeners think it was just a noise in the line? In
the end we had to abandon Wordsworth's brook for the sake
of Wordsworth's verse.

Next day we were all set, though it drizzled off and on all

day, and the hooded microphones were dripping rain. The church bells, a quarter of a mile away, were to be picked up by a microphone on a high telegraph pole by the road, but in our excitement we had forgotten the bell-ringers' crew. Church service was on, and an hour before the broadcast I sneaked down the aisle to where the 'captain' had been pointed out: he was doubling in baritone. We did a deal between prayers, and the eight men would be on duty after the service. (English church bells require one man per chime, and their teamwork is a traditional art.)

And now for the birds! We listened at our earphones; they twittered and sang very sweetly before nesting time. But the old Lakeland caretaker wasn't satisfied. 'Ye haavn't got the throosh,' he said. And where was the thrush? Why — in the caretaker's garden across the road. What *would* we do? ... Well, fifteen minutes before the broadcast he came back and asked us to listen, and there was — not one but a whole family of thrushes, mingling their notes with those of the blackbirds, finches, and larks. Grave as ever, he informed us that he had lured them over by spreading bread crumbs on Wordsworth's lawn!

But suddenly we heard too much: a motor car passing the house at full speed, then another and another. Nothing was audible but the whirr of their motors and the grinding of their gears, mounting the hill. Heavens alive, it was Sunday, and the trippers were enjoying an evening drive along the lakes. Could they be stopped? Was there no police? The caretaker's daughter, who up to then had been a nuisance, telling us the local scandal — which was about Wordsworth and his *real* sweetheart (not his wife), both of whom were dead these eighty-five years — now bethought herself of a good-looking young policeman, and we raced to find him at his cottage, taking his Sunday ease. He was the entire police force of Grasmere, he confided, as he carefully put on his helmet and tunic. Our strange request was for him to establish himself at one fork of the roads and a volunteer at the other, to divert the traffic to the highroad. We told him it was for Wordsworth's birthday and, law or no law, he did the job. Our broadcast was saved, for as we were talking the clouds were clearing away, and in the west the sun was painting them a glowing apricot pink.

Our program did us proud: we took a 'visitor' through the house, up to Wordsworth's bedroom, giving on the garden, where Ernest de Selincourt read Wordsworth's verses appertaining to the place; we opened up the tree microphones and our birds sang their symphony; we switched to the church at the end and the chimes rang out sweetly into the stillness of the evening, as we painted the landscape in words. Even the Lakeland dialect was not missing, for the caretaker also had his little say.

Wordsworth's drawing-room meantime was full of the village worthies; they sat still as mice, not even a creaking floor board was heard. And I have never seen a prouder lot of folks, whose claim to nobility lies in the familiarity with a poet's life and work. Only the caretaker's daughter was a little sniffy; talking to the B.B.C. driver, she couldn't understand all that fuss for just fifteen minutes. 'Aye,' said the driver, 'but after it rains all day and the sun comes out for fifteen minutes, it makes you happy, doesn't it?'

That was not our first poet's broadcast — nor the only one. I raked the calendar for centenaries, or jubilees or anything, so the 'special events department' in New York could be satisfied that the program had news value of a sort. We went to Anne Hathaway's cottage in Stratford on Will Shakespeare's birthday, and had a caretaker with her rich Warwickshire accent explain about the courting settle, the rushlights, and Anne's rushbottom bed, and the flowers in the garden, every one of which is named in Shakespeare's works. We went to Keats' house in Hampstead and read the 'Ode to a Nightingale' from the room in which it was written, and to Lord Tennyson's pretentious neo-Jacobean palace at Aldworth, on top of Blackdown, where you look down across the Sussex plain as far as Chanctonbury Ring, and the local choir sang 'Sweet and Low' among the bracken and the heather that Tennyson loved.

But the most ambitious of our broadcasts, to my mind, was the one from Milton's Cottage in Chalfont St. Giles, where we dramatized a scene from the poet's life, with actors and singers, with verses from 'Comus' sung to contemporary settings, and accompanied by the instruments of the time. The acoustic problems of that broadcast — in a low-roofed seventeenth-century cottage — with a harpsichord and strings in one room, actors and singers in another, myself as author-producer and monitor, with the engineers in a third, was as intricate as anything the B.B.C. does with its famous 'dramatic panel' and all the modern contraptions of Broadcasting House.

An experience, too, and great fun into the bargain was the program we put on for the centenary of Mr. Pickwick. It began and ended in Dickens's house in Doughty Street, where he started out on his meteoric literary career. Between this prologue and epilogue we switched to Broadcasting House and made Mr. Pickwick live by means of Clinton-Baddeley's dramatization, which is one of the best things of its kind.

CURFEW STILL RINGS

But eventually we ran out of anniversaries, so another type of atmospheric program had to be devised to convey an impression of the English scene. This formula — a friend of mine called it the 'picture-postcard broadcast' — which eventually begat a whole progeny of programs designed to give American listeners glimpses, in terms of sound, of places ranging from the North Cape to Pompeii, and from Cairo to Iceland and Seville, was born in the little town of Ripon, in Yorkshire.

Ripon, the second oldest town in England, has one of the smallest but most interesting English cathedrals, first built by Saint Wilfrid in the seventh century. It is the city for which Ripon, Wisconsin, is named and from which it has taken its coat of arms. On it is pictured the 'wakeman's' horn — the wakeman being the prototype of the modern mayor, whose chief business in the Middle Ages was to guard against fires. 'Unless ye Lord keepeth ye Cittie, ye Wakeman waketh in vain' is the motto over the town hall; and the horn, a replica of the ancient cow-horn, is still blown every evening at the town hall, just as curfew is still rung by a special curfew bell in the cathedral tower. To complete the illusion of antiquity, the 'news,' chiefly official announcements, is still cried out by a bellman whose hand-bell resounds in the market place. Ripon was the ideal place for a sound-picture and we managed to get it all — Cathedral choir, bishop, dean, mayor, bellman, curfew, and wakeman's horn — into a fifteen-minute program — a masterpiece of compression. There were seven microphone points and a control room in the famous Lady Loft: it all worked like a charm, and a dog accidentally barking in the market place added a poignant note of realism.

But the preliminaries to that broadcast were anything but simple, for the cathedral and the town (i.e., the municipal government) were found to be at war. The cathedral represented gentility, while the town was run by the common clay — Bottom the Weaver and Snug the Joiner being much what they were in Shakespeare's day. Difficult questions of precedence arose which were finally settled by a small financial transaction, in which the low-comedy characters turned out to be the nobility.

Which reminds me of another broadcast in which the question of caste played an important part. The neat, Scottish town of Dunfermline, where Andrew Carnegie saw the light of day in a miserable two-roomed cottage, now a shrine to the city's greatest benefactor, was celebrating the philanthropist's centenary. I arranged for a special transmission from the cottage itself, in which an eminent American, as well as the mayor of Dunfermline and a certain peer, were to provide the oratory. A representative of the noble lord, who called on me in London intimated that the mayor had better be left out, as his background wasn't appropriate to the occasion. I argued for this bit of genuine local color, but was sternly voted down. It was embarrassing to tell the honest mayor that he wasn't on the program after all, but it had to be done. Afterward I found that his Lordship had accepted not merely for the honor of Carnegie but for a very small fee, which he offered to divide with the American dignitary. I was flummoxed.

An English village church with its churchyard and its lych gate, its ancient square tower and no less ancient yews, set in the rolling green of its glebe lands, with cattle grazing at sundown and a tiny river slowly flowing in the dale, is one of the most serenely comforting scenes on earth. Here life has gone on unchanged for centuries, and every stone belies the transitory nature of man. I long wanted an excuse to transmit a word-picture of this serene peacefulness, with the simple religious service as the epilogue. America likes famous names and associations, so I thought of Stoke Poges, where Gray's 'Elegy' was inspired. But for some strange reason the vicar would not permit a broadcast to America (though a local broadcast had already been made from the church). The loss was made up by another church, at Purleigh in Essex, where the fact of Lawrence Washington's having been the rector, and the restoration of a set of bells donated by him, was enough to arouse some timely interest.

A grander broadcast — and one of the most beautiful I have ever heard — was the dedication service of the restored bell-tower of Boston Parish Church, the famous 'Stump' — the only church tower which at the same time serves as a beacon to the sailor at sea.

I was touched when a warden of the church came to my office to offer us this very costly transmission at the expense of the congregation, in gratitude for the help which the citizens of Boston, Massachusetts, had given to the ancient church in Boston, Lincolnshire, in restoring the damage caused by the 'death-watch beetle' in the woodwork of the tower. The singing in the great church, and the service of dedication, working up to the point where the long silent bells once more rang out, as the great beacon flashed its rays out to sea, must have left an unforgettable impression in the minds of anyone who heard the broadcast and realized the implications of the event.

Aside from the brilliant occasions when the Church of England played a spectacular part in transatlantic broadcasting — the wedding of the Duke and Duchess of Kent, the funeral of King George V, and the coronation of his son — I feel that the singing of English church music of the great centuries by the boys of Windsor's Chapel Royal and the annual singing of Christmas carols by the choir of King's College, Cambridge, stand out as memorable things. Personally I shall never forget standing in the richly carved box of Henry VIII in St. George's Chapel, looking up at the miraculous fan-vaulting and the incredible beauty of the Gothic traceries, and down at the riot of color made by the banners of the Garter knights, while the choir sang an evening service especially for America. Nor shall I forget the naïve answer of the choirmaster when I complimented him on the angelic voices of the boys: 'I told them to sing so as to melt the hearts of the gangsters in Chicago!' He meant it literally, too.

FIFTY THOUSAND DOLLARS' WORTH OF CORONATION

The quaint pageantry of a royal proclamation, the pomp and panoply of the coronation — these things show England from its 'unreal' side; they are the same make-believe England which has its daily resurrection in the changing of the guard at Buckingham Palace while the nursemaids and their charges look on. The coronation of King George VI — the first coronation ever to be broadcast — required three months of preparation and the services of a small army of engineers and executants. The equipment, costing $50,000, comprised 73 microphones, 7 tons of batteries, and 472 miles of wire. The program, lasting five hours, was broadcast throughout the British Empire and rebroadcast in most foreign countries (with the notable exception of Italy, which was nursing a grudge against 'sanctionist' England), ten of which sent their own commentators to report the proceedings in their own tongue. The two major American networks stationed announcers at positions opposite Buckingham Palace as well as Westminster Abbey, on the assumption that they would be better equipped to serve an American audience than their English colleagues of the B.B.C., and they made up in liveliness what they lacked in knowledge.

The B.B.C.'s arrangements functioned perfectly, and within the limits imposed by pious loyalty their men gave a remarkably clear picture of an event unprecedented in magnitude in the annals of broadcasting, which certainly succeeded in demonstrating the might of empire to a world which seemed in need of reassurance.

Having satisfied the American listeners' supposed desire for expert advance information and exalted names by providing a solid week of daily talks from all ranks of British nobility and learning, and having laid out an elaborate scheme of direct reporting of the great event in collaboration with the B.B.C., I had the pleasure of watching the 'works' from a fine vantage point opposite the palace. The most impressive moment to me was when the King and Queen, in their golden coach, swung through the wide-open gates of the palace to the cheers of the immense multitude. Strange to relate, the massed bands in front of the palace played them out to the tune of 'The Stars and Stripes Forever,' but most people were too excited to notice it — probably including the bandmaster. Altogether it was a patriotic orgy such as I have never seen outside a Fascist country, where such things are provided by command.

Excepting the usual number of fainting women — and men — exhausted from standing in the streets since dawn, nothing untoward happened, much to the disgust of some American reporters in search of a story. Complete contempt was expressed for the B.B.C.'s arrangements by one radio man because no provision had been made for the immediate broadcasting of an accident, should it occur, or a madman's attempt at assassination — or worse. It all depends on the point of view.

Besides giving the world a powerful impression of Britain's might, this broadcast demonstrated the world-wide appeal

Fred Bate, NBC commentator, outside Buckingham Palace describing the Coronation Procession of Their Majesties King George VI and Queen Elizabeth

The Foreign Control Room at Middlesex Guild Hall during the broadcast of the Coronation

of a pageantry and the power of a symbolism which can have little real meaning in the modern world. I think there was more of the real England in the broadcast of a Christmas dinner such as we managed to transmit one Christmas Day, for it conveyed the simple but unalterable customs which, despite all change, retain a valid meaning so long as the family remains the prime social unit of the race.

THE MAN IN THE STREET LETS HIMSELF GO

These things are mere indications of what international broadcasting can do: we have just scratched the surface, and there is a great deal below that surface which a little imagination and daring will reveal. Two or three times we have taken our microphones out into the street and let the ordinary passer-by, the man in the street, speak his mind. In the United States this has become a regular feature of broadcasting on all sorts of occasions, from an election to New Year's Eve. The first time it was done in London, the officials of the B.B.C. were palpably nervous, for might not the man in the street say things that decent ears should not hear? He might even use swear words. Well, he did.

The police were less dubious than the B.B.C., although we had picked as our 'stand' a spot just off Piccadilly Circus, in Regent Street, and as our time 11 P.M., when the theatre crowd would be beginning to liven things up. Inspector Prothero, then in command at Vine Street police station, a man of the world and a great detective in his day, brought his sense of humor to bear on the situation. I had explained our problem: we needed a permit to 'obstruct' the sidewalk; we needed a policeman or two to prevent disorder. He looked amused and very wise. To help him decide, my partner in crime, H. V. Kaltenborn, thought he'd encourage him by saying that there wouldn't be any obstruction really — no crowds or anything like that. The seasoned police officer, having presided over the hottest beat in London for many years, drew up his eyebrows and drawled: 'Mr. Kaltenborn, your modesty is disarming!'

Having thus put us into our places he said it would be all right and he would take precautions. When we told him that we wanted to ask all sorts and conditions of people about the economic situation (anent the Economic Conference) he volunteered, 'Well, you might ask some of "those" girls along Regent Street — you know?'

When we turned up with our microphone, crew and gear, outside the Piccadilly Hotel we found not one or two policemen, but twenty, with a sergeant at their head — and before we got through we needed them. It was the first man-in-the-street broadcast ever made in England, and at first the passers-by were shy. But once the ice was broken the fishing was grand. A crowd collected, and pretty soon people were struggling to get near that microphone or whatever it was; our stalwart bobbies did a noble and completely silent job, and their courtesy was a lesson to any gentleman. Various opinions on that frightful fiasco, the World Economic Conference, went across, from an intoxicated swell who insisted on introducing himself as Prime Minister Bennett of Canada, to a Cockney communist who compared it to 'an old sock — full of 'oles and the sweat runnin' out.'

As we were getting near the end of our time, a very pretty young lady was led up to the 'mike.' I asked her to tell the American audience what *she* thought about the econom——
'Oh, is that all you wanted, dearie?' said the lady of Regent Street. The crowd was slightly embarrassed, but they had a good laugh. Inspector Prothero was right. He knew we needed twenty policemen, and he knew we'd get one of 'those' ladies in our broadcast. The B.B.C. officials were duly shocked, and they haven't risked a street broadcast to this day! But *we* have — in London, and right in front of Broadcasting House.

When in search of England, don't forget the man in the street.

XX. THE TOURIST'S PARADISE

VIENNA IS STILL GAY

VIENNA is often referred to, by post-war writers, as the saddest place in the world. A city famed for its gaiety, the well-being of its citizens, the cosy comfort of its homes, the beauty of its women, and the prodigal brilliance of its society — a city lying in the midst of one of the sweetest landscapes, once feeding upon the wealth of a vast polyglot empire and the trade of half of Europe — was now deprived by the cruel fortunes of war of all those happy circumstances which gave it its prosperity. 'Wine, Woman, and Song' had been its slogan of happiness, but after the war the most ubiquitous woman was Dame Care.

Yet there are qualities in people which do not die. The war had taken from the Viennese everything they had — most of their land, their emperor, their wealth, and even their coffee, once the best in Europe, now replaced by *Ersatz*. When the Austrian delegation came to St. Germain after the war they were summoned only to sign the death warrant of their own once happy land. When they arrived at their Paris hotel, so the story goes, on a gray and dismal morning, and sat waiting for breakfast, no one was able to say a word. Not until some time after the waiter had left did the Prime Minister of the new Republic open his mouth for some deeply felt words. 'At last,' he said, 'once again a good cup of coffee.'

The coffee is good again in Vienna, its original European home (where it was introduced by the Turks), and the waiters who serve it are no different from the pre-war breed.

As for sentimentality — Vienna is more like itself than ever, for it can muse *ad infinitum* on the good old times.

At this no one is more expert than they. There is in Vienna a society which in effect does nothing else. The Federal Chancellor belongs to it, and many a solid citizen with a title before his name — titles which denote not so much a rank as an activity, and usually an activity long obsolete. Every now and again they foregather in a club-house which was once the home of an eminent patrician family, and which is still furnished in the style which Viennese call *Biedermayer* and the unfeeling outer world dubs '*incroyable.*' They dress up in the clothes of the Metternich period, dance the old dances, sing the old songs, and get tipsy on Grinzing wine. Early in the year — in carnival time — they usher in the season's dances with a *Fasching* ball, in the style of the long ago.

It was my privilege to attend one of these parties and to broadcast it to America, and next day the papers hoped that the Viennese in America who had heard it had wept tears of longing or of vicarious joy.

It was certainly Vienna at its most. The Chancellor couldn't come, but his wife, that ill-fated young Frau von Schuschnigg, who was destined to meet her death in a mysterious motor-car accident within a year, came in an *Empire* gingham dress, carrying a large bouquet, and got her hand kissed by innumerable 'court councillors,' barons and majors in colored tail-coats and stocks. Betty Fischer, the original 'Merry Widow,' now a prosperous Dutch lord mayor's wife, came to sing the songs that made her famous; a comic Viennese character, Ernst Arnold, well known to everybody, sang the '*Fiakerlied,*' the comic Viennese coachman's song which has made five generations of inebriates weep; and the illustrious Shrammel Quartet led by fat Pepi Wichart, with red face and his thick moustache curled into spirals at the ends, furnished the nineteenth-century equivalent of jazz. (A Schrammel quartet consists of two violins, accordion, and guitar.) As the party warmed up they sang, swayed to the music, and praised Old Vienna in many toasts. When the old clock on the mantelpiece played its ancient tune, the crowd hushed into silence and some wiped furtive tears from their eyes. When I left, there wasn't a dry eye — or glove — in the house, and for all I know they are still there...

Another time we went out to Grinzing — that sentimental suburb where Beethoven worked and Schubert imbibed while writing songs — and broadcast the crowd at their *Heurigen*, the new wine drunk outdoors in spring and summer, and indoors the year round. The result was much the same, only the songs were different. One of them, '*Fein, fein schmeckt der Wein*,' a particular favorite with the crowd, went something like this:

> 'Wine tastes good when you're twenty,
>   And so does love,
>   Wine tastes good when you're forty,
>   And kissing, by Jove.
> When you get older, and gradually colder,
>   Just wine alone
>   Tastes good.'

There was a scion of the Hapsburg family in our crowd, and when it came time to go home he refused to go by car. A *Fiaker*, the old-time hired carriage-and-pair, was the only thing fit to ride home from Grinzing in. When the carriage was found, our princeling discovered a finely engraved crown on each of the shining lamps, and recognized the carriage as having belonged to an old aunt, a Hapsburg long dead. The old cabby, with his bowler hat cocked on the side of his head, when questioned, confessed that he had been the old lady's coachman, and when he recognized her once royal relative he all but broke down. Leopold, the Hapsburg offspring, mounted the driver's seat with him and they talked about the good old times all the way to Vienna. For the rest of the night Leopold drowned his sorrow in a pseudo-modern Viennese bar, to the strains of strident jazz.

After the war, the cynical Viennese used to sing the old national anthem to these words:

> 'Gott erhalte, Gott beschütze
>   Unsern Renner, unsern Seitz,

Gott erhalt', man kann nicht wissen,
Unsern Kaiser in der Schweiz.'[1]

Renner and Seitz — the first Chancellor of the Austrian Republic and the first President of the National Assembly — became political exiles; Kaiser Karl is long dead. But the spirit is still the same. Vienna is still gay.

MOZART AND LEATHER BREECHES

Austria is a happy hunting ground for the picture postcard fan, but most of its landscapes are suffused with sound.

Take Salzburg as an example. Salzburg cherishes its Mozart and its architecture, which is music, too. During July and August it simply bursts with music and picturesqueness, while its fashionable tourists, in leather breeches and *Dirndl* dresses, almost burst with good food.

When I first knew Salzburg, just after the war, it was a different place. It was then the special preserve of Max Reinhardt and Richard Strauss and a mangy-looking crowd of composers, mostly Viennese, whose activities aroused the honest suspicions of the natives. One day two of these budding geniuses were actually discovered in the hall of the Mozarteum, playing on one piano at the same time, and as the piano was public domain, some worthy peasant trustees proposed their expulsion from the premises, for misuse of property.

There were two festivals in those days, one consisting of Mozart and Reinhardt's production of *Everyman* in front of the cathedral, the other of the most modern music of all the nations. The former was patronized by the tourists (mostly Viennese), and the latter almost exclusively by the modern composers themselves and their immediate families (also

[1] 'God preserve them, God protect them,
Our Renner, our Seitz,
God preserve — one can't be certain —
Our Kaiser, now abroad.'

mostly Viennese). It was an artistic maxim that one festival
did not know what the other was doing; but the natives
were equally hostile to both. 'We want our peace,' said they
— with the exception of the innkeepers and restaurateurs.
Everybody, including Stefan Zweig and a few genuine
Salzburgers, would meet in the afternoon at the Café Bazar
(nicknamed Café Megalomania) to shout at distracted
waiters and hear them shout back '*Komme gleich!*' (Coming
directly!) or '*Bin scho' da!*' (Am already there!).

There was no festival playhouse but the tiny municipal
theatre, though a hopeful band of 'founders' led by Strauss
and Reinhardt marched to a suburban meadow to watch the
Archbishop lay the foundation stone of a huge and fantastic
opera house which is still waiting to be built; and on the way
home Strauss turned to me to ask whether some rich American woman couldn't be found to sacrifice just one string of
pearls to make that great temple of art a reality.

But it needed no modern temple to listen to Mozart's
serenades in the open air, and Mozart's masses in the cathedral. Those who did, and drank cheap country-wine with
the friars in St. Peter's cellar afterwards, were mostly musicians, poets, and impecunious dreamers of all sorts; the
tourists were modest burghers, and the leather breeches
were worn only by natives and two or three show-offs from
Berlin...

Now all that has changed: there is just one Salzburg
festival, and it has become a flourishing industry. Toscanini
reigns supreme, Reinhardt lives in a reconstructed baroque
palace with a private chapel and a lake for swans; but
Strauss and the young composers are gone. There is a
gambling casino, the hotels are full to overflowing, the prices
are high, the predominant language is English, and the
leather breeches and Tyrolean hats have become *de rigueur*
— except for the natives, who dress in ordinary clothes, so
you can tell them from the socialites. Mozart's birth house
is still intact, and his Papageno tune is still played by the
town-hall chimes; but they are smothered by the 'functional'
American bars with indirect lighting, chromium-plated
railings, and 'swing.'

Now the microphone needn't hear any of that. It can pick up the operas and the serenades and the tinkle of Mozart's piano; it can go on a pilgrimage to the old real Salzburg hidden under the gaudy surface. The architecture, at any rate, is still there — that intriguing northern interpretation of Italian *motifs* — and the ruined castle surging up out of the middle of the town, and the bells of all the churches, and the sheer, snowclad mountains rising out of the plain. My first set of Salzburg broadcasts started July 25, 1931, and included the Mozart requiem from the cathedral; the last one, with Toscanini conducting, comprised Verdi's *Falstaff* and a promenade through the old Salzburg — a multiple 'pickup' of all its traditional charms. After that, commercialism stepped in and took what was left.

POLAND'S BROKEN MELODY

A favorite pre-war story about the Poles was the one concerning the elephant. A group of people of different nationalities agreed to write about the elephant and compare the result after two years. The Englishman wrote a handy volume entitled 'Elephants I Have Shot'; the Frenchman wrote a monograph on 'The Love Life of Elephants'; and the German a two-volume 'Introduction to a Study of the Psychology of Elephants.' But the Pole simply submitted a pamphlet on 'The Elephant and the Polish Question.'

There is no longer a Polish question in the old sense, but the mentality which produced that strange pamphlet lives on. There is nothing quite so sentimentally patriotic as a Pole, and his particular national touchiness is a thing apart.

Although Poland is supposed to be a republic, the shrine of national glory is Cracow, the city of Polish kings. Here the Palace of Wawel, used as a military outpost by the Austrians for nearly a century and a half, has been restored by the modern decorator's art to its medieval glory, and in its crypt lie the remains of Poland's kings, including John Sobieski, the reputed savior of Vienna from the Turks. But the most prominent position is now given to Marshal Pilsudski, who saved Warsaw from the Bolsheviks — with the help of Weygand.

It so happened that on the Sunday afternoon which we had chosen for a 'picture postcard' broadcast from Cracow, Pilsudski, dead only a few days, was lying in state in the crypt, embalmed in the manner reserved for modern dictators and Caruso, in a casket of silver and glass. Fifteen thousand people had passed around the Marshal's coffin that day, and a double line about a mile long was slowly snaking up the hill when we arrived to do our commentary. A microphone had been placed next to the Marshal, and I couldn't help feeling rather sacrilegious to be 'commentating' on the scene with the same kind of instrument that is associated by most people with crooners. Pilsudski's features, in death, were handsome and noble, and showed none of the choleric violence with which he was credited in life. The young Polish woman who was helping me — a graduate of Bryn Mawr and Oxford — broke into tears and could think of nothing but Pilsudski for days.

But the most dramatic part of that broadcast — aside from the way in which we ran it — was the watchman in the belfry of St. Mary's Church who, like his predecessors for six hundred years, every day and every hour of the day, plays a certain tune, the 'Heynal,' which stops abruptly before the end. It stops because one day, during the Tartar siege of the city in the thirteenth century, an arrow shot by a besieger pierced the trumpeter's throat at that particular point. Cracovians set their watches by the unfinished tune, which is supposed never to be a second off. It was the only punctual item in that broadcast of ours.

Patriotism takes time.

THE CITY OF THE DEAD

Nothing more incongruous could be imagined than the intrusion of radio into the silence of the dead city of Pompeii, which we picked for a broadcast early one spring. The good Neapolitans thought we were simpletons, for what could one tell people from the ruins of Pompeii that you couldn't tell them from the Naples Museum — or for that matter from the Metropolitan Museum of New York? Nevertheless their radio engineers humored us (just as they humored Max Jordan when a couple of months later he wanted to broadcast the rumble of Vesuvius), even though it involved expensive improvements in the fifteen-mile telephone line from Naples to Pompeii.

The nearest terminus, moreover, was at Pompeii station, about half a mile from the far end of the ruined city, which we wanted to describe. It was necessary to string two insulated lines of copper wire loosely over the jagged, ruined walls along the whole of one side of Pompeii. One of them was a fiery red, and sightseers craned their necks to see what they meant. Microphones were installed in five or six places in and around the recently and most perfectly excavated 'House of Menander,' and the broadcast was scheduled for late Sunday afternoon. My side-kick in Italy, Raymond Hall, and I managed to make a sort of relay pilgrimage from room to room, across walls and ruined swimming pools, into the 'House of the Painter,' the 'House of the Two Lovers,' and finally onto a balcony which brought us bang opposite the still unexcavated part of Pompeii, where twenty-three feet of earth, cut straight down like a layer cake, showed the strata of pumice, ashes, and soil deposited by Vesuvius and Father Time, crowned by a luscious crop of billowing wheat, under which lie the remaining secrets of Pompeii's tragedy.

Before we got there we came upon the skeletons of the rich owner's servants, caught and asphyxiated while guarding the treasures of their masters, who sought safety in flight. And the watchdog, whose skeleton is still chained, lies embedded in ashes three feet above the ground, showing how far he was able to climb with the mounting floor of ashes — an eternal postscript to stark tragedy.

Looking to the northwest from that balcony, we gazed upon Vesuvius, lazily smoking as always, its white cloud set afire by the setting sun. There was no sound in that broadcast but that of our voices, as we described our progress, step by step, save a resounding ring of a great bronze bowl in the *atrium* of Menander's House and the inconsequential tinkle of some Neapolitan tune at the end; yet I cannot help thinking that the tragic beauty of the place was made more poignant to our distant audience than ever before.

VENICE, CALIFORNIA, HEARS VENICE, ITALY

But Italy is full of beauty and curiosity — a paradise for broadcasters with an inquiring mind. Take the utterly medieval town of Siena, whence we broadcast a commentary on the Palio — that most ancient and most fantastic of all horse races in the world — while the heavy, caparisoned steeds hurtled around the cobbled market place. Armed with sticks their riders, each defending the honor of his city ward, think nothing of hitting out at their competitors' mounts in order to win the race, and each stable requires an armed guard to prevent what squeamish Anglo-Saxons call 'tampering.' Here is medieval gallantry in one of its more robust manifestations! And again, take Venice — that incredible defiance of nature; one of the most extravagantly creative boasts in the history of man.

We wanted to present Venice to the American listener — and to the prospective honeymooner — with all its romantic fascination, but with a realism that tourist catalogues and guide books do not attain. And we must have succeeded, for here is a fan-letter received some weeks later from Venice, California — some seven thousand miles away.

'It is 8.45 A.M. Sunday, May 19, 1935, in Venice, California,

U.S.A., and I am tuning in on Venice, Italy, for the first broadcast from that classic city. Now I hear the voice of the narrator ... describing the panorama spread out before him — St. Mark's, the four bronze horses, with their story, I hear the flutter of the pigeons, inseparable from St. Mark's, the bells, the great cathedral organ, and the sacred singing. Soon I hear the splash of water in the Grand Canal, the conversation of bride and groom (whether stage bride and groom doesn't matter) ... the traffic signals of the canal, and, to make it seem more natural, a near-accident occurs, accompanied by the quick, impatient staccato voices of the gondoliers, as they scold each other in their musical tongue. Now back to St. Mark's, with more description of the environment; the bells strike six o'clock in the evening, the sun is setting, and it is time to say good-bye.'

Perhaps our correspondent had no taste for music, for she might have mentioned the gondolier's song and the sound of guitars, and she was certainly too optimistic about radio's power to bring more sympathy and understanding to the tribes of humanity. What the poetic lady did not know was that the preliminaries were a most desperately sordid and harrowing experience, reminiscent of the days of Casanova, king of mountebanks and a Venetian among Venetians.

After encountering the various *bestie* of the Police Department, the Prefect's office, the Carabinieri, and the supposedly pious guardians of St. Mark's, not to mention the brotherhood of gondoliers, the café proprietors and the gentlemen in charge of the city's morals, we were ready to give up the ghost. A day before the broadcast the police ordered us to take down our lines and instructed the guards to remove microphones wherever they should be found! And all because, apparently, we hadn't tipped either the right people in the right sequence, or the right amounts. The guardians of St. Mark's had the greatest qualms about letting us profane the great church with microphones, and maybe put *americanata* (low-brow Americanisms) into our script. In the end they rang only the tiniest bell (instead of the famous great one as agreed), because the ducats had not reached the right hands. Luckily they couldn't stop the

Radio transmitted to the world the tragic beauty of the dead
city of Pompeii

bronze Moors, who, in the habit of striking the hour for centuries, could not be deterred.

The show was saved, it should be recorded, by Count Ciano, Mussolini's son-in-law (later Foreign Minister), who had been appealed to in Rome and sent a 'phonogram' to the Podestà inquiring who dared to obstruct us. But corruption is a tradition that goes back to the days of Othello, and Venice for all that is the City of Dreams...

'*Mila dollari per minuto*' (One Thousand Dollars a Minute) was the heading a leading Italian newspaper put over its report of our broadcast.

RIEN NE VA PLUS!

Turning from the sublime to the ridiculous, I come upon the following among my collection of scripts:

'Hello, America! This is Monte Carlo calling. We are going to take you on a flying trip through the world's most famous gambling resort. Sorry we can't win any money for you, but we'll have a look-in at the tables and see how others do it.' And we did. We were going to soften the blow with a little scene from the opera house, where the curtain was about to ring down on Glazounoff's ballet *Raymonda*, but the stage manager, after agreeing to retime his show, forgot that his watch was fast. So, without musical introduction we switched to the sumptuous Sporting Club, where French men about town, English aristocrats, Russian emigrés, and faded dowagers of all nationalities were trying to improve their economic status by staking all they could afford on the spin of the *roulette*. Among those present, too, were Prince Andrew of Greece, the Maharajah of Nepal, Lord de Clifford, Steve Donoghue, the jockey, H. G. Wells, Somerset Maugham, and Mr. and Mrs. Berry Wall of New York, dressed in the style of the gay nineties.

The croupiers were wonderful, and most obliging. We dangled a microphone over the table, to pick up the spinning ball and the click of the chips, and another one by the side of each croupier. They raised their voices as they shouted their '*Faites vos jeux!*' and '*Rien ne va plus*,' and offered to use real gold Napoleons instead of chips to make a more impressive noise. They poured a flood of gold out of a bag before my greedy eyes, but coming through the microphone the precious coins sounded like tin, so we decided to use chips in our 'demonstration game.' I then made the only running sports commentary of my career, except for the Olympic Games in Berlin, when Bill Henry suddenly handed me the microphone and asked me to tell the audience what *I* thought of a certain race. Both commentaries were of the same degree of expertness; they left the listener no wiser than he was before.

Our real trouble in Monte Carlo was not caused by the chips but by a bevy of 'girls' — *Les Girls* — just arrived from New York, who were doing a dancing show and were to greet the folks back home. They refused to take anyone seriously — except a weaselly little French ballet-master, who yelled at them and got kissed in return. This band of 'sugars,' used to working only with their legs, had to be taught even to giggle convincingly, and one of them just managed to say, 'This sure is a Ritzy place.' They nearly wrecked the show.

But it was all good, clean fun, and nobody in this Temple of Mammon needed to be bribed.

HOLLAND'S SILENT CHARMS

Holland, you would think, is full of things to broadcast. If it is not the most beautiful country in Europe, it is the most picturesque, and it has been almost entirely made by the hand of man. (The parts that were there before the Dutch came along, nobody seems to care about.) Holland, moreover, is a direct ancestor of America: New York was really New Amsterdam, and our highest claim to aristocracy is a Dutch name. The Dutch, enterprising as ever, were actually trying to produce broadcasts for us, while the rest of Europe just waited for us to come and make our own. But Holland is a silent land. William the Silent is the national hero, and Holland lives up to his name. It is a land of flat, hand-made squares of soil, called *polders*, of canals called *grachts*, of clean narrow brick houses on clean, brick-paved streets, of windmills and boats and vegetables and flowers, of large cheeses and wooden shoes — all silent things, except the clogs, and they are too monotonous for words. Even the cheeses are rolled along to be loaded on canal-boats, so they don't make any noise.

We investigated all these things, and finally the energetic Phillips's man (drumming up business for the short-wave transmitter) took me to the Island of Marken, where the people go about in the old Dutch costumes and get themselves photographed for money by gullible tourists. I never saw a sadder place; the inbred population of that little island has nothing to do but read books, so they are the most educated as well as the most picturesque peasants in the world. They used to fish, but now that the Zuider Zee is gradually being reclaimed and turned into more *polders* (for future generations of Dutchmen, who can either eat or export the surplus vegetables that will be grown), the water is turning sweet and the fish are getting soured on the locality.

We went to see the mayor of the little town — a wizened old man in shirtsleeves — but he had nothing to suggest. Weren't there any carillons in the church tower? No, the community is Calvinistic and very strict; there isn't any music in the church. We went away, sadder and wiser men, and got rather seasick on the shallow Zuider Zee. And yet we broadcast from Holland — several times. Once it was Hendrik van Loon, speaking from a diamond factory in Amsterdam, and a very interesting talk it was; another time it was from the tulip fields, ablaze in all the colors of the rainbow, and much more brilliant.

When Franklin Delano Roosevelt was inaugurated as President for the second time, I listened to the proceedings in a little Dutch town, together with some Dutchmen who took the fact that for the second time a member of the Roosevelt family had become President of the United States with remarkable calm, considering that his ancestors came from that very town — Oud-Vossemer, a mere hamlet on the island of Tholen, near the Hook of Holland. When the inauguration was over we had a little surprise party, to which we hoped the President would be able to listen, as millions of 'my friends and fellow citizens' did.

It took place in the little town hall of Oud-Vossemer, opposite the Dutch Reformed church and within sight of the house whence Claes Roosevelt, so they say, emigrated to the New World. Over the mantelpiece of the Council Chamber (where that afternoon I had seen clog-wearing Dutchmen collect their Depression dole) was the Roosevelt coat-of-arms, together with those of the other patrician families of the town; and the mayor, a mousy little man, dressed in his Sunday best, with his chain of office around his neck, was there to read a speech. So was the American Minister, who told the story of the Roosevelts of Oud-Vossemer.

But I never saw a stiller town. An immense Dutch flag hung over the town hall façade; it was Oud-Vossemer's great day. But not a sound, not a cheer!

Yes, Holland is a silent place.

WHAT PRICE GRANDEUR?

More and more European countries are organizing short-wave broadcasts for distant lands — primarily for their colonies, if they have any, secondarily for America, because America is full of 'colonies' of all nations. These American colonies have their value: at best they provide spheres of interest — thin wedges of economic penetration; and they are always customers for 'invisible exports' — remittances to relatives and purchases as tourists help the national exchequer. In any case national minorities have become a political preoccupation since the war, and some countries regard their hyphenated Americans as fit objects of governmental solicitude. Whenever European statesmen speak to America they have these prodigal sons in mind. And that leads to amusing episodes.

The Grand Duchy of Luxemburg is as proud of its independence as any power in Europe, possibly even more so — and it has reason to be. This musical-comedy monarchy has less than a thousand square miles of area, less than 300,000 inhabitants, an army of 250, and one radio station, which is the most powerful in western Europe, operating on one of the longest wave lengths in the world — but that is another story, belonging in Chapter XXIV. And it is ruled over by a charming young Grand Duchess, married to a descendant of Louis XIV. Its capital is a town of fairy-tale romance, with a moated castle high up over a river, and in its principal street you buy delicious pastries from a grand ducal purveyor, sporting the grand ducal arms over his door. A living picture postcard, in fact, and an ideal place for a picture postcard in sound.

When I asked the head of its government to say a few words — three minutes' worth — he replied with a full-length speech, which had to be cut down by very diplomatic maneuvering. When I discovered that the speech was to be made in two languages — the Luxemburg dialect and English — I almost passed out. 'But,' said the Minister of State, 'there are over 100,000 Luxemburgers in America' — a national minority, in fact. The one hundred and twenty million non-Luxemburgers were of minor importance: indeed, the dialect speech was to come first. The situation was desperate, so only desperate measures would do. We induced His Excellency to defer the dialect speech until the national anthem was played, and didn't tell him that the time would then be up and that American listeners (Luxemburgers and others) would be listening to something else. But as there was a distinguished audience in the studio, his oratory wasn't quite wasted. I hated to do it, for I never met pleasanter folks.

The American chargé d'affaires was even more romantic than the place. A Southerner, from Georgia, he was more royalist than the King. His courtly manners would have done honor to any Frenchman of the *ancien régime*, and he spoke of the Grand Duchess as Her Serene Highness, with a voice full of reverence. Walking me along the high river bank he told me the story of the fair Melusinde, who lived in a cavern by the river in the long-ago; she married a handsome prince, but the princess turned into a dreadful ogre, who plunged into the river where she lives until this day, and will live so until the perfect youth comes along, who has the courage to kiss the ogre; then she will be saved. In some way he seemed to believe that the prophesy would yet come true and a prince reign once more upon the Luxemburg throne.

When I left that night, on a modern railway train, seen off by the courtly American diplomat, I had to pinch myself to make sure it hadn't all been a dream.

The thing that stuck in my mind after leaving this midget state was that the people were extraordinarily prosperous, that there was no unemployment, and that the income tax was about the lowest in Europe. But then — despite its smallness — Luxemburg stands seventh among the world's producers of steel. Monaco, even smaller in territory, has hardly any taxes at all; but of course its government lives on the profits of the gaming halls. Let's have a look, I thought, at the rest of the Lilliputian states.

High up in the Alps, on the banks of the youthful Rhine, is the little principality of Liechtenstein, wedged between Austria and Switzerland, yet independent of both. Its capital is Vaduz, the *Vallis dulcis* — sweet valley — of the Romans, and its area of sixty square miles contains no minerals nor is its capital a gaming spa. There are plenty of rocky mountains, and the rest is peaceful farms. Well, I sent my friend Raymond Hall to make a broadcast from Liechtenstein, and he reported that the country supports some twelve thousand people in perfect comfort, and that the taxes are very, very low. Moreover, he found that Liechtenstein is perhaps the most democratic country on earth, for almost anything can be decided by a referendum of the whole people — a large town meeting at best. And the only soldier in the country, made of wax, is kept in the museum.

As for the country's octogenarian, six-foot-plus monarch, a Most Serene Highness who thoroughly knows his Vienna — he spends only a little of his time in the ancient battlemented donjon castle of Vaduz. Since Napoleon confirmed his country's ancient independence, his family is privileged to intermarry with the royal houses of Europe, but I seem to remember that one of his sons preferred the alliance of a good bourgeois Jewish family in London's West End.

So what do the large and powerful nations gain by being so grand? They can be patriotic. But so, we found, can the little ones. The Liechtensteiners who took part in our broadcast, from the head of the government down to the assembled peasants, sang the following anthem with much more gusto than the British put into 'God Save the King' — and to the same tune:

> 'Long live our Liechtenstein,
> A Jewel on the Rhine,
> Happy and true!
>
> Long live our country's Prince,
> Long live our Fatherland,
> In bond of brother-love,
> United, free!'

Smaller than either Luxemburg or Liechtenstein is the Republic of San Marino, which occupies the flat tops of two-thousand-foot Mount Titan and is completely surrounded by Mussolini. Since even Napoleon Bonaparte, defied by its doughty citizens and two guns, marched around it and left it intact, a Fascist dictator can do no less. *Noblesse oblige!* San Marino, ruled by two Captains Regent (one noble, one plain) joined the Allies in the World War and has not made peace with either Austria or Turkey to this day.

When King George V celebrated his Jubilee he received the felicitations of all the governments of the world, and from the hands of little Giovanni Sovrani, restaurateur and Vice-Consul of the Republic of San Marino, he received the order of that country's patron saint. Its insignia, in gold and enamel, are as gorgeous as any I have ever seen.

When we broadcast the inaugural ceremony of the Captains Regent that same autumn, the San Marinese went 'all out.' They posted official notices giving the details of the program; they tolled the palace bell when the announcer appeared on the palace balcony; had the national anthem played on time; fired the guns of the fortress as the guards saluted the flag, and tolled the great Rocca bell at the end, solely for the benefit of America. The crowd shouted '*Viva la Reggenza!*' '*Viva la Republica!*' and '*Viva l'America!*' after the newly elected Noble Regent addressed them thus:

'The friendship that unites the smallest and oldest republic in the world to the largest and one of the youngest does not date only from today ...'

Well, if most of the Americans who listened hadn't even heard of San Marino till that day, they were taught something; for, holding a faded letter written by the hand of Abraham Lincoln, he read:

'Great and good friends,

'Although your Dominion is small, your State is nevertheless the most honored in all history. It has by its experience demonstrated the truth, so full of encouragement to the friends of Humanity, that government founded on republican principles is capable of being so administered as to be secure and enduring ...' and so on for three or four pages.

The Marinese are as proud of that letter as Britain is of its Magna Carta, or America of its Declaration of Independence; and as proud of being Marinese as Englishmen and Americans are proud of being what they are. Nor are their ceremonies less impressive. The next issue of *Il Popolo San Marinese* carried a full account of the proceedings, including the broadcast to America. Just like an inauguration at Washington, D.C.

I am sorry to say that there is no broadcasting station in Andorra — not even a telephone line that could be used for a broadcast to the outside world. But the only thing that makes me doubt that Andorra is just as happy as the rest of Europe's tiny lands is a paragraph in my friend Negley Farson's book, *The Way of a Transgressor*. When Negley climbed up into the remote capital of the Pyrenean republic to interview its President (annual salary: $3.75), he asked him what his principal duties were. The answer was: 'Relations with foreign powers.'

XXI. VIVE LA FRANCE!

OF ALL the broadcasting organizations in Europe, Great Britain's is the most conscientious, Germany's the most efficient, Italy's the most ambitious. What shall we say of France's? The most casual? The most haphazard? It certainly is both of these, but at the same time the most amiable. Englishmen regard their radio as a great social force — religious, social, artistic, educational. The French, certainly, have no such ambitions about this latest contraption of the amusement world. The Frenchman is the world's individualist, and he refuses to take too seriously anything that is likely to disturb his own particular routine for the enjoyment of life. The 'T.S.F.' receiver [1] is by no means an indispensable furniture in the modern French home, nor has radio reduced in the slightest the clientèle of the corner café.

For years, therefore, radio was a stepchild, born of industry, and negligently fathered by the state. Successive governments advanced projects for a great central studio building, but none of them lasted long enough to get the money voted in Parliament, and by the time the new government came in, the experts decided that the plan was out of date. So official French broadcasting is still done from the backyard of the old post-office built under Napoleon III.

During the first year of international broadcasting no French programs were relayed to America. It was not until the opening of the Colonial Exposition of 1931 that France

[1] T.S.F. is abbreviation for Téléphonée sans Fil, literally 'wireless telephone.'

erected a short-wave station at Pontoise — for the benefit of the natives in Madagascar, Algiers, etc. If the opening of the Exposition, by Marshal Lyautey, was transmitted to New York (the first French broadcast heard in America), it was due only to the persistence of the American companies; and in the end it had to be taken via England and the transatlantic telephone because there was no suitable directional antenna at Pontoise.

JEAN PATOU TALKS TO THE LADIES

After this Colonial Exposition broadcast I thought it was about time that America should hear some characteristic French programs and the voices of French public men. The N.B.C. had broken the ice by rebroadcasting a concert of the Garde Républicaine band. What, aside from music — which didn't yet come across the Atlantic without considerable mutilation — could we import from France? What French things were Americans chiefly interested in? Fashions, for one thing; wine for another (America was still dry). Let's begin with fashions!

The most famous fashion creator of the moment was Jean Patou; let's have a talk on the autumn fashions — a forecast, 'inside stuff' — from Jean Patou, for the ladies of America. I was assured that Patou spoke English; his manager certainly did, and with him I worked out the details. The crucial day arrived, and the great man, handsome and temperamental as a film star, arrived at the old post-office building in the Rue de Grenelle, where a very primitive studio was placed at our disposal. He arrived rather late and I had not seen his script. It needed attention, and as for Monsieur Patou's English — a month would have been better than the fifteen minutes or so in which I tried to brush it up. But, worst of all, there was no forecast, no real information that was worth the expense of transmission, only some pretty words for 'ze American leddees' and some near-poetry about Patou's forthcoming perfume!

'What,' I asked prosaically, 'are the essential novelties for the fall? Give me some general principles and we'll work up an interview.'

'Ah! novelties,' he said. '*Il y a deux choses,* two cardinal innovations — *la mort du noir et la mort du derrière*' ('the death of black and the death of the backside').

I thought I hadn't heard right. He repeated it. 'But you can't speak of "the death of the backside,"' I said. 'Not to an American audience.'

'But why not?' — and he went on to explain how dresses would be 'straight up and down,' concealing all suggestions of curves at the stern. This was the Big News and I didn't appreciate it. We had to find an innocuous English circumlocution, but he remained skeptical. I began to be grateful for his Gallic pronunciation of English. While we were arguing someone rushed in from across the hall and said that we ought to begin (there was no starting signal). We did; we spoke into the most antediluvian and unconvincing microphone I had seen outside of Ireland.

Almost none of Patou's words could have been understood by the average high-school graduate, so I repeated his answers in paraphrased form — in language fitting for flappers' ears. I never heard whether anybody listened. I hope nobody did. That was our first 'special' from France, and the first fashion broadcast to be heard in America.[1]

BASTILLE DAY ON MONTMARTRE

But the Frenchest of French broadcasts came from the Quartier Montmartre, on the Fourteenth of July. The idea was to project across the Atlantic something of the spirit of the great national festival by which the French celebrate the fall of the Bastille. We chose the Place Clichy, where we found the unused upstairs room of a corner café, commanding

---

[1] There have been many transatlantic fashion broadcasts since then; in fact, they have become seasonal events.

a sweeping view of the Boulevard and the *Place*, and dominating the upper reaches of a comparatively quiet backwater — a favorite spot for the street-dancing that goes on all over Paris on the night of the Fête Nationale. This large, many-windowed room would make an ideal studio and control-room, permitting us to switch on and off at will the gaieties and noises of the street and square.

They were plenty — the usual attractions of a popular street fair, including side-shows, street vendors, two huge merry-go-rounds boasting steam calliopes of prodigious sonority, and at night (our broadcast would take place after dark) there were to be colored lights, fireworks, and the lurid brilliance of the Moulin Rouge, with its illuminated wings gyrating perilously over the heads of the passers-by. Street traffic didn't worry us, for on this day of days the accommodating Paris police divert motor cars or guide them adroitly around the orbit of couples waltzing in affectionate embrace.

The *clou* of our show would be a dance band in the side street, which was subsidized by the proprietor of our café. It was to be conducted by a dubious character known as the 'Clown of Montmartre,' who at desired moments would conjure up a community chorus from among the dancing couples under the sway of his bâton. For our special benefit Mlle. Floriot, a billowing blonde *vedette* of the Opéra-Comique, would sing the verses and lead the choruses of '*Les ponts de Paris*' and other favorite ditties of old-time Paris.

From all these riches of entertainment we would choose at will, tying them in with a little dramatization of café conviviality and a commentary by two American visitors — my Paris mate and myself. I was to run the show. By means of a 'mixing panel' we would fade in and out the various sounds of the street and the café, and the antics of the clown-conductor, who would take his cues from an electric torch signal through the nearly sound-proof windows of the studio. The arrangements were perfect: only the technical set-up and the general continuity had to be rehearsed in the early afternoon, when there would already be some goings-on. The engineering was in the hands of the P.T.T., the French department in charge of French telephones and radio.

In the morning the engineers were to be there, installing their microphones, amplifiers, and 'leads.' We arrived at the café; Père Vannoux, the *patron*, smiling cynical tolerance, was already behind his bar; Madame was supervising the cleaning up; chairs were piled on tables; odd characters of the *quartier* were standing about having an early bock. Some of them later turned out to be our engineers. There seemed to be some insurmountable technical difficulties; the local characters took a hand in the discussion, and pretty soon there was a chorus of gesticulation and shrugging of shoulders that boded ill for our enterprise.

Nobody paid any attention to us — until we proposed to stand a drink all round. That not only focussed the discussion, but gained us some auxiliary volunteers — local mechanics who had come to loaf but remained to work; one of them, in fact, saved the situation by some master-stroke which hadn't occurred to the official crew. After all — what would you? — this was a matter of advertising *la patrie.* So in the end, instead of the single microphone attached to an obsolescent telephone installation, we had cables slung across the street, special leads through cellars of private houses, and a veritable net of lines converging on the improvised studio over the corner.

We returned in the afternoon to rehearse and gather atmosphere. The street was alive with children and lookers-on. We waited for our chief actors; gradually they turned up, but no two of them were there together. People flitted in and out, but nothing happened. More shrugging of shoulders: *Malgré tout*, it was the Fourteenth of July!

Above all — no engineers; no possibility of trying out 'noises off.' Nobody thought they were important; everybody was concerned about his own piece. Our prima donna, in a frilly *création*, turned up complete with yellow-gloved, morning-coated husband, spreading an exotic perfume through the café; the 'mayor' of Montmartre made a visit of inspection; the hitherto mythical clown looked in between his turns at the Moulin de la Galette; Père Vannoux and

Madame, worried about the disturbance, were throwing ugly looks. We rewrote our script on a marble-topped table, moist with the remnants of liquid cheer. Darkness was coming on; we gave up the rehearsal and trusted to luck.

CHARM PLUS SPEED EQUALS EFFICIENCY

Presently the band arrived and started up. More than that: another band started up fifty yards further down the street, and the two produced a terrifying cacophony. What to do? The *patron* thought he might 'fix' things by indemnifying his competitor of the neighboring café for the loss in dance-minded customers. We agreed on a contribution, and with the diplomatic help of the *maire* were assured of a half-hour monopoly. About twenty minutes before the deadline, the engineers, holding smouldering cigarette-ends between their lips, sauntered on to the scene. The microphones had still to be connected up; also the earphones which were to enable me to listen to the entire output and so to stage-manage the show.

We mounted the dark stairs to the studio. Surprise number one: no lights in the room! While we sent out an S.O.S. for electric bulbs, the men began setting up their gear in the dark. A standard microphone was put in place for me near a strategic window.

'Now, what about the fireworks?' '*Mais, monsieur*, it's too early for those!' A twelve-year-old lad, named Hippolyte, turned up from nowhere and promised to set off some toy bombs on the glass and tin roof of the sidewalk café. How nice for the customers, I thought, but never mind! Everybody worked with a will, galvanized into action by the excitement. In an emergency Latins are at their best. (Remember Galliéni's taxicabs at the Battle of the Marne!)

At last we were ready to try just a few minutes of the program. I signalled to the maestro. The band started up; I listened through the engineers' phones. Great Apollo and the Nine Muses! The Mighty Barnum and Igor Stravinsky together couldn't have equalled this: the two merry-go-rounds, though 'way across the square, were drowning our show. Nothing could be heard but their steam calliopes, coming through the outside mikes.

Once again we appealed to the *patron*; this time nothing could be done. Not even by the *maire*. Stop the merry-go-rounds on the Place Clichy? Think of the loss, *Monsieur! Qui payera?* I was ready to throw up my hands when little Hippolyte, the fireworks expert, sidled up to me and whispered, 'You want the merry-go-rounds to stop?' 'Yes, for fifteen minutes.' 'I'll do it,' and off he was. In a few minutes he was back, having with his childish enthusiasm convinced the boss of the *carousels* that for the good of the *Quartier* and the glory of the French revolution he just had to lay off for a quarter of an hour. Moreover, a playmate had been posted near the merry-go-rounds who would watch for the first firecracker, by way of signal, and see that the armistice was carried out.

We were now as set as we could hope to be, everything considered. The street was crowded with dancing pairs. I took my position at the microphone, surrounded by the café characters, ready to flash signals at the maestro below. I now called for my earphones. Ye gods and little fishes! They were dangling off a short wire, far beyond my reach in a spot where I couldn't see the street. I exploded: '*Nom de Dieu!*' this was too much. Still chewing his cigarette, the engineer came up smiling. 'How many minutes have we got?' I pointed to my watch — exactly two and a half. It was marvellous to observe him and his helper — hauling wire, twirling, unscrewing, splicing, and twisting — a prestidigitator had been lost in this apparently blasé servant of the state. The seconds ticked off on my stop watch: one minute to go — silence — 'Hello, America!' As I said the words, a silent pair of hands slipped the ear-phones over my head. The show was saved.

Everybody came up to scratch — the prima donna, the dancers and singers, and even the surly *patron*, who had to contribute a few words in his rich *Auvergnat* accent, just to show that there were no Parisians in Paris — which was the point of the back-chat we had arranged. Hippolyte's firecrackers were a little too enthusiastic, perhaps, but even the merry-go-round added a touch of color, for out of sheer gratitude I waited just long enough before stopping them to give listeners a touch of bedlam at its best.

The end of the show was a clinking of glasses containing real champagne — by way of thanks to the helpers. There were six or eight of us in the room. After I signed off I saw that they had increased to thirty or more, and the *patron* was bringing up bottle after bottle of his best Veuve Cliquot. The prima donna had received a bouquet and went off dreaming of an American tour; Hippolyte refused all recompense except the remaining firecrackers, worth about ten cents. Madame, below, beamed at the crowded café, and as in the wee hours we gathered ourselves up to go, we had but one thought: 'Charming people, these French!'

MISS LIBERTY CELEBRATES

Franco-American amity is firmly based on history; its outward symbols to the Frenchman are Lafayette, Pershing, and Miss Liberty. Miss Liberty — meaning the gigantic bronze statue in New York Harbor, a gift of the Republic of France to the sister Republic across the sea — recently celebrated her fiftieth birthday in circumstances which her creator could certainly not have foreseen. Two Presidents, one speaking in the Élysée Palace in Paris, the other on Bedloes Island in New York, in the shadow of the statue itself, took part in the same ceremony and in the hearing of the peoples of both countries.

The occasion, impressive as it may have been, was not without a touch of comedy to those who could see the machinery. The American end was American enough, to be sure; but the French end was very, very French.

The ceremony on Bedloes Island was to include speeches

by the Mayor of New York, the Secretary of the Interior, and
the President of the United States, the usual salutes and
music by the United States Marine Band; in Paris the
President of the Republic would 'answer' President Roosevelt, after being introduced by the American Ambassador.
President Roosevelt would greet France and the 'Marseillaise'
would be played, while a guard of honor saluted the French
tricolor; then, from France, would come 'The Star-Spangled
Banner,' played by the Musique de la Garde — the crack
French army band. The ceremony was to start at two P.M.
New York time, corresponding to seven P.M. in Paris. The
United States Department of the Interior had approved the
program, and Ambassador Bullitt had been advised. All I
had to do was to go to Paris, superintend, and announce.

I arrived on the afternoon plane, about four, and started
to check up by telephone. First the American Embassy.
The officials had heard that a broadcast was taking place and
that the Ambassador was expected to speak, but he was in
bed nursing a cold, and while he *might* dose himself into
condition he certainly could not appear at the President's
Palace without an official invitation from the French
Government. No invitation had arrived!

It was evidently just one of 'those things' that happen in
official circles. The job was to get someone at the Quai
d'Orsay, the French Foreign Office, to 'invite' the Ambassador. Nobody was against it, I found; in fact it had
been intimated to the Embassy that if his Excellency would
like to be present it would be all right. The difficulty was,
first, to convince officials that that wasn't enough — for an
Ambassador — and second, to find a proper person who in
the Minister's absence could do more than 'intimate,' i.e.,
invite. French is the language of diplomacy; I mentally
thanked my school teachers for every word of it. After
many more calls from my bedroom telephone I was able to
try the Embassy again, and sure enough, word had come
from the Quai d'Orsay and national honor was saved. The
Ambassador was at that moment taking spirituous refresh-
ment and literally rising to the occasion.

By this time it had grown pretty late, and the next check-up — with the broadcasting people — was near closing time. Yes, everything was arranged, but what was this about the music? The President's private secretary had said something about the Garde. Yes, of course; I reminded him that the music had been requested weeks ago. 'Well, yes, but we thought that a recording would do. It's too late now to mobilize the band of the Garde Republicaine; they're all over town.' Time was getting short. All I could do was to repeat for the *n*th time that American broadcasting chains do not permit records. I had to leave it to the official to get the band — *a* band, anything that could play the American national anthem. After all, I had the President of the Republic on my side. I rang up his *Chef de Cabinet*: for all I knew the President himself might have walked out on me by now!

Thank God, he hadn't; but my respects were overdue. I rushed into my dress-suit, which had not even been unpacked, hopped into a taxi, and arrived, perspiring, at the Executive Mansion to make my peace with that impressively weighty dignitary, the *Chef de Cabinet*, chief secretary and major-domo of the Élysée. I found him in a rather nervous state, as the result of sundry wires that were trailing loosely all over his carpet, and a 'horrid' radio set (through which President Roosevelt's words were soon to be heard) usurping space in the sacred precincts where French heads of state since Napoleon Bonaparte had lived. As a studio, I found, we had been assigned a tiny waiting-room at the end of a long, long corridor. It would necessitate about a three minutes' walk for the President to take his cue. But what's time to the World's Exalted?

TWO PRESIDENTS AND A PHONOGRAPH

Suddenly the loud-speaker burst forth; the American program was on. Two o'clock in America: the announcer revealed that here we were on Bedloes Island, awaiting the

President's arrival. The Roosevelt party was late, so after some 'gagging' about the brilliant scene he gave it up and we went 'back to the studio for a little entertainment by Harold Levey's band.' American jazz blared out; the *Chef de Cabinet* bristled. Peering over the top rim of his gold pince-nez, he muttered words which happily no one understood.

The Ambassador arrived, and presently I was summoned into the presidential sanctum. Dapper Albert Lebrun, President of the Republic, affectionately known to his enemies as Pou-Pou, sat at an enormous desk. He was in excellent humor; the Ambassador, Mr. 'Bill' Bullitt, had evidently been telling an amusing story, possibly about having risen superior to his cold. . . . Although I had visited him in his Moscow embassy the year before, he didn't recognize me, which in the circumstances was not surprising.

Lebrun asked me if everything was arranged. 'Yes, President Roosevelt is due to begin; I'll let you know, so *Monsieur le Président* can listen to the speech.'

'*Et la musique est en place?*' ('The band is ready?') asked Lebrun. 'I don't know, *Monsieur le Président*,' — which was the honest truth.

'*Voilà!*' cried he, with a sweeping gesture, and turning to the Ambassador. '*Voyez-vous, c'est toujours comme ça; toujours les techniciens,*' meaning that the technicians never know. But he didn't seem to mind. We all laughed, and I blushed with pride, for the President evidently took me for a compatriot, with authority over the Republican Guards.

In the anteroom, the loud-speaker was still going strong; the announcer was again taking us back to the studio, for 'some entertainment by Harold Levey's band.' And more hot jazz, not improved by transmission, boomed forth. This happened three or four times — Franklin D. Roosevelt was very late indeed. At last we heard the booming baritone of Mayor La Guardia, then the other speakers, and at last the American President. Lebrun was duly notified, but evinced no special interest and continued to laugh at the Ambassador's yarns. We were listening intently when the weighty Major-Domo emerged. He seemed quite distraught by now.

Dragging his tired feet over the carpet he tripped and tore the wires — zip! — and the Rooseveltian eloquence was cut off short. There were vociferations and recriminations for '*les techniciens*,' and for some anxious minutes we thought we'd miss our cue. But finally the wires were tied, Mr. Roosevelt wound up with 'Liberty' and 'Democracy,' and 'our friends the citizens of France'; and to the sound of the 'Marseillaise,' drifting gustily from the loud-speaker, President Lebrun and the Ambassador picked their way to the improvised studio.

Outside its door was a pair of ear-phones for me. I introduced the Ambassador, who spoke his piece without a hitch. The engineer gave the signal to the '*musique*,' presumably *en place* somewhere in the inner courts. 'The Star-Spangled Banner' began; in my ear-phones it sounded magnificent. That was the Garde Républicaine, sure enough; no other band could play like that. 'The tune ended — a second verse began. My heavens, we're already twenty minutes late! Then, incredibly, the tune started a third time. I stormed at the engineer: where was the band — couldn't he stop it? He calmly pointed to an adjoining room. I rushed in and there, smiling sheepishly, was an official operating a portable gramophone. Words failed me, except to mutter that I would signal him when to stop. We arrived at the last line; I raised my hand for a vigorous down-beat and — without waiting for it — in the middle of the last phrase he stopped his wretched machine. He didn't know the tune — or any tune, most likely.

I now announced the President, who, blissfully ignorant of what was happening, began his oration — worthy of a Frenchman and an Academician. Nothing more mattered; we signed off, rather limp. I had visions of the United States Marines at present arms, the President of the United States, cabinet members, diplomats, state and city officials, Daughters of the American Revolution, and just citizens standing at attention, while my fat friend in the next room was running off a record on a portable gramophone! We had broken a rule, but we were innocent — a small consolation.

The beaming President came out and shook hands.

After he had gone the French engineer turned to me and said: 'You're too excited. Why get excited? Who cares?'

I suppose he was right. I stood him and his assistants a drink. Raising our glasses we murmured: '*Vive la France!*'

XXII. THE VOICE OF THE OLD COUNTRY

MIDNIGHT SUN BY RADIO

IN THE high summer nights of Europe's northernmost lands the sun never sets. A reddish-golden orb, suspended above the horizon, it traces a path of mysterious light upon the waters of the fjords. In these luminous nights the fisherfolk and peasants of the Arctic Circle light their bonfires and dance the old dances to the village fiddlers' tunes. At the summer solstice these nocturnal festivities reach their climax, and Midsummer Day has become the national holiday throughout the North.

Civilized nations that they are, Norwegians and Swedes have the comfort of their remotest citizens at heart; postman and telephone have done much to soften their isolation. A few years ago the Norwegian broadcasting administration opened a broadcasting station at Vadsö, almost as far north as the North Cape, so that even the remotest Laplanders might feel in touch with the world. All America heard the Vadsö station when it was inaugurated in 1934, for it was rebroadcast by the two principal American chains; and a year later the Norwegians organized, at my request, a broadcast of the festivities at midnight of Midsummer's Day.

From a lonely refuge on Rönvikfjeld Mountain a speaker described the splendor of nature's spectacle, awe-inspiring and full of mystic meaning to the simple man. Then, from the island town of Bodö came the sound of the dancers and fiddlers and of fireworks and beacons crackling in the wind, and finally the toll of midnight from the little Bodö church. Norwegians in the American Middle West heard the songs that their parents had learned from their mothers' lips, and many of them wrote to the old folks back home to tell them how they had been moved to tears.

Indeed, the voice of the Old Country is something that many millions in America would strain their ears to hear. Successive generations of emigrants from European countries kept the old songs and the old customs alive. Now that emigration is all but ended, a dimming memory is all that remains. Radio can — and should — help to preserve these elements of national life. In this endeavor it is restricted only by the public's insistence, or supposed insistence, on an unlimited amount of the currently fashionable variety of jazz (using the word in its broadest sense) and the constant demand for timeliness and news.

But programs can have news value by virtue of their nationality alone, and many an interesting program has been transmitted across the ocean from a country that happened to be 'in the news.' It was the tragedy of King Alexander's assassination that brought us not only the first broadcast from Yugoslavia but also a program of Serbian and Croatian folksongs that was full of beauty and interest. And to the eminence of Nicolai Titulescu, Rumania's great Foreign Minister — now a virtual exile — we owed a fascinating program of Rumanian national music from Bucharest, to which he added his first and only transatlantic speech.

The World War created no less than eight new independent states in Europe, and each of them, I found, had its Independence Day. That gave Americans a chance to hear not only the Fourth-of-July oratory of its leading statesman but — more pleasing by far — its national tunes. Poles, Czechs, Slovaks, Letts, and Lithuanians in America thus heard the Old Country sing, and so did — for similar reasons — the Hungarians, the Portuguese, the Swiss, and the Finns.

THE FINNS AND THEIR EPIC

For a thousand years and more the peoples inhabiting the lake shores and wide river beds of Finland or roaming its immense wooded plains have recited and sung the *runos* of a racial epic built by the imagination of their ancestors but never written down until a century ago. Today this 'Kalevala' is the greatest cultural possession of the Finns and the inspiration of its artists, and musicians. But now, as in centuries past, the primitive poets and rural composers of this extraordinary race go on creating their own verses and tunes, and come together to recite and sing them to the 'folk.' Two years ago a great assembly of these folksingers, as well as the flower of the country's men of arts and letters, met at Sortavala, on the shores of Europe's largest lake, Laaokka, to celebrate the completion of the manuscript of the Kalevala a hundred years ago, and a part of this great event was broadcast to America. Listening at their loud-speakers, thousands of Finno-Americans, as well as Americans in general, could hear four thousand Finnish singers intone the opening verses of the Kalevala, to a *runo* handed down by uncounted generations:

> 'Come and let us sing together
> Since at length we meet together
> From two widely sundered regions.
> Let us clasp our hands together
> Let us interlock our fingers
> While our dear ones hearken to us.

> 'While the young are standing round us
> Let them learn the words of magic
> And recall our songs and legends.'

And they heard, too, a tune played on the *kantele*, the ancient, many-stringed bardic harp, composed and played by the descendant of an old family of bards, and many other things beautiful in themselves and of deep significance to Finns.

HOLY WEEK IN SEVILLE

It was a fascinating task to learn about national festivals and religious customs peculiar to certain countries that could be transmitted to America in terms of sound. The processions of Saint Stephen's Week in Budapest, gorgeous as they are, were difficult to focus into a microphone; but nothing could surpass the splendor of the Holy Week processions in Seville.

For sheer barbaric fervor these open-air rites excel even those of the camp-meetings of the American negro, for they have in them elements of racial tradition going back through the centuries of Islamic conversion to an idolatry even more remote. It would be impossible to describe either the wild beauty of the picture or the mass emotion that grips the people of Seville in their *Semaña santa*, and that alone was good enough reason for projecting its sounds by radio. There are some seventy *pasos* in Seville — miraculously carved figures and groups each belonging to a church and cared for by a Holy Brotherhood whose competitive ardor is both religious and militantly artisan. For two years after the revolution of 1932 the Holy Week processions were forbidden; when they were once again allowed, they were also broadcast, for the first time in their history.

We placed our microphones on the balcony of the Town Hall on Good Friday evening, when the most famous images, the 'Virgin of the Macarena,' the 'Virgin of Hope,' and the 'Jesus of Great Power' make their slow, tortuous way through a billowing sea of humanity. What passed before the announcer's eyes was utterly fantastic: the weirdly hooded 'brothers,' completely covered by black and white mantles, with only slits for their eyes; the thousands of lighted candles; the crowd, seized with religious frenzy but hushed into silence when inspired singers suddenly intoned their rhapsodic, quasi-Oriental *saetas* — century-old wails that have defied all attempts at musical notation. No weirder, more incongruous running commentary was ever filtered through a microphone.

The commentator, a cultured young Spaniard, educated in England and married to an American girl, was, three years later, broadcasting insurgent bulletins from somewhere in Spain, having only narrowly escaped death in the early months of the Civil War.

It was in 1932 when the same Spanish friend took me from Barcelona to the mountain monastery of Montserrat, on Catalonia's sacred mountain, whose earliest traditions are lost in the mists of time. Up and up through vineyards and olive groves we went, then through forests of oak and pine until only shrubbery remains in the folds of those bizarre, tooth-like rocks, high up over the plain, like a mighty group of sentinels facing the Pyrenees to the north. According to a local legend the Devil in his fury tore these mountains out of the ground and turned them upside down; so what are now the mountain's peaks were originally its roots. Here the Benedictines have maintained a refuge for many centuries, and one of their pilgrims was the Ignatius of Loyola who afterward founded the Jesuit Order. Within its cloistered walls the monks still sing the age-old chants; but they had never been heard except by those who made their way to Montserrat.

We entered the sombrous church and by the mysterious light of hundreds of tiny candles saw the legendary Black Virgin, that weirdly beautiful image carved in ebony by unknown hands, which was discovered many centuries ago in a cave not far from the summit of the mountain and has been revered by the faithful ever since. She wore a golden crown and was clad in one of the richly ornate robes which sovereigns and popes and the Great of the Earth have bestowed on her through the ages. A young couple were praying silently before her, for no Catalan marriage, according to local belief, can be happy without the *Moreneta's* blessing.

We ascended the winding stairs to the quarters of the Father Abbot, benign Don Antonio, who interrupted his meditations to receive us, in cassock and scarf, incongruously nursing a cold. In awed whispers we arranged for a traditional service to be transmitted to America the following Christmastide; for the singing of the famous choir of monks and boys is especially beautiful then. The gentle abbot had never heard a radio, but he was a man of the world though living above it. He not only gave the permission; he even altered the hour of the service to suit American time. The idea must have fascinated him, as it did me.

Telephone lines had only recently been laid to the monastery (along with the rack-and-pinion railway which now — alas! — brought pilgrims to his hostelry without the effort worthy of a holy quest), and on this single line we based our hopes. With the enthusiastic Catalan radio people helping us, that line was made to carry music such as few telephone lines had ever carried before — thirty-odd miles to Barcelona, thence by telephone cable to Madrid, and by short-wave to America. The '*Salve Regina*' sung by the monks and the boys of the Escalonia, one of the most ancient singing schools in the world, was unique and unforgettable. No Christmas broadcasts have ever surpassed, in mysterious beauty, this service from Spain.

THE BELLS OF BETHLEHEM

Christmas is a religious observance in southern and Catholic countries; it is a family festival in the north. From France, therefore, America heard the *Messe de Noël*; from Italy the quaint children's nativity at the famous church of Ara Cœli in Rome. From Germany, as from England, we staged typical Christmas parties, in which the holly and the waits, the Christmas tree, and Father Christmas were essential ingredients. Christmas carols from various countries are now a regular adjunct to American programs at Christmastide. At one Christmas I joined ten European countries in a single broadcast, each contributing a carol and a Christmas wish in the native tongue, spoken by a child.[1]

[1] Christmas greetings were first exchanged by the N.B.C. with England, Germany and Holland, in 1929.

One of the genuine early successes of transatlantic broadcasting was the preview of Christmas toys from the world's most famous toy-town, Nuremberg, with its traditional toy market, its gold-tinsel Christmas angels, and its world-famous gingerbread. Most German toys make a noise, and we made them all perform before the microphone, against the background of the ancient town with its medieval ramparts and the tolling of its bells. Then some forty children intoned their Christmas songs as only German children can, and were one and all rewarded under a giant Christmas tree. We had to repeat this performance the following two years, and each time the benign democratic mayor of the city added his greetings in English with a quaint German accent.

Then, after a hiatus, we resumed this broadcast, by request. This time the jovial mayor had been replaced by a portly Nazi in brown shirt and gaudy insignia, and other party dignitaries provided atmosphere. The toys, which included miniature machine guns, howitzers, tanks, and airplanes dropping bombs, were duly 'demonstrated' before the microphone, to the delight of the bystanders, and so far as I know there were no complaints except from a lady in America who objected to our calling German children anything so disrespectful as 'kids.' . . .

But the children, all the same, were sweet kids, just as before; and they sang like little angels. Their teacher, who had brought sixty of them, instead of forty, explained that there were too many tears at the suggestion of any of them being left behind — so we had to buy an extra supply of *Lebkuchen* next day.

A new prospect of interesting broadcasts came with the opening of the radio-telephone link between London and Cairo, with good land-line connection to Palestine. Through the united initiative of the N.B.C. and the B.B.C., arrangements were made to transmit the bells of the Church of the Nativity in Bethlehem to England and thence to America, at Christmas, 1934. They sounded, of course, very much like other bells, since nothing was allowed to be added, to set the scene and identify the historic locality. But that did not detract from the sensation, and the idea of wrapping up this precious tidbit in elaborate Christmas music and peals of bells from London and New York was an excellent solution of the program problem.

What really was wanted, of course, was a complete Christmas program or service from Christianity's traditional birthplace. But the prospect opened by science could not be realized because, alas! the Christians who are in charge of this shrine of shrines do not practise the Golden Rule. The church, like that of the Holy Sepulchre in Jerusalem, is parcelled out among various Christian sects — Armenian, Latin, and Greek — who have been at loggerheads for centuries. The sacred grotto, with the manger, the silver star and the awe-inspiring inscription, '*Hic de Virgine Maria Jesus Christus Natus Est,*' is guarded by armed soldiers day and night, and the soldiers are Mohammedans; for it is the Christians who have tried, from time to time, to take possession by violence, and Christianity's treasure must therefore be entrusted to non-Christian guards . . .

In Jerusalem the matter is further complicated. Here, besides the Latin, Greek, and Armenian sections of the church built on the hallowed ground of Golgotha, part ownership is claimed by Protestants, Copts, and various other sects.

Broadcasts from the sacred interiors, both at Bethlehem and Jerusalem have been planned again and again; both the British Postmaster-General (in charge of all communications) and later the broadcasting authorities — eager young men sent out from London by the B.B.C. — did everything they could to help. But when a transmission was proposed from a part owned by one sect, the owners of the others would protest. If cable leads were to pass — unavoidably — through one section in order to connect up to a microphone in the next, it was in danger of being cut. So to this day no broadcast from any part of the church has yet been made.

The bells of Bethlehem have, however, rung for the two major American networks every Christmas since 1935. On the following Christmas Eve we managed to get a little further. The choristers of the Anglican church were actually allowed to sing their carols in the courtyard of the church, under the starry Bethlehem sky. And in Jerusalem we were able to transmit sermons and descriptive talks — and bells — from the safe vantage-ground of the English church. If the British succeed in partitioning Palestine and the holy places will be inside the British part, one may even be able to transmit an actual street scene, a trick that has been impossible until now for the simple reason that the local engineers have been too busy mending lines cut by rioting Arabs or Jews. Our unsophisticated executives in New York at one time ordered a program from the famous Wailing Wall. A broadcaster attempting that had better take poison, and die a *peaceful* death.

The Arabs, by the way, complained that Palestine is too much publicized from the Jewish angle already, and were not at all friendly to the various Jewish programs that have been short-waved to America. And except for the riots, we should have transmitted Arab and Bedouin programs long ago.

Indeed, the transmission of scenes from the Islamic world was a fascinating idea but difficult to carry out. The Egyptian broadcasting authorities came to the rescue in 1935, and with their help we constructed a program consisting of a street scene in Cairo, full of color and movement, a reading from the Koran by a famous sheik, and a concert of music on Arab instruments, all of which were clearly described. The Koran reading, a strange and to Western ears vaguely melodious performance, had a weird fascination, and students of such things might detect, if not a similarity, at least traces of a common ancestry between this Moslem ritual and the Christian *saetas* of Seville.

FOLKSONGS IN MANY LANDS

The voice of the Old Country lives most potently in its songs. Folksong revivals in many countries are a recognition of this, and both America and England have a strong ear for the music of the folk, to judge from their concert programs and the catalogues of the publishers. But nothing is more easily distorted, nothing more often debased to a mere pseudo-art, than these artless expressions of a people's soul. Strictly speaking, they are neither translatable nor transportable: you must go to the country of origin if you want to hear the genuine thing.

That is what I thought when, early in 1937, I undertook the most interesting broadcasting pilgrimage of my career. This was a folksong journey on behalf of the American School of the Air, resulting in the first series of transatlantic radio programs ever designed specifically for schools. But the interest lay not only in the tapping of these inexhaustible treasures but also in the human contacts to be made and the unexpected difficulties to be overcome. And most interesting of all was the discovery that some commonly held notions about these countries did not square with the facts: for instance, that all Italians are musical and most Englishmen are not; that Frenchmen are temperamental and Germans just efficient and disciplined; that Northerners are 'cold' and Southerners 'warm'; that the Orient begins east of Vienna, where European civilization is supposed to stop; and so on through the vocabulary of tourist lore.

Nearly all these notions are wrong. The English children proved to be very musical indeed, and thoroughly alive to the beauty of their songs. If Italian children are equally so we were not allowed to know it, for they are supposed to have 'forgotten' the old songs, being too busy with more important things (such as drilling with miniature rifles, marching, and singing Ballila songs). . . . The French kiddies didn't suffer from temperament so much as from discipline, administered by nervous schoolmarms, too anxious to make them behave; while the German *Mädchen* who sang for us so beautifully had the time of their life teasing the brown-shirted Nazi who conducted them.

The question of emotional temperature proved to be more personal than geographical; and the most ardent singers we found up north — in Scotland — where the songs are 'too passionate' to be entrusted to the bairns. So we had a man and a woman, with a wee choir — to save expense. But the conductor, a gaunt Scots nationalist, treated me to haggis and whiskey, to produce the proper frame of mind.

In short, the only people who seemed to regard their folk-songs naturally, and who understood just what was wanted, were the English, the Irish, the Poles, and the Czechs. And even the English were a little too artistic about the job.

The story of that journey through twelve countries can only be told with music, which I hope to do some day. But I cannot forego paying a tribute to willing helpers of various nationalities, especially that intelligent Mrs. Boylan, of Dublin, who has trained her little band of school-children to sing the traditional Irish songs with something of the old fantasy and without ironing out the quirks; also to Kárel Hába, that able Czech musician who is getting to the very heart of the folk, setting its songs in their simple purity; and to the passionate Czech and Polish schoolmasters who trained their boys and girls to sing them with such infectious zest.

The Germans seemed more interested in the new Nazi marching songs than in the beautiful folksongs of their child-hood days, but they finally gave us what we wanted, with one contemporary creation added, as a sop to fashion. In Italy, alas! we had to be content with a full-sized chorus and or-chestra, and professional soloists. (Everything had to be artistically elaborated, and even a Venetian gondolier's song could not be simply accompanied by a guitar, because the guitar is no longer considered a 'national' instrument.) And in Sweden they simply could not scrape up even a few chil-dren to sing their profoundly beautiful songs. But the per-formance, with an adult ensemble of sixteen, was the most efficient of all.

The grandest showing was made by the Hungarians, who promptly recruited a hundred boys from one high-school and a hundred girls from another and made them sing intricate *a cappella* settings by Bártok and Kodály, which they did as easily as rolling off a log. An astounding performance, though much too highbrow for the purpose.

All in all, I don't think that the voice of the Old Country had ever before been so effectively presented to American listeners as in this series of broadcasts, despite the sophisticated bias of some. But it was a mere beginning, a path to be trodden by people who are genuinely interested in education by radio. It was a pity to have to omit Wales, with its great Bardic heritage, and Norway and Belgium and Yugoslavia and war-torn Spain. (Bulgaria and Greece are still outside the broadcasting pale.) And above all Russia, richest in folksong of all the countries of the world.[1]

I have said very little in this book about the broadcasting of what is professionally called 'art music.' This, too, has its place in transatlantic radio exchanges, but I don't attach as much importance to it as do some. I incline to the opinion of those who believe that the international rebroadcasting of symphonic music, for instance, is very much like carrying coals to Newcastle. Art music is supernational — the heritage of the whole world — and with few exceptions is executed as ably abroad as in the country of its origin, depending upon the genius of its interpreters. This does not apply, of course, to the unique cultivation of certain musical species, such as the Tudor madrigal in England, Mozart operas in Germany and Austria, or the singing of polyphonic music of peculiar style by certain European choirs.

For that reason the great traditional festivals have a broadcasting value of their own. The Bayreuth and Salzburg festivals, first broadcast by N.B.C. and Columbia respectively; the Welsh national Eisteddfod, the Three Choirs Festival of England, and the great German *Sängerfest* are outstanding examples. Nor is it easy to duplicate the singing of Bach's music by the choristers of his 'own' church at Leipzig, which was rebroadcast at the Bach tercentenary and other occasions; nor the singing of Palestrina and other sixteenth-century church music by the Vatican choirs in Rome, which I was privileged to transmit for the first time early in 1932.

[1] Russian folk-music has, however, been transmitted to America on various occasions during the last three or four years, and in January, 1936, we managed to rebroadcast part of a great folksong festival — a kind of musical Olympiad — from Moscow. The difficulty about Russian transmissions to America is that the short-wave channel passes near the magnetic pole, and conditions are favorable only at certain times of the day.

Much remains to be accomplished, however, in the technical field of short-wave transmission before such broadcasts can be regarded as artistically reliable. And above all American stations must be prepared to take complete works and not just snippets, as now.

XXIII. FISHERMAN'S LUCK

TRANSATLANTIC broadcasting was a great adventure, especially in the earliest years when every successful transmission seemed like the miracle that it is. Nowadays people take too much for granted. Had they, sitting lazily at their loud-speakers and listening to us on the other side of the earth, known what was involved, they would have thought the miracle even more miraculous. To us, contending with a strange, untried instrument, in the hands of strange and temperamental people, often speaking languages one did not understand, it was a triumph when a broadcast came off — a heartbreak when it didn't. 'What an exciting life you have!' people would say when they heard about this new job. 'What interesting people you must meet!' Yes. But the fascination is often too exciting for the nerves; and an interesting man is never less interesting than just before he faces the mike. If he is new to the game, as often as not he is just plain scared.

That is one reason why some of the most carefully prepared broadcasts aren't better than they are. In the studio, everything is prepared, rehearsed, tried and tried again; out in the field nearly everything is impromptu. Sometimes you're lucky, sometimes not. And luck appears in strange guises, too; sometimes your luck will land you in the soup. And sometimes your worst licking will be a blessing in disguise. Here, then, are a few examples of both these dispensations of fate.

Sir Johnston Forbes-Robertson, the greatest Hamlet of

our day, matinée idol of two generations and two continents, the possessor of the finest speaking voice and noblest stage presence within living memory, had retired from the stage when radio came into its own. At seventy-eight, the great old actor was living quietly in his Bedford Square home, pottering about the house, dreaming of his past glories. I had an idea that Americans, even if they were not to see him again, might like to hear once more the sound of that magnificent voice, or what was left of it.

I went to call on him and found that the voice was feeble, but still vibrant. He spoke with feeling of America, the country that had been the scene of his mightiest triumphs, where he had made a fortune, where he was revered as the greatest tragic actor since Irving; and where he had found his idol too — Gertrude Elliott, who became his wife and the mother of his talented children. His memory dwelt on these things, though otherwise it had a tendency to ramble. He was getting very old.

But he agreed to speak: he would do a short talk on Shakespeare on the poet's birthday, and read Hamlet's advice to the players. It was an experiment, not without its hazards, and to support the program I engaged the famous English Singers, who would sing Shakespearean madrigals. There was no chance for a rehearsal, and I trusted to the fortunes of the moment. Anyhow, as long as I was there it was all right: I was always prepared to fill in.

The Sunday afternoon chosen for the program was very wet. As luck would have it, my watch was slow. When I realized it, it was twenty minutes to air time. I jumped into my small car and fairly flew down Regent Street toward the B.B.C. Suddenly something came out of a side street, I jammed on the brakes, skidded into an iron sand box, and smashed the front of the car. The windshield was shattered into a thousand bits, but by a lucky chance I escaped without a scratch. The street was empty except for a cruising taxi. There was nothing to do but hail it, and with the cabby's help I pushed the wreck to the side, left it, and taxied to the studio. I walked in a couple of minutes before the signal to start. There was only time to place the singers and

shake hands with my 'star.' I didn't see that he was quivering with mike fright. The old stager, who had thrilled
millions in thousands of performances, was in terror of that
tiny object dangling in front of him.

The introduction over, the old routine came into action;
he pulled himself up straight; he read his speech, though
haltingly here and there. Everybody was on edge, expecting
something awful to happen. But he reached the last word
in safety, then with a deep sigh he turned to me and asked,
pointing to his huge Shakespeare folio, 'Is there still time
for this?' — not realizing that all America could hear his
whisper.

I motioned 'yes'; he braced up again, and then the old
Hamlet voice came forth, apparently strong as ever, with
its old bronze glamour, and the lines rolled forth in the grand
manner of the prewar tragedian. It was fascinating — and
touching — to see the old man. Once finished, he seemed
to shrink in size; then, with utter exhaustion in his voice,
said 'Thank God, that's over!' and all America heard that,
too. Then the English singers burst into their fa-la-las and
we began to cheer up.

When it was all over and Forbes-Robertson had been
tucked into his car, I thought of my own flivver, up in Regent
Street, and expected to be in for a fine for obstructing one
of London's busiest streets. I taxied up to it; a policeman
had just passed along and when he saw me he turned his
back. It was a complete wreck, not worthy of his notice.

Well, that broadcast probably cost me a year of my life:
first, the worry about the old man; the nervous strain of
running an improvised program, after arriving in the nick of
time; then the wrecked car and the near-catastrophe! But
anyway, I had put over what I thought a unique show —
something that could never happen again: the greatest actor
of our time was nearing eighty; he had never broadcast
before and never would again. Surely I would get some
swell fan mail after that. . . .

A week or so later it came: three or four letters from elderly
ladies, complaining about Forbes-Robertson's 'blasphemous'
remarks.

Well!

NO *PAPIER*, NO BROADCAST

At the beginning of 1934 Paris was in an ugly mood. The Stavisky scandals stank in the nostrils of good citizens; the economic crisis was at its peak; Fascism, as preached by Colonel de la Rocque and his 'Croix de Feu,' was arrogantly raising its head. On February 6, seventeen people were killed and thousands injured in the riots on the Place de la Concorde. Fascists, communists, socialists, war veterans, and just angry Frenchmen had tried to force the bridge leading to the Chamber of Deputies, and except for the drastic shooting by the police (after *provocateurs* in the crowd had fired the first shots) the Chamber might have been fired, with the Deputies inside. This was France's 'little revolution,' following upon a period of corruption and a series of ineffectual governments which preceded the 'national' government of Doumergue. It was the crisis which decided, for the time being, whether France would go Fascist or find a way to law and order and yet preserve its heritage of liberty.

On Wednesday (the seventh) the morning papers in London were full of the bloodshed across the Channel; that night it broke out afresh and I was on my way to Paris, to see if I couldn't broadcast an eye-witness account from there. I decided to get Percy Philip, correspondent of the *New York Times*, who had been in the thick of the fighting, to tell his story that night, and myself give a follow-up next day. The great advantage was that Philip had already got permission from the Quai d'Orsay for a similar talk he was making for Great Britain; he was a highly respected and trusted man. Next thing was to get the telephone lines set up — via England, for the sake of safety, for the French short wave was still risky then. London and New York agreed; the chief of Radio-Coloniale (our usual studio) agreed, provided the order came through in time.

Between six and seven the London telephone service called me at my Paris hotel; said they had telegraphed the order to the Paris telephone service but had had no answer. They tried to reach French officials by telephone, but everybody at the Paris end had gone home; could I help them to deliver the order by giving them a 'live' address? I suggested the chief of Radio-Coloniale, with whom I had dealt. An hour later, at the studio, I checked up and heard that the message had come through; it was now merely a question of getting the necessary *papier* (document, permit, or whatever) from the telephone official — which would be attended to.

At ten o'clock Philip and I, script in hand, arrived. The director was gone; his office door locked. Two jovial engineers were on duty. They informed us that there were no lines. Why not? They had heard nothing; they had no *papier*. We remonstrated, talked, argued; millions of listeners were waiting in America, the programs of a hundred stations would be upset. Nothing moved them; they tried telephoning to somebody — but it didn't sound convincing. The hour came and passed — no lines. The engineers working the repeaters were gone for the night, said the engineers. Here we were, with the most graphic and exciting story of the biggest thing then happening in the world, and New York, after waiting in vain, switching on a cinema organ instead! And all because two French minor officials refused to work without a written order — a scrap of paper from somebody higher up. The sworn word of two Americans representing a world-renowned newspaper and a universally known radio chain was not enough. We tore our hair — and left.

Next morning I stormed the office of the broadcasting service, and told my story to the man in charge of foreign *liaison*. 'So it was you who wanted lines last night?' he said. 'If I had only known that! The studio telephoned me, but all they said was that some newspaper man (*un journaliste quelconque*) wanted to talk to America. He didn't give the name, so I couldn't authorize a *papier*. "No *papier*, no broadcast"; you know — those are the rules!'

Next day, after seeing the great demonstration at the Place de la République, at which Léon Blum was cheered as the leader of the *Front Commun* (which later became the 'Popular Front'), watching the French police clean up the workingmen's quarters with armored cars and truncheon charges, and feeling the heavy boot of an enraged Paris *agent* in my rear, I thought I had enough local color: so I flew back to London and told America my story from there.

THE CASE OF BARON ALOISI

When Mussolini, in the summer of 1935, was getting the Italian steam roller ready to invade Abyssinia, the name of Mr. F. W. Rickett began to figure dubiously in the British and American press. The presence in Ethiopia of this oil prospector started the dogs of scandal barking at John Bull's heels, thanks to the Italian press campaign. Overnight this hitherto obscure Mr. Rickett became the symbol of British mercenary designs. He had secured a concession from Hailie Selassie, the value of which in the circumstances seemed very doubtful indeed; but presently it became known that he was acting for American concerns, and the name of Standard Oil was being bandied about on the front pages. There were rumors and denials, accusations and counteraccusations; the American Government took a hand and extracted a disclaimer from the suspected tycoons. The British were worried.

Meantime Mr. Rickett got home to London, having given an interview on the way, and my smart secretary in my absence had promptly arranged for a transatlantic talk from the famous mystery man himself. I thought there might be trouble, but the order for facilities was duly booked by the British Post Office, and New York was keen. I bearded the lion in his den — a windowless office at the end of a long corridor in London's financial district. Rickett was a typical Englishman of the go-getter type, ruddy-faced, rather elegant, and close-mouthed about his affairs. He had made piles of money in the Mosul oil fields and the outposts of empire and had now achieved the dignity of an M.F.H.

(Master of the Foxhounds), which in England is almost a title of nobility. To the mineral wealth of Ethiopia, he assured me, Mosul was a mere puddle.

An obsequious ex-Fleet Street journalist, acting as his publicity man, produced the script of the proposed talk. It was quite innocent; had eloquent words in it about peace, economic co-operation, and so on. The pioneers of Big Business were the real champions of civilization — shades of Cecil Rhodes and all that.

Next day it got noised about that Rickett was going to speak. My telephone began to be busy; not mere secretaries or subalterns, but some pretty weighty personages themselves got on the wire to convince me that a talk by Rickett would be a nasty bomb. Britain, it is true, had nothing to do with it, except to supply some telephone facilities on the usual terms, but would Italy understand that? Italy was a friendly country; did we want to jeopardize Anglo-Italian relations? We certainly did not, and the talk was cancelled at very short notice. A perfectly good scoop gone west, and New York getting excited because the newspapers were yapping for an explanation. Where was our vaunted free speech?

I didn't care a whoop about Mr. Rickett, but it was a bitter pill.

Well, despite Britain's generous gesture the friendly relations didn't last very long. The famous Peace Ballot, organized by the League of Nations Union, showed that Britain was overwhelmingly not only for peace (11,000,000 votes) but also for sanctions against the aggressor; the National Government pushed sanctions at Geneva; Sir Samuel Hoare made ringing speeches pillorying Italy; on October 9 fifty-odd nations condemned her, and Baron Pompeo Aloisi left Geneva in a huff.

Two nights before his departure, Edgar Ansell Mowrer, Chicago *Daily News* correspondent, made a talk from the Geneva studios for Columbia listeners, stating the case for sanctions and describing the League's historic action, and for a minute or two he interviewed Tacle Hawariat, the dusky Abyssinian envoy whose day of triumph this was.

His English was limited, but he did manage to say what he did in perfectly intelligible words. We were delighted; here was the Man of the Hour, and radio made him real.

Next night it was Italy's turn. The delegation was packing up to go; the die was cast. Mowrer was speaking again; it was obvious that he must let Aloisi have his say. We worked hard, and by midday the Baron had decided to talk. A microphone interview was prepared.

Both Hawariat and Aloisi were controversial matter, of course. According to the rules attaching to the League's use of the Swiss short-wave station we had to give twenty-four hours' notice and submit the manuscript if required. Since that was impossible in this case, we ordered telephone facilities via London and a radio telephone channel from Rugby to New York. I notified the British Post Office that the Baron would speak.

About 6 P.M. — five hours before the broadcast — I was told that no facilities would be available for Aloisi or any other Italian. No argument would convince the officials in charge that this fiat would have a bad effect. In Rickett's case we had agreed to cancel a broadcast because the Italians were a friendly nation; now we were asked to cancel one because they weren't. It was bewildering.

For the next five hours I was in a stew. I tried to find officials of the League to see whether we could use the Geneva transmitter after all; we even tried to set up a channel via Berlin. Everybody had gone underground. Sitting in London, I kept the telephone hot all evening; but not even my friend Mowrer could be located. To calm his nerves he'd gone to a cinema! At five minutes to eleven I reached him as he walked into the Geneva studio, with the Baron on his arm. I told my tragic tale. The talk was off. The Baron, speech in hand, had to be told. He acted like a gentleman, pocketed his script and stalked out. Next morning he was en route to Rome.

I never felt so 'licked'; and wired an apology to New York. Back came the answer:

CONGRATULATIONS GETTING HAWARIAT STOP
NOT GETTING ALOISI EVEN GREATER SCOOP

The American front pages carried streamer headlines reading 'First Sanctions on Italy Imposed. Aloisi Forbidden to Talk,' in many variations.

Somebody had blundered, no doubt. And it was costly. For three days later the suave Baron (who had distinguished himself in the war by organizing an amazing burglary of Austrian secret documents from a consulate in Switzerland), walked into the Rome studios, whence the same interview, with added spice, was short-waved to America on a Sunday afternoon. In the interim the publicity had been tremendous and all America was on tiptoe. He gave the Italian case, in polished, noble-sounding phrases. It was almost convincing.

Nothing like this is likely ever to happen again. Firstly, because British government officials — human though they are — rarely make the same mistake twice. And secondly, the United States-European telephone monopoly, held by Great Britain and the American Telephone and Telegraph Company for years, has been split in two at the European end. The second terminus is Paris. It's an ill wind . . .

MODERN MUSIC, VESUVIUS, AND SHORT WAVE

There is just one more episode which illustrates the lingering imperfection of our instrument — or the frailty of the human ear. The International Society for Contemporary Music, which I had helped to found in Salzburg fourteen years before, was giving its annual festival in Barcelona in 1936. The civil war hadn't yet broken out, and everything was as peaceful as could be. Telephone lines were intact and the short-wave station at Madrid was working very well. There was no reason why the route which had carried the singing of ancient music by the monks of Montserrat should not also carry the music of our day.

We arranged for the transmission of one orchestral work

— the only one by an American in this musical Olympiad. It was Carl Ruggles's symphonic piece, 'Sun Treader.' Carl Ruggles is a middle-aged musical Gandhi whose word is law to a faithful band of disciples and whose every note is — to the initiates — like a rare pearl; also, it takes about as long for these musical pearls as for real pearls to mature. And they come in strange clusters, too, like seed pearls, producing the weirdest harmonies — or cacophonies — ever imagined.

The first piece by Ruggles I ever heard was called 'Angels' and was scored for six trumpets. When it was played, at one of the earliest Contemporary Music Festivals, in Venice, no six trumpeters could be got together until somebody thought of the Municipal Band, playing the 'Aïda' overture on the Piazza of St. Mark's. So they were recruited and drilled to play Ruggles: it is said that their ears haven't been right since.

Well, this new piece of Ruggles' was, if anything, even more advanced. When the time came for the broadcast — a difficult one to arrange, because no Barcelona concert had ever been known to start on time — I listened at my receiver in London. The radio channel from Madrid to New York was perfect, and the engineers who were chatting over it by way of test said 'O.K.' Then came the telephone line from Barcelona; it wasn't quite so clear, but that too was finally passed. Then started the announcement of the program from Barcelona; I understood every word. And then the music.

Suddenly the circuit was interrupted; New York was inquiring of Madrid what was wrong, and Madrid was scolding Barcelona. They tried again; they tried a third time. Each time the New York engineers made some remark which could not be heard on my little receiver, but could be guessed from the worried answers of the Spanish engineers. Finally New York, after listening to some more of the strange harmonies, decided to cancel and cut off. I — a powerless bystander — had no means of warning them. But I felt sure I knew what was wrong: I had heard 'Angels' twelve years ago, when there was no short wave. And Ruggles by radio sounded just the same. The radio engineers didn't know ultramodern music; they were like the nearly deaf old lady at a modernist concert, who after shaking her ear trumpet again and again, shook her head and walked out. They weren't inured to 'atonality,' and mistook the music for interference, or static, or something worse.

I thought this very bad luck, especially as I remembered that not long ago the same engineers had accepted the explosions of erupting Vesuvius as legitimate program material from my friend, Max Jordan, of the N.B.C., though he certainly deserved his luck, after all the effort and preparation of months.

Vesuvius hadn't made a respectable noise for years. The minor explosions in its crater are just so many gassy puffs. The Neapolitan engineers laughed when I asked them about that broadcast from the fiery mountain — one of Max's long-nursed pet ideas — when it was first projected. 'Ha!' they said; 'it's no good. We've been up there several times and each time it's the same: pfff, pfff — that's all. And the deeper you go down the softer it gets, because the real crater is behind the corona, and nobody ever gets to that.' Moreover, the Italians had no equipment that could be carted up the steep, lava-strewn slope.

Well, Max got the New York engineers to send over a specially light American portable transmitter and the requisite gear. It was hoisted up and put into place. A half-hour before the broadcast all was as quiet as ever: only 'pfff!' Then, just as they get started, Vesuvius opens up, for the first time in years, to please the American listener, and goes 'boommmm.' And again — 'boom-boom' and so on through the repertoire. It was a great success, so much so that one of the microphones got swallowed up by the fury of Vesuvius's bad temper — which made the show more realistic to the folks at home.

'But how,' said a skeptical Italian to me some time after, 'did they know it was Vesuvius and not just blasting on the roads? Are your American listeners so trusting?' (Well, they are; some people might even call them gullible.)

Now I have a grudge against those above-mentioned New

York engineers. They passed 'boom-boom' as authentic, but they didn't believe the modern American composer...

Yes, people do take too much for granted. They drink in a dictator's words or a roar produced in the African jungle as though these were being run off in an effects room around the corner. And when they've heard them, they say a-hum and turn over to the next selection of 'swing.' Also, if the ether waves crackle, or your broadcaster (who may have braved death to tell his tale) has a cold, they sniff, and turn the dial again. Ten or twenty years later they'll be acting the same way when a picture of Vesuvius in action or a gray-haired Mussolini is flashed on the television screen.

Maybe, after all, it's only the player who really enjoys the game.

PART FOUR

Systems and Policies

XXIV. RADIO OVER EUROPE

IN THE year 1913 two young engineers working in the electrical laboratories of the Royal Palace of Laeken, near Brussels, were experimenting with the new wonders of the wireless telephone. The world's first wireless telephone circuit had recently been established in Germany, and amateurs everywhere were constructing strange-looking contraptions for the capturing of radio waves. The two young engineers, pupils of the great French pioneer, Ferrié, were transmitting daily, first Morse, then actual sound, using a grotesquely primitive device — a jet of water impinging on a rotating copper electrode to produce the requisite electrical oscillations. To vary the monotony — and save their voices — they conceived the idea of transmitting phonograph records in their tests. Presently letters came in from grateful amateurs, asking for more; and, for a lark, Messrs. Raymond Braillard and Robert Goldschmidt began transmitting a series of 'concerts' every Saturday afternoon.

Soon the Royal Family became interested, and one day a real concert, with live artists, was given under the patronage of Queen Elisabeth of the Belgians. It was 'broadcast' to the amateurs in the presence of a select audience; and the amateurs with their home-made receivers — their musical 'Aladdin's lamps' — thought they were in the Arabian Nights indeed. That was the first true studio broadcast on record; and might have been the beginning of great things — had not the sound of cannon, coming from the east, cut the young pioneers short. It was August, 1914. The two

young men, like everyone else, went off to war, and radio,
having groped its way to the very threshold of its great joy-
giving task, went to work in Europe's charnel house.

Twenty years later Raymond Braillard, one of the two
pioneer broadcasters, reproduced that historic first concert
on its anniversary day for the amusement of radio fans; and
all Belgium listened. Braillard, by then, was the chief engineer of the International Broadcasting Union, Europe's
'traffic policeman of the air,' patrolling the ether lanes of the
world from a point not far from where their first experiments
intrigued the amateurs. Much — very much — had happened in the intervening years.

To understand the history of European broadcasting one
must never forget the World War. From the firing of the
first gun in August, 1914, radio became the hand-maiden
of the destroyer; the war departments, the strategists, the
military engineers determined its further course, developed
one side of its possibilities, just as they developed one side
of the possibilities of aviation — to the detriment of the
future of both. And they also developed a fear — a morbid
dread — of science's latest child, if it should ever leave the
tutelage of those in charge of a country's defence. That in
part explains why the governments of Europe, once their
hands were on radio, first refused to loosen their grip, and
then continued to hold over it a 'protecting' hand, which
was later to tighten into a stranglehold.

First in France, then in one country after another, the authorities opposed the introduction of broadcasting by radio.
Severe restrictions were placed in the way of amateurs: playing with radio waves which travelled across frontiers as
easily as within them was — to the war mentality — worse
than playing with fire. Even the postal authorities made
trouble. In June, 1920, when Melba's voice was radiated
from the Marconi station in England, in a historic concert
organized by the *Daily Mail*, the postmaster-general protested against this 'frivolous' use of a potential national
service. In Germany, Dr. Hans von Bredow, the radio
pioneer who had demonstrated the radio diffusion of music
in America before the war, tried to persuade the German

government in 1919 to institute broadcast entertainment, but wasn't successful until 1923!

When they finally yielded to popular pressure, it was the authorities themselves who had to regulate broadcasting, at least on the technical side. By that time the state of chaos which overtook the American air after the first scramble for ether channels, or wave lengths, had already set in. The European chaos would have been even worse, had the door been opened wide to private enterprise. As it was, each country took what it could, anxious primarily to avoid confusion within its own borders and escape interference from abroad — a forlorn hope in view of the strides by which radio grew up, in terms of watts and kilowatts. Soon it was realized that the European air had to be apportioned as a whole, and it was a comfort at least to realize that not more than about thirty national claims had to be reconciled, instead of the thousand-odd individual claims to be dealt with in the United States.

DIVIDING UP THE AIR

The development of European radio is an interesting story, and it can perhaps be best understood by comparison with America. The United States is a country almost exactly the size of Europe (difference: 12,000 square miles in favor of Europe). It has forty-eight states, against Europe's forty. In area and division, therefore, the two are similar, and if their populations differ as one to four (in favor of Europe), their racial basis is almost the same. But there are two vital differences. The United States has one official language, while Europe has twenty-five, not including dialects; and American states have only partial autonomy while European states boast complete sovereignty, backed up by force. It is no use discussing here why they adhere to this troublesome privilege; it happens to be rooted in the soil of ages, and is as dear to them as personality is to the individual man.

Now when Americans came to divide up, among private individuals, the most recently discovered of the nation's domains, the ether, none of the forty-eight states had a thing to say. No one in Santa Fé, New Mexico, or Cheyenne, Wyoming, for instance, got worked up about states' rights, or even state pride, when most radio channels were assigned to broadcasters in the eastern states. But when Europeans, armed with state sovereignty, and loaded with national pride, came together for a similar purpose, imagine their difficulties when asked to relinquish a wave length or to reduce the power of a station for the benefit of a foreigner and a potential enemy! Great Britain, first in the field, and 'in possession' of twenty-two frequencies, had to sacrifice eleven of them in the interest of Europe as a whole.

Moreover, if there was any trouble among American broadcasters, the Federal government could settle it out of hand, by virtue of its constitutional power. In Europe there was no central authority that could settle anything except by going to war. The wonder is, not that the ideal solution was not found, but that a workable plan was established at all. It was established through peaceful negotiation, on the principle of give-and-take, by a private and voluntary organization, the International Broadcasting Union (U.I.R.).[1] European ether waves are today being projected without serious interference, and broadcasting traffic is being regulated by a common 'policeman' — the Union's checking centre at Brussels — maintained at the common expense.

In other words, radio has achieved — unofficially — what the European governments profess to be striving for, a League of Nations which works. By successive 'plans,' worked out — from 1926 to 1929 — by the engineers of various nations (Geneva Plan, Brussels Plan, Prague Plan) they apportioned the available frequencies within the so-called broadcast band among the broadcasting countries, and these became the basis of the more recent Lucerne Plan, adopted by the governments themselves. By virtue of its

[1] Union Internationale de Radiodiffusion, with its central office in Geneva, and its technical department *Centre de Contrôle* in Brussels.

work the U.I.R. became the official broadcasting 'expert' to the governmental bodies regulating radio services as a whole. (Communications, marine, aviation, army, navy, police, etc. occupy overwhelmingly the available ether space.)

Significantly enough, the U.I.R. was founded (in 1925) in the old building of the League of Nations, where it now maintains its headquarters, while the League has moved to its immense white palace further up the lake. Under the presidency, first of Admiral Sir Charles Carpendale of Great Britain, then of M. Maurice Rambert of Switzerland, it has increased its influence through the world, and broadcasting in the European area would be unthinkable without it. Its *Centre de Contrôle*, or checking centre, where the operation of all broadcasting waves is observed day and night, and where all necessary rectifications are initiated, is still located on the outskirts of Brussels — not far from the spot where the first attempts at broadcasting took place before the war. It is the nerve centre of European broadcasting, the Greenwich of the Air.[1]

The U.I.R., besides regulating the ether traffic, has other important functions, such as the common discussion of legal questions and the various problems with which a professional body deals on behalf of its members, insofar as they are susceptible of international treatment. And above all, by virtue of the natural *cameraderie* which develops among colleagues, it has pursued with considerable energy the aims of international understanding and good will, by organizing program exchanges and collective transmissions designed to promote world solidarity.

First there were 'national evenings,' then 'European concerts,' and finally world programs, of which 'Youth Sings Across the Frontiers' in 1936, comprising over forty nations in all the continents, was the first. In 1936 there have been

---

[1] Accuracy in maintaining frequency oscillations is all the more important since in the crowded European ether there are only 9 cycles of separation between broadcasting waves. (In the United States the separation is 10 cycles.) Also, it must be remembered that there is no central authority to limit the power of stations, some of which develop up to 500 kilowatts.

no less than 1550 exchanges of programs among European countries, nearly all of which were due to Union initiative.

These multiple relays are the nearest European approach to 'chain' broadcasting on a continental scale, such as exists in America but which is ruled out by the existence of national frontiers in Europe. In order to make them possible, the Union has exerted a constant influence on the national telephone administrations, with the result that the European telephone network has greatly improved in quality and most of the great international trunk lines have been adapted for the transmission of music. The wider activity of the organization, on behalf of Peace, will be touched upon in Chapter XXV.

Once broadcasting got into its stride in Europe, its development, if more orderly, was no less prodigious than in America. After some abortive French attempts in 1921 and 1922, Great Britain was the first in the field. The Marconi Company started its experiments at Writtle in the latter year; and the British Broadcasting Company (later called Corporation) was founded, with stations in London, Manchester and Birmingham. France, Denmark and Russia followed; then, in 1923, Germany, Belgium, Finland, Norway, Switzerland and Czechoslovakia. By the end of 1925 eighteen European countries had organized services; there are now thirty, operating about 400 medium and long-wave stations on 357 frequencies. Albania, Liechtenstein, Monaco and Andorra have no broadcasting of their own as yet.

According to the latest available licence figures there are nearly twenty-eight million stationary radio sets in operation in Europe (including the U.S.S.R. and Turkey), as against twenty-five million in the United States, and it is estimated that there are between two and three million undeclared sets in addition. The actual European radio audience is, of course, much larger than the American, since owing to the lower economic status of most countries, and the development of group listening in some, an immeasurably greater number of people are served by the average set.

Group listening is the rule rather than the exception in

Russia, where one loud-speaker often serves a whole village; it is widely developed in Germany, where every school, every factory and numerous public places are equipped with loud-speakers, and listening to certain 'official' broadcasts is obligatory. It is common in Italy, where a group or crowd listening outside the local store or inn, especially at times of football matches and other sporting events, is a common sight. Finally there are in many countries so-called radio exchanges or local relay systems by wire, through which the poorer public is being served from a central set.

To give a picture of broadcasting in the various countries of Europe would require a large volume in itself. No such book has yet appeared in English, though to French-speaking readers I should recommend Arnold Huth's *Radiodiffusion Puissance Mondiale*,[1] a work of encyclopedic proportions. What I shall attempt to do very briefly is to give the outstanding principles on which European radio is organized and operated, and point out the characteristics of the outstanding prototype of each system.

American radio is run by private enterprise; European radio is, almost without exception, either operated or controlled by organs of the government. We have seen how the war was largely responsible for this: but even if private enterprise had been given a larger share, it is still certain that in the absence of a central European authority the governments would have had to regulate transmissions as a part of the communications system of the continent. And it is an interesting speculation whether the 'older' mentality of many European countries would ever have allowed the complete freedom of 'juvenile' America, the great playboy of the west.

HOW EUROPEAN RADIO IS RUN

Europe never could regard radio as just another entertainment industry: it was too inclusive, too universal, for

[1] Paris, 1937.

that; and universality imposes responsibility. Radio has everything except the power to select its audience; it must provide for all or for none. The people who go to the cinema do so because they wish to be amused or instructed; those who listen to the radio are animated by every sort of human desire — some want diversion, some instruction, some want solace and others information. The instrument which supplies all these, to all, and at all times, is first and foremost a public service — a public service which can do even more, can make the community conscious of itself, fortify the national character, rally people to a common task, warn them of danger, avert a crisis and alleviate distress. On the other hand there are conceivably people who will deny that any such obligations exist.

Be that as it may, it is certain that government operation is not exclusively associated with dictatorship, nor is it in itself any indication of the degree of political restriction to which broadcasting is subjected. There are, for instance, democratic countries like Denmark and Norway, where government ownership is preferred to private exploitation, after both forms have been tried. On the other hand, there is Italy, where private ownership does not prevent the state from exercising the severest control. France, a country in which democracy and individual liberty are the fundamental principles of society, has given a wide scope to private enterprise; yet has found it advisable to add a governmental system in order to secure something more than the kind of entertainment with which the advertiser attracts an audience.

Between the two extremes of government control there is the system of operation by a chartered public service corporation, which escapes the disadvantages of close government interference on the one hand, and of the profit system on the other. Of this Great Britain, with its genius for compromise, is the prototype. And finally there is the unique system of Holland, where the listeners themselves, organized in voluntary societies, provide the program organizations, while the government merely shares ownership of the transmitters, which are leased for alternate periods to the five societies. Since these are supported by the voluntary contributions of their members, in the absence of either advertising or compulsory payment of any kind, it is in the last analysis the interested amateur who determines the intellectual bill of fare.

In virtually all the other European countries except Luxemburg, broadcasting is financed by the so-called licensing system, by which every person operating a receiving set pays an annual fee, ranging from $2.00 to $3.00, for the privilege of receiving programs. The most usual fee is an equivalent of about $2.50. In every case this is collected through the postal authorities, who usually retain a proportion for collection expense, and in most cases deliver a part of the total fee to the national treasury. The proportion in Great Britain at present is a total of 25 per cent total government deduction.

It is important to distinguish between a radio license (which corresponds to a motor-car license) and a tax. It is not a tax, since it is not based either on the price of a product or the income level of the citizen (though there are remissions for invalids, crippled veterans and the like). It is, in effect, an entrance fee to a year's performances supplied through the facilities or the franchise of the government.

Germany, Russia and Italy, in their several ways, illustrate the system of government-controlled radio in the authoritarian state. Germany, perhaps, is the best example of all, for radio reached a certain development there even before the advent of the Nazi dictatorship.

GERMANY

When the government of republican Germany finally yielded to the importunities of its radio pioneer, Dr. Bredow, backed by pressure from radio clubs and press, it allowed private enterprise considerable scope in the various component parts of the Reich, with the idea of preserving local autonomy and regional characteristics. Companies were formed in which the government owned the controlling half of the shares, to operate transmitters erected in various parts by the technical staff of the postal administration and owned by the government. There was also a central holding company, the Reichs-Rundfunkgesellschaft (R.R.G.), headed by two joint directors, and there were various committees to supervise program material and exercise political vigilance. Dr. Bredow became Federal Commissar to supervise radio on behalf of the postal authorities.

Despite the heterogeneous structure of this complicated organization, a high degree of artistic quality went into the making of programs, and Germany's great treasure-house of music was tapped for the benefit of the masses with the help of a host of first-rate artists, orchestras and opera houses in various parts of the country. There was a fair balance of political discussion and a minimum of propaganda. Technically the organization, thanks to German ingenuity and efficiency, soon stood in the front rank of the world's radio. Artistically it encouraged research and contributed original experiments, such as special forms of radio drama and music specifically composed for radio. Nowhere were the young leaders of music and literature more keenly interested in developing new ideas and new art forms for broadcasting.

The Nazi coup of 1933 destroyed the old organization at a stroke. The new régime substituted an almost completely new personnel, which had been built up as a sort of 'shadow administration' within the Nazi-dominated Listeners' League while the party was still in militant opposition. Dr. Eugen Hadamowsky, the head of that revolutionary organization, became the new 'leader' of the R.R.G., and the old directors, as well as the eminent Dr. Bredow, were soon under arrest on a variety of charges. But the supreme head, above everybody, was and still is Dr. Josef Goebbels, minister of 'propaganda and public enlightenment,' who immediately proclaimed the right of the state to 'supervise the formation of public opinion' and asserted that the purpose of all art was to serve the state and exalt the National-Socialist ideal. Henceforth the policy of German radio was uniform, totalitarian, and subservient to one idea — the dissemination and inculcation of the Nazi doctrine and the aggrandizement of the German state.

This idea is carried through with the thoroughness for which Germans are noted. Even music, the 'language of humanity,' is given a political bias: not only is German music exalted above any other, but some German composers are regarded as more German than others. The heroic theme is emphasized, and military marches given a predominant share in entertainment, to foster the martial spirit. Beginning with physical culture 'jerks' in the morning, numerous transmissions are designed to make Germans into a sporting athletic nation. The Olympic Games at Berlin gave a new impulse to this movement. Conveying an indubitable impression of Germany's world supremacy in sport, the radio has ever since kept up the pace.

Being at all times under orders of the propaganda organization, German broadcasting throws every political event into the desired relief. Announcers and commentators have made the *reportage* of open-air demonstrations a fine art, strictly in accordance with the model set by Nazi orators. Pitching their voices in a high lyrical key, these word-painters not only describe every important meeting or triumphal appearance of their Leader in radiant colors, but aim to make every German feel the thrill of actual presence and comradeship. Since on such occasions all German stations form a single unit, the citizen has no choice but to listen, for even a switched-off loud-speaker might be regarded as disloyal.

Not content with one transmission, recordings of day-time events are re-broadcast in the evening. On the day of a Nuremberg rally, for instance, the entire time is filled with high-flown descriptions of triumphant scenes, against a background of cheering masses and the music of military bands — a cumulative effort at mass suggestion such as the world has never witnessed before.

The climax to such a day is, of course, the speech of the Führer himself, and radical precautions are taken throughout the land that it is heard by all. Sirens in factories call men together; loud-speakers in public squares and villages make listening obligatory to the passer-by. In order to make the voice of authority more ubiquitous still, loud-speakers are being installed in street-corner kiosks, the familiar feature of every German town. The complete regimenting of an entire population of nearly seventy million people — nothing less — is the unique achievement of German radio during the first five years of the present régime.

It would be giving a false picture of this remarkable country to omit mention of the still excellent and sometimes superlative broadcasting of operatic and symphonic performances, which are listened to not only in Germany but beyond its borders. No country had so highly developed and decentralized a cultivation of musical and dramatic art, and even the ruthless removal of 'undesirable' talent has not destroyed all these values, created through the tradition of centuries. From the Munich and Bayreuth Festivals down to the studio performance of classical chamber music these broadcasts are exemplary; but beside them is a dreary waste of 'light' music and banal comedy, cut to the taste of the provincial low-brow and the yokel.

The spoken word, on whatever text, is tuned in the key of propaganda. Whether it is a book review or a talk on furniture or the fire brigade, it extols the national revival, and mostly it is pitched in the explosive style of the Nazi orator. Normal speech, except in the reading of news bulletins, is a rare exception; and news bulletins, read with studied objectivity, rely upon the arts of interpretation and omission for their effect. What the ultimate effect of all this is likely to be one can only surmise; but the fact that nearly 40,000 schools receive six daily half-hour lessons by radio per week means that virtually the entire youth of Germany has its mind tuned to the nationalistic key.

ITALY

In Russia and Italy, as in Germany, the radio is the complete servant of the state and the protagonist of its political doctrine. But in both of these countries the régime antedated the coming of radio; it was not, therefore, necessary to destroy in order to build; and the fervor of destruction is always likely to out-run discretion. Soviet and Fascist broadcasting was conceived as such from the ground up.

Thus in Italy, whereas state supervision is complete in the political sphere, essentially nothing was altered on the artistic side. The E.I.A.R.,[1] a private company working for only nominal profit, is in the position of a concessionaire operating a national monopoly; by virtue of a government decree it has unfettered access to the output of all the musical, operatic, dramatic and other entertainment organizations in the country, for which it pays with cash subsidies through the various professional 'corporations' (syndicates). It broadcasts the best performances of the Scala and other opera houses, the leading orchestras, musical societies, etc., and during the 'dead' season provides its own series of studio operas with first-class artists. Opera is outstandingly the favorite entertainment of the Italian masses, and it is the pride and glory of Italian radio, which devotes nearly 45 per cent of its time to serious music. These transmissions leave little to be desired. So-called 'light' and dance music is a negligible quantity in Italian broadcasting, and the comic element is virtually non-existent.

The E.I.A.R.'S purely artistic offerings are not unduly influenced by the political régime, which, however, exacts a considerable amount of time for rural and agricultural education — of prime importance to a country like Italy. Mussolini, himself a child of the Italian village, decreed that 'the village must have radio'; and despite his poverty the Italian peasant is, by dint of community listening, becoming radio-minded.

[1] Ente Italiana per Audizione Radiofoniche.

But the Fascist government also takes a large share of available time for its own propagandistic purposes: two hours daily for official statements, three periods a week for 'special transmissions' of political complexion. A quarter of all broadcasting time is devoted to news, 'news' and 'propaganda' being virtually synonymous in dictatorship countries. However, as Italy's sixteen stations are divided into two parallel chains, listeners may have a certain amount of choice, except on days when the great demonstrations of party and régime overshadow all else.

Be it noted, for what it is worth, that in the proportion of radio sets to population, Italy is at the bottom of the world list.

RUSSIA

Geography and language combine to make Russian broadcasting — aside from short-wave propaganda — a closed book to the western world. It would be presumptuous to deal in a few paragraphs with a subject so vast. The following remarks are inadequate and aim to indicate only the general trend.

Soviet radio organization represents state paternalism in its most undiluted form, for the state not only owns and runs everything — from technical construction and research to program production; it must also provide the means of program reception and organized listening, down to the last factory, farm and village school. Since there was no private capital or enterprise in Russia, the soviets had to be manufacturer and artist, producer and consumer, in exploiting the new discovery for the benefit of 170,000,000 people, settled on an area of 8¼ million square miles (in Europe and Asia) — more than twice the size of the United States and about eighty-five times the size of Great Britain. If we bear in mind that 95 per cent of these people were illiterate up to twenty years ago, that they comprise two hundred nationalities, speaking sixty-five languages and dialects, we get a mere inkling of the task that is involved.

Allowing for the undeniably important share of communist and nationalist propaganda, the keynote of Russian radio today is and must be education. Its mission — the most prodigious ever entrusted to a single organization — is the tutoring of this multi-nation, left intellectually prostrate through the centuries. And this is a country where communications were, and still very largely are, in a primitive state, where telegraph and telephone did not lie ready to hand to link up a network of stations, and where the ether alone provided a clear path to the remoter regions of the land.

Today, by means of some forty-odd stations, ranging from the 500-kilowatt giant at Moscow to the little 10-kilowatt transmitter of the localities, Russia is after a fashion 'covered' from end to end, and even the dweller of the Arctic regions is supplied with programs especially designed for him. The program service is provided by a central Committee attached to the Council of People's Commissars, aided by some seventy regional committees — twenty-seven in Russia proper, the rest in the 'autonomous' soviets, where broadcasting is done in the languages of the various nationalities and tribes. According to official figures, nearly sixty per cent of all time is devoted to classical and folk-music, over 17 per cent to genuine education, for children and adults, exclusive of physical training, and roughly 16 per cent to news and politics. Sovietism is twenty years old; hence over 30 per cent of the population has grown up under the present régime. Propaganda, therefore, need not be so all-embracing as in the younger dictatorships.

One interesting detail should be mentioned. Listening in Russia, with less than a million individual radio sets in operation, must needs be predominantly communal. The vast majority of listening is done, therefore, either in the village hall or school and at loud-speakers connected by wire to a local 'radio exchange.' Every collective farm, every factory is, or will eventually be, equipped in this way. Capital for programs and operation is provided by a sliding scale of charges, ranging from three rubles for a crystal set

to fifty rubles for the best valve set or a radio exchange for
collective use.

State monopoly, accompanied in the three 'totalitarian'
states by complete 'ideological' control, ranges through
various degrees of supervision down to free democratic
functioning, as in Denmark and Norway, where broadcasting
is wholly non-political (except for election purposes) — a
civil service designed in the public interest and with the public's benevolent collaboration. The profit motive is elimi-
nated in these countries; there is of course no advertising, and
revenue is collected in the form of licenses. Denmark, largely
by virtue of a well-balanced program schedule, in which informative lectures occupy an uncommonly high percentage
of time, stands first on the list of European countries as to
density of audience. Its proportion of radio homes is only
slightly less than in the United States, although sets are far
more expensive and the license is 10 crowns ($2.50 per year).
These small countries enjoy a special advantage in the proximity of other countries which afford ample opportunity of
program choice. Reciprocally they provide a welcome variety
to the listeners of their neighbors, including those of Great
Britain and Germany.

GREAT BRITAIN

Between the all-political and the non-political extremes
lies the ingenious compromise devised by Great Britain —
an autonomous chartered corporation, non-profit making,
licensed to provide a public service, and financed by a 75
per cent share of listeners' licenses collected by the Post
Office. Though its Board of Governors is appointed by the
Crown with the advice of the government of the day, it is
non-partisan, like the civil service; but unlike the civil
service it has complete freedom in the choice and promotion
of its employees, thus giving ample opportunity for enterprise and ability.

Whatever one may say about the B.B.C., whose programs are internationally better known than those of any other European broadcasting organization, it does reflect the character of the British nation and the British conception of democracy. British patriotism is a compound of pride, complacency and benevolence: orderly habits and relaxed tolerance, pious confidence and easy humor make up a mentality which dislikes all exaggeration, avoids excitement and eschews undue competitive effort outside of sport. The B.B.C. appeals to all these characteristics of the British citizen, as well as to his philanthropy.

British radio programs are the only ones which begin every news period with S.O.S. messages; no Briton need die in loneliness if any of his relatives are within reach of the ether waves. Every Sunday sees not only its religious services but its appeal for a good cause. A million dollars was the response to these appeals during a single year. Every day begins with morning prayer, ends with a comforting epilogue. Every year, through B.B.C. appeals, charity procures more radios for the blind.

By means of fourteen principal stations (three of them synchronized) ranging from one hundred and fifty kilowatts to five kilowatts, plus four small relay stations, the B.B.C. affords effective coverage to the territory under its jurisdiction (all Great Britain and Northern Ireland) in such a way that two alternate programs are everywhere available (National and Regional), while many localities theoretically can tune in to six. While the six 'regions' provide a large part of their own programs, with due regard for 'national' interest and language in the case of Scotland, Ireland, and Wales, it is rare that all of them differ at one time, and at many periods — especially Sundays — there is no alternative to the national program. This is the subject of much criticism, but here, too, charitable toleration is exercised, for it is recognized that broadcasters require leisure, like other men.

Artistic and technical quality is as high as any in Europe and, in some respects, America. The B.B.C. Symphony Orchestra, the musical pride of the country, playing either under its own conductor or distinguished foreign guests such as Toscanini, is today reckoned in the front rank of the world's orchestras. Several smaller orchestras, for lighter music, and choral organizations achieve similar standards. Light music occupies a rather high percentage of time; out-and-out dance music as a rule is available only at late hours. Radio drama is taken very seriously and has reached a high degree of production technique, while musical comedy and vaudeville are regular favorites with the public. Altogether music occupies 69 per cent of the time.

Someone has remarked that the 'news' is the Mickey Mouse of the B.B.C., meaning that it is the most popular of all radio programs. It is certainly listened to in all circles of society with almost religious constancy and that is due both to its unfailing regularity and to the impartiality with which it is edited. It is often supplemented by 'flashed-in' talks of observers on the spot, and feature talks by experts, in the manner of newspaper commentary or editorial comment.

But the highest standard has been established in the department of lectures on every conceivable subject, with the collaboration of the greatest experts and personalities in the country. Controversial matter, at first excluded, is now permitted, with speakers on both sides of the question, or in the form of debates. The pleasant British fiction that there must be two sides — and no more — to every argument works as admirably on the air as in Parliament. Contrary to most other countries, there is no direct government supervision, and the spectacle of an Advisory Council with an archbishop as chairman and George Bernard Shaw as an active member gives an indication of the broad-minded impartiality which obtains. School broadcasting has been developed to a high standard of efficiency, and adult education, supplemented by the organization of 'discussion groups' among listeners is regarded as especially important.

The social service interests of certain members of the B.B.C. staff, at one stage especially, gave rise to some outstanding series of talks; for instance, unemployed men of all kinds were asked to the microphone to tell their stories —

a deeply moving human document which had serious repercussions in Parliament.

THE ENFANT TERRIBLE OF EUROPE

When British listeners get bored with the B.B.C. — and there is no doubt that some do, especially on Sundays — they turn the dial an inch or so to the right and get Luxemburg. Luxemburg, as a country, is one of the smallest and most charming on the continent. In terms of radio it is the Bad Boy of Europe. The very name is anathema to the radio nabobs; it is not admitted to membership in the U.I.R.; its programs are boycotted by the 'official' radio magazines.

The reason for all this is twofold. Luxemburg, as 'sovereign' a state as any in Europe, a few years ago chose a wavelength, just as everybody else had chosen while the choosing was good. But most of the previous choices had received the Union's blessings, and when Luxemburg awoke to the possibilities of radio, there was just one good long wave left unassigned, because the merits of the various big claimants had not been decided. Without a 'by your leave,' Luxemburg took the wave, put one hundred and fifty kilowatts of power behind it and so became the smallest broadcasting country with the loudest voice.[1]

The motive behind this manoeuvre was, for once, not political but commercial. Luxemburg station is a commercial enterprise — a radio station *à l'Américaine*, financed by advertising. It advertises patent medicines and a few other things — not of course to attract merely the 300,000 Luxemburgers but chiefly and frankly the forty-odd millions of inhabitants of the British Isles, for the 'announcements' are mostly in English. Its programs are the most unexacting in Europe; it makes little pretense at cultural values; it gives the British low-brow what it thinks he wants, and

[1] 'Long' waves in Europe are those over 1500 metres (which in the U.S. are not available for broadcasting); those under 1000 metres are known as medium waves.

apparently its efforts are crowned with success. Luxemburgers, whose government benefits by a fat share of the profits, get radio programs without paying for them, especially on weekdays, when the sponsored programs give way to something more in keeping with the local taste. Having applied the 'American system' to the European scene, Luxemburg represents the single 100 per cent example of untrammelled private enterprise. Its inhabitants tolerate it, as the inhabitants of Monaco tolerate gambling, but there is no evidence that they like it.

Luxemburg, incidentally, is not the only European country where radio advertising is permitted. Advertising is 'authorized' in twelve out of thirty, but only two or three have made any extensive use of this source of revenue. The most prominent of these is France.

FRANCE AND EUROPE'S LITTLE COUNTRIES

France is not merely a democracy; it is truly democratic. It is the classical country of personal liberty and equality, of individualism and commercial *laissez-faire*. Despite the experience of the War, despite its incipient socialism, it could not abandon the new industry wholly to the state, without giving private commercial enterprise a run for its money. Hence it decided — temporarily — in favor of both. It established a system of public service broadcasting, run by the state, and even persuaded the thrifty French citizen to pay an annual licence, after he had the experience of free radio for several years. And at the same time it continued to authorize private companies, privileged to finance themselves by selling 'time.' It is a tribute to French tolerance that the lion could lie down with the lamb. Only one other European country presents a similar spectacle, and that is Yugoslavia.

There are in France today fourteen government (P.T.T.) broadcasting stations (not counting the Colonial short-wave service) and twelve private ones. The government stations are connected by cables into a 'chain'; further additions will make it possible to diffuse two concurrent programs, national and regional, throughout France, while at present the national program depends on one station of medium power, Radio-Paris. The private stations have no cable connection and each works on its own. The government stations, animated by the spirit of public service, specialize in serious music and drama, lectures and news; the private stations, having no cultural obligations, go in for light entertainment with a dash of higher class material for sweetening. News also forms an extensive part of the schedule, and there is apparently no attempt at censorship.

The inspiration of French radio is the theatre — opera, drama, and comedy. Classic beauty alternates with lyric sentimentality and a generous dose of humor and gaiety. The national genius for comedy has free play; full-length operetta has an important place. The government stations have access to the productions of the subventioned theatres and there is a large proportion of direct pick-ups from these, as from the leading symphony orchestras. Poetry readings, lectures on cultural and artistic subjects rather than 'educational' subjects predominate. News interpretation, frank and fair on the whole, supplements the frequent news bulletins; together they furnish the largest single item on the government schedule. Outdoor pick-ups and commentaries on public events occupy a moderate place; regional programs add the flavor of the old provinces of France. There is very little dance music in the government programs; and only a little more in the commercial ones. School broadcasting does not exist, nor adult education as such: Frenchmen evidently consider they are educated enough.

Up to 1933, before radio was organized on the licence principle, radio listening in France was rather listless; since the introduction of the licence system it has gone up by leaps and bounds, rising from a little above one million to three within three years — thus shattering another popular notion about the French, namely, that they refuse to pay for amusement when it can be had for nothing.

Comprised within the types I have described are virtually all the European broadcasting systems — allowance being made for variations due to national characteristics. Except for lack of space I should like to mention in greater detail Austria where, with an abundance of high-class material, an exemplary program service has been developed, culminating in such achievements as the Salzburg Festival. Also Belgium and Sweden, like Austria private monopolies, with high cultural aims; and Holland and Switzerland, each giving satisfaction to a serious-minded audience, with comparatively modest means. Switzerland has an added complication in the necessity to furnish tri-lingual entertainment, which it accomplishes through semi-autonomous regional organizations; while Belgium provides concurrent programs to satisfy two national language groups. Finland, Hungary, Poland, Czechoslovakia, Rumania, and Turkey all have private or semi-private companies working government-operated transmitters; while Bulgaria, Esthonia, the Irish Free State, Iceland, Latvia, Lithuania, and Portugal have state-controlled radio throughout.

As for Spain, it was, up to the Civil War, served by private companies subsisting mainly on advertising; after the outbreak of hostilities all radio was commandeered by the contending sides. What will happen eventually lies in the lap of the gods.

To sum up, broadcasting in Europe is, for the most part, either government operated or government controlled. The reasons for this are partly, though not altogether, political — either national or international. And the uses to which broadcasting is put, the policy which determines its operation, and the degree of government supervision are not determined by the economic structure or the system of operation, but by the nature and policy of the government itself, as will be seen in the next chapter.

Any mental picture of Europe today must, however, include not only the land and the people but the ether above them. Day in, day out, night and day, that ether is suffused with signals and messages and intellectual projections of every kind — a stupendous, close-meshed network of speech in many tongues, of music, of significant sounds, the throbbing of a mighty continent breathing out its kaleidoscopic soul. And in his watch-tower outside Brussels the watchman of the ether wakes, preventing interference and collision. By a delicately tempered tuning fork he daily measures every wave, though its content is beyond his control. So long as this watchman is at his task, the chaos of Europe is at any rate not complete.

XXV. THE SPEECH-POISONED AIR

ANCIENT 'CHAMPION' AND MODERN EQUIVALENT

IN ANCIENT times, when warring tribes met on the field of battle, their leaders went forth to challenge the enemy with opprobrium. The fiercer the champion's defiance, the more contemptuous his insults and the more bombastic his boasts, the more warlike would be the spirit of his followers and the fiercer the enemy's hate, until at last their armies would join in combat, to show that actions speak louder than words. With the introduction of firearms, actions spoke not only louder but faster; and with the invention of strategy the leader's life became too valuable to be risked in the front line. The warrior-challenger became obsolete, so the recriminations had to be carried on by diplomats or newspaper editors, reaching their mark with much troublesome delay.

But with the invention of radio, the old-time champion has come into his own once more. Instead of going out into the field and shouting himself hoarse, he or his minions may sit comfortably at a microphone and let their voices go forth to their own people to work up pride, and to the enemy to demoralize his ranks. There is just one difference: in the old days the people who did the talking had to make good their talk; nowadays, those who order the talking done can send others out to risk their lives.

If anyone thinks that this interpretation of history is merely facetious, let him sit at any good radio set in Europe, preferably one that will tune to both long and short waves. At various times of the day and evening, right into the night, he can hear from many countries what is usually announced as 'news,' given very accommodatingly not only in the language of the country but in languages which foreigners understand, notably English, Spanish, and French. The reason for this solicitude toward the foreigner becomes clear only when one compares the news of some important event — say a battle in China or the sinking of a merchantman in the Mediterranean — as given by the radio interpreters of the different countries. It soon becomes apparent that their interpretations are just the subtle modern equivalent for the opprobrium of the past.

And as for the boasts? We have a longer word for them now, commensurate with their greater sophistication and variety, but fundamentally the meaning is the same. The word is Propaganda. Broadcast propaganda, both national and international, economic and political, is the bane of European radio today. The European ether is suffused with excellent things — beautiful music, drama, ethics, and poetry; but all this is shot through with propaganda, just as American radio is shot through with advertising. Only, while you can always detect advertising, the cloven hoof of propaganda is often more subtly concealed.

IS THE AIR FREE?

Before we examine the various kinds of propaganda, and hostile broadcasting generally, it is well to be clear about who 'owns' the European air. At the risk of repetition, let us summarize thus: out of thirty European national broadcasting systems, thirteen are state-owned and operated, nine are government monopolies operated by autonomous public bodies or partially government-controlled corporations, four are physically operated (engineered) by the government and privately serviced as to programs, while only three are privately owned and run. In two countries (France and Yugoslavia) government and privately owned companies exist side by side.

But all these organizations, whether government or private, are under more or less rigorous state supervision as to their policies. In fifteen of them (including the Vatican City, which is non-political) political broadcast matter is forbidden outright, except that which is broadcast by the Government or at its behest. This, it is needless to add, includes all the authoritarian countries, as well as some others, including Germany, Italy, the U.S.S.R., Austria, Bulgaria, Estonia, Finland, Hungary, Danzig, Poland, Portugal, and the Irish Free State. In at least two more countries, namely, Czechoslovakia and Yugoslavia, all political controversial talks are censored by the state, and in most other countries, democratic or otherwise, some sort of censorship is exercised by the broadcasting officials themselves, though in most cases simply by the standards of law and good taste.[1]

In Great Britain all supervision is suspended during election campaigns, and the same is true of some other democratic countries. Turkey — a phenomenon in this respect — boasts a total absence of supervision, but considering the undeveloped state of radio in that dictatorship, the boast need not be taken too seriously.

Even non-political talks are subject to one kind of control or another. Aside from the state-operated organizations, some, such as the Czechoslovakian and Yugoslavian, must submit *all* manuscripts to government censorship, and in many cases there is a direct control of the actual words as they are spoken over the air. Far from regarding it as a disadvantage, most countries seem to approve of all this supervision and control. Broadcasting officials are glad to escape responsibility, both internally and especially vis-à-vis their foreign colleagues. Commendatore Gino Montefinale, radio chief of the Italian Ministry of Communications, giving his expert opinion to an international committee,[2] made

---

[1] Holland, one of the eleven 'free' countries, is a curiosity: this little country contains five broadcasting organizations (not counting the short-wave service to the colonies); and two of these, owned respectively by the Catholics and the Socialists, permit political speeches favoring their own parties and principles only.

[2] The Committee on Intellectual Co-operation, studying the question of broadcasting in the cause of peace.

a point of saying that Italian radio programs are 'rigorously controlled by the state,' that even economic and financial news must be previously submitted to the government, and that 'nobody is allowed to speak before the microphone of the Italian stations unless the E.I.A.R. has previously obtained government permission.'

It would seem, then, that there is precious little freedom on the European air. In the authoritarian states we know that the motive of control is political, and the object is the total elimination of opposition or criticism of the government, the country, and its institutions; further than that, the elimination of favorable comment on certain other countries and their institutions, acts, and policies — in short, complete dictation for nationalistic ends.

On the other hand, in democratic countries such as the Scandinavian kingdoms, even state control does not necessarily mean the abrogation of free speech, any more than the state operation of posts and telegraphs necessarily means the censorship of communications. Denmark, for example, has a state-owned and operated broadcasting system; yet the control exercised over speakers is wholly on the basis of decency and good taste. Norway considers that all propaganda, whether political or religious, is out of place on the air; hence the only political speeches allowed are those at election time. The B.B.C., through its license arrangement with the British Post Office, is subject to a certain amount of parliamentary control. Yet there is no greater liberality anywhere in Europe when it comes to the broadcasting of controversial matter. Speakers from the extreme right to the extreme left, including Fascist and Communist, have had access to the microphone; though, as in the United States, one opinion must be balanced against another if violent protest and attack are to be avoided.

But in the last analysis the air belongs to the governments, and it is the policies of the governments which determine the degree of freedom, or otherwise. In dictatorship countries, and in countries living in the shadow of dictatorship, freedom in the air does not exist.

ACROSS THE FRONTIERS

So much for 'internal' broadcasting, subject to internal laws and regulations and policies. But strictly speaking no exclusively internal broadcasting exists: no way has yet been discovered by which ether waves can be restricted in their radius so as to conform, even remotely, to the eccentric boundaries of European states. This tremendous thing — the power of radio waves to pass all man-made boundaries, both physical and spiritual — was welcomed at first as a great new factor for peace. But soon after the setting-up of broadcasting systems in Europe it was found to be a new and incalculable element in the propagation of war. Indeed, the intercepting of radio waves was forbidden for some time after the World War; and this prohibition, dictated by fear, delayed the setting-up of radio services in the European area.

It must not be forgotten that this circumstance, as much as any, brought about the various measures of control which today give such an unsatisfactory picture of European broadcasting from the point of view of freedom. 'Thus it soon happened,' says Mr. A. E. Burrows, Secretary-General of the International Broadcasting Union, 'that most broadcasting organizations, certainly those in the highly complex and politically sensitive European area, found it necessary to ask for a previous submission of the manuscript from all invited to broadcast from their studios.' [1]

As early as 1926 the International Broadcasting Union, which without legislative power of any kind has brought order into the European ether and maintained it without government aid for upwards of eight years, negotiated a gentlemen's agreement to the effect that the member organizations would adopt all possible guarantees against transmissions which would harm the spirit of co-operation and good international understanding. Ever since then an important part of the Union's activities has been directed to

[1] 'Broadcasting and Peace,' International Institute of Intellectual Co-operation, Paris, 1933.

the restriction of propaganda, hostile comment, and incitement of political unrest.

The first flagrant example of hostile broadcasting came in 1926 and — significantly enough — as the result of the minorities question created by the more well-meaning of the statesmen responsible for the Treaty of Versailles. As a result of the plebiscite in Upper Silesia, decided in favor of Poland, more than 200,000 Germans found themselves on the Polish side of the border, and their alleged treatment by the Poles became the subject of border strife. The powerful German transmitter at Breslau took a hand in the fight by broadcasting to the expatriated Germans, and the Poles were furious. The result was that at Geneva Polish and German statesmen made faces at each other while fiery protests were aired. In the meantime German and Polish broadcasters, friendly co-members of the I.B.U., settled the matter by a regional agreement of non-aggression over the air — the first step toward what was to become known as 'moral disarmament.'

This agreement has worked, as between Germany and Poland, to this day; and for years only minor infractions of the earlier gentlemen's agreement occurred, to be adjudicated by the I.B.U. Then in 1933 the Nazis came to power in Germany, and within a short time there started the radio war which has been described in Chapter XIV. It illuminated in lurid colors what hostile broadcasting really meant — how it could precipitate a national tragedy in a neighboring country. The lesson was taken to heart — if not by Germany, then by others. Austria, unable to come to terms with her most powerful neighbor, concluded a radio non-aggression pact on the Polish model with Czechoslovakia. And in far-away South America, six countries concluded agreements to the same effect. Broadcasting had gained recognition as a breeder of war.

THE RACE FOR POWER

This recognition was in fact already being accorded in more sinister ways. It started a race for power in the ether. At the beginning, when it was just a question of frontier stations, the Union exerted its influence for the reduction of power; the new power competition concerned not merely single frontiers but the whole of Europe, for distance was no longer a serious handicap in the high-power era that had begun to dawn.

In 1930 the 238 stations of Europe developed an aggregate power of 1813.9 kilowatts; in 1937 there were 336 medium and long-wave stations alone with an aggregate power of 7290.8 kilowatts. The average power of the single station had nearly trebled in the intervening space of time.

Overwhelmingly the greater part of this increase is accounted for by high-powered and super-powered stations, such as would be neither permitted nor practicable in the United States. This development is sensational when one realizes that in 1930 the 100-kilowatt station was unknown. Then, after the construction of the 120-kilowatt stations at Warsaw and Prague in 1931 (presumably in answer to the previous erection of high-power stations in Russia), the race began. Stations went up to 100, to 120, even to 150 kilowatts all over Europe, and Russia, to top everything, built Europe's most powerful station at Moscow, developing 500 kilowatts. The following table will show more clearly what has happened within the short space of five years — years which coincide with the recrudescence of aggressive nationalism and the greatest armaments race in history:

	1932	1937
Stations of 20–29 kw.	9	16
Stations of 30–39 kw.	4	7
Stations of 40–49 kw.	2	1
Stations of 50–59 kw.	8	9
Stations of 60–69 kw.	6	9
Stations of 70–80 kw.	1	4
Stations of 100–119 kw.	5	27
Stations of 120–129 kw.	2	27
Stations of 130–150 kw.	0	13
Stations of 200–500 kw.	0	3
Total high-power stations	37	116

The great propaganda machine was nearing completion: the voice of the modern 'champion' was acquiring dynamics commensurate with the power of the guns.

'MORAL DISARMAMENT'

But alongside the 'armament' of the ether, ways were being sought to ensure peace. The very people that set the new pace in transmitters — the Poles — also took the lead in moral disarmament at the World Disarmament Conference in 1932. Bearing in mind their bitter experience in Silesia six years before, they made an ambitious proposal for a treaty affecting not only radio, but press, theatre, film, and school; and this met with such hostility on the part of various countries that it was abandoned, like all the other beautiful projects of that most ambitious effort of League of Nations history.[1]

But not quite. The League, foiled everywhere else, salvaged the idea of restricting hostile radio activity and commissioned its subsidiary body, the Committee on Intellectual Co-operation, to work out a convention which could be adopted by the Powers. In 1933 the first text was submitted by the League to the various governments. At a Conference held in the autumn of 1936 twenty-eight nations signed the convention, and eventually thirty-seven executed the final act, among them most European countries, including the U.S.S.R., but not including Germany and Italy.

This 'Convention for the Use of Broadcasting in the Cause of Peace' provides that the high contracting parties mutually undertake to prohibit the broadcasting of anything which is detrimental to good international understanding, or which will incite the population of any of each other's territories; undertake that nothing which is transmitted by

---

[1] Among the most bitter opponents was the American Government, which quite naturally saw in this scheme an attempt to curtail the sacrosanct right of free speech.

their broadcasters shall incite to war; that nothing harmful shall be broadcast which is known — or ought to be known by the responsible persons — to be incorrect.

Like most international agreements, this first European radio treaty is as important for what it omits as for what it contains. The real 'disarmament' clauses, which the idealists responsible for its promotion finally managed to embody in a series of attached recommendations, concern two very important things. One of them demands vigilance against broadcasts which, even though they may not incite a foreign population, may give offence to its sentiments — national, political, religious, or social. The other calls particular attention to transmissions in foreign languages. Recent history has shown that it is just these two points that have led to international conflict; yet to convert them into treaty obligations would undoubtedly mean a further restriction of the freedom of the air.

Now, so long as this Convention is not signed by Germany and Italy it has, of course, very little practical value for Europe, since the nations who adhere to it are precisely those who are least likely to give offence in any case. But whatever its restraining influence may be, it does not affect the more important, because the more far-reaching, activities of those Powers which have developed that last word in stentorian champions, the high-powered short-wave transmitter, with its literally unlimited range. This development has taken place, in very recent years, without legal or conventional restriction of any sort. No international regulation within the short-wave broadcasting band exists; a wild scramble for wave lengths has resulted in a wholly arbitrary and lopsided status quo. Politically this is a major problem in the world today.

BALLYHOO BY SHORT WAVE

The peculiarity of short-wave transmission, which at first was thought to be only of local importance, is that it is most efficacious over ultra-long distances — thousands of miles — and especially in transoceanic work. The direct wave, or so-called ground wave, fades after a short distance, but the sky wave, reflected from the Kennelly-Heaviside layer of the atmosphere, encircles the earth. Through the device of directional antennæ (beam system), these waves can be aimed at any desired section of the globe, thereby increasing audibility in that region. Thus it came to be used for transoceanic communications.

As the abstruse science of short-wave transmission came to be mastered (adaptability of certain waves to light or darkness, seasonal cycles of efficiency, sun spot activity, etc.), broadcasters began to exploit the new domain in hitherto unsuspected ways. In 1930 only three short-wave transmitters were used for broadcasting in Europe; today there are over forty sizable ones, and more are being built. Short waves require proportionately less power to project them: a two-kilowatt transmitter in Addis Ababa carried the Negus's voice to America, over seven thousand miles away. Yet many short-wave transmitters now in use are of the order of 40 and 50 kilowatts; others now being built will go up to 100 kilowatts and probably more.

The value of this method of long-distance transmission in creating a new link between parts of a far-flung community like the British Empire is obvious. Great Britain therefore took the lead; the British Empire station at Daventry, with its six transmitters, reaches virtually every British dominion and possession with a carefully timed cycle of transmissions. But the Germans, whose 'empire' is of different nature, were not far behind. Prior to the Olympic Games of 1936 they increased their small but very efficient short-wave station at Zeesen to comprise eight powerful transmitters — two more than the British — thus making it the largest and most potent propaganda machine in the world. After the Games were over, this giant station, by virtue of highly intelligent engineering and very astute publicity technique, became the most terrific agency for the spread of political doctrine that the world has ever seen.

THE MODERN TOWER OF BABEL

Having no colonial territories, the policy of the German short-wave service is, first, to reach 'colonies' of overseas Germans wherever they may be, make them conscious of their ties to the Fatherland, and preach to them the Nazi philosophy of national greatness; secondly, to promote 'good will' and create German markets in competition with other exporting countries; and thirdly, to convince the rest of the world of German greatness and the justice of German aspirations. This is being done consistently in six languages — and more, as required. It is carried out with tremendous thoroughness, broadcasts being aimed with great accuracy and efficiency at definite communities to be cultivated: German-Americans in the United States are showered with brotherly love from 'home'; the South Africans, in Afrikaans language, are mollified on German colonial claims; the South Americans, in Spanish and Portuguese, learn to revere German music and incidentally German machines; and so on. Nobody is forgotten. A series of broadcasts aimed at Tasmania — opening with 'Hello, Tasmania, beautiful Apple Isle' — is but one example of this new 'spot' propaganda.

Italy, both master and pupil to German Fascism, is not far behind the big brother in this field. The short-wave station at Prato Smeralda, always one of the best-functioning in Europe, is, according to official announcement, being supplemented by two short-wave transmitters of 100 kilowatts each and three of 50 kilowatts each, besides an ultra-short wave at Monte Mario. This will carry the Italian 'empire station' far beyond its British prototype, although the Duce still considers his empire in its infancy. The use to which these transmitters will be put is not in doubt. Even now the Rome transmitters emit a fairly steady stream of Fascist propaganda, mostly in the guise of news, history lessons, and reports regarding the march of Italian civilization in Africa and elsewhere. During 1937 the Italian short-wave station was broadcasting regularly in Italian, English, Spanish, Portuguese, Arabic, Chinese, Japanese, and Hindustani. As a result, the British felt themselves politically menaced in the Mediterranean, in India, in the Near and Far East, and along their trade routes everywhere, and soon announced their policy of world-wide broadcasting in six foreign languages. For this purpose additional powerful short-wave stations have been authorized, a step which is bound to be answered by further increases in Germany, and so on.

Other countries with colonial empires — the Dutch, the French, the Belgians, and the Portuguese — are all using short-wave broadcasting to provide their colonists and natives with news and entertainment from home. In none of these cases does there seem to be a determined effort at propaganda outside the legitimate scope. But France, which already broadcasts a cultural program to the United States, soon ordered the construction of a 100-kilowatt short-wave transmitter at Pontoise. The French Radio-Coloniale, run by the Colonial Ministry, today transmits in French, English, Arabic, Italian, and Portuguese, all of which languages are spoken in French territories. Of non-colonial countries the first to enter the short-wave field is Czechoslovakia, with its excellent station at Podebrâdy (35 kilowatts), which at last accounts was broadcasting in Czech, Slovak, and — for the United States — in English.[1]

When we give all this activity its right name, we must not forget that propaganda, in the nationalistic countries of Europe, is regarded as an entirely praiseworthy endeavor. Even the regional non-aggression pacts specifically provided for a certain amount of legitimate propaganda. But much of this short-wave propaganda is not legitimate by any liberal

[1] The foregoing paragraphs are reproduced from the author's 'Radio as a Political Instrument,' published in *Foreign Affairs* for January, 1937.

standards, and some of it is openly hostile. Russia (which uses all the leading European languages in its short-wave transmissions) attacks Germany, and Germany retaliates; both accuse each other when giving 'information' about Spain. The air is filled with recriminations of this sort.

THE VOICE OF THE LEAGUE

The only non-nationalist short-wave transmitters of any importance, at the present writing, are those of the Vatican, which is nevertheless ideological, and of Prangins, in Switzerland, which for broadcasting purposes is leased to the League of Nations. This, the only neutral short-wave outlet in Europe, is available for program traffic to any foreign broadcaster who wishes to hire it and submit to the rules (due notice and submission of manuscript if required); and it has been largely used on this basis by the American radio chains. The League itself has made a practice of broadcasting bulletins of its own activities in the principal languages at least once a week for some time. During the League Assembly of 1937 daily transmissions were broadcast for the first time, and parts of the actual speeches were interpolated, either directly or by the recording method, to add program value. A broadcasting expert, lent by the B.B.C., was attached to the staff, and the new broadcasting budget provides for an increased service. No attempt was made, however, to broadcast League propaganda, or in any way to counter the propaganda of anti-League countries; in other words, international democracy is even less vigorous than the national democratic governments in defense of its principles in the air.

Apart from these mild, academic effusions the earth's ether is suffused with political venom, projected with ever-increasing efficiency by those countries which profess anti-democratic creeds. The dictator countries have, roughly, pre-empted thirty out of the ninety-four effective short-wave frequencies now operated for broadcasting, with an aggregate of 1,033,000 watts out of the available 1,484,000 watts of short-wave power in the world (1938). In assaying the opposing forces in this 'war of words,' and comparing the effectiveness of the authoritarian stentors with the democratic ones, it must also be remembered that the advantages of initiative and unscrupulousness are on the side of the former. It is not likely that any of the Fascist dictatorships will sign or ratify the 'moral disarmament' pact. Their mouths — as well as their hands — are therefore free.

EPILOGUE: TOWARD THE FUTURE

THE RACE BETWEEN SCIENCE AND POLITICS

TWO main currents of thought were reshaping the social fabric of the western world in the decades preceding the World War, both issuing from the materialistic philosophy of the nineteenth century. One found its expression in scientific discovery and invention which promised great material and moral benefit to mankind. The other, postulating a new conception of human relationships, resulted in a re-awakening of the social conscience, increased the class struggle and finally precipitated international strife. Both of these thought-forces responded in the last analysis to the deepest needs of human nature: the mitigation of loneliness and the dispelling of fear.

The inventions of the late nineteenth and early twentieth centuries tended to bring people closer together. They centred on efforts for faster transportation and better communication. The development of motor traction — the automobile, the aeroplane — helped to annihilate space; telegraph, telephone and finally radio brought cities, states and continents within the hearing of each other. The last remnants of spiritual separation were being removed. The integration of man on this planet had begun.

Political activity of the corresponding period was bent, first, on securing the benefit of the new inventions for nations and for special groups within nations, and to the claiming of a greater share in these benefits by the masses whom industrial expansion had separated from their tools. Internationally, politics supported the struggle for material supremacy by tightening the countries' grip on colonies, on raw materials, on means of scientific and industrial exploitation, on markets for the new and ampler products of science and labor at home.

Science, then, was tending to bring men together; politics, to tear them apart. It is possible to view this era as a race between the two. If science — unhindered by economic strife — could have perfected its devices, could have adapted the new tools to the works of peace, we might conceivably not have had the war. But political thought was not alive to the new implications, either of science or of social change, and war came. Science was subjected to the purposes of war and made it more destructive than ever before. Aviation and radio, the latest gifts of inventive genius, were harnessed to the war machine; both played their grim part in the struggle; both were perfected under the stress of military demand; both received a new and sinister direction through war. Science helped to decide the war, but war solved no problems; it created new ones for science to solve.

Radio was still in its infancy when war broke out, but its beneficent works of peace had already written a glorious page in history. In 1909 the radio telegraph saved the lives of the 761 passengers of the sinking American steamer *Republic,* three years later 703 more from the ill-fated *Titanic,* and other remarkable feats of salvage followed in quick succession. A new type of hero, the marine wireless operator, was presented to the world. In 1911 the first radio telephone service was established between Berlin and Vienna; in 1915 the human voice, carried by ether waves, had spanned the ocean, and the trans-Atlantic radio telephone was in sight. Meanwhile, in 1910, the De Forest radiophone had relayed the voices of Caruso and Destinn from the Metropolitan Opera in New York to listeners outside, portending a great expansion of artistic enjoyment. In 1913 — a year before the war — the first tentative radio transmissions of music were instituted in Brussels, and broadcasting had virtually begun.

RADIO IN WAR

But the War cut short these peaceful endeavors; the wireless telegraph was used, not for friendly messages but to carry military intelligence through space; the radio telephone was used for establishing contact between men-of-war, between battleship and shore, and for directing the aeroplanes which, soaring overhead, spread destruction with new and terrifying force.

Since then radio technique has advanced with gigantic strides. Industry and business are exploiting it for profit; governments for offense. Radio, which might have been free — the freest mode of communication yet discovered — was shackled; after the experience of the War no European government could permit its unhampered development; no country in the world could afford to ignore its sinister potentialities. Aside from its peaceful functions it is being used to spread propaganda and hatred through the world. Radio communications are being perfected and organized to be capable of terrific efficiency in 'the next war.' The Powers who in 1914 were isolated from the outer world because their cable communications were cut, are fortifying themselves against a similar loading of the dice next time. 'The greater the number of channels of communication under a country's control, the stronger the position of that nation in the event of war,' says O. W. Riegel in *Mobilizing for Chaos.*[1] The most important channels of communication today are in the air.

These ether channels have the advantage, not enjoyed by other methods of communication, that they cannot be effectively cut. They can be interfered with over a limited field, but not consistently, since the unlimited possibility of changing frequencies would require foreknowledge of every change. Secrecy, moreover, can be maintained by the technique of 'scrambling' speech, which, again, is susceptible to infinite variation. Broadcast messages between governments

[1] Yale University Press, 1934.

and their agents in hostile or neutral countries can, under modern conditions, be picked up over thousands of miles, with instruments so minute as to escape detection. A mere bar of music or a prearranged quotation from literature might convey important instructions to those in possession of the code. Thus, no country in the world is safe from the tentacles of war. The aeroplane will find out the last noncombatant; the radio will penetrate every defense of neutrality.

The Civil War in Spain has shown in a small way to what other uses radio may be put in war. Military authorities took over the radio immediately after hostilities broke out, and hostile propaganda was emitted from stations on both sides in a steady stream. General Queipo de Llano, the 'broadcasting general' of the insurgents, quickly became as important as the generals at the front. All pre-war arrangements regarding wave lengths were thrown overboard, regardless of the rights of combatants and neutrals alike. The defenders of the Alcazar were prevented by Loyalist 'jamming' from receiving messages informing them that relief was on the way. Madrid broadcast on Seville's wave length, to drown the rebel propaganda; and the rebels tried to jam Madrid. Broadcasting to the opposing army by means of loud-speakers in the trenches has also become a feature of modern war. Radios were placed in trenches and by means of a 'loud-speaker offensive' military leaders sought to spread terror and demoralization in the opposing ranks. The sinister potentialities of radio defy our imagination, which has not grasped even its full possibilities in peace.

DEMOCRACY'S CHANCE

What of the future? Will science, having lost the first heat in the race, recoup the balance in the next? It is barely possible that science may eventually discover some way to disperse hostile radio waves and screen populations from verbal attack, just as it aims to screen them against poison gas. But failing this rather unlikely consummation, it would seem that the only course would be to meet like with like, propaganda with propaganda, attack with attack.

The dictatorship states, as we have seen, have already perfected their machine. Democracies, at the moment of writing, have made only a half-hearted effort at retaliation. In Great Britain the government has taken a hand by giving to the B.B.C. a mandate to broadcast in foreign languages to the neutral world. The United States government, afraid of the charge of authoritarian leanings, is leaving the initiative to private hands. Private radio, sponsored by industry, is assumed to be in a better position for this patriotic service than the government, which is the elected spokesman of the people's will . . .

In a world divided into two ideological camps what chance has democracy against dictatorship, projecting its 'ideals' and its own idealized portrait to the world?

Democracy cannot adopt totalitarian methods or modes of expression without escaping the charge of totalitarianism itself. Its only way to counter the verbal batteries is by words of tolerance and truth. The truth may not always be pleasant, or complimentary to the country itself, but nothing else will carry conviction in the long run. Biased news and partisan argument will not do. Democracy cannot afford to justify itself by ready-made doctrine; shibboleths and slogans are not enough. It can demonstrate its freedom only by acting free — by admitting differences of opinion, even confessing mistakes. The best it can do is to show that, far from being 'bankrupt' it has genuine vitality, a will to progress, a capacity for adjustment to social needs, for neighborliness and generosity. Campaigns of propaganda and untruth in the end are likely to cancel each other out; democracy has nothing better to show than faith in itself.

But there is more than the spoken word. Propaganda, political as well as commercial, is made palatable by entertainment, by the 'harmony of sweet sounds.' When those who listen are to be rewarded, or enticed to listen again, what do they hear? Beethoven symphonies from Germany, Verdi operas from Italy, Russian folksongs from Soviet land.

By drawing on the artistic glories of the past, these countries lay claim to a civilization superior to any other. Rightly or wrongly, the word has gone forth that the cultural content of European radio is higher than our own. Whatever the treatment meted out to political minorities, the intellectual minorities are said to be catered for as well as the great mass. Yet in this the radio of the western democracies can compete on more than equal terms. Like the Fascist countries they may draw with equal right on that great heritage which only the free spirits of a better time could have produced. Like them they can disseminate the cultural gifts which today are the legacy of all instead of the privilege of the few.

Owing to economic stress and politico-racial persecution an overwhelming majority of the world's eminent artists are gathered together in the democratic countries of the world. The greatest singers and instrumentalists, the finest orchestras, the most gifted writers are here, ready and willing to devote their talents and their wisdom to the spiritual recreation and enlightenment of all the people. To release these intellectual forces for the benefit of the world and in defense of freedom is, it seems to me, the noblest mission of radio in a democratic society.

Here, and in radio's ability to integrate the community, to bridge the gap between high and low, rich and poor, nation and nation, man and man, lies its incalculable power for good — its greatest potential contribution to the unifying of mankind. Science has solved many problems of war; will science, allied with art and the higher manifestations of the human spirit, ultimately solve the problem of peace?

In the preceding chapters I have attempted to give a picture of radio in Europe, as it is today. In the earlier sections of this book I have recounted my own experiences with an experiment which in a modest way represents a step in the direction of better international understanding. If a few more people in the English-speaking world have, by means of that experiment, become conscious of Europe's problems and a little more familiar with its personalities and its genius; if, by the same token a few additional thousands of people in

Europe have become aware of America's problems, as well as its unlimited possibilities, the effort has been justified.

The exchange thus inaugurated is going on. The American radio chains are rebroadcasting a certain number of events from Europe every week; European countries are rebroadcasting an increasing number of American programs all the time. If these programs follow a little too closely the drift of the news, this is to be expected, with the ephemeral appeal of radio as it is today. But with a more homogeneous organization of radio programs in America, in the direction of useful information and genuine enlightenment, the things that are of lasting value are bound to be forced to the front.

On the other hand, with the gradual perfection of short-wave technique and the constant increase in the use of short-wave receivers, the ordinary listener will become increasingly Europe-conscious — and in time world-conscious — on his own account. When that time comes, some way may have been found by which the treasures of the human mind will come to us without strident political accompaniment. Then, too — always supposing that there will be peace — may Europe, in the still undreamed-of splendors of the future, receive from America a complete — or at least a representative — projection of American civilization at its best.

THE END

INDEX